W9-AXM-377

# Virginia

A Guide to Backcountry Travel & Adventure

OTHER TITLES AVAILABLE FROM OUT THERE PRESS

North Carolina: A Guide to Backcountry Travel & Adventure

# Virginia

A Guide to Backcountry Travel & Adventure

James Bannon

Maps by

Jennie Treeger
&
James Bannon

out there press
post office box 1173 • asheville. nc 28802

Virginia:
A Guide to Backcountry Travel & Adventure

Copyright © 1997 James Bannon

All rights reserved. No part of this publication may be reproduced, stored in a retrieval system or transmitted in any form by any means, electronic, mechanical, photocopying, recording or otherwise, except brief excerpts for the purpose of review, without the written permission of the publisher and copyright owner.

Library of Congress Catalog Card Number: 96–070792
ISBN   0–9648584–1–X

Although the author and publisher have made every attempt to insure the accuracy of the information provided herein, they accept no responsibility for any loss, damage, injury, or inconvenience sustained by any person using this book. Users of this book should be aware that wilderness travel carries certain inherent risks and can be dangerous or even fatal.

Cover photo: fly-fishing on the lower Jackson River

Cover photograph and design: James Bannon
Back cover photograph: Robert Jakubik

Manufactured in the United States of America

10 9 8 7 6 5 4 3 2 1

For my father,

Who loved the mountains and wide-open spaces

It was of the wilderness, the big woods, bigger and older than any recorded document:—of white man fatuous enough to believe he had bought any fragment of it, of Indian ruthless enough to pretend that any fragment of it had been his to convey...It was of the men, not white nor black nor red but men, hunters, with the will and hardihood to endure and the humility and skill to survive, and the dogs and the bear and deer juxtaposed and reliefed against it, ordered and compelled by and within the wilderness in the ancient and unremitting contest according to the ancient and immitigable rules which voided all regrets and brooked no quarter.

– William Faulkner
"The Bear"

# Contents

# Maps

# Map Legend

| | |
|---|---|
| • • • • • •• | ........................... Hiking Trail |
| o o o o o o o | ........................... Mountain Bike Trail |
| ⟨W⟩ | ........................... Wild Trout Waters |
| ⟨H⟩ | ........................... Hatchery Supported Waters |
| ⟨CR⟩ | ........................... Catch & Release Waters |
| ▲ | ........................... Developed Campground |
| ⟂ | ........................... Primitive Campground |
| △ | ........................... Backcountry Camping Area |
| ▲▲ | ........................... Group Campground |
| ⊤⊤ | ........................... Shelter |
| ⌣ | ........................... Boat Ramp |
| (40) | ........................... Interstate |
| (64) | ........................... U.S. Highway |
| (70) | ........................... State Highway |
| (3651) | ........................... Secondary Road |
| [411] | ........................... Forest Service Road |
| ⌂ | ........................... Ranger Station/Park Office |
| ⬆ | ........................... Other Building |
| — — - - — — | ........................... State Border |
| — — — -. — | ........................... Forest/Park Boundary |
| ☀ | ........................... Bald |

# Acknowledgments

A book such as this one is the work of many hands, although only one name ends up on the cover. Such are the vanities of authorship. First thanks are owed to all the people who manage and promote Virginia's natural areas. Their numbers are far too great to list here and most of their names are unknown to me, but without their contributions this book would not exist in its present form. They are employees of the state parks, national parks, national forests, national wildlife refuges, regional parks, state forests, and wildlife management areas in Virginia who supplied me with brochures, maps, lists, and suggestions and graciously answered my questions. In addition to the many, a few went to extra lengths to provide me with information that was essential to ensure the book's accuracy. Special thanks are therefore owed to the following people: Harry Fisher, Donna Wilson, and Nadine Pollack at the George Washington and Jefferson National Forests; Spike Knuth and Don Hinchey at the Virginia Department of Game and Inland Fisheries; Michelle Menendez–Scanlon at the Department of Conservation and Recreation; and Deborah Jerome at Fort Belvoir. Any errors that remain in the book are my own.

At the production end of the project, huge thanks to Jennie Treeger for doing such a fine job on the maps and for working under absurd deadline pressures. Thanks to Morrison for accomanying me on research expeditions, for holding down the fort at Out There Press, and for his wise input and proofreading skills. Thanks again to Jake for the author photo.

Personal thanks to my family for their encouragement and support. And to Marina, for everything else.

# Preface

This is the second book in the series of outdoor guidebooks published by Out There Press. It is also the second one I've written. The basic idea behind the series remains the same: to provide outdoor enthusiasts with a single guide that covers all the major backcountry areas of a particular state, focusing on five primary activities: hiking, camping, fishing, canoeing & kayaking, and mountain biking. As the book's subtitle suggests, it's a travel guide, but with some obvious differences from the standard travel guides available for Virginia. Inside you'll find no resorts, no four-star restaurants, no descriptions of historic downtown areas. In their place are hiking trails, scenic rivers, trout creeks, and campgrounds. In short, it's a guide to traveling through Virgnia's natural regions. Whether you want to travel on foot, by canoe or kayak, or on a mountain bike, this book will provide you with the information you need to decide where to go and to plan your trip once you do. The adventure part comes in because when you're traveling in remote backcountry, no matter how you do it, you're never entirely sure what's going to happen. When you leave your car at the trailhead or boat launch, you also leave behind the highly-regulated, well-lit, air-conditioned world of civilization. Out there, there's no one else to rely on because no one's really in control. You're on you own, more or less. Which is, I think, most of the appeal.

As you use this book, keep in mind that some of the information included will become dated rather quickly. Quickest of all to change will of course be prices. They'll rise. But other changes occur too. Recreation areas and campgrounds close due to budget cuts (a particularly pressing problem in recent years), trails are rerouted, fishing regulations change. Violent storms or floods wipe out roads and campgrounds. As this book was going to press, in fact, Virginia was struck by Hurricane Fran. The storm was one of the most devastating in recent memory, causing substantial flood damage in the northern mountains. Shenandoah National Park was closed for a week and several ranger districts on the GWNF suffered extensive damage to roads, trails, and recreation areas.

If you find that some of the information in the book is inaccurate, please let us know. Our goal at Out There Press is to produce the most accurate, most useful guides possible to backcountry travel. After all, we use them too. See ya out there.

Asheville
October, 1996

# Abbreviations

| | |
|---|---|
| 4WD | four wheel drive |
| BRP | Blue Ridge Parkway |
| CCC | Civilian Conservation Corps |
| E | east |
| ft | foot/feet |
| FS | Forest Service |
| GWNF | George Washington National Forest |
| hr | hour |
| jct | junction |
| JNF | Jefferson National Forest |
| I | interstate |
| L | left |
| mi | mile/s |
| mp | milepost |
| mtn | mountain |
| N | north |
| NF | national forest |
| NHP | national historical park |
| NP | national park |
| NPS | National Park Service |
| NRA | national recreation area |
| NS | national seashore |
| NWR | national wildlife refuge |
| ORV | off road vehicle |
| PATC | Potomac Appalachian Trail Club |
| R | right |
| RD | ranger district |
| rec | recreation |
| RS | ranger station |
| S | south |
| SF | state forest |
| SP | state park |
| SR | secondary road |
| SRA | state recreation area |
| USFS | United States Forest Service |
| USGS | United States Geological Survey |
| VDGIF | Virginia Dept of Game and Inland Fisheries |
| W | west |
| WMA | Wildlife Management Area |

# Introduction

Due to a providential combination of location, geology, and border placement, Virginia possesses a diversity of geographic regions and habitats that translates into a minor paradise for lovers of the outdoors. Like most of the states on the south Atlantic coast, Virginia has three distinct geographic regions—coastal plain, piedmont, and mountains. Each offers backcountry travelers and outdoor enthusiasts its own unique pleasures.

In the mountains you'll find hundreds of miles of hiking trails that wind through some of the oldest uplands on earth; whitewater rivers to challenge the skills of the most ardent kayaker; dozens of remote creeks that harbor both native and stocked trout; and campgrounds sprinkled throughout waiting to be used as bases for backcountry exploration. The piedmont is home to Virginia's largest recreational lakes and a large number of parks, wildlife management areas, and state forests that are all working to restore some of the magnificent forests that covered the entire region just a few centuries ago. Hunters and anglers have long appreciated the area's natural resourses, and now hikers, paddlers, and other outdoor enthusiasts are beginning to catch up. The coast practically begs to be explored from a canoe or kayak. With the Atlantic Ocean, Cheaspeake Bay, and four major tidal rivers, water is a natural medium of travel. And navigating them in silent boats allows visitors to share the habitats of the hundreds of bird species that live in or pass through the region. In short, Virginia's diverse natural habitats offer backcountry travelers and adventurists an unsurpassed wealth of opportunities.

Virginia covers 40,815 square miles. At its widest point, it is almost 500 miles across. North to south, it is 220 miles from West Virginia to North Carolina. The population of roughly six million is clustered in several urban areas in the eastern part of the state. Virginia Beach is the largest city, though it's located in one corner of a much larger metroplex that extends west and includes Norfolk, Newport News, and Hampton. The northeastern corner of the state across the Potomac River from Washington, D.C. forms another such metorplex. Richmond, the state capital, is the third large urban area. Much of the rest of the state is a combination of agricultural areas punctuated by small cities and towns. The exception is the mountain region. The mountains there remain heavily forested, with small farms and small cities nestled into the valleys between mountain ridges. This is also the region in the state with the most possibilities for outdoor recreation.

## Climate & Weather

Virginia is located in North America's temperate zone; the seasons are clearly defined, but none are particularly extreme. Spring and fall are the most pleasant seasons. Across the state, summertime highs average 85°–90°; in winter the average high is about 45°. Summer is hot and humid across most of the state except in the mountains, where temperatures generally remain 5° to 10° cooler than on the piedmont or coast. Winters are short, with just a few days each year when daytime temperatures remain below freezing. That is less true of the mountains, where winter is longer and snow and freezing temperatures more common. For the backcountry adventurer that simply means another mode of travel: cross-country skiing. Virginia has no wet and dry seasons. It does lie within the area affected by hurricane season, however. Severe coastal storms are not uncommon from May to November. The effects of these storms are often felt throughout the state, with floods the typical result further inland. In addition to tropical storms, late afternoon thunderstorms are a common occurence across most of the state in late spring and summer. These storms are often accompanied by lightning.

# The Backcountry

Approximately 4 million acres of publicly owned land are included in this book. If all this land were placed in a single tract, it would occupy an area about equal in size to Hawaii. These lands represent federal, state, and local holdings. Although management objectives differ in the various jurisdictions, outdoor recreation is a primary goal at all of the areas covered. Among these areas are national park holdings, national forests, state forests, state parks, national wildlife refuges, state wildlife management areas, regional parks, Corps of Engineers lakes, and county parks.

## National Forests

In terms of acreage alone, the national forests account for the largest percentage of public lands open to outdoor recreation in Virginia. There are two national forests in the state, the Jefferson NF and the George Washington NF. They stretch almost the entire length of the state's mountain region. The JNF extends southwest from Roanoke to near the Cumberland Gap; the GWNF runs northeast from Roanoke to Front Royal. The two forests are similarly managed for a variety of—and often competing—purposes. In addition to outdoor recreation, the best known and most controversial management objective is timber extraction. Conservationists, outdoor lovers, and companies that make their profits selling the forests' resources continue to battle in the courts and other public forums.

The forests are divided into eleven ranger districts and one special area, the Mt. Rogers National Recreation Area. All of these areas offer outstanding opportunities for backcountry recreation. Individual locations vary from developed recreation areas that offer facilities such a swimming beaches on small lakes, bath houses, and picnic areas to designated wildernesses where the only signs of human presence are the primitive hiking trails. For additional information contact the George Washington NF, Federal Building, 101 N Main St, Harrisonburg, VA 22801; 540/564-8300 or Jefferson National Forest, 5162 Valley Pointe Parkway, Roanoke, VA 24019; 540/265-6054.

## National Parks

Four areas included in this book are administered by the National Park Service: Shenandoah National Park, Cumberland Gap National Historical Park, the Blue Ridge Parkway, and Great Falls Park. The national parks differ from the national forests in that their primary purposes are resource conservation and outdoor recreation. No logging takes place on the national parks or other properties administered by the NPS. Which isn't to say that signs of human presence aren't abundant. All of these areas were intensively logged and otherwise altered by people over the course of the last few centuries. Only during the latter half of this century have their lands begun to return to a more natural state. That conversion will never be complete, however, nor is it intended to be. Roads run through and define the two largest, most popular parks. The Blue Ridge Parkway, in fact, is a linear park defined by one of the nation's most scenic drives. The parkway runs for 469 miles between Shenandoah NP and Great Smoky Mountains NP. Along its lazy, winding route, it passes through some of the most stunning mountain scenery on the east coast. Although there are numerous backcountry areas and miles of hiking trails along its corridor, the road remains the park's defining feature. Shenadoah National Park has a much vaster backcountry, but Skyline Drive is still central to the park and, sadly, the way that most visitors experience it. The backcountries of Shenandoah NP and Cumberland Gap NHP are open to backpacking excursions and offer excellent opportunities for extended trips. If you want to camp on the BRP, by contrast, you have to stay at one of the designated campgrounds. Great Falls Park is a day-use only park with no camping facilities.

## State Parks

There are twenty-four state parks in Virginia, with several more currently under development. The focus of the state parks is different from either the national parks or the national forests. To start with, the backcountry areas are typically much smaller, and therefore offer more limited opportunities for off-road travel. Pocahontas SP is the largest at 7,600 acres; most are between 1,000 and 4,000 acres. Facilities at the parks vary considerably, though an emphasis on family recreation is common to all. Many of the parks feature developments such as picnic grounds, swimming areas on lakes or pools with bath houses, cabins for rent, and campgrounds. Backcountry travel is often of secondary importance. These parks closely resemble county parks and seem to fulfill a similar role in their communities. At the other extreme are a small handful of parks where conditions are primitive and where a premium is placed on backcountry travel. The parks rival any area on the national parks or forests for scenic beauty and quality of backcountry experience. The state parks are managed by the Department of Conservation and Recreation, which also manages the two natural areas and the state recreation area included in this book. For more information on these areas or on the parks, you can contact the DCR at 203 Governor St., Suite 302, Richmond, VA 23219; 804/786-1712.

## The Appalachian Trail

One of the quintessential American outdoor experiences is still hiking a section of the *Appalachian Trail*. An increasingly popular—and ambitious—undertaking is to hike the entire trail from end to end, a distance of 2,150 miles. The *AT* is the world's longest continuous foot path, and probably the most famous. It passes through Virginia for 540 miles between Harpers Ferry, WV and Damascus, or one-quarter of the trail's total length. Most of that mileage in on Shenandoah NP, the GWNF, and the JNF. There are dozens, if not hundreds, of access points along the route. No single chapter in this book is devoted to the trail; rather sections of it are described in the areas through which it passes. The trail passes through some of the most rugged and spectacular mountain scenery in Virginia, if not on the entire east coast. No hiker or backpacker should forego a chance to hike at least part of this magnificent footpath. The trail is maintained largely through the work of volunteers organized by local trail clubs. Although several state and federal agencies have a hand in the trail's management, day-to-day operations are handled by and information is available from the Appalachian Trail Conference, P.O. Box 807, Harpers Ferry, WV 25425-0807;304/535-6331.

## Wildlife Management Areas

The twenty-nine wildlife management areas scattered across the state offer hikers, anglers, and backpackers opportunities for outdoor travel that they may have overlooked. The WMAs are managed to provide hunters and anglers with high-quality hunting and fishing grounds. Since hunting only takes place in fall and winter, however, for much of the year these areas are virtually deserted. Conditions on the preserves are primitive, with few amenities and none of the developed recreation facilities found in the parks and national forests. Even signed hiking trails are few. This primitive state offers hikers and backpackers the challenge of traveling through backcountry without the customary advantages of clearly marked trails and well-mapped wildernesses. The WMAs cover a total of 175,000 acres, with individual sites ranging in size from 400 to 33,000 acres. For information contact the Virginia Department of Game & Inland Fisheries, 4010 W. Broad St, Richmond, VA 23230; 804/367-1000.

## National Wildlife Refuges

As their name suggests, the nation's system of national wildlife refuges are managed primarily to provide habitat to wildlife, particularly birds. Low-impact outdoor recreation consistent with these goals is permitted on the refuges. This does not include camping, however; all of the refuges are open during daylight hours only. It does include hunting, though, and visitors should be aware that hunters are likely to be present in fall and winter. Five NWRs are included in this book, all of them located in the coastal region. Unless you're hunting or fishing, these areas are best suited to activities that somehow center around the abundant wildlife—nature photography and birding are two of the most popular activities. Chincoteague Bay NWR, the Virginia component of the Assateague Island National Seashore, is an exception. It has a network of hiking and biking trails and a large beach on the Atlantic that is popular with swimmers and sunbathers. Since the refuges are all located on water, canoes and kayaks provide an excellent means of exploration.

## State Forests

Virginia's 3 state forests are all located on the central piedmont. The forests are managed for timber extraction, resource conservation, education, and study. Each of the forests has at least one designated natural area. Hunting is the major outdoor activity on each forest. Other visitors such as hikers, anglers, and campers tend to stay in the state parks that are adjacent to each forest. The forests are included here, however, because they offer visitors traveling on foot or bike an extensive backcountry to explore if the smallish state parks prove too confining. Conditions are very primitive, and only one of the forests even has a designated hiking trail, but each forest has a large network of unpaved roads that are open to hiking and mountain biking. Most of these roads are also open to motor vehicles, though there are also many gated roads that are not.

## Regional and County Parks

On the piedmont and coast, a handful of regional and county parks round out the backcountry areas covered in this book. These parks vary in size from 500 to 8,000 acres. All have some sort of developed recreation area, usually with an emphasis on family activities such as picnicking or swimming in pools or small lakes. At first glance backcountry travelers may find little that appeal to them at these parks, but the ones that have been included either have an extensive undeveloped natural area, high-quality fishing or paddling, or a campground in a region where there are no others.

# Backcountry Travel

On its face, backcountry travel should not require any specialized knowledge. At its most basic it's no more than walking in the woods. While there is an element of truth to that, it's also true that every year dozens of adventurers get themselves into situations from which they have to be rescued by others. These operations risk lives and cost considerable amounts of money. In addition to these well-publicized misadventures, there are the more mundane mishaps that endanger outdoor enthusiasts and the natural world they value. Although each of the five activities featured in this book requires at least some specialized knowledge and preparation unique to it, what follows is a basic outline of helpful information and potential hazards common to all backcountry pursuits.

How much preparation you need to do before setting out on your trip and how much you need to bring in the way of supplies will of course depend on a number of factors: time of year, location, length of trip, and planned activities. Short, summertime hikes require little more than the clothes on your back and a water bottle. Longer trips and even short wintertime trips require more preparation and more supplies. The items in the first list below should be included on all but very short hikes on well-marked, heavily-traveled trails. Items from both lists should be included on any trip that involves at least one night spent in the backcountry.

## The 10 Essentials

| | |
|---|---|
| Topographic Map | Compass |
| Warm Clothing | Adequate Food |
| Flashlight | Fire Starter & Matches |
| First Aid Kit | Water |
| Knife | Whistle |

## 10 More Essentials

| | |
|---|---|
| Insect Repellent | Sunscreen |
| Sunglasses | Rain Gear |
| Hat with brim | Hiking Boots |
| Camera | 50–100 ft Nylon Cord |
| Backpack or Daypack | Tent |

## Clothing

During the past quarter-century, a revolution in outdoor clothing has occurred with the invention of waterproof-breathable materials such as Gore-Tex and synthetic fabrics that wick moisture away from the skin. Utilizing these technologies, clothing is now made for the most extreme climatic conditions, from the subzero temperatures of the poles and the planet's highest peaks to the hot, humid soup of the tropical rain forests. Fortunately, Virginia's climate is pleasantly distant from these two extremes. For much of the year, in fact, shorts and a T-shirt are about all you'll need to be comfortable outdoors. During the colder months, of course, more specialized clothing is required, and raingear should always accompany any trip of more than an hour or two.

In outfitting yourself for hiking or backpacking, there are two points to keep in mind: 1) Hiking boots are the single most important piece of equipment; and 2) Clothing should keep you comfortable and dry under the worst weather conditions you're likely to encounter. This means carrying raingear on almost every outing. In the mountains especially, but also on the coast, storms can seem to come out of nowhere, materializing from blue skies in a matter of hours. The large majority of backcountry tragedies involve hypothermia, the condition that resutls when the body's core temperature drops below a critical level. Wet clothes, fatigue, and cool or cold temperatures are usually the main culprits. In general, avoid wearing cotton, except during the hottest months. Cotton retains moisture and is extremely slow to dry, which means that if you're wearing jeans and a sweatshirt and get caught out in a rainstorm, you can expect to stay wet until you change clothes. In winter, wearing the right clothes can mean the difference between misery (not to mention frostbite) and comfort. The appendix at the back of this book lists all of the outdoor stores in the state. They can help you outfit yourself so that your next outing will be an enjoyable one.

## Water

It's no longer safe to assume that water taken from rivers, lakes and streams is safe to drink. Regardless of how crystal clear the water of a cool mountain creek may look, odds are good that it contains bacteria and viruses. Giardia, a microscopic organism, has become the number one culprit in illnesses resulting from drinking untreated water. If you're going to drink surface water, you'll need to treat it first. There are currently three main methods of treatment. The oldest, and probably safest, is to boil the water for several minutes (some sources recommend 10 minutes). This is the method usually recommended by park and forest rangers. Another method, increasingly popular with backpackers, is to filter the water through a portable water filter. Many different models are available; most cost between $50 and $150 and weigh less than 20 ounces. If you choose this method, be sure to buy a filter that eliminates organisms as small as 0.5 microns. One that also eliminates bacteria is preferable to one that doesn't. The third method is to treat the water with iodine tablets. The tablets impart a taste to the water that many find unpleasant. This is probably the least effective method, particularly if the water is very cold.

## Hypothermia

Hypothermia is the condition that results when the body's core temperature drops below normal. If untreated, it is fatal. Symptoms include disorientation, lack of coordination, slurred speech, shivering and fatigue. To treat a victim, change him into warm, dry clothes, give him warm drinks, and put him in a sleeping bag. Building a fire can also help. In most cases of hypothermia, a combination of cold temperatures and wet clothes are responsible. The best way to prevent the condition is to be prepared. Bring clothes that will keep you dry and warm during the worst weather you might encounter.

## Snakes and Insects

Four species of poisonous snake inhabit Virginia. The copperhead is the only snake whose range covers the entire state. The timber rattlesnake occurs in the mountains, while the canebrake rattlesnake and the cottonmouth inhabit the wetlands of the state's southeast corner. There is little reason to fear these snakes, as they are nonagressive unless provoked. The greatest danger is in stepping on one or placing a careless hand on one without realizing it. When hiking in snake territory, always be aware of where you're putting your hands and feet. A snakebite kit, available at most outdoor stores, should be part of your first-aid kit.

Although insects are considerably less dangerous than snakes, they can turn an otherwise pleasant trip into a maddening ritual of swatting, itching, and cursing. The coastal region has the greatest concentration of biting insects in Virginia, with the piedmont second. A good repellent should be considered essential equipment between the months of May and October.

## Bears

Black bears inhabit the mountain and coastal regions of Virginia. Their numbers are relatively small and the odds of seeing one of these shy creatures are quite low. Black bears are not naturally aggressive toward humans, and they should not be feared. Instances of bear attacks on people are almost always the result of the bear having been acclimatized to people from food or garbage, a camper sleeping with food in his tent in bear country, or a bear being threatened. If you're camping in bear country, be sure to store all food in a manner so that bears (or other animals) cannot get at it. If no food storage container is available, suspend the food between the limbs of two trees at least 10 ft off the ground and 5 ft from the nearest tree branch. Do not under any circumsances sleep with food in your tent.

## Getting Lost

If you become lost while in the backcountry, the most important thing to do is to avoid panicking. Wherever you are, stop. Relax for a minute or two. Try to remember how you got where you are. If you're on a trail, backtrack and look for familiar landmarks. If it's getting dark or you're injured or exhausted, don't move. The universal distress signal is three of anything—shouts, whistles, flashes of light (a mirror works for this). If you've left or lost the trail, follow a creek or drainage downstream. Eventually it will lead to a road or trail. The best way to avoid getting lost is always to carry a topo map and compass and to know how to use them. Also, be sure to leave plans of your trip with a friend or relative. Give them specific locations so they'll know where to send rescuers if you don't return on time.

## Hunting

Hunting is one of the most popular outdoor activities in Virginia. White-tailed deer, wild turkey, ruffed grouse, black bear, wild turkey, quail, pheasant, and fox are all hunted in the state. Hunting seasons vary, but generally the larger game species can be hunted with guns for short periods in fall and winter. Hunting is permitted on the national forests, state forests, wildlife management areas, and national wildlife refuges. If you're going to travel on one of these areas in fall or winter, be sure to wear at least one article of blaze orange clothing. Deer gun season varies by region, but it's advised that you avoid backcountry travel during these periods unless you too are hunting. For information on hunting licenses and seasons contact the Virginia Department of Game and Inland Fisheries, 4010 West Broad St, Richmond, VA 23230; 804/367-1000.

## The No-Trace Ethic

The no-trace ethic is neatly summarized in the oft-quoted phrase, "Leave only footprints, take only photographs." Where once the untraveled portions of the country were true wildernesses, unvisited regions where the principal dangers were to the traveler, today the situation is reversed. When we speak of wilderness now, we mean a designated area protected by law from development and set aside for natural resource protection and backcountry recreation. The greatest dangers are to the wilderness, not to those who visit. Far from the mysteries and dangers that the word wilderness conjures, these places too often show abundant signs of human presence. Littering is of course inexcusable anywhere. But other, less obtrusive signs of human impact can also diminish the quality of a trip into the backcountry—and of the backcountry itself.

Campfires are first among these unsightly blemishes. Although the appeal of an open fire is undeniable, so too is its impact. Fire rings and the tramped-down, scarred earth that inevitably spreads around them remind us that we are not in the wilds, but are merely following in the footsteps of many others. Burning firewood deprives the soil and forest floor of important nutrients. Whenever possible, a portable camp stove is preferable. It may lack the visceral, romantic appeal of an open fire, but it preserves resources that are unfortunately jeopardized by our numbers. If you do build a campfire, keep it small and contained within an already existing fire ring. If no fire ring exists, build your fire on soil cleared of vegetation; a fire ring is not necessary. When you break camp, make sure the fire is extinguished; scatter the fire ring and any remaining wood and return the surrounding area to a natural state.

In choosing a campsite, it's best to select a site that already exists, but has not deteriorated into an obviously overused state. Minimize impact in making camp. Do not alter the site by digging trenches or creating log benches. When you break camp, return the area to a natural state by scattering leaves, twigs and other forest debris over the area.

To dispose of human waste, dig a hole six inches deep at least 100 feet from trails, campsites and water sources. After use, fill the hole in with soil and lightly tramp it down. Toilet paper should be burned or packed out.

Anything you bring with you into the backcountry should be packed out. When hiking, avoid using shortcuts on switchbacks.

# Using this Book

This guidebook has two main purposes: 1) To catalog and describe all of the major backcountry areas in the state open to the public for recreation; and 2) To provide all the information you need to decide where to go, to get there once you do decide, and to know what to expect when you arrive. The book is divided into approximately 140 different backcountry areas covered in three main sections—The Mountains, The Piedmont and The Tidewater & Eastern Shore. Within each section the areas are arranged geographically, from west to east and from south to north, with a few minor exceptions. This layout is intended to enable you to plan trips where you visit more than one area.

Each listing begins with a description of the backcountry area. Information such as size, location, major natural features, outdoor recreation potential, and open dates is included here. The main purpose of these descriptions, however, is to convey a general sense of the area—whether it's isolated, roadless wilderness; an easily accessible park frequently crowded on weekends; a busy recreational lake; or a remote region of the Outer Banks where water is scarce and mosquitoes abundant. Also included is the nearest town or city and the direction in which it lies.

A number of the areas have accompanying maps. These maps are intended to give a very general overview of an area. They are for illustration purposes only and should not be used for navigation or backcountry travel.

**contact:** Each entry includes the address and phone number of the administrative office that manages the area. This is your best source for additional information. If you have questions about local conditions or are uncertain about opening dates or times, this is the number to call. For all areas where there's a main listing followed by sublistings (i.e. national parks, national forests, state recreation areas, etc.) the address and phone number are only given once, under the main listing.

**getting there:** Directions to each area are from either a nearby town or city or from a major highway. I measured all distances in my car. Because odometer readings vary, you should start looking for turns several tenths of a mile before where they're indicated.

A good road map is necessary to locate the starting point of the directions. You can buy one at any service station or get one free from the Department of Transportation, 1401 E. Braod St, Richmond, VA 23219; 804/786-0020. Ask for the state road map and the *Map of Scenic Roads in Virginia*. The latter shows most of the areas included in this book. If you're going to be doing a lot of traveling in Virginia, a good investment is DeLorme's *Virginia Atlas & Gazetteer.*™ It's an 80-page atlas with large-scale maps that are particularly useful for finding and navigating back roads.

**topography:** This section is intended to give you a rough idea of the type of terrain you can expect to encounter. Major geographical features—rivers, lakes, mountains, forest cover—are described, and high and low elevations are given where they have an impact on backcountry travel or are of interest. Hikers will find this section useful in determining the level of difficulty to expect on the trails. **maps:** A good topographic map should be considered essential equipment for backcountry travel. Maps listed under this heading are only those that have a large enough scale to be useable as topo maps for backcountry navigation. There are 3 major types of topo maps that cover the backcountry areas described in this book: The 7.5 minute series published by the

United States Geologic Survey, district maps and wilderness or recreation area maps published by the USFS, and maps published by private companies that cover Shenandoah NP. USGS topo maps are listed for every area covered in the book. Maps listed as USGS-FS are USGS topo maps modified for Forest Service use. For areas where other maps are available, those are also listed. The list of outdoor stores at the back of this book indicates which stores sell the USGS topo maps. USGS-FS maps are available at each of the district ranger stations.

**starting out:** The primary purpose of this section is to indicate what you can or must do, once at an area, before heading out into the backcountry. Facilities, such as restrooms, water, pay phones, picnic areas, etc., that are located in the area are always mentioned here. Also included is any on-site source of information, such as a ranger station, visitor center, or park office. If you need to obtain a permit or pay a fee, that's indicated as well.

The last paragraph of the section lists some of the more important restrictions, such as rules against alcohol use and pet regulations. Don't assume that because something isn't included here it's allowed. Complete lists of restrictions are available from the various administrative contacts.

**activities:** This guidebook describes the Virginia backcountry from the point of view of five major activities: hiking, camping, canoeing & kayaking, fishing and mountain biking. I've attempted to list these activities in order, beginning with the one that is the most popular attraction of any area. Although most areas are suitable for other outdoor activities, such as horseback riding, rock climbing, cross-country skiing, nature study, and photography, only those five are listed under this heading. If one or more of the other activities is a significant attraction, it's typically mentioned as part of the main description or under *starting out*.

**hiking:** There are more than 2,500 miles of hiking trails in Virginia. The large majority of these are located in the state's mountain region, with a substantially smaller number on the piedmont and coastal region. Descriptions under this heading are intended to give a general idea of hiking opportunities and conditions at each of the areas. Mention of individual trails is fairly uncommon. An attempt has been made to indicate trail mileage, conditions, allowed uses, location of trailheads, level of difficulty and any improvements, particularly bridges across rivers or streams. Mileages have been taken from administrative sources. In many instances I've rounded them to the nearest half-mile.

There are a number of good trail guides available for different parts of the state, including put out by the Potomac Appalachian Trail Club.

**camping:** Camping facilities have been divided into three main categories: developed campgrounds (usually referred to here as car campgrounds), primitive campgrounds that are accessible to autos, and backcountry camping. Dates for campground openings and closings should be considered estimates, as they vary from year to year depending on the weather, and in some areas, Congressional funding. Fees were accurate as of the summer of 1996.

**canoeing/kayaking:** Opportunities for paddling in Virginia fall under three broad categories: flat water on enclosed bodies of water such as lakes and coastal rivers, whitewater on the rivers of the mountains and piedmont, and open water, encountered on the ocean, bays and major tidal rivers. The intention of this section is to make you aware of the general conditions you can expect to encounter on a body of water and to indicate where access points are. Whitewater classifications, where given, are subjective. They are based on first-hand experience and official sources. This section is not intended as a primer on paddling techniques. If you are inexperienced or uncertain about whether conditions on a particular body of water are within your capabilities, you should seek instruction or advice from a reputable paddling school. Every year canoeists and kayakers become stranded or are seriously injured or killed because they put themselves in dangerous situations. The inevitable rescues cost money, risk lives and give the sport a bad name.

Paddling in winter requires specialized equipment. Because the human body can not stand exposure to frigid water for any but the shortest times, mishaps on winter paddling trips can quickly turn into disasters. No one should be canoeing or kayaking in cold weather without being fully prepared for the consequences of capsizing.

**fishing:** Fishing in Virginia can be broken down into three main categories. In the mountains, brook, rainbow and brown trout are the primary species of game fish. Approximately 2,800 miles of creeks and rivers contain trout, with 2,200 of those designated as wild trout waters. Only the brook trout is native to Virginia. Browns and rainbows were introduced from Europe in the 19th century. Other species sought by anglers in the mountains are smallmouth bass, walleye and the very large, elusive muskellunge. On the freshwater rivers and lakes of the piedmont and coastal plain, largemouth bass is the most ubiquitous game fish. Other species popular with anglers include striped bass, northern pike, crappie, bluegill, perch, chain pickerel, and several species of catfish. The tidal rivers, Chesapeake Bay and Atlantic Ocean surf offer renowned fishing for species such as bluefish, Spanish and king mackerel, seatrout, flounder, red and black drum, amberjack, shad, cobia, croaker, spot, and tautog. To fish the Virginia's freshwater lakes and rivers a freshwater fishing license is required. You can get one from an authorized seller or from the Virginia Department of Game & Inland Fisheries, 4010 West Broad St., P.O. Box 11104, Richmond, VA 23230-1104. To fish in Chesapeak Bay or on the tidal portions of the coastal river a marine fishing license required. They are available from authorized sellers or from the Virginia Marine Resources Commission, 2600 Washington Ave., P.O. Box 756, Newport News, VA 23607; 804/247-2200 or 800/541-4646. When you get your license you will be give a complete list of regulations, size limits, and creel limits. Out There Press and the author support a policy of catch-and-release fishing.

This section is intended primarily to list most of the major game species found in a particular body of water; to describe the most appropriate angling methods, whether from a boat, bank or by wading; and to describe access. Information for trout waters is more specific, and includes stream characteristics and special regulations.

**mountain biking:** This section should be used in conjunction with information included under *hiking*, where most trail information is given. Supplemental information found under this heading includes type of trail, whether single track, gated forest road, or road open to motor vehicles; traffic level; typical conditions; and difficulty level. Most opportunities for mountain biking are on the national forests and at several of the national wildlife refuges.

# The Mountains

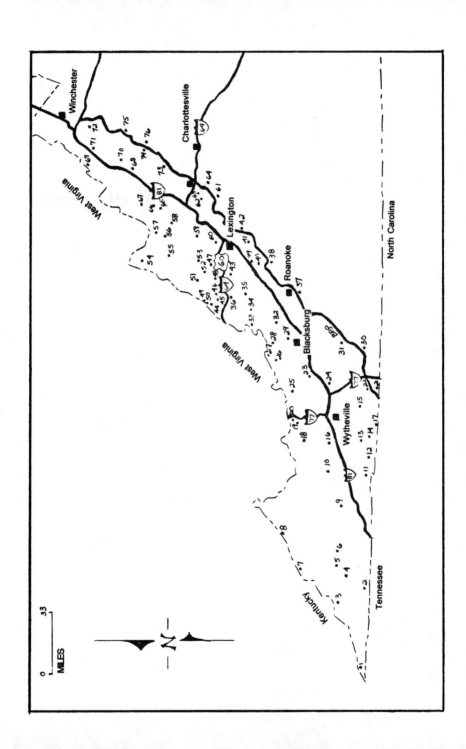

# Mountains Region Key Map

1. Cumberland Gap NHP
2. Natural Tunnel SP
3. Lake Keokee Area
4. Devil's Fork Area
5. High Knob/Little Stony Creek Area
6. Guest River Gorge Area
7. Pine Mountain Area
8. Breaks Interstate Park
9. Hidden Valley WMA
10. Clinch Mountain WMA
11. Virginia Creeper Trail
12. Whitetop Laurel Creek Area
13. Iron Mountain Area
14. Highlands Area
15. Little Dry Run Wilderness
16. Hungry Mother SP
17. Grayson Highlands SP
18. Beartown Wilderness
19. Walker Mountain Area
20. Little Wolf Creek Area
21. Stewart's Creek WMA
22. Crooked Creek WMA
23. Claytor Lake SP
24. New River Trail SP
25. Dismal Creek Area
26. Cascades Rec Area
27. Peters Mountain Wilderness
28. Mountain Lake Wilderness
29. Blacksburg Area
30. Pinnacles of Dan
31. Rocky Knob Rec Area
32. North Mountain Area
33. Potts Creek Area
34. Barbours Creek Wilderness
35. Patterson Creek Area
36. Roaring Run Area
37. Roanoke Mountain Rec Area
38. Peaks of Otter rec Area
39. James River
40. North Creek & Middle Creek Area
41. James River Face Wilderness
42. Otter Creek Rec Area
43. Lake Robertson SRA
44. Lake Moomaw Area
45. Jackson River
46. Fore Mountain Area
47. Rich Hole Wilderness
48. Douthat State Park
49. Gathright WMA
50. Lake Moomaw Area
51. Hidden Valley Area
52. Beards Mountain Area
53. Rough Mountain Wilderness
54. Locust Springs Area
35. Highland WMA
56. Shenandoah Mountain Area
57. Ramsey's Draft Wilderness
58. Great North Mountain Area
59. Goshen–Little North Mtn WMA
60. Goshen Pass Natural Area
61. Mt. Pleasant Scenic Area
62. St. Mary's Wilderness
63. Sherando Lake Rec Area
64. Crabtree Falls Area
65. North River Area
66. Little River Area
67. Hone Quarry Rec Area
68. Massanutten Mountain Area
69. Wolf Gap Area
70. Camp Roosevelt Rec Area
71. Little Fort Rec Area
72. Elizabeth Furnace Rec Area
73. Rockfish Gap to Swift Run Gap
74. Swift Run Gap to Thornton Gap
75. Thornton Gap to Front Royal
76. Rapidan WMA

# Introduction

The mountains in Virginia are the Appalachian Mountains, the oldest mountain range in North America and among the oldest on the planet. They stretch from Canada to eastern Alabama, following a line from northeast to southwest for more than a thousand miles. Although they are dramatic, stunning, spectacular, choose an adjective, they are only shadows of their former selves. In Virginia they reach a peak of only 5,729 ft. In North Carolina, where they attain their highest elevations, they top out at 6,684. For millions of years the forces of wind, weather, and erosion have worn the mountains down from far greater heights. Despite their diminished size they attract millions of admirers every year. The blue haze that clings to the Blue Ridge Mountains. The remote summits and snug pastoral valleys of the Alleghenys. Something about their human scale seems to welcome those who would hike their ridges, fish their streams, or camp in small clearings.

Geographically, the mountains rise in a long continuous ridge from the rolling hills of the piedmont plateau. This first line of mountains is the Blue Ridge, home to Shenandoah National Park, Skyline Drive, and the Blue Ridge Parkway. These parklands extend almost from one end of Virginia to another. They are something of a unique approach in the concept of large parks, All are centered around the easy accessbility offered by a road, with large tracts of wilderness flanking it and the summit crest of the Blue Ridge. Since these projects were completed in the 1930s, the once logged-out, misused land has rapidly regenerated the forests that occur naturally. And with the forests have come the wildlife that are native to the region and once held dominion. White-tailed deer, bobcat, black bear, wild turkey, ruffed grouse. The species that helped define a young nation as different from its European heritage are back in substantial numbers.

These forests occur in a climatic zone that permits two main types: the southern Appalachian forest and the boreal, or northern forest. The former occures throughout the mountainous part of Virginia and is the most common. At its climax stage oak and hickory are the dominant species. This is the forest that draws millions out onto the scenic drives and into the woods every October for the brilliant displays of color put on by the hardwood species. And again in the spring when buds reappear on the branches and then the whole forest explodes into a million shades of green. The boreal forest, on the other hand, is predominantly an evergreen forest. The spruces and firs that are the chief species are adapted to the harsh climates of New England and Canada. In

Virginia, this forest type is relegated to the highest elevations. The presence of this forest should give notice to backcountry travelers that they have entered a region where the climate can be less than hospitable. Summer temperatures rarely exceed 80° at these elevations. Storms can be a common occurrence at any time of year. Winters are bitterly cold with plenty of snow.

The large bulk of this book covers the mountainous region of Virginia, despite the fact that the region is not considerably larger than the piedmont, and not much larger than the coastal plain. Why? Because most of the publicly owned land in Virginia is in the mountains. The two national forests and Shenandoah National Park account for the large majority of the state's public land-holdings. These lands are managed for a variety of purposes, outdoor recreation chief among them. The forests and parks of the mountains therefore provide the best opportunities in the state for outdoor recreation. In the vast backcountry areas there are thousands of miles of trails. More than 500 miles in Shenandoah National Park Alone. Another 300 miles in the Mt. Rogers National Recreation Area. 540 miles on the *Appalachian Trail*, more than in any other state along its route from Georgia to Maine. For fly-fishermen there are 2,800 miles of trout streams to fish, including one of the largest native brook trout fisheries on the east coast in Shenandoah National Park. Canoeists and kayakers can choose to paddle the placid waters of mountain lakes such as Lake Moomaw, or run the rapids of whitewater rivers such as the Jackson or Maury. Campers can choose between developed car campgrounds with electrical hookups or primitive campgrounds with a rustic atmosphere, Or they can leave their cars at a trailhead and backpack into a backcountry that covers well over 2 million acres. Regardless of your taste in outdoor recreation, it's a good bet that Virginia's mountains can satisfy it.

# Cumberland Gap National Historical Park

This long, narrow park straddles three states: Kentucky, Tennessee, and Virginia. Although a scenic area with an extensive backcountry, the park's primary significance is historical. For centuries Cumberland Gap provided travelers—first animals, then native Americans, and finally European settlers migrating westward—the only route through the barrier formed by the Appalachian Mountains. As with so many other parts of the eastern "frontier", Daniel Boone's name is associated with the area. Although not the first white man to travel through the gap, he blazed the trail that became known as the Wilderness Road. The gap itself is located near the southwest corner of the park, where the three states meet. From there, the park stretches almost 15 miles northeast along the main ridge and flanks of Cumberland Mountain. If you approach the park from the east along US-58, you'll get a good sense of the impenetrable wall formed by the mountain and how important a natural opening such as Cumberland Gap was to settlers eager to migrate to the fertile hunting and farming lands of Kentucky. The roadless, forested backcountry is accessible via a network of well-maintained trails. Aside from the area's natural beauty, of interest is the Hensley Settlement, a small, isolated community of self-sufficient farmers that flourished in the first half of this century. Some of the buildings have been preserved and can be reached by hiking trail. In addition to the extensive trail system, facilities in the park include a visitor center, several picnic areas, a car campground, and primitive backcountry campsites. The park is open all year.

Middlesboro, KY (W), and Harrogate, TN (S) are the closest towns.

**contact:** Superintendent, Cumberland Gap NHP, Box 1848, Middlesboro, KY 40965; 606/248-2817

**getting there:** The visitor center is located on US-25E just E of Milddlesboro, KY. In VA, US-58 follows the S border of the park.

**topography:** Cumberland Mtn rises more than 2,000 ft above Poor Valley to the SE. Terrain is rugged in places, with sheer cliffs known as the White Rocks near the park's E edge. Elevations are between 3,500 and 1,200 ft with most of the terrain covered by hardwood forest. **maps:** USGS Varilla, Ewing, Middlesboro South,

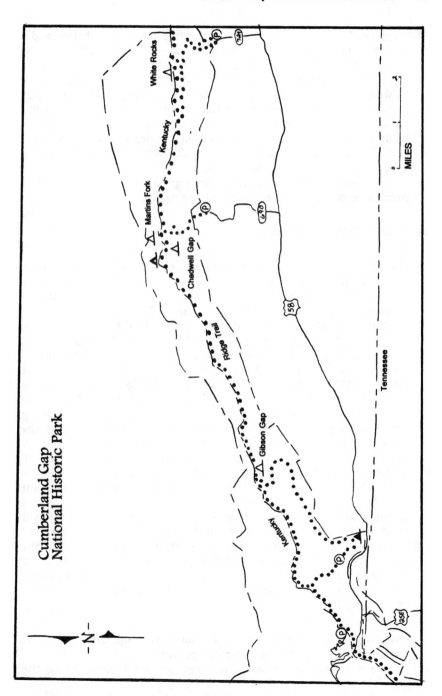

Cumberland Gap
National Historic Park

**starting out:** The visitors center can provide you with brochures and a trail map of the park. There are also exhibits on the area's history, and a small selection of books of local interest is for sale. Hours are 8 AM to 5 PM daily. Restrooms and water are on the premises, as well as at the Pinnacle parking lot and at the picnic area. A pay phone is at the campground. Although crowds are a rarity in the park, most people cluster at the Pinnacle, where a short hike leads to an overlook with stunning, long-range views into KY, TN, and VA. The park has a large picnic area with tables, grills, and a single shelter set in a wooded area.

Pets are allowed, but must be kept on a leash. Alcohol is permitted in the picnic area and campground.

**activities:** Hiking, Camping

**hiking:** Park trails range from short, paved paths that lead to scenic overlooks, to steep mountain ascents, to the 16-mile *Ridge Trail*, which follows the VA/KY border along the crest of Cumberland Mtn. In all, there are roughly 50 mi of trails. On the VA side, several trails make the steep ascent to the summit crest of the mountain where they join the *Ridge Trail*. These trails are between 2 and 5 miles long. Although park trails are not blazed, they are well maintained and easy to follow. All trailheads are clearly signed. Improvements include footbridges and steps in a few places, as well as signs at trail jcts. Hiking is mostly through hardwood forest, with rock outcrops that provide outstanding views into VA and KY. Other highlights include Skylight Cave, the Hensley Settlement, and the tri-state marker where KY,TN, and VA meet. Although loop hikes are possible, multi-day hikes will involve either backtracking or a vehicle shuttle. Trail use is relatively light, with some trails open to horse travel. Hiking on most trails is moderate to strenuous. Trailhead to the *Ridge Trail* is at the Pinnacle Overlook (from the visitors center, follow signs 4 miles to the parking lot). At its other end, the trail can be reached by hiking the short, strenuous *Ewing Trail* from Civic Park at the park's E end (from the jct of US-25E and US-58, take US-58 E 13.7 mi to SR-724. Turn L and go 1 mi to the parking area). Other trailheads on the VA side of the park are at the picnic area and the campground.

**camping:** Campers at the park have two options: primitive backcountry sites or a large car campground.

The 4 backcountry camping areas are all located along the

ridge of Cumberland Mtn. The only improvements at the sites are pit toilets. Although water is sometimes available from creeks near a couple of the sites, you should plan on carrying in a sufficient supply. The sites are fairly small, but don't receive very heavy use; crowding is rarely a problem. Getting to the sites requires a hike of from 2 to 5 miles, on trails that are moderate to strenuous. Backcountry campers are required to register and pick up a free permit at the visitors center before heading out. Backcountry camping outside of the designated sites is not allowed.

The large car campground has 160 sites laid out in a number of smaller loops. This pleasant campground is situated in a large forested area. Sites are fairly large and well spaced in a wooded area with a dense understory; privacy at the sites is quite good. Each site includes a picnic table and grill. Shower/restroom facilities with hot water are centrally located. The camping fee is $10/night. Finding a site should not be a problem, even on summer weekends. Group sites are also available, with fees of $1/person ($20 minimum). The campground is located on US-58 1.3 miles E of US-25E.

# Natural Tunnel State Park

The natural tunnel that gives this park its name was declared by William Jennings Bryan to be the "Eigth Wonder of the World." It's a monicker that has stuck, at least locally. The 850-foot tunnel, which geologists believe to be at least a million years old, was formed by the force of water over tens of thousands of years. Railroad builders took advantage of the natural opening in the mountain to lay tracks which are still in use today. Although you can't enter the tunnel, yoiu can get a good up-close look at it, thanks to several hiking trails and a new chairlift. Although the lift has spoiled some of the wilderness appeal of the area, the tunnel has been a tourist attraction for more than a century, drawing thousands to the area. And with as many as ten trains passing through it daily, its pristine natural appeal was already more or less shot. The 850-acre park exists mainly to protect the tunnel and to make it available to the public. Most visitors come to see the tunnel and then leave, though the park does offer several other attractions. A small network of hiking trails winds through the area's rugged, forested terrain, and there's a car campground, picnic area with tables, grills, and shelters, and swimming pool (open seasonally). The park is worth a stop to see one result of nature's implacable forces, or to take a pleasant stroll through mountain scenery. Just don't expect backcountry solitude. The park is open all year from dawn to dusk.

Gate City (SE) and Big Stone Gap (N) are the closest towns.

**contact:** Natural Tunnel State Park, Route 3, Box 250, Duffield, VA 24244-9361; 540/940-8674

**getting there:** From Gate City, take US-58 W 12 mi to SR-871. Turn R and go 1.3 mi to the park entrance, R.

**topography:** Park terrain is rugged and mountainous. Natural tunnel is carved out of a steep groge. Gorge walls are a 400 ft vertical drop. Most of the park is forested, though a few large areas have been cleared and landscaped. **maps:** USGS Clinchport.

**starting out:** Information is available in two locations: the park office at the entrance or the visitor center next to the chairlift. A pay phone, restrooms, and water are all located at the visitor center. The chairlift drops 500 ft from the visitor center into the gorge. It costs $2 reound-trip. The gorge can also be reached on a short, steep hiking trail. If you want to use the swimming pool or picnic areas, you have to pay a parking fee of $1/vehicle on weekdays, $2 on weekends.

Public use of alcohol is not allowed in the park. Pets must be kept on a leash.

**activities:** Hiking, Camping

**hiking:** The small network of trails in the park exists primarily to provide access to the park's scenic attractions and to vantage points that allow outstanding views of the gorge and surrounding mountains. 5 trails cover just 2 miles in all. You can start your hike from the visitor center, the campground, or the picnic/pool area. The trails all connect, so you can take in all the main attractions on a single short hike. Since the trails receive very heavy use, improvements such as paved treadways, fences, boardwalks, steps, and benches have been added. Although you won't escape into the wilderness here, you might come away with some great photos. The *Lover's Leap Trail*, which begins at the visitor center, is an interpretive trail with a guide available at the trailhead. Hiking on the trails is easy to moderate.

**camping:** The car campground has 22 sites squeezed into a small clearing beside a forest and field. The sites are small and closely spaced, offering almost no privacy. A few sites located at the edge of the forest are fairly large and secluded. If you're lucky enough to score one of these sites, a pleasant camping experience is possible; if not, expect to be squeezed by neighbors on all sides. Each site has a picnic table and a grill. A shower/restroom facility is available. Sites cost $11/night, $15 with hookup. Pets cost $3 extra. The campground is open Apr 1 to Nov 30.

# Clinch Ranger District

## Jefferson National Forest

The westernmost district on the Jefferson National Forest, the Clinch encompasses 90,000 acres in three major sections. The northern section borders Kentucky along the summit and southern flank of Pine Mountain in Wise and Dickenson Counties. The Pound River parallels the mountain to the south, and the North Fork of Pound Reservoir offers water-based recreation. The John W. Flanagan Reservoir, at the district's southeast end but maintained by the Army Corps of Engineers, is considerably larger and a popular fishing and boating spot. A second section, similar in size and shape, is located north of the town of Big Stone Gap. The long summit ridge of Stone Mountain forms the backbone of this area, with the Powell River forming the southern boundary; Kentucky is again adjacent to the north. The largest section spreads out south of Norton. The Clinch river flows nearby to the south, with the Powell running to the northwest. This area includes High Knob, the highest point on the district. Recreational facilities on the district feature several networks of hiking trails (including a rail-trail conversion, a national recreation trail, and three long trails), remote dirt and gravel roads well suited to mountain biking, stocked trout streams, three car campgrounds, and three lakes with boat ramps.

The towns of Norton, Big Stone Gap, Appalachia, and Pound are all adjacent to forest lands. Wise and Coeburn are in close proximity to areas described below.

**contact:** Clinch Ranger District, 9416 Darden Dr, Wise, VA 24293; 540/328-2931.

**getting there:** US-23 and US-58 are the major highways that provide access to the district. The district ranger station is in Wise across the street from Clinch Valley College. To get there: take US-23 to US-23 Business and go 1.3 mi N to SR-640. Turn R and go 0.6 to Darden Dr NE. Turn R and go 0.9 mi to the ranger station, R.

**topography:** The disparate lands of the district are mostly mountainous, with elevations between 4,000 and 2,000 ft. Forest cover is mixed Appalachian hardwoods, with some conifer species interspersed. **maps:** USFS Clinch Ranger District; USGS maps are listed below under individual headings

**starting out:** If you haven't brought maps with you or want to check on current conditions, a stop at the district ranger station is worthwhile. They sell district maps and have free brochures and fact sheets that describe many of the rec areas. It's open weekdays from 8 AM to 4:30 PM. While the district map is useful for locating trailheads or rec areas, its scale is too small to be of much use as a topo; you're better off with the USGS topo quads listed for each entry below.

**activities:** Hiking, Camping, Fishing, Mountain Biking, Canoeing/Kayaking

**hiking:** There are 110 miles of trails on the district. 4 of the 5 areas described are anchored by a single long, straight hiking trail, with shorter spur trails that branch out. The exception is the Devil's Fork Area, which features a series of trails that form a loop. Except for the *Guest River Gorge Trail*, all of the district's long trails offer outstanding opportunities for multi-day backpacking trips. While most of the trails offer scenic highlights that include mountain vistas, the lush hardwood and hemlock forests through which they pass are major attractions themselves. On the district's trails it's possible to escape into a world that seems primeval for its dense vegetation. For the most part the trails are well maintained, with signed trailheads and clearly-defined footpaths. Much of the terrain is mountainous, providing hikers and backpackers with challenging conditions.

**camping:** Campers on the district have a wealth of options. Since 4 of the areas described below feature an extensive backcountry served by hiking trails, there are plenty of opportunities for multi-day backpacking trips. Canoe or kayak campers can overnight at the backcountry sites on the N Fork of Pound Reservoir. Primitive backcountry camping is permitted anywhere on NF lands, except where posted. Generally areas where you can't camp are next to developed rec areas and within 100 ft of roads.

Car campers have 4 campgrounds to choose from. Each of these campgrounds is small and fairly primitive, offering a nice compromise between the convenience of car camping and the solitude of backpacking. The campgrounds are all located in attractive settings, with trail networks and access to small lakes nearby. A fee is charged at each, and the campgrounds are all open from May 15 to Oct 15.

**fishing:** Anglers can fish for both cold water and warm water species on the district. A pair of stocked trout creeks run through the large backcountry between the High Knob Observation Tower and the Hanging Rock Rec Area. These are small, intimate waters that flow through an exceptionally scenic forest. Another small trout creek is located in the Devil's Fork Area.

3 of the areas featured below have small lakes that harbor largemouth bass and other warm water species. North Fork of Pound Reservoir is the largest of these lakes. All can be fished from the banks or from a canoe or kayak.

**mountain biking:** The district's newest trail—the *Guest River Gorge Trail*—is a rail-trail conversion that's ideal for short bike trips. Riding elsewhere on the district is mostly on forest roads, both gated and open to motor vehicles. Traffic throughout the district is light, so that doesn't really pose a problem for riders. The best areas for riding are the High Knob/Little Stony Creek Area and the Devil's Fork Area. A large network of unpaved roads runs through both areas, allowing for rides both short and long.

**canoeing/kayaking:** Paddling opportunities on the district are found on 3 small lakes. Backcountry travelers will be most drawn to the N Fork of Pound Reservoir. Not only is it the largest lake on the district, but there are facilities for backcountry camping as well. Paddlers wanting a larger body of water can head E to the John W Flanagan reservoir, located in the shadow of Pine Mountain.

# Lake Keokee Area

Scenic Lake Keokee sits in the middle of this long, narrow parcel of forest service land located to the north and northwest of Big Stone Gap. Marsh grasses and forest surround the small lake, and the trunks of dead trees rise from its waters like eerie sentinels. Stone Mountain, which runs through the area SW–NE, is the defining topographical feature of the area. The Powell River traces the line of the mountain to the south. Although this area is relatively small, it contains some of the most impressive scenery on the district. Lush forests of hardwoods and hemlocks, cliff faces, massive boulders, mosses, ferns, and large rhododendron slicks are all present on and around the mountain. The backcountry here is fairly isolated, with access via a hiking trail that runs the length of the area and passes through an exceptionally beautiful woodland setting. A couple of rec areas provide facilities for camping, picnicking, fishing, and paddling. Crowds are minimal. The Lake Keokee area is best suited to a one or two day visit, with backpacking or hiking trips into the backcountry highly recommended

Big Stone Gap (S) is the closest town.

**getting there:** All directions are from downtown Big Stone Gap. To reach Cave Springs Rec Area, take US-58 ALT W 4.1 miles to SR-621. Turn R and go 2.3 miles to a jct with SR-622. Keep R on SR-621and go 6.7 miles to the rec area entrance, R. • To get to Lake Keokee, take US-23 BUS N 2.8 miles to VA-68. Turn L and go 8.1 miles to SR-623. Turn L and go 0.6 miles to the lake and parking lot.

**topography:** The terrain is rugged and mountainous, with rocky slopes and sheer walls present. Forest cover is dense across most of the area and consists primarily of southern Appalachian hardwoods and hemlocks. Elevations are between 1,500 and 3,000 ft. **maps:** USGS-FS Big Stone Gap, Appalachia.

**starting out:** Access to this area is at 2 rec areas and a trailhead. Facilities are located at Lake Keokee (pit toilets) and Cave Springs Rec Area (water; toilets in campground). Both areas have picnic tables and grills. You won't find this area crowded on many days, but visitors are usually concentrated at the rec area and lake.

Alcohol is not allowed at Cave Springs Rec Area.

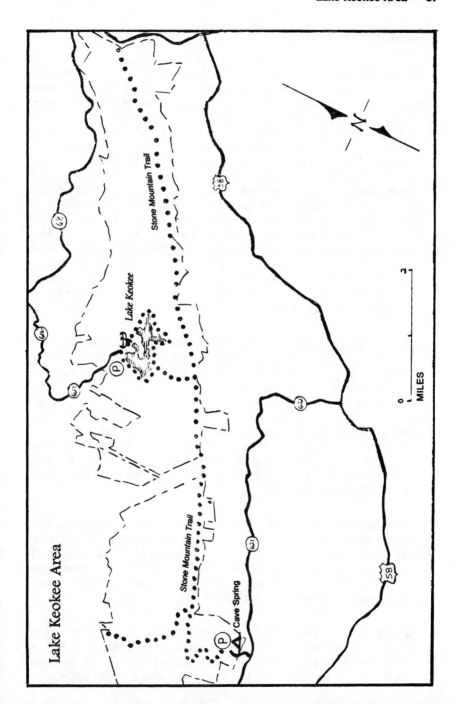

**activities:** Hiking, Camping, Fishing, Canoeing/Kayaking

**hiking:** The 12.5-mi, arrow-straight *Stone Mountain Trail* stretches from one end of this area to the other, with a couple of spur trails branching off from it. If you're only hiking a part of the trail, make sure it's the E end. From the E trailhead, the trail rises up a series of rugged stone steps constructed by the YCC beside Roaring Branch. Almost immediately, you enter a cool, lush cove forest dominated by towering hemlocks and vast rhododendron slicks. Underneath, the creek slides through massive rock formations and under looming cliffs. Further along the trail is a stand of old growth hemlocks and excellent views of the surrounding countryside. A 1-mi connector trail leads to Lake Keokee, where the easy, 3-mi *Lake Keokee Trail* circles the lake. The *Stone Mtn Trail* ends in the Cave Springs Rec Area. The trail is blazed and easy to follow. Use is light to moderate. To reach the E trailhead, take US-58 ALT N from Big Stone Gap 1.4 miles to the trailhead, L. Park on the R another 0.2 miles up the road near some dumpsters. Hiking on the trail is moderate to strenuous.

**camping:** Backcountry camping is permitted throughout the area on NF lands, except where posted. In practice, this means along the *Stone Mountain Trail*. Camping is not allowed at the lake or rec area except at designated sites.

A car campground is located at Cave Springs Rec Area. 41 large sites are spread out on a heavily wooded hillside. The dense forest growth affords plenty of privacy. Each site has a picnic table, grill, and lantern post. Flush toilets are centrally located. The campground is rarely crowded. Come on a weekday, and you might have it to yourself. The campground is open from May 14 to Oct 15. The fee is $8/night.

**canoeing/kayaking:** Although it's unlikely anyone would want to make a special trip to Lake Keokee just to paddle it, the 92-acre lake does offer a pleasant setting for a short paddle. Particularly if you happen to have rod and reel with you. One of the advantages of the lake is that you're not likely to see more than one or two other boats on it. Boats with gasoline motors are not allowed.

**fishing:** Lake Keokee contains largemouth bass, sunfish, and catfish. The lake's small size and remnant trees keep the fish in a pretty limited area. There's a small cleared area on shore from which you can cast, but angling from a canoe is a better option.

# Devil's Fork Area

Although not far from Norton, this small, rugged mountainside is one of the most remote backcountry areas on the Clinch Ranger District. Except for the road that leads to the trailheads and the hiking trails themselves, it is entirely undeveloped, without facilities or roads. That wasn't always the case, however, as signs of fairly recent logging activitiy are plain. Today the attractions are the hardwood and hemlock forest, scenic trout creeks that tumble through carved chutes and over waterfalls, and picturesque views out over the surrounding landscape. It can also be used as a base for exploring the surrounding region on a mountain bike. This seldom-traveled area is best suited to a day-hike or a single overnight.

**getting there:** From Norton, take SR-619 S 15.4 miles (at 9.4 miles the pavement ends and the road becomes a narrow, winding, gravel road) to an umarked road at a white house with a fenced yard, R. Turn R and go 0.3 miles to the end of the road and trailheads at a small parking area. • Or, from Big Stone Gap, take US-23 S 14 miles to SR-871. Turn L and go 2.1 miles to SR-653. Turn L and go 12.3 miles to SR-619. Turn L and go 0.6 miles to the gravel access road at the white house.

**topography:** Rugged, mountainous terrain interlaced by small creeks and runoffs defines the area. Forest is cover is mixed conifers and hardwoods. Elevations are between 2,750 and 1,750 ft. **maps:** USGS-FS E Stone Gap, Fort Blackmore.

**starting out:** There are no facilities in the area. Water sources along the trails are plentiful, but surface water should be treated before drinking.

**activities:** Hiking, Fishing, Camping, Mountain Biking

**hiking:** All trails are accessed at the single trailhead. From there, you follow the 5.5-mi *Devil's Fork Trail*, heading either up Straight Fork Ridge or following Devil's Fork upstream. Either way, you end up back at the starting point. A spur trail, the 2-mi *Straight Fork Ridge Trail*, branches off the main trail on the ridge that gives it its name. The trails are blazed and the trailhead is signed, but the trails are obscure in places and following them can be difficult, particularly near the trailhead. Hiking is moderate to strenuous. Trail use is light.

**fishing:** Although not a major trout fishing area, Devil's Fork does contain some native trout and a short section from the trailhead to SR-619 is stocked. This segment of the creek is reached from the access road, upstream from there access is from the hiking trail. The creek is small with plenty of cover from rhododendrons. Its gradient is mild with lots of small pools.

**camping:** Backcountry camping is permitted throughout the area on NF lands, except where posted. There are a couple of good sites along the *Devil's Fork Trail.* There are no developed camping facilities in the area.

**mountain biking:** The hiking trails are all closed to bikes, and there are no designated bike trails, but that doesn't mean there are no riding possibilities in the area. SR-619, the long, winding dirt and gravel road that leads up and over Stone Mountain to Norton, and SR-653, the unpaved road that follows the base of the mountain, offer pretty good rides. In combination with other forest roads in the area, loop rides of up to 25 miles can be pieced together. Riding is easy to strenuous in the area, depending on the route chosen and direction of travel. Use the Jefferson NF road map or the topos for navigating the back roads.

# High Knob/Little Stony Creek Area

Extending from just south of Norton to the Clinch River, this is the largest backcountry area on the district. Three separate recreation areas and the generally dispersed lands of this area are united by a single long trail. Actually, it's two trails—the *Chief Benge's Scout Trail* and the *Little Stony National Recreation Trail*—connected end-to-end and covering a total distance of more than nineteen miles. At the northeast end of the trail is the High Knob Observation Tower, providing outstanding 360° views into five states. Adjacent is the High Knob Rec Area, with car campground, picnic area, and lake with small swimming beach and bathhouse. Midway along the trail is the Bark Camp Recreation Area, with car campground, 60-acre lake with boat ramp and fishing docks, and picnic area. At the trail's eastern terminus is the Hanging Rock Recreation Area, a large day-use area with extensive picnic grounds. All three rec areas have vehicle, as well as foot, access. The two trails follow a pair of exceptionally attractive creeks that meander through thick growths of mountain laurel and rhododendron—Mountain Fork and Little Stony Creek. Both are stocked trout streams. The hardwood forest that surrounds them provides haven to white-tailed deer and beaver. The short, paved trail and views from High Knob make it the busiest spot on the district. The trails in the area are typically less crowded. With several scenic highlights and an extensive backcountry, there's enough to see and do to fill a weekend visit.

Norton (NW) and Coeburn (NE) are the closest towns.

**getting there:** Directions are to the 3 rec areas. To reach High Knob Rec Area, from the jct of US-23 and SR-619 in Norton, go S on SR-619 4 miles to FR-238. Turn L and go 1.4 miles (or at 0.5 miles turn R and go 0.2 mi to a parking area for the High Knob Observation Tower) to gravel FR-233. Turn R and go 1 mile to the campground and lake. • To reach Bark Camp, from Coeburn, go S on VA-72 4.7 mi (5.8 mi N of Hanging Rock Rec Area) to SR-664. Turn R and go 1.1 mi to gravel SR-700. Turn L and go 1.3 mi to a jct with gravel SR-701 (ahead it's 1 mi to the Falls of Little Stony). Turn R on gravel SR-700 and go 4.9 mi to gravel SR-822. Bear R and go 1 mi to gravel FR-993. Turn L and go 0.8 mi to the campground and lake. • Another route is from the jct of US-23 and US-58 ALT: go E on US-58 ALT 5 mi to SR-706. Turn R and go 4 mi to SR-699. Turn L and go 0.3 mi to SR-822. Turn R and go 1.6 mi (at 1.1 miles the pavement ends) to FR-993. Turn R and go 0.8 mi to the rec area. • To reach Hanging Rock, from Coeburn, take VA-72 S 10.5 mi to the entrance, R.

**topography:** At 4,000 ft, High Knob is the highest point on the Clinch RD. Elevations drop as low as 1,500 ft along Little Stony Creek at the area's SE edge. Except for the bald on High Knob and clearings around the 2 lakes, the area is heavily forested, with southern hardwoods and hemlocks the dominant species. **maps:** USGS-FS Norton, Wise, Coeburn, Fort Blackmore, Dungannon.

**starting out:** Facilities (water, toilets, picnic area with tables and grills) are at all three rec areas. In addition, there's a nice bathhouse and small swimming beach at High Knob Lake. A $2/vehicle entrance fee is charged. Despite the attraction of the nearby High Knob observation tower, this area keeps pretty quiet. Solitude shouldn't be hard to find on the trails.

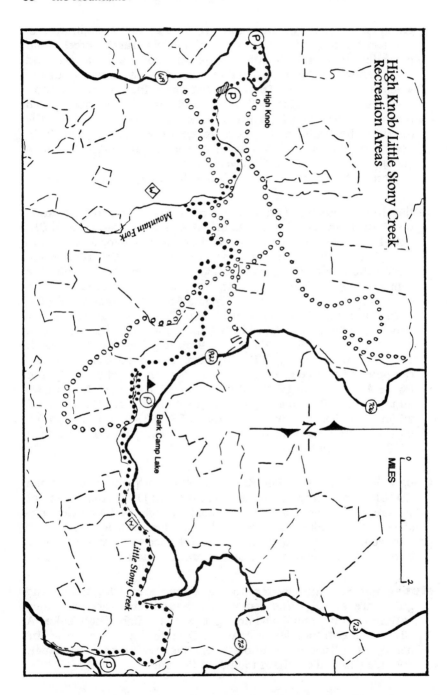

High Knob/Little Stony Creek
Recreation Areas

High Knob

Mountain Fork

Bark Camp Lake

Little Stony Creek

N

MILES

0

2

Alcohol is not allowed at Hanging Rock, Bark Camp Lake, or High Knob rec areas. Swimming is not allowed in Bark Camp Lake. Boats are not allowed on High Knob Lake.

**activities:** Hiking, Fishing, Camping, Canoeing/Kayaking, Mountain Biking

**hiking:** The single, 19-mi trail formed by the *Chief Benge's Scout Trail* and *Little Stony National Recreation Trail* provides the main opportunity for hiking in the area. Although it starts out with the stunning views on High Knob, for most of its length it travels through the deep, cool forest that surrounds Mountain Fork and Little Stony Creek. With towering hemlocks and hardwoods, lush rhododendron slicks and the rocky creeks, this is one of the prettiest hikes on the district. Since the trail follows a crooked line from one end of the area to the other, all hikes involve either backtracking or a vehicle shuttle. Access to the trail is at any of the 3 rec areas, making it possible to hike shorter segments. The well-designed, well-maintained trail is not difficult to hike, with creek crossings the only major difficulty (there are footbridges in some areas). Yellow blazes point the way. At Bark Camp Lake, the trail joins an easy 3.7-mi loop trail that circles the lake. Trail use is heavy at both ends of the trail, light in its long midsection.

**fishing:** Fishing in the area is at one lake and two stocked trout creeks. Mountain Fork begins at High Knob Lake and flows E and then S. It's a small creek with an average to mild gradient. It has a very rocky bed and rhododendron and mountain laurel press in on both banks, making fly-casting very tight in spots. The *Chief Benge's Scout Trail* follows the creek for about 3 miles; most of that portion of the creek is stocked.

At the area's other end is Little Stony Creek, another small, very rocky creek with tight cover. Its gradient is mild to average, with a course that twists under and around some massive boulders, forming some good pools and adding to the scenic beauty. Little Stony begins at Bark Camp Lake, flowing SE about 8 miles before joining the Clinch River. The *Little Stony Trail* and *Chief Benge's Scout Trail* provides access along the entire route.

Finally, Bark Camp Lake is a smallish (60 acres) body of cool water that supports populations of bass, northern pike, trout, and sunfish. Fishing is either from the banks, where there's a large area that's been cleared, or from a boat. In addition, a couple of handicapped-accessible fishing piers have been constructed on the lakeshore. The trout in the lake are stocked.

**camping:** Campers can spend the night in the backcountry along the 2 main hiking trails, or at either High Knob rec area or Bark Camp rec area, both of which have car campgrounds.

At High Knob 14 sites are spread out on a wooded hillside. The sites are large and well spaced, affording plenty of privacy. Each site has a picnic table, grill, and lantern post. There are modern restrooms at the campground, with showers a short walk away at the bathhouse beside High Knob Lake. The fee is $8/night. The campground is open May 14 to Oct 15.

Bark Camp campground has 21 sites spread out along two prongs of the campground road. The sites, set in a hardwood forest, are large and well-spaced. Each site has a picnic table, grill, and lantern post. There are modern restrooms, but no showers. The camping fee is $5/night. The campground is open May 14 to Oct 15.

**canoeing/kayaking:** 60-acre Bark Camp Lake offers the only paddling opportunity in the area. The lake is small and scenic; a nice place to spend a lazy couple of hours paddling, or maybe longer if you bring rod and reel. The lake is usually pretty quiet, and boats with gasoline motors are not allowed. You might see another boat or two with fisherman, but probably not much more in the way of traffic. Look for white-tailed deer along the shore.

**mountain biking:** Although there are no specifically designated bike trails in the area, the numerous dirt and gravel forest service roads that lace the area make a nice network for a day's ride. The best area is around Bark Camp Lake. Start out at the parking area there and head either E or W along the lightly-traveled roads. Most of the riding is easy to moderate, but if you get off the main routes and follow a gated logging road the going can get a little rougher. With at least 100 miles of unpaved roads in the area, it's possible to piece together some pretty long rides.

# Guest River Gorge Area

The Guest River Gorge is the area on the Clinch most recently developed for its recreational potential. In 1994 the *Guest River Gorge Trail*, a rails-to-trails conversion, was dedicated, opening the scenic gorge to hikers, bikers, equestrians, anglers, and other outdoor lovers. The trail follows more than five miles of the route of an old Norfolk–Southern line. The railroad paralleled the Guest River, which has been designated a State Scenic River. With whitewater sliding through rock formations and cascading over ledges, it provides a stunning backdrop to the trail. A forest of hardwoods and hemlocks mingles with both river and trail. Although the trail is new and relatively unknown, it's already attracting a fairly high number of visitors. Most people come to spend an hour or two; in three or four you can hike the trail from start to finish and back again.

Coeburn (N) is the closest town.

**getting there:** From downtown Coeburn go S on VA-72 (at 3.7 miles is the Flatwoods picnic area, R) 3.9 mi to a paved access road, L. Turn L onto the road and go 1.3 miles to the parking area and trailhead.

**topography:** The mountain slopes that surround the trail and gorge are forested with both pines and hardwoods. The trail drops about 500 ft from start to finish. Elevations are between 2,000 and 1,500 ft. **maps:** USGS-FS Coeburn.

**starting out:** Facilities are at the Flatwoods Picnic Area (toilets, water, picnic tables and grills, shelter) across the road from the entrance to the *Guest River Gorge Trail* and at the trailhead (port-a-toilets). The only access point to the area is at the trailhead. This is becoming a popular day-use area, particularly along the first mile or two of the trail.

**activities:** Hiking, Mountain Biking

hiking/**mountain biking:** The 5.3 mi rail-trail parallels the Guest River, which flows north to south. Although the river is always within earshot of the trail, it's often out of sight. The trail is wide, with a bed that's alternately cruched cinders, dirt, and gravel. Scenic wooden trestles cross the river in several spots. Hiking or biking along the trail is easy, as the grade is mild. From the trailhead, it's downhill; since the trail is straight with no connectors, you have to hike or bike on a slight uphill to return to the trailhead. Scenic highlights along the trail include the river, with whitewater and waterfalls; sandstone cliffs; a long railroad tunnel; and a hardwood and pine forest. Trail use is heavy.

# Pine Mountain Area

This part of the district is defined by Pine Mountain, a long narrow ridge that rises where Russell Fork passes through The Breaks and continues southeast for 125 miles. Here, the mountain forms the border with Kentucky, and national forest lands occupy the upper reaches of its southern flank. The other natural feature defining the area is the Pound River, which flows through the valley below Pine Mtn. Although this part of the district is in the heart of coal country, and large, gaping scars mar large segments of the surrounding landscape, Pine Mtn itself is today covered in a dense forest of mixed Appalachian hardwoods. Despite this area's relatively small size, a good mix of outdoor recreation potential exists. The length of Pine Mtn from Pound Gap to The Breaks is traced by a hiking/biking trail, while the N Fork of Pound Reservoir provides an intimate, scenic setting for paddling or fishing, with a couple of rec areas for camping and picnicking on its perimeter. In general, the Pine Mtn area is best suited for a daylong or weekend visit. The John W Flanagan Reservoir (operated by the Army Corps of Engineers) is adjacent to forest lands and is a popular boating and fishing area.

Pound (S) is the closest town.

**getting there:** Most trailheads and rec areas are a short drive from downtown Pound. US-23 runs along the W edge of town. VA-83 parallels Pine Mtn, providing access to the area's E end. Directions to trailheads and rec areas are given below.

**topography:** The long, narrow spine of Pine Mtn reaches elevations of 3,000 ft. N Fork of Pound Reservoir is at 1,570 ft. The mountain is heavily forested with both pines and hardwoods present. **maps:** USGS-FS Flat Gap, Jenkins E, Jenkins W, Clintwood, Elkhorn City, Hellier.

**starting out:** The area's only facilities are at N Fork of Pound Reservoir. Across from the dam are restrooms, water fountain, and a couple of picnic tables. This area doesn't receive a whole lot of use, so crowds shouldn't really be a problem.

**activities:** Hiking, Camping, Fishing, Canoeing/Kayaking, Mountain Biking

**hiking:** The main hiking trail in the area is the 23-mile *Cumberland Mountain Trail*, which follows the ridge of Pine Mtn between Pound Gap and The Breaks at Breaks Interstate Park. The mountain is dominated by a hardwood forest, yet openings and rock outcrops afford impressive views of the surrounding countryside. Although neither trailhead is signed or particularly easy to locate, the trail itself is blazed and relatively easy to follow. Hiking along the trail is moderate to strenuous. To reach the W trailhead: from Pound take US-23 3.1 mi N to Pound Gap at the KY state line. Park across the road near a small grocery. The unmarked trailhead is up a short paved (then gravel) road on the northbound side of the highway. Don't judge the trail by its first half-mile; on an unattractive dirt road it passes a construction site, a radio antenna station and a cluster of satellite dishes. After that it enters the forest and leaves civilization behind. Hiking on the trail is strenuous. Trail use is moderate. Several spur trails branch off the main trail and descend the S side of the mtn to additional access points. The trail is open to horses and mountain bikes, although use is generally light. The E trailhead is in Breaks Interstate Park. To get there go to the park entrance and head W on VA-80 4.9 miles to a sharp curve in the road and a small, unmarked parking area, L. Follow the short, steep, unmarked trail down to the RR trestle. Cross the trestle to the start of the trail.

Several short trails are also in the area around Pound. To reach the 1-mi *Red Fox Trail*, take US-23 N 1.2 miles out of Pound to SR-667 (Potter Town Rd). Turn L and go 0.6 mi to a gated road L and a small parking area across from it. Hike 0.2 miles up the gated road to the trailhead. The single-track trail is an easy hike through a hardwood, hemlock, and rhododendron forest to the site of the ambush where on May 14, 1892 5 members of the Mullins party were gunned down. The assailant, nicknamed the Red Fox, was hanged at Wise courthouse the following autumn. He dressed all in white and vowed to rise from the dead, a promise he apparently failed to keep.

The *Phillips Creek Trail* is a 1.3-mi nature trail that begins and ends in the Cane Patch campground. Attractions along the trail include wildlife clearings, a homestead site, and a waterfall. To get there, follow directions below to the campground.

**camping:** Campers have 3 choices: backcountry camping at undesignated sites, primitive backcountry camping at Laurel Fork on N Fork of Pound Reservoir, or a developed car campground at Cane Patch.

Backcountry camping is permitted anywhere in the area on NF

lands, unless posted otherwise. In practice this means camping along the *Cumberland Mtn Trail.* Hiking the entire trail at a reasonable pace takes 3 days.

Another attractive backcountry option is the Laurel Fork primitive camping area at N Fork of Pound Reservoir. The half-dozen lakeside sites are situated in a large clearing and marked by permanent fire rings. The area is surprisingly remote and quite scenic. The sites can be reached by a moderate 1.5-mile hike through a hardwood forest or by a 1-mile paddle on the reservoir. There's space to dock or beach a canoe or kayak. Whether you hike in or paddle, the starting point is the boat ramp 0.5 mile past the dam.

At the other end of the reservoir, car campers can overnight at Cane Patch Campground. 34 large sites are spread out across an expansive meadow. The lack of forest cover minimizes privacy. Each site has a table, grill, and lantern post. Facilities include modern restrooms with showers, pit toilets, and water. Sites cost $5/night. The campground is open May 15 to Oct 15. Use is light to moderate. To get there take US-23 S out of Pound 0.7 mi to SR-671. Turn R and go 5.8 mi to the campground entrance, R.

**fishing:** Largemouth bass, muskie, and bluegill all inhabit the N Fork of Pound reservoir. Although it's possible to fish from the banks in several places around the lake, including at the primitive camping area, fishing from a canoe is your best bet.

**canoeing/kayaking:** Although it's a fairly small body of water, N Fork of Pound Reservoir offers paddlers an enjoyable setting for a day-long paddle or a single overnight. The reservoir has a serpentine profile, with plenty of narrow coves to guide a canoe or kayak into. Emerald waters and a dense hardwood forest lining the shore provide a scenic woodland setting, and although a dam looms at one end of the lake, it is out of sight from most of the lake.

Access to the reservoir is at 2 launch sites. The Pound Boat Launch (near the dam) is located at the end of SR-630, which begins at the jct of US-23 and US-23 BUS just W of downtown Pound. The Wise Boat Launch is located on SR-671, 4.4 miles W of US-23.

**mountain biking:** the Cumberland Mountain Trail is open to mountain bikes. The narrow single-track trail is strenuous to bike; some steep, rocky sections will need to be walked. See above for additional information.

# Breaks Interstate Park

The 4,500 acres of this park sprawl across the Virginia/Kentucky border, encompassing the largest canyon east of the Mississippi, billed as the "Grand Canyon of the South." Although the geology really doesn't approach that level of grandeur, the Russell Fork River has carved the surrounding mountains into some impressive forms, with towers of paleozoic sandstone rising 1,600 feet from the river. As with so many areas in this part of the state, Daniel Boone's name is linked to The Breaks; he is credited with having "discovered" them in 1767. The park itself has something of a schizophrenic nature. On the one hand, it features an extensive, pristine backcountry with superb scenery. On the other, a motel, restaurant, gift shop, and olympic-size pool are all main attractions. Fortunately, the park's two natures seem not to intrude too much on one another. The tourist facilities are concentrated in a relatively small area, leaving most of the park's backcountry remote and unspoiled. In fact, most of that acreage is entirely inaccessible, as hiking trails cover only the eastern half of the park. The large majority of park lands are covered by a lush mixed forest of hemlock, yellow poplar, white oak, dogwood, and magnolia. Outdoor enthusiasts will find a whole spectrum of options in the park, including hiking trails with rocky vantages, a large whitewater river for fishing or paddling, a full-service campground, and mountain bike loop. Ther are also numerous picnic facilities in the park. A day is enough time to fully explore any one of these options. Without the possibility of backcountry camping, longer trips have to be based in the car campground or motel.

Elkhorn City, KY (W) and Haysi, VA (S) are the closest towns.

**contact:** Breaks Interstate Park, P.O. Box 100, Breaks, VA 24607; 540/865-4413 or 800/982-5122

**getting there:** From the jct of VA-83 and VA-80 (Sand Lick Rd) in the town of Haysi, go W on VA-80 8.5 mi to the park entrance, L.

**topography:** The Russell Fork has carved the mountainous terrain into a 1,600-ft gorge, with sheer cliffs and towering pinnacles looming over the river. Elevation on the river is 850 ft. Where the terrain is gentle enough for trees to gain a foothold, a hardwood forest is present. **maps:** USGS Elkhorn City, Harman.

**starting out:** The park entrance fee is $1/vehicle. Before heading out into the backcountry, a stop at the visitor center is worthwhile. There's a small museum with exhibits that explain different facets of the area. There's also an information desk where you can get park maps and brochures. Facilities (restrooms, water). Hours are 9 AM to 5 PM daily. The park is open daily year round. It closes at 11 PM.

Alcohol is not allowed in the park. Pets must be kept on a leash.

**activities:** Hiking, Mountain Biking, Fishing, Camping, Canoeing/Kayaking.

**hiking:** The park's hiking trails provide views out over the impressive geological formations of the breaks, traverse steep mountainsides, and follow beside the stunning Russell Fork River. In all, a network of 13 interconnecting trails covers a total of 8 miles. Most of the trails are short paths ending at overlooks that afford various perspectives on The Breaks. Most of the signed trailheads are located along the main park road. Since the trails interconnect, it is possible to string several together into loops of varying distance. All of the trails are well-designed and-maintained, with improvements that include stone and long steps, benches, and handrails at overlooks. Trail jcts are signed, with distances to other trails or landmarks indicated. Hiking on most trails is easy, though a couple trails that descend to the river are strenuous. Also in the park is the E end of the 23-mi *Cumberland Mountain Trail*, which traverses a section of Pine Mtn on the Clinch ranger district. To reach the E trailhead, leave the park and go W on VA-80. Go 4.9 mi and park L at a small, unsigned parking area at a sharp curve in the road. Follow a short, steep, unmarked trail to the RR trestle. Cross the trestle and follow the trail W.

**mountain biking:** All hiking trails in the park are closed to bikes. There is, however, a separate 2-mile trail designed for and used almost exclusively by mountain bikers. The moderate trail follows a narrow single-track dirt path and sections of an old roadbed through a dense hardwood forest. The trail forms a loop, with access directly across from the rental shack. They rent mountain bikes there for $5/hr or $30/day.

**fishing:** The Russell Fork is a large river with a flow that varies considerably, depending on the water release schedule at

Flanagan Dam upstream. It flows through the park for about 5 miles. The gradient there is mild to average, with plenty of massive boulders and rocky ledges that create churning whitewater when the water is up. For anglers, the river offers a chance to fish for a whole array of fish. Smallmouth bass, trout, walleye, and suckers are all taken from the river. Access in the park is via hiking trail, with a strenuous, 1-mi descent required to reach the river. Fishing pressure is light, but kayakers and rafters are a common presence on the river.

**camping:** Primitive camping is allowed in the extensive backcountry, but backpackers are requested to check in at the visitor center before heading out on their tip.

The park also contains a large car campground. 138 sites are laid out in loops and along short spurs in an area that is mostly covered by a hardwood forest. The sites are fairly close together, however, which diminishes privacy. On the plus side, the campground is rarely very crowded. The sites come in a variety of configurations, with some designated as tent-only, while others have different combinations of water, electrical, and sewage hookups. All sites have a picnic table and grill. Tent sites cost $7/night ($14/night for 2 tents), with prices rising in $1 increments for additional services. Tent sites cost $7/night for 1 tent, $14/night for 2 tents. Shower/restroom facilities are at the center of each loop. Firewood is for sale. The campground is open from Apr 1 to Oct 31.

**canoeing/kayaking:** The 5-mi section of the Russell Fork River between the Garden Hole put-in and the take-out in KY is one of the premier whitewater runs in the southeast. The river is wide and when the water is up, it tumbles over and around house-sized boulders and dozens of rock ledges. The water is mostly class III & IV, with some rapids reaching class V. The water level depends on the release schedule of the Flanagan Dam. This is not a run for novices. If you're inexperienced at whitewater, but still want to experience the thrill of descending through The Breaks, book a trip with one of the local rafting companies. The put-in is at the Garden Hole access. From the park entrance, go E on VA-80 0.9 mi to a gravel road, R. Take the gravel road 1 mile to the parking area and boat launch area. Cars *cannot* be left there overnight. The take-out is 4.7 miles past the park entrance on KY-80.

# Hidden Valley Wildlife Management Area

This 6,400-acre mountain oasis occupies the shoulders of Brumley Mountain and a narrow, secluded valley that cradles a 60-acre lake. The immensely scenic area is known mostly by local hunters and fishermen, who come to pursue game through the forested mountain slopes or to fish for bass and walleye in the lake. Its remote location off the well-traveled outdoor recreation circuit makes it an ideal spot for backcountry enthusiasts eager for some isolation and the challenge of a backcountry where none of the trails are marked and pathfinding is a required skill. There are few restrictions on outdoor activties here, as long as they are consistent with the low-impact ethic. You can hike, backpack, make camp just about anywhere you please, paddle a canoe or kayak on the lake, or cast for fish on Brumley Creek or Hidden Valley Lake. And if it isn't hunting season, odds are good that you'll have the place to yourself. Venture into the backcountry and you're more likely to encounter a black bear, white-tailed deer, or wild turkey, than another hiker. This area is best suited to a day-trip or a single overnight.

Lebanon (N) and Abingdon (SE) are the closest towns.

**contact:** Hidden Valley WMA, Route 1 Box 107, Marion, VA 24354; 540/782-9051

**getting there:** From downtown Abingdon, take US-19/US-58 ALT N 10.7 mi to SR-690, R. Go 2.4 mi to a fork in the road and a small parking area and trailheads, L. To reach the lake and boat ramp continue down the L fork (unpaved) 1.1 mi to an unsigned jct. Turn R and go 0.2 mi to the lake.

**topography:** Although the terrain surrounding Hidden Valley Lake is mountainous, the lake's position in a high alpine valley puts it above most of the mountain slopes. The rounded peaks around it are not unlike the rolling hills of the piedmont. A climax hardwood forest covers the mountain slopes. Elevations are between 2,000 and 4,000. **maps:** USGS Brumley.

**starting out:** This is an undeveloped backcountry area with no facilities or information center. You can call the WMA at the above phone number for a map of the area that gives a pretty decent overview, though it doesn't show all the hiking trails. Surface water is abundant in the area, but should be treated before drinking. Hunting is a popular fall and winter activity here; if you come during those seasons wear blaze orange.

Swimming in the lake is not allowed.

**activities:** Canoeing/Kayaking, Fishing, Camping, Hiking.

**canoeing/kayaking:** Nestled in an alpine valley that seems cut off from the rest of the world, Hidden Valley Lake is one of those special outdoor places that seem unlikely in such a heavily developed part of the country. Its only downside for paddlers is its size. At only 60 acres it really doesn't offer a whole lot of room to explore. You can compensate for that problem by bringing a rod and reel and combining a day on the water with angling for bass, bluegill, and walleye. Lake traffic is minimal to nonexistent depending on when you come. Boats with gasoline motors are not allowed on the lake.

**fishing:** You can fish Hidden Valley Lake from the shoreline or from a small boat. A boat will allow you to cover more water, but there's plenty of open space along the shore for casting. Even fly-casters shouldn't have much of a problem. The lake supports populations of smallmouth and rock bass, walleye, and bluegill.

Another option for fly-fishermen is Brumley Creek, which flows E down Brumley Mountain from the lake. It's a small creek on the WMA with a rocky bed and an average gradient. Cover on both banks is dense. The creek supports a native population of rainbow trout. It can be fished for 4 miles downstream from the dam. Access is from a small parking area next to the dam.

**camping:** Primitive backcountry camping is allowed anywhere in the WMA except within 100 yds of Hidden Valley Lake. Many good campsites are located in groves of towering hemlocks not far from the lake's perimeter. You can either backpack in to a site or car camp along the main WMA road that runs near the lake. No-trace camping is of course the rule.

**hiking:** Hiking on the WMA is best suited to the adventurous or those who don't mind spending some of their backcountry time following unmarked trails to unknown destinations. None of the trails is signed, blazed, or regularly maintained, though there are several trails that receive a moderate amount of use. 2 of these trails go to overlooks from the first parking area at the WMA entrance. They provide excellent 180 views encompassing the long ridge of Clinch Mountain. Trails follow a combination of narrow footpaths and seeded roadbeds. Most are the result of use by hunters and fishermen. Hiking is moderate to strenuous. There are probably as many as 10 miles of trails on the WMA.

# Clinch Mountain Wildlife Management Area

This 25,477-acre upland preserve occupies lands on four counties: Russell, Smyth, Tazewell, and Washington. The vast backcountry is well known to hunters and trout anglers. Laurel Bed Lake is a 330-acre impoundment set in the middle of stunning alpine scenery. The lake is stocked with trout and is part of the management area's fee fishing program. Big Tumbling Creek and Laurel Bed Creek, two of the most attractive mountain creeks in Virginia, are also part of the program. Access to the creeks and lake are easy, making this a popular area with families. The mountainous backcountry is home to a wide variety of flora and fauna, including black bear, white-tailed deer, beaver, and wild turkey. Visitors wanting to spend more than a day in the area can make camp in the primitive car campground or in the backcountry. Hiking is available, but requires a bit of effort, as there are no regularly maintained trails.

Saltville (S) is the closest town.

**contact:** Clinch Mountain WMA, Route 1 Box 107, Marion, VA 24354; 540/782-9051

**getting there:** From I-81, take exit 29. Turn N onto VA-91 and go 10 mi to Saltville. At a traffic light downtown turn L onto Allison Gap Rd/Perryville Rd (SR-634). Go 1.4 mi to SR-613. Go 3.9 mi to gravel SR-747. Turn R and go 1.3 mi to the entrance of the WMA. At 1.6 mi reach the WMA office and snack bar, R.

**topography:** Rugged, mountainous terrain is blanketed by a mature hardwood forest. Numerous areas have been left open to facilitiate wildlife habitat. Elevations are between 1,600 feet on Tumbling Creek and 4,700 ft on Beartown Mtn. **maps:** USGS Saltville, Broadford, Elk Garden.

**starting out:** You'll probably need to stop by the snack bar/permit station before starting your trip. They issue camping and fishing permits. Facilities there include restrooms, water, vending machines, and a snack bar. Unfortunately, no decent maps of the WMA are available here. Bring the USGS topo or get a WMA map from the VDGIF district office in Marion. You should have one or the other, particularly if you're going to be doing any hiking.

Public use or display of alcohol is not allowed.

**activities:** Fishing, Canoeing/Kayaking, Hiking, Camping

**fishing:** Most people who come to the WMA come to fish. Trout are the main quarry here, and the major trout waters—Big Tumbling Creek, Laurel Bed Creek, and Laurel Bed Lake—are fee fishing waters that require a $4 permit from Mar 16 to Labor Day to fish. Big Tumbling Creek is a medium to large creek with an average to steep gradient. Lush forest cover, a series of cascades and small waterfalls, and numerous rocky ledges make this one of the region's most attractive trout fisheries. Access is from SR-747, where there are numerous pullouts. Laurel Bed Creek is somewhat smaller with an average to steep gradient and excellent forest cover. Access is also from the road, which runs high above the creek. Fishing on the 330-acre lake is best done from a small boat. The lake is stocked each spring; by summer warm temperatures have often depleted the trout populations.

**canoeing/kayaking:** 330-acre Laurel Bed Lake was constructed in 1968. The alpine lake is nestled among the forested peaks of Clinch Mountain, making it one of the most scenic paddling environments in the mountains. Lake elevation is 3,600 ft and it's stocked with trout. Boat traffic is rarely heavy on the lake; it's busiest during spring when the trout fishing is at its peak. Since gasoline motors are not allowed on the lake, you're assured of a quiet environment. Put-in is at the boat ramp.

**hiking:** Although the WMA doesn't maintain a regular network of hiking trails, that doesn't mean that there are no opportunities for trekking through the backcountry. In fact, the WMA is crossed by a number of hunter access roads that are easy to follow and offer foot access to the large backcountry. The road access points are signed along the main WMA road. In addition to these roads, several single-track dirt footpaths wind through the hardwood and conifer forests that blanket the mountain slopes. One such trail begins across from the dam. Hiking is moderate on most trails and roadbeds. Trail conditions on the hunter access roads are better than on the footpaths, which often require pathfinding skills.

**camping:** Primitive backcountry camping is permitted on the WMA, except where posted.

A primitive car campground is located 6 miles past the permit station/concession stand. 20 large sites are laid out on a hillside shaded with stands of hemlock and hardwoods. Each site has a picnic table and grill. Privacy is minimal, due to the open nature of the area. The only facilities are a hand water pump and pit toilets. Sites cost $6/night. Permits must be purchased from the permit station near the WMA entrance. Patterns of use are seasonal, with the busiest periods during peak hunting and fishing days.

# Virginia Creeper Trail

The Virginia Creeper Trail is part of a movement that has had stunning success across the country in the past couple of decades: the conversion of old, unused railroad lines into multi-use trails and parks. Along the Virginia Creeper urban landscape and remote backcountry are fused by a corridor with historical significance and outstanding opportunities for outdoor recreation. The 34-mile trail runs between downtown Abingdon and Whitetop Station along a former route of the Norfolk-Southern Railroad. It earned the nickname "Virginia Creeper" for the slow pace with which it wound through the rugged mountains of North Carolina and Virginia. The train's engine is now stationed beside the trailhead in Abingdon. Before the railroad tracks were laid in the early 1900s, the path had been used by Native Americans and European settlers. Today, a trip along the trail reveals two natures. The sixteen-mile segment between the towns of Abingdon and Damascus passes through rolling countryside cleared for pastures and residential developments. West of Damascus, the trail continues eighteen miles to the North Carolina border, passing through lush hardwood forests and alongside gurgling trout creeks in the Mt Rogers National Recreation Area. The trail is open to hikers, mountain bikers, and equestrians. It is also popular with joggers and people out for a leisurely stroll. With so much to offer, the trail deserves at least two or three days of exploration, though you can cover the whole length in a single day-long bike ride.

Either way, you won't forget it.

The trail starts in Abingdon (W) and passes through Damascus.

**getting there:** There are almost a dozen access points to the trail. The most popular 5 are listed here, from W to E. The W trailhead is in downtown Abingdon. Turn S off of E Main St onto Pecan St and go 0.2 mi to the trailhead, L. • In Damascus, the trail parallels US-58 (Main St). There's a large parking area at the W edge of town next to the red caboose and iron bridge. • To reach the Creek Jct access, from Damascus take US-58 E 10.1 miles to gravel SR-728. Turn R and go 1.5 miles to the parking area. • To Reach the Green Cove access and info center, from Damascus take US-58 E 15.2 miles to SR-600 (Green Cove Road). Turn R and go 0.3 miles to the parking area, R. • To reach Whitetop Station (1 mi W of the trail's E end), from Damascus take US-58 E 16.7 miles to SR-726 (Whitetop Gap Rd; another SR-726 is 3.2 miles previous). Turn R and go 1.7 miles to the parking area.

**topography:** Elevations along the trail are between 1,750 ft at S Holston Lake (mile 8) and 3,576 ft at Whitetop Station (mile 33). The W half of the trail is basically flat; the E half climbs almost 2,000 ft from Damascus to Whitetop Station. **maps:** USGS Abingdon, Damascus, Konnarock, Grayson.

**starting out:** The USFS runs info centers in Damascus and at Green Cove (directions to both above). They're open May to Oct with hours Th–Sa and holidays 9 AM to 5 PM, Su 1 to 4 PM. You can pick up trail brochures and buy maps at either location. Facilities (water, toilets, pay phone) are also there. A trail map and brochure can also be picked up at the Abingdon trailhead. If you'll only be traveling the *Virginia Creeper Trail*, a topo map really isn't necessary. If you want one for the E half of the trail that shows connecting trails, pick up the USFS Mount Rogers NRA topo.

**activities:** Mountain Biking, Hiking, Fishing, Camping.

**mountain biking:** Although I'm not aware of any hard statistics, my guess is that mountain bikers make up the largest group of trail users on the Virginia Creeper. The reasons are obvious: from Whitetop Station it's a 34-mile ride through some of the most stunning scenery in the state. And it's almost all downhill. The surface of the wide trail is mixed: cinders, dirt, crushed gravel, and wooden boards on the numerous trestles are all encountered.

The level of difficulty depends on which way you travel. The climb is from Damascus to Whitetop Station. Most riders choose to go the other way, virtually coasting for the first 18 miles. This is one of the most popular trails in the state, so expect company. Bike rentals or shuttles can be arranged at one of the outfitters listed in Damascus or Abingdon (see appendix). Access points are given above.

**hiking:** The *Virginia Creeper Trail* offers two fairly distinct hiking experiences. W of Damascus, the more or less flat trail passes through rolling countryside that is given over mostly to farm pasturage and intermittent residential development. No other trails intersect, and the segment is more popular among casual strollers than backpackers. E of Damascus, however, the trail enters the Mt Rogers NRA and ascends through dense forest before emerging on the grassy balds of the highlands area. Between Damascus and Creek Jct the trail is intersected and joined several times by the *Appalachian Trail*. This allows for connection with many of the other trails in the Mt Rogers NRA, creating the possiblity for loop hikes of varying length. Hiking along the Virginia Creeper itself is easy, regardless of which way you travel. Trailheads are clearly signed and easy to locate. Use is heavy, especially by mountain bikers.

**fishing:** The Virginia Creeper passes over and along rivers and creeks that hold both warm- and cold-water species of fish. Beginning in Abingdon, the trail first reaches S Holston Lake at mile 8 and then follows the S Fork Holston River until mile 13, where it joins Laurel Creek, which it follows through Damascus and into the Mt Rogers NRA. Both S Holston Lake and S Fork Holston River hold plenty of fish: largemouth and smallmouth bass, trout, crappie, suckers, and catfish. The problem is access. The river flows through private property and the boat ramps on the lake are away from the trail. Backpackers and bikers are better off waiting to fish the waters of the NRA, where several blue ribbon trout streams await.

Along the 13-mi section between Damascus and Green Cove, the trail closely follows two creeks—Whitetop Laurel and Green Cove. The former is a medium-sized stream that joins the trail at Creek Jct and hugs it for 10 miles until its waters join those of Laurel Creek just E of Damascus. This is one of the most renowned trout waters in the state. Even non-anglers passing by stop at the trestles above the big pools to watch the trout hold in the current or rise to feed. Although the stretches near trail access points can get pretty busy, if you're willing to hike a mile or two you should be able to find a long stretch all to yourself. The creek is stocked and only artificial lures with single hooks are allowed. At Creek Jct, Whitetop Laurel is joined by Green Cove Creek, a small to medium stream that joins the trail 4 mi upstream at the old Green Cove RR depot. At the upper end Green Cove is small with a mild gradient and very tight conditions. As you move downstream toward Creek Jct conditions become more amenable to fly casting. The stream is stocked, with only single hook artificial lures permitted.

**camping:** Backcountry camping is permitted along the entire trail. Between Abingdon and Damascus, where the trail passes through private property, the permission of the landowners should be sought before selecting a site. In all areas, campers should choose sites at least 100 ft from the trail.

# Mount Rogers National Recreation Area
## Jefferson National Forest

With more than 119,00 continuous acres in the Virginia highlands, this vast parkland is one of the premier backcountry areas in the state. Only Shenandoah National Park can match it for popularity, size, and opportunities for outdoor recreation. The centerpiece of the area, which stretches out along the line of the Appalachians from Damascus to the New River, is Mt Rogers, at 5,729 ft the highest point in the state. Although the Mt Rogers Rec Area is a part of the Jefferson National Forest, it is administered as a "special" area, one whose primary focus is recreational, as opposed to resource management or timber extraction. A recent plan to widen US-58 to a 4-lane highway has been abandoned, insuring, for the near future at least, that the area's natural beauty will remain relatively intact.

Despite its current popularity as an outdoor playground and backcountry oasis, the Virginia highlands area has a long history of settlement. Some of this history protudes into the present, and visitors to the area will find not only roads and small settlements, but extensive tracts of land still used for limited pasturage. A herd of wild ponies is also maintained withing the rec area. The grazing of animals and intermittent burns maintain the open character of much of the land. Rather than detracting from the wilderness experience, however, these accommodations to human economies help maintain one of the more unusual environments in the state. Admittedly, the term "natural" must be used loosely to describe an area that would soon revert to hardwood and spruce-fir forest if nature were left to take its course. But the open fields of grasses, blackberry shrubs, mountain laurel, and other ground cover afford the opportunity—rare in the southern Appalachians—to travel through mountains were long-range views are the norm, rather than a rare treat. Not that forests are completely absent from the area. 3 designated wilderness areas are almost entirely covered by forests in various stages of succession. At the highest elevations is found the damp, lush environment of a spruce-fir forest, one of the few occurances in Virginia.

For hiking, trout fishing, mountain biking, cross-country skiing, and backcountry camping, the Mt Rogers area simply affords some of the best opportunities in the state. In addition to the vast backcountry, there are 7 developed car campgrounds, a small recreational lake with swimming beach, and numerous picnic areas and roadside pullouts. Although a trip of any length is worthwhile, if you're looking for a place to spend a week tramping through backcountry without having to retrace your steps, this is it. Keep in mind that Mt. Rogers is a popular area. Peak weekends can get pretty crowded, particularly in the scenic highlands area and along the *Appalachian Trail, Virginia Creeper Trail* and shorter trails that lead to area highlights.

Damascus (W), Marion (N), and Wytheville (N) are the closest towns. The small community of Troudale is near the center of the rec area.

**contact:** Mount Rogers National Recreation Area, Route 1, Box 300, Marion, VA 24354; 540/783-5196.

**getting there:** I-81 parallels the rec area not far to the north, providing access from all parts of the state and from TN. Within the rec area proper, US-58 enters the rec area at Damascus and runs along the S edge of the W half. VA-16, US-21, and VA-94 all bisect the rec area in a N–S direction. Directions to specific areas are given below under the individual listings.

**topography:** Although the terrain within the NRA is generally mountainous, such a large area encompasses much topographical variety. Plant communities include mixed deciduous forest, boreal forest, alpine meadow, and pine/hardwood forest. The highlands area includes the highest mountains in VA, though they are no longer the rugged, jagged peaks they were millions of years ago. Eons of weather and erosion have softened their edges and rounded their peaks. Elevations range between 2000 ft on the New River and 5,729 ft on Mt Rogers. **maps:** USFS Mt Rogers NRA; USGS maps listed below under each heading.

**starting out:** There are 3 locations in or near the rec area where info is available. Maps (for sale and free), brochures, and some guidebooks are available at all 3. The Mt Rogers NRA headquarters is located on VA-16 S of Marion. Hours are M–Th 8 AM–4:30 PM, F 8 AM–6 PM, Sa & Su 9 AM–5 PM. The USFS operates an info center out of a red caboose on US-58 on the W end of Damascus. It's at the jct of the *VCT* and the *AT* beside the iron bridge. You can't miss it. Another USFS info center is in the old Green Cove RR depot along the *VCT*. It's located on SR-600, which is off US-58 14.7 mi E of Damascus. Both are open Th–Sa and holidays 9 AM to 5 PM, Su 1 to 4 PM between May and Oct. Facilities (water, restrooms, pay phone) can be found at the campgrounds, picnic areas, and at many small stores and service stations within and adjacent to the rec area. The USFS topo map of the NRA provides an excellent overview of the area; it's scale is too small, however, to be useful for backcountry navigation.

At all times of year, visitors should be prepared for extremely volatile weather. A beautiful sunny day in Damascus or Marion can be stormy, windy, and cold on the flanks of Mt Rogers or Whitetop Mt. Raingear and warm clothes are essential gear for all visits.

activites: Hiking, Camping, Fishing, Mountain Biking

**hiking:** A network of more than 300 mi of trails extends into all regions of the NRA. Among these trails are some of the best in the state, if not the nation. First is the world-famous *Appalachian Trail*, which winds through the western half of the area for approximately 60 miles. Entering the NRA on the same path in Damascus is the newer *Virginia Creeper Trail*, which spends the last 17 miles of its route in the Mt Rogers NRA. A former RR line that has been converted into a multi-use trail, the *VCT* is probably the most popular trail at Mt Rogers. Other long trails are the 50-mi *Iron Mtn Trail* and the 80-mi *Virginia Highlands Horse Trail*. These trails, together with literally dozens of shorter trails, provide an impressive range of backcountry travel options. Scenic highlights include rushing trout creeks, alpine meadows where wild ponies and cattle graze, boreal forests, stunning mountain views, and former RR trestles converted to bridges for hikers and bikers. The many overlaps and connections of trails long and short make possible loops of almost any length. There are trails to accommodate trips of an hour, a day, a weekend, a week, or longer. Trail conditions vary too, with the most popular trails blazed, signed, and well-maintained. Others require greater skill with map and compass to find and follow. Although this is mountain country, the mountains are old and the ages have worn them down and rounded them off. As a result, hiking falls generally in the easy to medium range, with few strenuous stretches. Trailheads to most of the major trails are signed, and are described below in the separate sections.

**camping:** Campers have almost as great a range of options as hikers, with backcountry camping, primitive car camping, and developed car camping all possible.

The best way to experience the magnificent backcountry of the Mt Rogers NRA is to spend a night in it. Except in a very few areas where it is posted otherwise, campers have the whole 118,000 acres plus of the rec area to choose from. No trace camping is of course the rule, with campers requested to choose sites at least 100 ft from water sources. There are 5 shelters along the *AT*, 2 along the *Iron Mtn Trail.*

If you can't spend the night in the backcountry, but want to spend more than a day in the NRA, car camping is the next best option. In addition to some limited places where roadside camping is possible, there are 7 car campgrounds in the rec area. 3 are fully developed with showers and modern restrooms; 4 are more primitive with pit toilets and water. Each of the 7 campgrounds is fully described below.

**fishing:** Angling for trout is one of the most popular activities at the Mt Rogers NRA. There are 2 small lakes and 100 miles of creeks that support populations of rainbow, brown, and brook trout. About half of the trout waters are hatchery supported; the rest support native populations. Most of the stocked creeks are accessible along their lengths from a road, usually dirt or gravel. Creeks with native populations are generally accessible via a hiking trail; a few require upstream wading. Creeks range in size from small to medium. Many of the creeks that support native stocks are very small with very tight conditions, making fly-casting a real challenge.

**mountain biking:** A large percentage of the trails in the Mt Rogers NRA are designated multi-use, with many open to mountain bikes. Longest of these are the *Iron Mountain Trail*, *Virginia Highlands Horse Trail*, and the unsurpassed *Virginia Creeper Trail*, which may be the most popular backcountry bike trail in the state. Trails follows a variety of treadways, including single-track, gated logging road, gravel and dirt roads, and a converted rail line. Difficulty levels cover the whole range from easy to strenuous, with trail conditions varying considerably depending on the weather (which seems to change every half hour) If you can't bring a bike with you, rentals (and vehicle shuttles) are available from local outfitters (see appendix A). Specific trail networks are described below under each heading.

# Whitetop Laurel Creek Area

This relatively small corner of the Mt Rogers NRA, bounded by US-58 and Tennessee, boasts some of the best opportunities for trail travel and trout fishing—not only in the rec area, but in the entire state. Entry into the area is typically through the attractive small town of Damscus, which bears the distinction of having two of the state's most famed trails pass right down Main Street. Both the *Appalachian Trail* and *Virginia Creeper Trail* (see separate entry above) follow the corridor of the old Virginia & Carolina Railroad line behind the storefronts and homes along Main Street. A major gateway to the NRA, the community has adapted to the continual flow of hikers and bikers, with shops and restaurants catering to their needs. The dominant features of this part of the Mt Rogers NRA are Whitetop Laurel Creek, a trophy trout stream that's among the most highly regarded in the state, and the picturesque rail line, which closely parallels the course of the creek, crossing over it twenty times on scenic trestles that recall an earlier era. Between the two main trails and the renowned trout fishing, this part of the NRA sees plenty of activity, with many visitors passing through on the long trails. Visits of a day or two are best, with longer trips possible by connecting to other parts of the NRA.

Damscus (W) is the closest town.

**getting there:** Vehicle access points are along 15 miles of US-58 between Damascus and SR-600 at Green Cove. Another option is to hike or bike in from downtown Damascus on either the *AT* (no bikes) or *VCT*. By vehicle, take US-58 E out of Damascus. At

4.1–4.3 mi reach parking areas for the *AT* and *VCT*, R. At 9.8 mi reach Creek Jct Rd (SR-728). Turn R and go 1.5 mi to another access to the *VCT* and *AT*. Continuing along US-58, at 15.2 mi come to SR-600. L it's 0.2 mi to the Green Cove info station and *VCT* trail access.

**topography:** Whitetop Laurel Creek tumbles 1,000 ft as it drops through the area flowing west. The surrounding terrain is rugged, mountainous, heavily forested, and generally inaccessible. Elevations are between 2,000 ft in Damascus and 3,800 on Chestnut Mtn. **maps:** *AT* Mt Rogers NRA; USGS-FS Konnarock, Damascus, Grayson, Laurel Bloomery.

**starting out:** Before heading into the backcountry, stop by the USFS info center in Damascus or at Green Cove Station to pick up maps, brochures, or check current conditions. Both spots sell a good selection of rec area maps. Water and restrooms are available at each both info stations. There are no other developed facilities in the area, though the Beartree Lake Rec Area is very close by on the other side of US-58. There are restrooms, water, and a pay phone there, as well as a developed campground.

**activities:** Hiking, Mountain Biking, Fishing, Camping

**hiking:** Hiking is primarily on either the *Appalachian Trail* or the *Virginia Creeper Trail*, with few other trails in this relatively small area. The former is more popular with hikers, the latter with mountain bikers. Both trails are long: The *VCT* runs 34 miles between Abingdon and Whitetop Station near the border with NC and the *AT* is of course more than 2,000 miles long—the world's longest continuous trail in fact. Starting in downtown Damascus, where they follow a single path, the trails join each other and separate 3 times, offering the chance to hike both trails consecutively or to form loops of varying distance. Connections to trails on other parts of the Mt Rogers area are also possible. Hiking on the trails is easy to moderate, with the *AT* providing the more challenging terrain. Trail access points are in Damascus and along US-58. No trail lover should forego a chance to hike in this particular corner of the state, as these trails are unsurpassed in history, construction, and natural splendor.

**mountain biking:** The *Virginia Creeper Trail* may just be the most popular backcountry mountain biking track in all Virginia. The

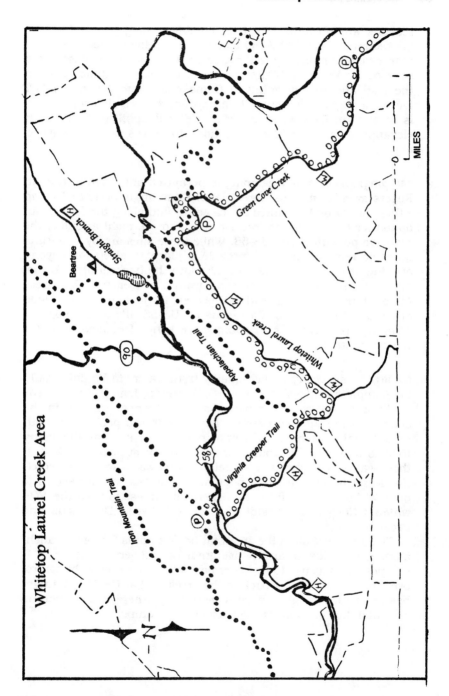

reasons are obvious. The trail combines magnificent forested backcountry, railroad history along an exceptionally scenic stretch of tracks, and proximity to the area's towns and cities. Most riders start out at Whitetop Station or one of the other highpoints along the trail and ride downhill to Damascus. From there, the *VCT* follows a slight uphill grade to Abingdon. A more challenging ride is to start in Damascus and ride the trail uphill to its end, an elevation gain of 1,600 ft. Directions to access points are given above.

**camping:** Backcountry camping is permitted anywhere in the Mt. Rogers area on national forest land. Camping is permitted along either the *AT* or *VCT*. Sites are easier to find along the former. An option for those wanting to car camp is to overnight at one of the roadside pullouts along US-58. While these sites are by no means quiet or remote, they will provide a place to sleep for anyone arriving in the area too late to hike into the backcountry. A final option is the developed car campground at Beartree Rec Area. Although not technically within this area, it's just on the other side of US-58, 7.8 mile E of Damascus on US-58. It's a very popular camping area that fills on summer weekends (see next entry for full description).

**fishing:** No summary of high-quality trout waters in Virginia would be complete unless it included Whitetop Laurel Creek. The medium-sized creek flows over a mild to average gradient in the shadow of the *Virginia Creeper Trail*. Cover and pooling are both exceptional. Hikers and bikers on the trail stop at the many trestles to watch the trout laying in pools or surfacing to feed. If there was a time when the Whitetop Laurel was a well-kept secret, the secret is out. This is a popular stream that always seems to draw at least a handful of fly-fishermen. Access is from the *VCT*, which follows close beside the creek between Damascus and Creek Jct.

The other stream in the area that holds trout is Straight Branch, a smaller creek with an average gradient and very dense cover. It can pose a challenge to fly-fishermen, who must keep tight control over their casts. A drawback to the creek is that US-58 runs right beside it. This makes access very easy (there are numerous pullouts), but diminishes the backcountry setting.

# Iron Mountain Area

Iron Mountain is a long, narrow ridge that extends the entire length of the Mt Rogers NRA. The area described here accounts for about half that length, with boundaries formedy by US-58 and SR-603 to the south, Damascus to the west, and Wythe County to the east. A vast area with several centers of activity, the Iron Mountain Area offers backcountry travelers a dizzying array of options. There are three developed recreation areas included under this heading, with facilities for camping at each. The Bear Tree Lake Rec Area is the most heavily developed; it features a lake with beach and swimming area, large picnic grounds, bathhouse, and 2 campground loops that are the busiest on the NRA. The area is a good destination for families, but those seeking backcountry solitude will want to give it a pass. The other 2 rec areas—Hurricane and Raccoon Branch—also have campgrounds, but on a smaller, more intimate scale. These areas make good basecamps for those wanting to explore the eastern half of this area without backpacking. As with other parts of the NRA, however, the real attraction of the Iron Mountain Area is the backcountry. More than 100 miles of multi-use trails wind along mountain slopes, ridges, and through valleys, including a segment of the *Appalachian Trail*. A few of the shorter trails provide access to stocked trout waters; others lead to mountain vistas. With the whole backcountry open to primitive camping, you could spend a week exploring the environs of Iron Mountain.

Troutdale (S) is the closest town.

**getting there:** Road access to this long area is along US-58 and SR-603, which together form the area's S boundary. VA-16 forms the E boundary and provides access to the rec areas located near the area's E edge. To reach the Cressy Creek Area, from the town of Sugar Grove, take SR-601 S 0.3 to a fork and jct with SR-676. Bear L and go 2.1 mi to the trailhead to the *VA Highlands Horse Trail* and parking on an unmarked road spur, R.

**topography:** Although the elevations are lower than on Mt Rogers and the highlands area to the S, the terrain is steeper and more rugged. Elevations reach more than 4,600 ft on Round Top. Forest cover includes northern and southern species of hardwoods and conifers. **maps:** USGS-FS Konnarock, Whitetop Mtn, Troutdale, Damascus.

**starting out:** The 3 campgrounds in the area make good basecamps for exploring the region. Even if you're backpacking, you can still fill up on water or use the pay phones there. To get into Bear Tree Lake Rec Area you have to pay a $3/vehicle parking fee. Limited facilities (water, pit toilets) are available at Skulls Gap Picnic Area.

**activities:** Hiking, Camping, Fishing, Mountain Biking

**hiking:** A pair of long hiking trails—the *Iron Mountain Trail* and the *Appalachian Trail*—both pass through this area. Actually, the 50-mi *Iron Mountain Trail* crosses it intermittently from one end to the other between Damascus and The Little Dry Creek Wilderness Area. Another long trail is the *Highlands Horse Trail*, which also traverses most of this area. Hikers might want to avoid it, however, as it receives very heavy use from equestrians. All of these trails cross each other at various points, and numerous shorter trails connect. The possibilities for forming loop hikes in this area—or combining other NRA areas—is almost limitless. A full range of hiking experiences are available in this area, from short, heavily-used trails that lead to scenic attractions or overlooks to remote, overgrown trails that require strong backcountry skills and determination. One such trail is the *Iron Mountain Trail*. Although maps show it crossing the entire area, large segments of it are difficult to locate, overgrown, or just too much trouble to hike. The *AT*, on the other hand, offers conditions that are uniformly excellent. Hiking in the area runs the gamut from easy to strenuous, with most trails somewhere in-between. Access to the trails is at many locations in the area, but the rec areas are a good place to start. A good topo map is essential for traveling through this area. Trail use is moderate; the area is a good bet when the trails on and around Mt Rogers become too congested.

**camping:** The Iron Mountain Area has the widest selection of camping facilities on the NRA. In addition to backcountry camping, which is permitted throughout the area, There are 3 developed car campgrounds.

The car campground at Beartree is probably the most popular in the Mt Rogers Rec Area. It's divided into 2 separate areas separated by a short drive: Beaver Flats and Chipmunk Circle. Combined, there are 79 sites at the 2 areas, with roughly half in each area. There's little difference between the 2 areas. Sites are medium size with average spacing and don't afford much privacy. This problem is compounded by the both campgrounds often being full on peak weekends. The dense understory of rhododendron does help to alleviate the sense of camping with your neighbors. Each site contains a picnic table, grill, and lantern post. Restrooms with showers are centrally located. The fee at either area is $10/night. The campground is open from mid-Mar to Dec 1. To get there, turn N off US-58 (3 mi W of the jct of SR-603 and US-58) onto FR-837.

Raccoon Branch is another, smaller car campground that's located on VA-16, 5.8 mi S of the NRA HQ and 5.6 mi N of Troutdale and SR-603. Each of the 20 sites here is rather smallish, and some are in open areas with almost no privacy. Each site has a picnic table, grill, and lantern post. Modern restrooms (no showers) are centrally located. The fee is $8/night. This campground is particularly popular with RVers. It's open all year.

The third car camping area is the Hurricane Rec Area, also located on VA-16, 2.4 mi N of Troutdale and 8.9 mi S of the NRA Headquarters. Turn W onto gravel SR-650 and go 1.4 mi. Bear L and go 0.3 mi to the campground. With 27 large, well-spaced sites in a woodland setting, this is the nicest campground on the NRA. Each site has a picnic table, grill, and lantern post. Restrooms/showers are located in the campground. Sites cost $8/night. The campground is open from Mar 1 to Oct 31.

**fishing:** Although the area isn't a major destination for anglers, there are a few small trout waters to choose from. The most popular—and least remote—is Bear Tree Lake. Located near the busy campground and with a swimming beach on its shore, it doesn't really qualify as backcountry. Still, anglers cast for the stocked trout from a pair of large piers.

Further east, in a less-traveled region of the Iron Mountain Area, are several small stocked trout creeks. Hurricane, Comers, Dickey, and Cressy Creeks are all small streams with mild gradients that flow over rocky streambeds through dense forests. Each offers a mile or two of stocked trout waters. Except for Dickey Creek, which is paralled by VA-16, access to all of these creeks is on dirt and gravel forest roads. To get to the first 2, follow directions above to Hurrican Campground. Cressy Creek is reached by taking SR-601 S from VA-16 in Sugar Grove.

**mountain biking:** The Iron Mountain Area offers mountain bikers a wealth of riding options, particularly for those willing to face the challenge of uncertain trail conditions and piecing together different rides. Riding on the area is on a combination of old roadbeds, gated roads, unpaved roads open to traffic, and single-track. Most of these conditions are found on just one trail, the 50-mi *Iron Mountain Trail*. The trail crosses the area from one end to another, following roadbeds, roads, and narrow single-track. Numerous access points, however, make is possible to ride short sections or combine sections of the trail with other area trails and roads. Almost all trails in the area are open to mountain bikes, with the notable exception of the *Appalachian Trail*. Riding conditions are moderate to strenuous on the trails, easy to moderate on the roads. Trail use is moderate.

# Highlands Area

Probably the most popular part of the Mt Rogers NRA, this area encompasses two designated wildernesses, long stretches of the *Appalachian Trail* and *Virginia Highlands Horse Trail*, and the two highest peaks in the commonwealth—Mt Rogers and Whitetop Mountain. Aside from the maximum altitude, the main attraction here is the terrain and ecology. Almost unique in the southern Appalachians, the highlands area is largely devoid of forest cover, causing it to resemble alpine terrain in New England or the Rockies. Formerly pasture, most of the mountainsides have only grasses and shrubs for cover. Horses and cattle still graze here, part of an effort to maintain the open setting. At the highest elevations, northern spruce-fir forests blot out the sun and leave the forest floor covered in a lush green carpet of mosses and ferns. The 2 wilderness areas—5,730-acre Lewis Fork and 3,855-acre Little Creek—offer large roadless tracts coivered with dense hardwood and conifer forests. Recreation in the area centers around the magnificent backcountry; hiking and backpacking are the most popular activities. Grindstone Campground, located at the northern edge of the area on SR-603, is the single developed recreation area. If there's a drawback to the area, it's that with so much to offer, it can get rather crowded on weekends during peak season. If you can, plan your visit during the week or at slow times of year. But at any time of year, the Highlands Area is worth a visit.
    Troutdale (NE) is the closest town.

**getting there:** To reach Whitetop Mtn, take US-58 18.8 miles E of Damascus to SR-600 (Whitetop Mtn Rd). Turn L and go 1.7 miles to gravel FR-89. Turn L and go 1.8 miles to a parking area, R. At 2.6 miles bear R at a fork. At 2.8 miles is the parking area, L. • Elk Garden is the main access to the *AT* and Lewis Fork Wilderness.

It's on SR-600 2.9 miles N of US-58 and 3.7 miles S of SR-603. •
To reach the Little Wilson Creek trailhead, take US-58 E of
Grayson Highlands SP 3.1 mi to gravel Briar Run Lane (SR-817)
(VA-16 is 4.6 mi ahead). Turn L and go 0.3 mi to a fork. Bear L
and go 0.9 mi to a cluster of buildings. From here on the road is
impassable, but there's room to park.

**topography:** Elk Garden is at 4,500 ft. Mt Rogers, the state's highest
peak, is at 5,729 ft. Vegetation varies widely in this region. Coves
and riparian areas are dominated by lush hardwood forests with
dense understories of rhododendron. Mountain ridges and slopes
are mostly open, with small shrubs such as wild blackberry
prominent. **maps:** USFS Mount Rogers High Country; AT Mt Rogers
NRA; USGS-FS Whitetop Mtn, Troutdale

**starting out:** The only USFS facilities in the area are at Grindstone
campground. There's a day use area there with picnic facilities.
The fee is $3/vehicle. Non-campers are permitted to shower in the
campground for $2. Hikers and backpackers traveling through the
Highlands Area should expect extremely unstable weather.
Temperatures here are often 10° or more cooler than in Damascus
or Marion. High winds, fog, and rain are all common, and can arise
quite unexpectedly.

**activities:** Hiking, Camping, Fishing

**hiking:** The Highlands Area is the premiere hiking and
backpacking area in the Mt Rogers NRA, and one of the most
popular areas in the state. The main attraction here is the
magnificent combination of northern and southern forest types and
vast swaths of open land grazed by small herds of horses and
other livestock. You won't find a more scenic area in all of Virginia.
The backcountry is well served by an extensive network of hiking
trails, including a segment of the *Appalachian Trail*, which crosses
the area from US-58 near Green Cove to SR-603 and the Iron
Mountain Area. Approximately 90 miles of trails wind through the
backcountry here, not counting the *Virginia Highlands Horse
Trail*, which is not recommended for hikers. Although trails
provide access to almost every corner of this area, major
concentrations are found in the 2 wilderness areas. Hiking on the
trails is moderate in most places. Most of the trails follow single-
track footpaths that are blazed and easy to follow. Creek crossings
in the wilderness areas are unimproved. Most trail jcts are signed.

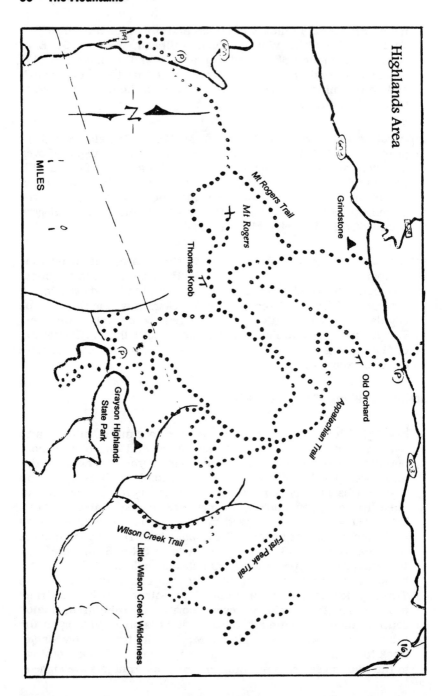

Highlands Area

Trail use is heavy, and on weekends the more popular trails can become quite crowded. Access points to the trail network are on Whitetop Mtn, at the Elk Garden Trailhead, in Grindstone Campground, and at an *AT* access on SR-603 E of the campground.

**camping:** Most campers in Highlands Area opt to spend the night in the backcountry, and rightly so. Backpacking in the southeast just doesn't get much better than this. Campers can choose sites anywhere, but should avoid camping within 100 ft of water sources. There are 2 shelters along the *AT*.

Car campers can overnight at Grindstone Campground. The large campground has 100 sites spread out in 3 loops across a heavily wooded area. Despite its size, the campground is quite attractive and the large, well-spaced sites offer a comfortable degree of privacy. Each site has a picnic table, grill, and lantern post. Shower/restroom facilities are centrally located. Sites cost $10/night. Some sites can be reserved by calling 800/280-CAMP The campground is open from May 1 to Dec 1. To get there: From the jct of SR-600 and SR-603, take SR-603 E 4.4 to the campground, R.

**fishing:** Because of its lofty elevation, trout fishing in the Highlands Area is fairly limited. The exception is the Little Wilson Creek Wilderness, which offers fly-fishermen one of the most exceptionally attractive backcountry settings in the NRA. Although you have to drive outside the NRA on US-58 and then take a bumpy dirt and gravel road to reach it, it's worth the effort. Big Wilson Creek is medium to large and flows over moss-covered boulders and ledges down an average gradient. Pooling is excellent. The forest cover on both banks is dense, with lots of rhododendron, offering a challenge to fly-fishermen. The stream holds native populations of rainbow trout, with brook trout near the headwaters. It can be fished for about 5 miles upstream from the access described above. A hiking trail follows the creek upstream.

Little Wilson Creek offers similar conditions on a slightly smaller scale. It is reached via a hiking trail which follows it all the way to its headwaters and can be fished for about 3 miles. Both creeks make an excellent destination for a backpacking/fly-fishing expedition.

# Little Dry Run Wilderness Area

Located at the relatively quiet eastern end of the Mt Rogers NRA, this area includes the wilderness area proper (2,858 acres) as well as adjacent lands to the south and east. It's a good area to visit on busy summer weekends and holidays, when the roads and trails of the highlands area are more crowded. Iron Mountain, which traverses the entire NRA, reaches its eastern limit here. Attractions here include forests of hardwoods, hemlock, and pine; a couple of trout streams and a stocked lake; a pair of isolated car campgrounds; and fairly large network of hiking trails. Most of the trails are open to mountain bikes, with some good stretches of dirt and gravel forest road that don't see much in the way of traffic adding to the possibilities for extended trips and loops. In winter, many of the roads and trails make good cross-country skiing tracks. At the eastern edge of the area is the New River and the New River Trail State Park.

Wytheville (N) and Independence (S) are the closest towns.

**getting there:** From Wytheville, take US-21 S 13 mi to the trailhead and parking area for the Little Dry Run Wilderness, L. Directions are given below to additional points of interest in the area. Continue S on US-21 another 1.5 mi to FR-14 and access to the Hussy Mtn campground. Or continue S another 1.1 mi on US-21 to gravel FR-57. Turn R and go 3.8 mi to Comers Rock campground.

**topography:** The mountains here are considerably lower than in the central part of the NRA. Elevations do not exceed 4,000 ft, with a low point of about 2,100 ft on Cripple Creek at Raven Cliff rec area. Forest cover is predominantly hardwoods and hemlock, with an understory of rhododendron and mountain laurel. **maps:** USGS-FS Cripple Creek, Speedwell.

**starting out:** Facilities in the area are limited. You'll find water and pit toilets at Comer's Rock and Raven Cliff Rec Areas, but that's about it. Both areas also feature picnic grounds. The one at Raven Cliff is beside Cripple Creek and has numerous tables and grills and a single shelter in a large meadow. Comer's Rock is a bit run down, but there are a few tables and grills, as well as a small shelter.

**activities:** Hiking, Mountain Biking, Fishing, Camping

**hiking:** The trails in the area branch out on either side of US-21, which runs through the area N–S, cutting it in half. In all, the trails cover about 60 miles, with most of that mileage on segments of 2 long trails, the *Virginia Highlands Horse Trail* and the *Iron Mountain Trail*. In addition to these 2 trails, a number of shorter trails are also in the area. They can all be connected to form a single large network or loops of varying length. The easiest access points are at the Little Dry Run Wilderness parking area, at Comer's Rock Campground, and along FR-14 near the Hussy Mountain Horse Camp. Trails connect all of these areas to one another. Because these trails receive relatively little use, some sections have become obscure or are frequently overgrown. Blazes and signs do occur, but only intermittently. A good topo map and compass should be carried for any but the shortest trips.

**mountain biking:** With a number of trails open to bikes, and the traffic on the gravel forest roads generally light, this is a good area for mountain bike rides. Using Comers Rock as a base, it's possible to put together a couple of pretty long rides. FR-57, which passes through the campground, is an easy 5-mi run between Hale Lake and US-21. From US-21, it's possible to ride on the *Iron Mtn Trail*, FR-14 (another lightly traveled gravel road) the *Henley Hollow Trail*, or the *Virginia Highlands Horse Trail*. FR-14 is an easy, almost flat 8-mi ride beside East Fork and then Francis Mill Creek. Along the way it connects to all 3 of the other trails, providing the option for some more strenuous single track riding. There are plenty of parking pull-outs along FR-14. Mountain bikes are not allowed in the Little Dry Run Wilderness.

**camping:** Backcountry camping is permitted throughout the area on NF lands, except where posted. In addition, campers have 2 primitive car campgrounds to choose from: Comer's Rock and Raven Cliff. The former is the more centrally located, with easy access to all area hiking trails. The campground has 9 sites in a cleared semi-circle. Each site has a picnic table and grill. Privacy at the sites is minimal, and the campground is less than attractive, but use is very light. There are pit toilets and a water pump. No fee is charged. To get there, from the parking area at Little Dry Run Wilderness, take US-21 S 2.6 mi to gravel FR-57. Turn R and go 3.8 mi to the campground.

Raven Cliff is a little more out of the way. From the Little Dry Run Wilderness parking area, take US-21 N 2 mi to SR-619. Turn R and go 7 mi to the gravel entrance road, R. 20 well-spaced sites are arranged in a loop beneath a forest of hardwoods, offering a good degree of privacy. Each site has a picnic table, grill, and lantern post. There are flush toilets and water. Sites cost $4/night.

Another option for car campers is to overnight at one of the primitive roadside sites along gravel FR-14. There are no designated sites here, but signs of previous campers are fairly frequent. East Fork runs beside the road.

**fishing:** Although not a major fishing destination, there are several small trout creeks, a small stocked lake, and a smallmouth bass river to choose from. To reach Hale Lake follow directions above to Comers Rock, but continue on FR-57 1.2 mi past the campground to an unsigned jct. Keep L and go 0.3 mi to the lake and parking area, L. It's a small, scenic alpine lake with a shoreline dominated by spruce, hemlock, with hardwoods. An angler's trail circles the lake at the water line, providing access. In addition, there are several large clearings for bank fishing. The lake is stocked with trout.

E Fork is a small creek with a rocky bed and mild gradient that forms some small pools. Dirt and gravel FR-14 runs beside it for about 5 miles until it reaches Francis Mill Creek. This is a small stocked trout creek. In meanders through rhododendron thickets over a rocky bed. The gradient is mild, with a mostly shallow flow. It can be fished from pullouts on the side of FR-14 for about 1.5 miles.

Cripple Creek is stocked trout water that would appear to be poor habitat for cold-water fish. It's a slow-moving stream with a bottom that is heavily sedimented in place. Smallmouth bass are the native species, and seem better adapted to the creek's conditions. Access to the river is at the Raven Cliff Rec Area. The best way to fish it is by wading. It passes through national forest land for less than 2 miles.

# Hungry Mother State Park

This unusually named park is located just north of Marion in Smyth Country. The name comes from the legend of Hungry Mother, a settler woman who escaped an Indian attack with her small daughter. When she collapsed and her daughter went to seek help, the only words the young girl could manage were "hungry mother." Like many Virginia state parks, Hungry Mother is divided between a very busy area where outdoor recreation centers around a sandy beach on a lake, and an extensive backcountry that is much less traveled. While the beach area attracts families in large numbers between Memorial Day and Labor Day, a network of hiking trails and the 108-acre lake provide backcountry travelers the chance to escape the madding crowd. In all, the park covers 3,051 acres, most of it forested mountain slopes that rise steeply from the lake. The woods and lake provide a haven for wildlife, particularly small mammals such as beaver, raccoon, and woodchucks, and birds such as great blue herons, warblers, and loons. In addition to the beach and bathhouse, park facilities include overnight cabins, rowboat and paddleboat rentals, an extensive picnic area with tables, grills, and shelters, a restaurant, and car campground. The park is open year round.

Marion (S) is the closest city.

**contact:** Hungry Mother State Park, Route 5, Box 109, Marion, VA 24354; 540/783-3422

**getting there:** From I-81, take exit 47. Turn S onto US-11. Go 1.1 mi to US-16. Turn R and go 3.7 mi (at 1.8 mi R is the road to the boat ramp) to the park office, L and main entrance, R.

**topography:** Elevation on the lake is 1,350 ft. The surrounding terrain is mountainous, with some very steep ridges. Elevations in the park's NE corner reach 3,600 ft. Hardwood forest predominates, with hardwoods and pines along the parts of the lakeshore that have not been cleared and landscaped. **maps:** USGS Chatham Hill, Marion.

**starting out:** The park entrance fee is $1 on weekdays, $2 on weekends. Facilities are located in the bathhouse and restaurant area, where you'll find restrooms, water, pay phone, and food concessions. You can pick up a small park map and brochure at the park office.

Pets must be kept on a leash. Public display and use of alcohol is not allowed. Swimming outside of the designated area is prohibited.

**activities:** Hiking, Fishing, Canoeing/Kayaking, Camping.

**hiking:** Across the lake from the busy beach area, a network of hiking trails winds through the forest and climbs the mountain slopes that define the park's terrain. There are more than 10 miles of trails in all, with most trails connecting, allowing for loops of various length. Hiking on the trails is easy to moderate, with the main highlights being the woodland setting and some nice views of the lake and surrounding area. The trails are all easy to follow, with trailheads and trail jcts signed. Access to the main trail network is past the picnic grounds and cabin area. Another smaller network of trails is located behind the restaurant and picnic area. Trail use is heavy.

**fishing:** Hungry Mother Lake is noted for the high quality of its northern pike fishery. In recent years, heavy stocking of walleyes has taken place. Other game species in the lake include largemouth bass, crappie, bluegill, mukellunge, and catfish. The last two are stocked annually. The best fishing is from a canoe, though there are a few areas along the shore from which it's possible to cast and there's a handicapped-accessible fishing pier as well.

**canoeing/kayaking:** Although you wouldn't know it from driving past the crowded beach area, most of Hungry Mother Lake is quiet and serene. On the other side of the lake, in fact, you might not know you're in a park at all, so quiet is it at times. Summer weekends are of course an exception. The lake is small, so any paddling excursions will have to be relatively modest. The woodland mountain setting and the high quality of fishing on the lake make it a pleasant place for a morning or afternoon paddling/fishing trip. Paddleboat and rowboat traffic can get pretty heavy during peak days. To reach the boat ramp, follow directions above to the park, but after 1.8 mi on US-16 turn R onto SR-617. Go 1 mi to SR-750. Turn L and go 0.5 mi to the boat ramp.

**camping:** The car campground has 43 sites arranged in 3 loops that are in separate areas. All 3 loops are somewhat similar, with smallish sites set close to one another amidst a canopy of oaks, hickories, hemlocks, and pines. Privacy is minimal, though on most days the campground is not very crowded. Sites cost $12/night, $17 with hookup. Each site has a table and grill. A shower/restroom facility is at the center of each loop. In loop C, most sites sit on elevated wooden platforms. The campground is open from Mar 1 to Dec 1. Reservations are available by calling 800/933-PARK.

# Grayson Highlands State Park

This 4,935-acre rugged highland oasis is one of the real gems in the Virginia state park system. Bordering the Mount Rogers National Recreation Area and located just 4 miles south of Mount Rogers, Virginia's highest peak, its lands encompass a wide array of habitats: lush hardwood forests, grassy balds where wildflowers, ferns, and shrubs proliferate, northern spruce-fir forests, and rocky outcrops that offer the hiker magnificent views across the tops of three states. At the beginning of this century, these highlands provided local German and Scotch-Irish farmers pasturage for their livestock herds. Today, the open character remains, offering the rare opportunity in the southern Appalachians to backpack through mountainous terrain that is largely unforested, permitting long-range views and an increased likelihood of observing wildlife. Wild ponies roam the highlands, as do white-tailed deer, black bears, wild turkey, and groundhogs. You're likely to see one or more of these species on even a short visit. Several species of hawk, including red-shouldered and red-tailed, are frequently seen too. Several forest types cover some parts of the park, including the only native growth of Fraser firs in the state. Yellow birch, red spruce, hemlock, sugar maple, and oaks are all common. Rhododendron, hawthorne and witch hazel contribute to the understory. With facilities that include two picnic areas, a car campground, visitor center, horse stables and camping area, and trails for bikes and hikers, including easy access to the *Appalachian Trail*, Grayson Highlands is ideal for day visits or as a base camp for longer expeditions.

Volney (E) and Troutdale (NE) are the closest towns.

**contact:** Superintendent, Grayson Highlands State Park, Route 2, Box 141, Mouth of Wilson, VA 24363; 540/579-7092

**getting there:** From I-81, take exit 45 at Marion an go S on VA-16 24.4 miles to US-58. Turn R and go W 7.8 miles to Grayson Highlands Ln (SR-362) and the park entrance, R.

**topography:** Elevations in the park reach 5,089 ft on Little Pinnacle, at the peak of Haw Orchard Mtn. Low point is 3,000 ft on Wilson Creek. Several forest types inhabit the park, including northern spruce-fir and southern Appalachian hardwood. Much of the upland is open or "bald", with wildflowers and rhododendron abundant. **maps:** USFS Mount Rogers High Country; USGS Whitetop Mtn, Troutdale, Park, Grassy Creek.

**starting out:** Entrance fee is $1/vehicle on weekdays, $2 on weekends. Stop by the visitor center to pick up maps, brochures, and a trail guide; it's open daily 10 AM to 6 PM Memorial Day to Labor Day, same hours weekends 'til Nov 1. A few good exhibits inside highlight local history, and there's a small shop that sells local crafts and books. Facilities (restrooms, water) are there too. The best topo map for traveling the backcountry is the USFS High Country one listed above.

Alcohol is not allowed in the park. Pets must be kept on a leash. The park is open year round.

**activities:** Hiking, Camping, Fishing, Mountain Biking

**hiking:** The park's trails will take you to stunning views from the rock formations known as Big Pinnacle and Little Pinnacle, through dense stands of rhododendron to sparkling trout creeks with scenic falls, or across open meadows graced with wildflowers and gardens of massive stone. In all 9 trails cover 9 miles. Although park trails are short, longer trips are made possible by connecting with the *Appalachian Trail*, which passes through the park. The *AT* provides access to the extensive network of trails in the Mount Rogers NRA, adjacent to the N. Hiking on most park trails is easy to moderate, with the trails well established and blazed. As most trails are short and lead to park highlights, use is moderate to heavy. The signed trailheads are at several locations throughout the park. Small shelters are found along some of the trails.

**camping:** Although the park is a popular starting point for backpacking trips, backcountry camping isn't allowed in the park. It is permitted on the *AT*, however, and throughout the Mount Rogers NRA, little more than a mile hike from the Massie Gap trailhead. There's a parking area nearby to leave your car overnight. Backpackers must register at the contact station before heading out.

There's also a 73-site car campground in the park. The small sites are located in a sparsely wooded area not far from Wilson Creek. The lack of heavy forest growth and the proximity of the sites to each other leaves little privacy. Nevertheless, the campground is very popular, and almost always fills on summer weekends. Sites cost $11/night, $3 more if you bring a pet. Each site has a picnic table and grill. Shower/restroom facilities are centrally located. A small camp store is located just outside the campground. The campground's open May 1 to Nov 1, with primitive camping until Dec 1 ($8/night, pit toilets only). You can reserve sites by calling 800/933-PARK.

**fishing:** A couple of creeks in the park offer a nice opportunity for backcountry fishing. Cabin Creek is a small, tight stream with a steep gradient and lots of little pools. Cover is very tight, and fly-casting is difficult in most places. Access is via the *Cabin Creek Trail*, with a half-mi hike from trailhead to creek. Cabin Creek passes through the park for 2 miles, with its headwaters just outside the park on Pine Mtn. It's worth fishing as much for its scenic beauty as for the trout it holds, which are generally small.

Wilson Creek, which forms most of the E boundary between the state park and the Little Wilson Creek Wilderness, is medium in size with an avg gradient. Massive boulders and rock ledges afford outstanding pooling. streamside cover is dense, and the surrounding forest lush and beautiful. The creek begins N of the park on Pine Mtn and flows S through the park for about 3 mi. You reach it by hiking 0.7 mi on the *Wilson Creek Trail*, which begins just outside the car campground.

**mountain biking:** A small network of dirt and gravel gated park roads are open to mountain bikes (horses and hikers too). In all they cover about 6 miles. Riding on these paths is easy to moderate, with some fairly rugged conditions and small creek crossings. Access is at the picnic area and at the start of the campground road. A trail map is available at the visitors center.

# Wythe Ranger District

## Jefferson National Forest

The Wythe Ranger District covers 173,400 acres in the Blue Ridge Mountains between the Mt Rogers National Recreation Area and

West Virginia. With lands extending into seven counties, it is the largest district on the Jefferson National Forest. The district includes 2 desiganted wilderness areas—5,609-acre Beartown 5,542-acre and Kimberling Creek—though neither has a large network of trails to facilitate backcountry travel. Despite the district's vast acreage and the scenic combination of rugged mountains and pastoral valleys, opportunites for outdoor recreation are somewhat limited. The *Appalachian Trail*, which passes through the district for almost 60 miles, provides hikers and backpackers the best means for exploring a large section of the district's backcountry. There are no large developed recreation areas on the district. A single campground and a couple of small picnic areas provide bases for exploring the district on foot or bike. The proximity of the immensely popular Mt Rogers NRA may explain the lack of opportunities for outdoor recreation on the Wythe. In fact, the lightly-traveled trails on the district are a good alternative on days when the trail on Mt Rogers are too congested.

Wytheville (S), Tazewell (NW), and Bluefield, WV (N) are the closest towns.

**contact:** Wythe Ranger District, 1625 W. Lee Highway, Wytheville, VA 24382; 540/228-5551.

**getting there:** Major highway access to the district is from I-81, which parallels it to the south, and from I-77, which bisects it running N–S. The district ranger station is located on US-11 in Wytheville. From I-81, take exit 67 and go 2 mi E on US-11 to the RS. A USFS information center is located 9 mi E of Wytheville in a factory outlet shopping center. From I-77/81, take exit 80. Turn E on Factory Merchants Dr and go 1.2 mi to the outlet mall access road, R.

**topography:** District topography is dominated by a pair of long, narrow mountain ridges separated by valleys the are agricultural centers. Clinch Mtn runs along the N half of the district; Walker Mtn runs along the S half. Elevations exceed 4,600 ft on the former. Forest types are varied, with southern Appalachian hardwoods most prominent. **maps:** See below under each listing for USGS maps.

**starting out:** District maps and brochures are available at the ranger station in Wytheville. Hours are M–F 7:30 AM to 4 PM. A much broader selection of information—with maps and brochures available for all of the national forest ranger districts in VA—is available at the info center just off I-81 9 mi E of Wytheville. It's open M–Sa 9 AM to 5 PM, Su 12 to 5 PM. A pretty good selection of guidebooks is also available.

**activities:** Hiking, Camping, Fishing, Mountain Biking.

**hiking:** The primary hiking opportunity is on the *Appalachian Trail,* which is on the district for 58 miles. It enters from the south on the adjacent Mt Rogers NRA, traveling N on narrow easements of USFS land around heavily trafficked I-81 and continuing N through more remote areas until reaching the Beartown Wilderness. There it turns E, following a more or less continuous set of ridges until exiting the district at the boundary with the Blacksburg RD. The focus below is on the latter half, which is more remote and offers a higher quality backcountry experience. Other trails on the district account for only another 70 miles, with most offering hikes of 5 miles or less. Several of these trails do connect with the *AT,* with a few possibilities for loop hikes. Hiking is generally easy to moderate, with a few strenuous sections on the *AT.*

**camping:** Backcountry camping is allowed anywhere on the district, except where posted otherwise. The lack of a large trail network, however, diminishes the possibilities for long trips into the backcountry. The *Appalachian Trail* is, of course, an exception. Shelters are located at regular intervals along the trail, each about a day's hike from the next.

For car campers, there's just one developed campground on the district: the very attractive and well-maintained Stoney Fork Campground. It's located on the south side of Walker Mtn not far from downtown Wytheville.

**fishing:** Anglers will find several small creeks with stocked trout and a couple more with native populations. Most of these creeks are accessible from roads and better suited to spot fishing trips than to longer backpacking/angling treks. Of the areas described below, only Roaring Fork in the Beartown Wilderness is worthy of a backcountry trip in seach of trout.

**mountain biking:** The limited number of trails on the district applies to bikers even more than hikers. That said, however, the district really does offer some pretty good riding. The reason is the large network of dirt and gravel roads that lace the backcountry. These roads see very little auto traffic, and with a little imagination they can be connected to form routes of almost any length. Pick up a copy of the district map and head out on the state routes that run through forest service land; almost all of these are suitable for biking. Several routes are described below.

# Beartown Wilderness Area

Located in the northwest corner of the district, the centerpiece of this area is the remote, roadless 5,609-acre designated wilderness. On a district with few large tracts of untrammelled backcountry, the Beartown Wilderness demands a certain amount of dedication from those who would visit; the only way to get to it is on foot. Although not quite as remote, the forested ridges to the south that comprise the rest of this area are barely more traveled. Gravel SR-625 provides the only vehicle access; the *Appalachian Trail*, which traverses the area, probably accounts for more traffic. The *AT*, in fact, is the area's defining feature, winding over mountains and valleys and briefly skirting the wilderness for a total distance of 17 miles between VA-42 and SR-623. The area's ridges and mountain slopes are covered in forests of mixed hardwoods, hemlock, and pockets of spruce-fir. A sphagnum bog is also located within the wilderness. With no facilities, a remote location, and little traffic, the Beartown Wilderness area offers the best opportunity on the district for a primitive backcountry excursion.

Tazewell (NW) and Bland (E) are the closest towns.

**getting there:** From I-81 in Marion, take exit 45. Turn N onto VA-16 and go 0.8 mi to a jct. Turn R and continue on VA-16 1.2 mi to another jct. Turn L, still following VA-16 and go 13 mi to VA-42. Turn R and go 13.1 mi to SR-625. Turn L and go (at 0.5 mi the pavement ends; at 7.8 mi is access to the *AT*) 8 mi to a small parking area, R. • From I-81 in Wytheville, take exit 70. Turn N onto US-52 and go 16 mi over the crest of Walker Mtn to VA-42. Turn L and go 13 mi to SR-625. Turn R and follow directions above to the parking area.

**topography:** Chestnut Ridge—it runs NE–SW—forms the wilderness' S boundary. The slopes of the ridge are mountainous, but relatively mild. Within the wilderness itself, however, the terrain is considerably steeper in some places. Elevations in the wilderness top 4,600 ft; on SR-625 they drop to 2,300 ft. **maps:** USGS-FS Hutchinson Rock; AT Wythe Ranger District.

**starting out:** There are no facilities in the wilderness or surrounding area. Water is generally available along the AT from intermittent springs, though the trail follows a ridgeline above most headwaters for 15 miles. Inside the wilderness, Roaring Fork is the primary water source. Be sure to treat all surface water before drinking. The AT map is the best topo for the area, though it doesn't show all of the Beartown Wilderness (it does show the hiking trail and Roaring Fork).

Group size is limited to 10 in the wilderness.

**activities:** Hiking, Fishing, Camping

**hiking:** The only way to get into the wilderness is on foot. A single short trail enters into the heart of the wilderness, while the *Appalachian Trail* skirts its S border for 3 miles. From the south, the AT enters the area when it crosses SR-625 (see above for directions), follows a winding route N for almost 2 miles to the Beartown Wilderness, turns E and then follows a pair of ridges for 9 miles until it reaches SR-623, the area's E border. Several places along the ridgeline afford good views. As elsewhere, the AT is blazed with a white bar and very well maintained. Trail access points are signed. Hiking this section of the trail is moderate.

A second trail starts on Chestnut Ridge at the wilderness boundary and follows a narrow dirt footpath 1.5 mi to Roaring Fork, a native trout creek. To reach the trail, walk 50 yds up SR-625 from the parking area described above, turn R onto a dirt and gravel road (not recommended for cars), and continue 2 mi to the wilderness boundary. There's a blockade and signboard there, as well as the start of the trail. Hiking is moderate on the road and trail. Trail use is light.

**fishing:** The only fishing in the area is on Roaring Fork, a native brook trout creek that can only be reached by hiking into the Beartown Wilderness. It's a small creek with an average gradient, located in the middle of a remote forest. Once you reach Roaring Fork, the only way to fish it is to wade it upstream or down. It can be fished for about 5 miles. As might be expected, fishing pressure is light. See above for directions to the trailhead.

**camping:** Backcountry camping is permitted throughout the area on national forest lands. The Chestnut Knob shelter is located on the *AT* at the SE corner of the Beartown Wilderness. The shortest distance to the shelter is from the trail access on SR-625, a moderate, 5-mi hike.

# Walker Mountain Area

Located to the northwest of Wytheville and spreading out along the summit ridge and southern flank of Walker Mountain, the trails, creeks, and recreation areas of this region are dispersed over a fairly large region. To visit them all requires some driving on dirt and gravel backcountry roads, but the payoffs are isolation, scenic vistas, and a good chance to observe wildlife, particularly wild turkey, ruffed grouse, white-tailed deer, and cottontail rabbits. There are facilites for camping at the Stony Fork Rec Area, and picnic grounds at Dark Horse Hollow and Big Bend. Without a large trail network nearby or access to the *Appalachian Trail*, which passes through other portions of the district, these areas are all best suited to short visits. At the region's western end, however, there are a couple of long trails (and a connection to the *AT*), which makes longer treks possible.

Wytheville (SE) is the closest town.

**getting there:** From Wytheville, take US-52 N 7.8 mi to SR-717. Turn R and go 0.5 mi to the Stony Fork campground, R. • Continuing N on US-52 from SR-717, go 0.4 mi to SR-686 (ahead it's 3.6 mi N on US-52 to a large lookout tower at the crest of Walker Mtn and FR-206, R). Turn L and go 1.2 mi to a jct with FR-221, L and the end of the pavement. Bear L on the forest road and go 6.9 mi to SR-625. Turn R and go 0.5 mi to a fork. Bear L and go 1.9 mi to the end of the road and trailheads to the *Crawfish* and *Channel Rock* Trails. • Another access to the area is via I-77. Take exit 47 and turn W onto SR-717. Go 3.8 mi to the Stony Fork campground. • The Dark Horse Hollow picnic area is on US-52, 2.3 mi S of SR-717.

**topography:** The terrain is generally mountainous, though the mountains are not especially rugged or steep, with elevations that do not exceed 3,850 ft. Highest elevations are on Walker Mtn at the area's N perimeter. Forest cover is heavy through most of the area, with tracts of pines and extensive hardwood forest. **maps:**

USGS-FS Big Bend, Garden Mtn, Rural Retreat.

**starting out:** Facilities in the area are at 3 separate rec areas, all accessible via US-52. The Dark Horse Hollow Picnic Area has pit toilets, but no water. A $1/vehicle fee is charged there. At Stony Fork Campground are modern restrooms, water, and a pay phone. Both areas are open Apr–Nov. Big Bend Picnic Area on FR-206 has pit toilets but no water. It's open all year.

**activities:** Hiking, Camping, Fishing, Mountain Biking

**hiking:** The trails on this part of the district are dispersed over a large area, allowing for several shorter hikes over varied terrain. For the best views of the area, hike the 0.75-mi section of the former *Walker Mountain Trail* that has been redesignated the *Monstor Rock Trail* in honor of the massive boulder which affords panoramic views S. The blazed trail begins on a dirt construction road behind the large lookout tower beside US-52 atop Walker Mtn.. Hiking is easy to moderate. You can continue hiking along the trail past the rock, though it is no longer blazed and is overgrown in places.

Near the Stony Fork Campground area is a pair of trails that connect to cover about 6 miles. The *Stony Fork Nature Trail* is a 1-mi loop that passes through a forest of pines and hardwoods. Access is in the Stony Fork campground, at sites #32 and #44. The *Seven Sisters Trail* is a 5-mi trail that roughly parallels Stony Fork in a lush, beautiful forest. Trailheads are on the Stony Fork Nature Trail and 2.6 mi E of the Stony Fork campground on SR-717. Little Walker Mtn and East Fork are highlights. The trail is blazed with red bars and easy to follow. Hiking is easy.

The longest, most remote trails are located at the W edge of this area. Combined, the *Crawfish Trail* and *Channel Rock Trail* cover 10 miles, with 2 crossings of the AT offering the possibility of hikes of almost any length. The trails share a trailhead at a gated forest road that soon gives way to single-track. Together the trails form a loop, with highlights along the way that include a good chance to observe wildlife, remote hardwoods forest, fields of wildflowers, and mountain ridges. Hiking is moderate. The trails are open to mountain bikes, but use by all users is light.

**camping:** Backcountry camping is permitted throughout the area, except where posted otherwise. The best areas for a short overnight trip are along the *Seven Sisters Trail* or off FR-206. For longer trips, the area along the *Crawfish Trail* and *Channel Rock Trail* is best, with extended expeditions possible along the *AT.*

Stony Fork, the only car campground in the area, is also one of the nicest on the national forest. 52 large sites are dispersed over a wide, heavily forested area, affording a good measure of privacy. Each site has a picnic table, grill, and lantern post. Facilities include bathhouses with hot showers. Sites cost $8/night. Double sites cost $12/night. The campground is open from Apr 2–Oct 29.

**fishing:** Although the small creeks in the area don't really merit a visit on their own, they do add another dimension to hiking or mountain biking trips. The 2 creeks of interest to the trout fisherman are Stony Creek and East Fork. Stony Fork is the larger of the two, with a mild gradient and some good pools, but it flows through USFS land for only a short distance. Access is from a trail at Dark Hollow picnic area. Streamside cover is heavy, but the creek is wide enough to allow for pretty easy fly-casting. The fishable section is about a mile long.

East Fork feeds into Stony Creek near the jct of US-52 and SR-717. It flows down off Walker Mtn and follows the latter road for almost 5 miles. This is a small creek that flows down a rocky bed on a mild gradient. Lush thickets of rhododendron line the banks, adding an element of natural beauty to the creek, but create very tight conditions that can frustrate the casts of fly-fishermen. Access is along SR-717, where there are numerous pullouts. Both creeks are stocked.

**mountain biking:** There are two areas in the vicinity NW of Wytheville with good mountain bike tracks. The first is in the valley S of Walker Mountain. 2 trails described above—*Channel Rock* and *Crawfish* Trails—and a number of rarely-traveled dirt and gravel roads—FR-221, SR-625, SR-727—combine to form a 30-mi network of easy to moderate rides. The roads pass through a combination of hardwood forest and scenic farmland, with a good opportunity to observe wildlife on the USFS portion of the route. Riding is generally easy, with a few moderate stretches.

The other area with biking potential is on the other side of US-52, and follows the crest ridge of Walker Mountain on FR-206, a rugged dirt and gravel road. Views along the road are good, especially in winter, and traffic is very light, making this one of the better rides in the area. Since the road starts out at the top of the mountain, you get the benefits of the mountaintop scenery without the usual arduous climb. The road follows the summit for 10 miles, before connecting with unimproved SR-656. By following this road a couple miles north or south, it's possible to make connections with a number of other backcountry dirt roads. Parking is on US-52 just N of the jct with FR-206 or at Big Bend picnic area. The picnic area is located 3.7 mi E of US-52.

# Little Wolf Creek Area

This area is defined by a pair of roads and the *Appalachian Trail*. The forested ridges of Garden Mountain and Brushy Mountain are bounded by I-77 to the east and SR-625 to the west. Between them runs a 17-mi segment of the world's longest and most famous hiking trail. A couple of other trails connect with the *Appalachian Trail*, and there's a trout creek that runs right through the heart of the area. Rhododendron line the creek beds and wildlife can sometimes be seen in the clearings along the trails. Come for a day of hiking or fly-fishing. If you want to cover more ground, just keep going on the *AT*.

Bland (E) is the nearest town.

**getting there:** From I-77 at the town of Bland, take exit 52. Go W on VA-42 3.2 mi to SR-615. Turn R and go 2.8 mi (at 1.2 mi the pavement ends) to the *AT* trail crossing and small parking area, L. Another parking area and access to the *High Water Trail* is ahead 0.6 mi, L.

**topography:** Terrain is predominantly mountainous with second growth forest of hemlocks, hardwoods and pines covering the ridges and spine of two gentle mountains. Elevations are between 2,500 and 3,000 ft. **maps:** *AT* Wythe Ranger District; USGS-FS Garden Mtn, Big Bend.

**starting out:** Despite fairly easy highway access, this is a remote backcountry area with no facilities. Water is avilable along the *AT*, except on the mountain ridges. Be sure to treat all surface water. The *AT* topo map is the best guide to the area.

**activities:** Hiking, Fishing, Camping.

**hiking:** The primary hiking trail here is the *Appalachian Trail*, which enters the area at SR-623 and leaves when it crosses I-77 and passes S of the Kimberling Creek Wilderness. A couple of other trails connect with the *AT* at the main trail access, allowing for side trips or loop hikes. The longer of these trails is the 3.5-mi *High Water Trail*. The trail is blazed and follows an old roadbed that mostly parallels the *AT*. A 7-mi loop is formed by hiking the 2 trails together. The 1.5-mi *Trail Boss Trail* also connects with the *AT*, forming a loop of 3 miles. The trailhead is 0.2 mi further up SR-615 from the *AT* access. Like the *AT* here, it starts by crossing a scenic footbridge. Hiking on all 3 trails is easy to moderate. Trail use is light, except on the *AT*, where it's moderate to heavy.

**camping:** Although backcountry camping is allowed throughout the area, it can be hard to find good sites along the trails because of the dense understory and topography. Nevertheless, there are a few good sites along the *AT*, with a shelter located 5 mi W of the trailhead described above. Primitive roadside camping is possible at a few sites along SR-615 near the trailheads.

**fishing:** Laurel Creek is a small to medium trout stream with a mild to average gradient and decent pooling created by a series of rock ledges. Cover is generally tight, though there are a few open areas that permit unencumbered casting. The creek is stocked. Access is along SR-615. It can be fished for about 2 miles.

# Stewart's Creek Wildlife Management Area

Stewart's Creek WMA is a secret that few people besides trout fishermen and hunters know about. Perched on the eastern flank of the Blue Ridge not far north of the North Carolina state line, the area comprises 1,087 acres of hardwood forest laced by cool, clear mountain creeks. Although hunters know the area for its populations of white-tailed deer, wild turkey, and ruffed grouse, the area's real prize is the two-forked Stewart's Creek, a native brook trout fishery. With no roads running beside the creek and access only by wading or hiking trail, this is one of the best area's for a backcountry fishing expeditions under conditions that existed in centuries past, before the introduction of brown or rainbow trout, or stocking programs. Other possible activities on the WMA include hiking, nature photography, and backpacking. With no facilities and a low concentration of visitors, this is a good destination for a backpacking-for-trout trip.

Galax (NW) is the closest town.

**contact:** Stewart's Creek WMA, Route 1, Box 107, Marion, VA 24354; 540/782-9051

**getting there:** From I-77, take exit 1. Turn W onto SR-620 and go 1.5 mi to SR-696. Turn L and go 0.7 mi to SR-795. Bear R at a fork and go (at 0.5 mi the pavement ends; at 1.5 mi is a ford across the creek) 1.6 mi to the end of the road and parking area. • From the BRP, exit at milepost 206.4 onto SR-608. Go 0.3 mi to SR-620. Turn R and go 3.3 mi to SR-696. Turn L and follow above directions to the WMA.

**topography:** The WMA occupies the eastern flank of the Blue Ridge, overlooking piedmont terrain dotted with small farms. The forested ridges are rugged and steep. Elevations are between 3,000 and 1,600 ft. **maps:** USGS Lambsburg.

**starting out:** There are no facilities at all on the WMA. Reaching the trailhead can be difficult during high water on the creek, as there is an unimproved crossing. If you don't have 4-wheel drive, park at the edge of the first crossing, where there's room for a car or two. Hunting takes place on the WMA in fall and winter. If you visit during that time, wear blaze orange.

**activities:** Fishing, Camping, Hiking

**fishing:** In many way Stewart's Creek represents the quintessential southern Appalachian trout stream—fishing the way it was a hundred years ago. Stewart's Creek is a native brook trout fishery that begins high on the Blue Ridge and tumbles over rocks, boulders, and flumes as it descends to the piedmont below. It's a medium-sized creek as it reaches the bottom of the WMA, with exceptional pooling and good forest cover. The only way to fish it is by wading upstream from the WMA entrance or to follow the hiking trail that runs beside it. Its 2 forks can be fished for about 5 miles. Regulations are single-hook artificial lures only and all fish caught must be immediately released.

**camping:** Primitive backcountry camping is allowed anywhere on the WMA except where posted.

**hiking:** Although most visitors who hike the old roadbeds that follow the creeks do so to get at the trout, the trails pass through attractive hardwood forests that are worth a visit in their own right. The trails are not maintained, but repeated use by hunters and anglers keeps them relatively well defined. Hiking is moderate. Trail use is light to moderate, depending on the season. Access is from the main trailhead described above.

# Crooked Creek Wildlife Management Area

The Crooked Creek WMA covers almost 1,800 acres of lazy mountain slopes and riparian habitat in Carroll County. Most visitors come to fish, hunt, or simply enjoy the natural setting. Crooked Creek offers sections of stream that are both stocked and native trout waters. On a spring weekend the stocked section can get pretty crowded with hopeful anglers. In the backcountry, a hardwood and pine forest is gradually reclaiming the land from the small farms that once populated the area. Some old fields still remain, and a section of Crooked Creek flows through meadow. The woods and fields are prime habitat for the many species of wildlife that inhabit the area, including wild turkey and white-tailed deer. Outdoor recreation here centers around the trout fishing. There's a concession stand that's open only during the fishing season. A small picnic area is also on premises, or you can stake out a shady spot along the banks of Crooked Creek. All told, this is a nice place to introduce young sportsmen to the pleasures (and frustrations) of fly-fishing.

Galax (W) and Hillsville (NE) are the closest towns.

**contact:** Crooked Creek WMA, Route 1 Box 107, Marion, VA 24354; 540/782-9051

**getting there:** From the Blue Ridge Parkway, exit at milepost 206.4 onto SR-608. Go 0.3 mi to SR-620. Turn L and go 0.7 mi to a jct. Turn R, continuing on SR-620, and go 4.6 (at 3 mi the pavement ends) mi to SR-712. Turn R and go 0.2 mi to the entrance, L. • From I-77, take exit 14. Turn W onto US-58 and go 3.5 mi to SR-620. Turn L and go 3.5 mi to the WMA entrance, R.

**topography:** The broad valley W of the Blue Ridge is characterized by rolling hills that have been mostly cleared for agriculture and residential development. Within the WMA, most of the land is forested, though there are large swaths of open land near the main

entrance and creek. Elevations are between 2,400 and 3,000 ft.
**maps:** USGS Woodlawn

**starting out:** All visitors inevitably start out at the concession area, where you purchase fishing permits. Access to the creek is there, as is a small picnic area, restrooms, and water. Hunting takes place on the WMA in fall and winter. Visitors should wear blaze orange during those seasons.

**activities:** Fishing

**fishing:** The main action on the WMA in spring and summer is trout fishing. Crooked Creek is a fee-fishing area that offers about 6 miles of fishable water on 2 creeks. A daily permit costs $4 from the 3rd Saturday in March to Labor Day. Crooked Creek is a medium to large stream with a mild gradient and a gravel bottom. Unlike many of the neighboring mountain trout streams, sections of its banks are mostly open field. A narrow band of forest lines part of one bank. Access is from the large parking lot behind the concession. Crooked Creek is stocked trout waters.

Anglers wishing to fish in more natural conditions can try Crooked Creek above its confluence with East Fork, or East Fork itself. Both waters contain native trout, with brookies most prominent. The gradient on these creeks is a little steeper than on the stocked portion of Crooked Creek, and the cover is considerable denser, providing a challenge to fly-casters. Access is from the main WMA road and then by wading. Fishing pressure on the WMA is heavy, though it's much lighter on the unstocked portions of the creeks.

# Claytor Lake State Park

Located in the scenic New River Valley in Pulaski Country, Claytor Lake is a 472-acre park that sits on the north shore of the lake of the same name. 4,500-acre Claytor Lake was created in 1939 with the completion of a dam across the New River. One of only several large lakes in the southwest highlands, Claytor Lake is also one of the most popular with outdoor recreationists. Waterskiers, jetskiers, sailboats, bass boats, and other pleasure craft often crowd the lake's 21-mile length. The state park is geared primarily toward accommodating water-based recreation, with facilities that include a marina, swimming beach, boat launch, large picnic grounds, full-service car campground, and rental cabins. So many facilities and so much activity can leave backcountry enthusiasts feeling a bit crowded. The majority of park acreage, however, is woodland, with a pair of trails providing a chance to get away from all the summertime bustle. And off season, when most of the power boats are back in their slips, can be an ideal time to explore the park and lake in a quieter setting.

Dublin (N) and Radford (E) are the closest towns.

**contact:** Claytor Lake State Park, Route 1, Box 267, Dublin, VA 24084; 540/674-5492

**getting there:** From I-81, take exit 101. Turn S onto SR-660 and go 2.3 mi to the park entrance.

**topography:** The park and lake are part of the New River Valley. The terrain is generally rolling countryside covered by a young pine/hardwood forest. Around the lake and in the park, tracts of land have been cleared to accommodate development or to create a park-like setting. **maps:** USGS Dublin, Radford South.

**starting out:** An entrance fee of $3/vehicle on weekends, $2 weekdays is charged. Facilities (restrooms, water, vending machines) are lcoated at the marina and near the picnic areas. The marina sells the usual beach and boating supplies.

Public use or display of alcohol is not allowed. Pets must be kept on a leash.

**activities:** Hiking, Camping, Canoeing/Kayaking, Fishing

**hiking:** Although most park activity centers on the lake, a couple of trails wind through the hardwood and pine forest that covers most of the park land. Neither trail is very long, and both are best used as a quiet, solitary respite from the often busy activity along the lakeshore. The 1.6-mi *Claytor Lake Trail* and the 0.6-mi *Shady Ridge Trail* form loops. The latter is a nature trail, with a guide pamphlet available at the trailhead. The 2 trails do not connect. Access to the *Claytor Lake Trail* is between the marina and beach; the trailhead to the other is in the picnic area parking lot. Both trails are blazed and easy to follow. Hiking is moderate. Trail use is moderate to heavy.

**camping:** The large car campground has 132 sites in 4 loops. A shower/restroom facility is at the center of each loop. Most of the average-sized sites are laid out in sparsely wooded areas, with sites in loop D in a more open setting. Privacy is minimal to average at best. Each site has a picnic table and grill. Sites cost $12/night, $17 with hookup. The campground is open from Mar 1 to Dec 1. Reservations are available by calling 800/933-PARK.

**canoeing/kayaking:** From the point of view of the backcountry paddler, Claytor Lake is something of a mixed bag. First of all, it really doesn't fit any definition of backcountry at all. Although it's 21 miles long with a 100-mi shoreline and offers the canoeist or kayaker plenty of water to cover, much of the shoreline is developed and the lake is very popular with recreational boaters of all stripes. In other words, if you decide to paddle Claytor Lake, expect company. In general, solitude seeking paddlers are better off on the New River—on either side of the lake. A boat ramp is located in the park.

**fishing:** The lake is stocked with walleye and striped bass. Other game species include largemouth, smallmouth, white, and spotted bass, crappie, and catfish. Fishing from the shore is possible, with large open areas along the shore and a fishing dock. Fishing from a canoe offers better water coverage, although without electronic equipment locating fish on such a large body of water can be a real challenge.

# New River Trail State Park

Winding through four counties along North America's oldest river (and most inappropriately named), New River Trail is Virginia's longest and skinniest state park. The park is one of the rails-to-trails conversions that have recently been transforming the nation's old and abandoned railroad corridors into a vast network of greenways and linear parks. Opened in 1987, the park quickly became a popular destination for hikers, bikers, equestrians, and other lovers of the outdoors. The nearly level trail follows a wide bed of crushed cinder through an 80-foot corridor that passes through forests, meadows, farmland, towns, and along the river, which it crosses several times on scenic RR trestles. It has two southern termini—one in Galax and one in Fries. At Fries Junction the two trails meet and the trail then follows a single path for another 40 miles to its northern terminus in Pulaski. Park headquarters is at Shot Tower, located near the mid-point along the trail. Hiking and mountain biking day-trips are the most popular ways to experience the trail. If you decide to spend more than a day on the trail, you can camp at a new campground in the Mt Rogers National Recreation Area or on lands that border the trail.

In addition to the towns at the three traiheads, there are numerous small towns along the trail's route.

**contact:** New River Trail State Park, Route 1, Box 81X, Austinville, VA 24312540/699-6778

**getting there:** In Fries, from the jct of VA-94 and SR-1001, take SR-1001 0.1 mi to the park entrance, trailhead, and boat launch area, R. • In Galax, the trailhead is downtown on US-58. • To get to Shot Tower, from I-77, take exit 24. Turn N onto VA-69. Go 0.2 mi to US-52. Turn L and go 1.4 mi to SR-624. Turn L and go 0.2 mi to the historical park and trail access. • To reach the Pulaski trailhead, from I-81 take exit 94B. Turn N onto VA-99 and go 1.9 mi to Xaloy Way. Turn R and go 100 yds to the trailhead, R.

**starting out:** Information centers are located at Shot Tower and in a red caboose at the Fries trailhead. Shot Tower Historical SP is open daily Apr–Nov 8 AM to dusk. Overnight parking is not allowed in the park. Entrance fee is $1/vehicle weekdays, $2 on weekends. Facilities are restrooms, water, and picnic tables. Trail maps are available at the tower or at the park office. Hours are M-Th 8 AM to 4:30. It's located at mile 25 on trail.

Alcohol is not allowed on the trail. Pets must be kept on a leash.

**activities:** Hiking, Mountain Biking, Kayaking/Canoeing, Fishing, Camping

hiking/**mountain biking:** As one of the rail-trail conversions that have become so popular in recent years, the *New River Trail* offers hikers and bikers an experience that is different from the more traditional foot and bike trails found in national forests and parks. The trail follows the wide corridor of a former RR line for its entire length. Since the grade had to be suitable for trains, it is rather mild. Hiking and biking on all parts of the trail is easy, regardless of which direction you go. The treadway is made up primarily of crushed cinders. The trail passes through a variety of environments, including urban areas at the trailheads, the long pastoral valley that the New River flows through, and narrow bands of forest. The scenery in many places along the trail is exceptional. Access points, in addition to the 4 described above, are located at frequent intervals. The trail has quickly become a favorite destination for hikers, mountain bikers, and other outdoor enthusiasts. Though it doesn't get as busy as the *Virginia Creeper Trail*, trail use is heavy.

**kayaking/canoeing:** In VA, the New is divided into 2 distinct sections, with Claytor Lake in the middle. The upper New, which enters VA from NC near Mouth of Wilson, flows E and N about 80 mi before emptying into the man-made lake. The river here meanders through scenic countryside that is alternately forested and cleared for cow pasturage. The water is flat along most of this section, with intermittent rapids mostly in the class I-II category. A few rapids, near the start and end of the section, may reach as high as class III-IV, depending on water levels. Aside from the most challenging rapids, this section of the river is ideal for novice to intermediate paddlers, as well as for those wanting to take a multi-day trip. (Even longer trips are possible by beginning on the 26-mi New River State Park, just across the border in NC. See *North Carolina: A Guide to Backcountry Travel & Adventure*). Thrill seekers will be mostly disappointed. 4 dams are located on this part of the river, 1 at Mouth of Wilson (easy portage) and 3 in a 15-mile stretch between Fries and Ivanhoe (these sections are best suited to short day trips, as a couple of the portages are difficult). River access points are spaced approximately every 10 miles along the route, allowing for trips of varying length. Boat traffic throughout the section is relatively light.

**fishing:** The New is regarded as one of the best smallmouth bass rivers in the state. Despite this reputation, fishing pressure is relatively light, due in part to the isolated character of most of the river. Fishing is mostly done by wading or from a canoe. There are very few places along the banks easily accessible to anglers. A boat will allow you to cover the most water, though you'll probably want to get out and wade the river's shallow water when you come to a promising pool. Other spicies of game fish in the river include muskellunge, catfish, largemouth bass, crappie, and sunfish.

**camping:** Primitive backcountry camping is permitted along the *New River Trail*. Keep in mind, however, that the trail passes through a very narrow corridor of publicly owned land. If you go outside that corridor without first seeking the permission of the landowners, you're trespassing and subject to prosecution. In other words, use common sense. Don't camp on private property unless you check with the owners first. Camping in town parks and towns along the trail is not allowed.

The New River campground is actually located within the Mt Rogers Rec Area. It's included here because it was constructed to served users of the New River and *New River Trail*. 22 sites are spread out across a large area that has been cleared and landscaped. This has created an attractive setting but reduced privacy when the campground is full. Each site has a picnic table, grill, and lantern post. Pit toilets and water are in the area. Sites cost $5/night. The campground is located near Buck Dam 5 miles above Fries Jct. It's open all year. To get there by car, From I-81 take exit 80 (US-52 S). Go 1.3 mi to VA-94. Turn R and go 14 mi to SR-602. Turn L and go 3.6 mi to gravel SR-737 (Buck Dam Rd). Turn L and go 2 mi to the campground.

# Blacksburg Ranger District

## Jefferson National Forest

The Blacksburge Ranger District encompasses 115,630 acres in three major tracts. The New River, considered by geologists to be the oldest river in North America, flows north through the district. One tract of district land is west of the broad New River Valley; it borders the Wythe Ranger District to the west. The other 2 tracts are east of the river and valley: the larger occupies the southern slopes of Peters Mountain on the West Virginia border as well as the ridges of Fork Mountain, Potts Mountain, and Johns Creek Mountain. The third tract occupies the long, narrow valley of Craig Creek between Blacksburg and the New Castle Ranger District. The thread that binds these disparate land holdings is the *Appalachian Trail*, which crosses the district for 85 miles. The trail passes through three of the areas described below and skirts a fourth, providing a link to the district's recreation areas and designated wildernesses. The district includes two designated wilderness areas—3,881-acre Peters Mountain and 10,753-acre

Mountain Lake. The wildernesses and other large backcountry areas harbor wildlife that includes black bear, white-tailed deer, and wild turkey. There are several stands of virgin timber on the district as well as a bog. Outdoor recreation centers around the excellent network of hiking trails. Developed recreation areas are few. Cascades is the most popular, with facilities for picnicking beside Little Stony Creek. There are two campgrounds on the district, though one is little more than a clearing with space for half a dozen campers. Fly-fishermen will find several mountain streams worth visiting, containing both hatchery-raised and native populations of trout.

Narrows and Pearisburg are both located at the district's N end; Blacksburg is close by to the S.

**contact:** Blacksburg Ranger District, 110 South Park Drive, Blacksburg, VA 24060; 540/552-4641.

**getting there:** US-460 runs through the heart of the district N of Blacksburg, providing the major highway access. The The district ranger station is located just off US-460 BUS (S Main St) near the S end of Blacksburg.

**topography:** Terrain throughout the district is mountainous, with elevations generally topping out at about 4,000 ft. The New River is the one of the largest rivers in the mountains and the district's major drainage. Elevation where it leaves the district is 1,600 ft. **maps:** USFS Blacksburg Ranger District; see individual listings below for USGS maps.

**starting out:** If yoiu need maps, information, or want to check on current conditions, stop by the district office before heading out. They sell a complete selection of USFS maps and can offer free brochures on the different parts of the district. Hours are M–F 8 AM to 4:30 PM. Located off US-460 BUS (S Main St) near the S end of Blacksburg).

**activities:** Hiking, Camping, Fishing, Mountain Biking

**hiking:** The district's trail inventory lists 162 miles of trails. Just more than half of the total is covered by the *Appalachian Trail*, which charts a circuitous path through the district from one end to the other. Along the way it crosses the New River, ascends mountain ridges that offer magnificent vistas, meanders through hardwood forests, and passes through both of the district's wilderness areas. It offers the best opportunity for extended backpacking trips on the district, and many of the other trails connect to the *AT*. In addition to the *AT*, each of the areas described below offers from 5 to 15 miles of other trails. Loop hikes are often possible by combining trails with short sections of the *AT*. Due to the mountainous terrain, hiking on most district trails is moderate to strenuous. Trail use is light to moderate, except at the Cascades Rec Area, where it's heavy.

**camping:** Primitive backcountry camping is permitted anywhere on NF lands, except where posted. The Appalachian Trail and the 2 wilderness areas all offer exceptional environments for backpacking. There are 7 shelters spread out along the *AT* on the Blacksburg RD.

**fishing:** Anglers have several locations with outstanding trout fishing to choose from. These streams are not large, but they are exceptionally scenic and offer miles of crystal clear waters to fish. The only drawback is that roads run beside most of them. This makes access very easy, but it also eliminates the possibility of multi-day backpacking/fly-fishing expeditions. Fishing pressure across most of the district is light.

**mountain biking:** Although many of the district's trails prohibit mountain bike traffic, the networks of gated and unpaved forest roads in a couple of the areas described below are well suited to riding. Long-distance trips may not be a possibility, but shorter rides through remote backcountry on roads that see almost no traffic are. Riding is easy to moderate. The Jefferson NF road map or the relevant topos are recommended as navigational aids.

# Dismal Creek Area

This is the only backcountry area on the district located west of the New River. Forest land here encompasses Flat Top Mountain, the southern slope of Wolf Creek Mountain, and the northern slope of Brushy Mountain. Dismal Creek, which lies in the shadow of the latter, is the area's major drainage. A long stretch of the *Appalachian Trail* is what brings most backpackers and hikers to the area. With a primitive car campground nearby and plenty of room to camp along the trail, multi-day trips can be arranged from a base camp or with backcountry camping. The other major draw is Dismal Creek, which is a stocked trout creek. The creek also features a scenic falls where the water tumbles over several ledges. A short trail leads from the parking area to an overlook.

Bland (W) and Pearisburg (NE) are the closest towns.

**getting there:** From I-81, take exit 98. Turn N onto VA-100 and go 11.6 mi to VA-42 (Pearisburg is 11.1 mi N on VA-100). Turn L and go 10.1 mi to SR-606. Turn R and go 1 mi to FR-201. Turn R and go (at 0.4 mi the pavement ends; at 0.9 mi reach the Falls of Dismal, R) 1.7 mi to Walnut Flats campground, L.

**topography:** The terrain in the area is mountainous, but less than rugged. The mountains have been logged, and the forest that now covers them is relatively young, with a mixture of pines and hardwoods. Rhododendron are present in the coves and valleys. Elevations are between 2,100 and 4,000 ft. *AT* Blacksburg Ranger District; USGS-FS White Gate, Mechanicsburg.

**starting out:** The only developed facilities in this remote backcountry area are at Walnut Flats, where there's a pit toilet and hand water pump. Dismal Falls is the major attraction in the area, though the entire area is lightly traveled.

**activities:** Hiking, Fishing, Camping, Mountain Biking

**hiking:** The *Appalachian Trail* affords the primary hiking opportunity in the area. It enters the area from the S on SR-606 where it crosses Kimberling Creek. From there, it follows Dismal Creek to its headwaters on Sugar Run Mtn, which it follows to Flat Top Mtn before turning NE and going 10 miles to Pearisburg and a bridge crossing on the New River. This segment of the *AT* measures 23 miles. Hiking on this segment of the trail is generally easy, with a few moderate to strenuous stretches. Apart from the endpoints, two more access points are described below. The other hiking trail in the area is the *Ribble Trail*, a moderate, 2-mi trail with access to the *AT* at both ends. A loop hike of almost 10 miles is possible by hiking on both trails. Both trails are blazed and have signed trailheads. Access to the *Ribble Trail* and *AT* is as follows: from Walnut Flats, continue E on FR-201. At 2.2 mi reach a sharp L and a gated road, R. The trailhead to the *Ribble Trail* and a 0.5-mi connector to the *AT* are just R of the gate. To reach the N terminus of the *Ribble Trail* and another access to the *AT*, continue following FR-201 4.1 mi to FR-612. Turn R and go 1 mi to a gated road and small parking area, R. The *AT* crosses the road about 100 yds back down FR-201 from the gate.

**fishing:** Trout fishing in the area is on 7 miles of Dismal Creek. It's a small to mid-sized creek with a mild gradient. The cover is good on both sides. Although the *AT* parallels the creek, as does FR-210 for several miles, access is only available at a few points. As a result, it's necessary to wade upstream in most places. Dismal Creek is stocked trout waters. Fishing pressure is light.

**camping:** Backcountry camping is permitted throughout the area on national forest land. There are 2 shelters along the *AT*. The most easily accessible is the Wapiti Shelter, which is located about 2 miles from the first FR-201 access described above.

Primitive car camping is available at Walnut Flats. The campground is little more than a large forest clearing with 4 sites marked by picnic tables, lantern posts, and fire rings. 2 of the sites have grills too. Sites are spread out across the clearing, with shade provided by pines, oaks, and hickories. There's a pit toilet and hand water pump in the area. With only 4 sites (and those often unused) privacy is not a problem. No fee is charged.

**mountain biking:** The Dismal Creek area is the best backcountry biking locale on the district. Riding is primarily on the dirt and gravel forest roads that are open to motor vehicles but receive little use. The best riding is at the area's upper end, where the roads are very rugged and mostly dirt double-track. Riding is easy to moderate.

# Cascades Recreation Area

The 66-foot waterfall on Little Stony Creek that is the centerpiece of this area may be the most photographed attraction on the district. To reach it, you hike along a 2-mile national recreation trail beside the rushing waters of the creek, a strikingly scenic attraction in its own right. Visit in January or February when the falls freeze and you'll get to see a whole other dimension to their beauty. Aside from the falls and hiking trails, the rec area features a large, handsomely landscaped picnic grounds with tables and grills. Fly-fishing for trout in stocked Little Stony Creek rounds out the outdoor activities in the area. The Cascades Rec Area is located east of the New River not far from the West Virginia state line.

Pembroke (W) is the closest town.

**getting there:** From US-460 in downtown Pembroke, turn E onto Cascade Dr (SR-T623). Go 3.3 mi to the rec area entrance.

**topography:** Butt Mountain overlooks the rec area and Little Stony Creek to the north. Apart from the picnic area, which has been cleared and landscaped, the gorge and mountain slopes are covered in forests of hemlock, hardwoods, and rhododendron. Elevations are between 4,000 ft on Butt Mtn and 2,100 ft on Little Stony Creek. **maps:** USGS Eggleston.

**starting out:** A parking fee of $2/vehicle is charged to enter the rec area. Facilities there include modern restrooms and water.

Pets must be kept on a leash in the rec area. Public use of alcohol is not allowed.

**activities:** Hiking, Fishing, Camping

**hiking:** 2 hiking trails laid end-to-end provide 5 miles of one-way foot travel. The *Cascades National Scenic Trail* ascends the gorge for 2 mi from the picnic area to the falls, where it is joined by the 3-mi *Nature Conservancy Trail*, which follows a ridge to the crest of Butt Mountain, where there's a lookout. The trails are well defined from heavy use and easy to follow. The signed trailhead is located near the restrooms in the picnic area.

**fishing:** Fly-fishermen have a short stretch of fishable water on what may be the most beautiful stream on the district. Little Stony Creek is a mid-sized creek with an average to steep gradient. The cover is exceptional on both sides, and ledges and boulders create excellent pooling. The creek can be fished for about 3 miles; access is from the hiking trail and secondary road that runs beside it. It's wild trout waters.

**camping:** Backcountry camping is permitted on national forest lands except where posted otherwise. It is not allowed within the rec area.

# Peters Mountain Wilderness Area

Pressed up against the West Virginia state line, the 3,881-acre Peters Mountain Wilderness and adjacent backcountry area occupy the southeastern slope of the mountain that lends its name to the area. Peters Mountain is a long mountain ridge that runs northeast from the New River Valley all the way to Covington, WV. Rocky outcrops along its crest allow views of the surrounding area. The mountain is mostly covered in a forest of southern Appalachian hardwoods and hemlocks, including one stand that is 250 years old. Wildlife favors the remote location; white-tailed deer, black bear, wild turkey, ruffed grouse, and bobcat all inhabit the mountain slopes. With no facilities, the wilderness area offers visitors an outdoor experience at its most primitive. Hikers and backpackers can follow miles of trails, including a 20-mile segment of the *Appalachian Trail*. Trout anglers can try their luck along five miles of Stony Creek, a stocked trout stream. The Peters Mountain Wilderness area is ideal for a day or weekend visit.

Pearisburg (W) is the closest town.

**getting there:** From the jct of US-460 and VA-100 in downtown Pearisburg, take US-460 E 3.9 mi to SR-635. Turn L and go (at 6 mi enter the NF) 9.8 mi to a parking area and trailhead to the *AT*. L. At 13.3 mi reach gravel FR-722. Turn L and go 0.2 mi to gated Kelly Flats Rd and the trailhead to the *Flat Peter Loop Trail*.

**topography:** Peters Mountain is the dominant topographical feature of the area, with elevations that reach 4,000 ft at the E end of the region. Elevations on Stoney Creek drop to 2,200 ft. The terrrain is rugged and steep, with forest cover of hardwoods and hemlock. **maps:** AT Blacksburg Ranger District; USGS Interior, Lindside.

**starting out:** There are no facilities in the area. Water is readily available from creeks along all of the area trails. Be sure to treat all surface water before drinking. The Interior Rec Area has picnic tables and grills beside Stony Creek, but no facilities.

**activities:** Hiking, Fishing, Camping

**hiking:** Hikers and backpackers traveling in the area have their choice of 3 long trails. A 20-mi segment of the *Appalachian Trail* tracks the summit crest of Peters Mountain before descending through the wilderness to Stony Fork near the Interior Rec Area. The *Alleghany Trail* connects with the *AT* on top of Peters Mountain and follows the ridgeline northeast along the state border for almost 13 miles to VA-15. The trail is part of a 330-mile trail that travels southwest from the Mason–Dixon line. The segment on Peters Mtn, however, is overgrown and does not seem to be receiving regular maintenance. For information on the *Alleghany Trail*, write the West Virginia State Scenic Trail Association, P.O. Box 4042, Charleston, WV 25304. The third long trail in the area is the 8-mi *Flat Peter Loop Trail*, part of which passes through the wilderness. The main attraction on the trails is their remoteness and the opportunity for a multi-day backpacking trip. For even longer trips, hike 5 miles on the *AT* S to the Mountain Lake Wilderness (see separate entry below). Hiking on the trails is mostly moderate, with some strenuous areas. Trail use is light, except on the *AT*, where it's moderate. Trailheads are located as described above.

**fishing:** Stony Creek is a beautiful, medium-sized creek with a mild to average gradient. The only drawback is that SR-635 follows close beside it for its entire length. Frequent roadside pullouts do make access easy, but the road spoils some of the backcountry flavor of the area. The creek can be fished for the 5 miles it flows through national forest property. It is stocked trout waters. Cherokee Flats is a very nice handicapped-accessible fishing area located on Stony Creek. To get there take SR-635 11.4 mi E of US-460.

**camping:** Backcountry camping is permitted throughout the area, except where posted. A shelter is located on the *AT* less than a quarter mile N of the trailhead on Stony Creek.

# Mountain Lake Wilderness Area

10,753-acre Mountain Lake Wilderness in named for the only natural lake in the Virginia mountains. The lake isn't actually in the wilderness or even on national forest land; it's part of a large, upscale private resort. The wilderness itself is located northeast of the lake on a high mountain plateau that drops off on steep slopes to the east and John's Creek. It's the largest roadless backcountry area on the district, with the only access via the *Appalachian Trail*

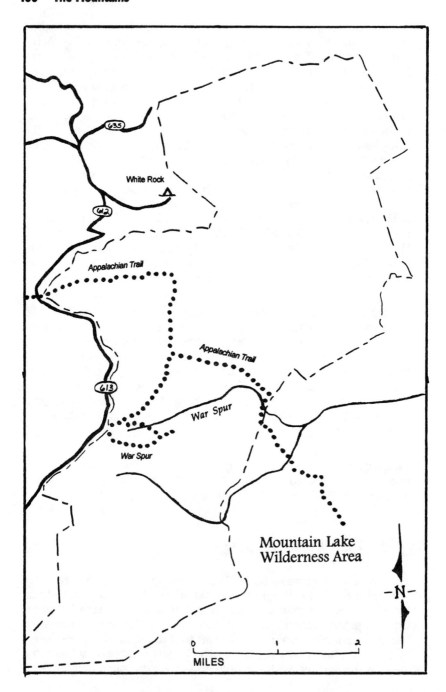

White Rock

635

612

Appalachian Trail

Appalachian Trail

613

War Spur

War Spur

Mountain Lake
Wilderness Area

-N-

0          1          2
MILES

or a pair of other hiking trails. Despite its remote location, several scenic attractions make it a pretty popular area for hiking and backpacking. A pair of scenic overlooks provide views that surpass those anywhere else on the district. Proximity to the trailheads means that they are easily accessible too. A tract of virgin forest features hemlocks and spruces that dwarf the other trees of the forest. Traveling among them is like going back in time to a primeval world. Mann's Bog—a sphagnum bog—is another interesting natural feature of the area. In addition to the rare fauna, the wilderness provides habitat to many wildlife species, among them white-tailed deer, black bear, bobcat, fox, wild turkey, ruffed grouse, and woodcocks. Although the wilderness is best suited to daytrips and the trails can all be easily hiked in a day, give yourself plenty of time to explore some of the area's amazing habitats up close.

Pembroke (SE) and Blacksburg (S) are the closest towns.

**getting there:** From the jct of US-460 and VA-100 in downtown Pearisburg, take US-460 E mi to SR-635. Turn L and go 16.3 mi to gravel SR-613. Turn R and go 0.7 mi to the campground entrance, L. Ahead it's 1 mi to the campground. To reach the AT access, continue past White Rocks which is also SR-613 and go 0.5 mi to an unsigned L, which is the continuation of SR-613. Take the L and go 2 mi over the rough, rugged dirt road to a large parking area. 2.1 mi further is a parking area and trail access to the War Spur Trail and Chestnut Trail.• From Blacksburg, take US-460 W mi to SR-613. Turn R and go 4.9 mi to SR-700, R. Turn L continueing on SR-613. Go 3.3 mi to the trailhead to the War Spur Trail, R.

**topography:** The wilderness consists of a mountain plateau and the steep slopes that drop down beside small creeks that feed John's Creek, the area's major drainage. Elevations in the wilderness are between 2,100 and 4,120 ft. Forest cover includes oak-hickory, hemlock, and spruce. Rhododenron, mountain laurel, azalea, and blueberry are prominent in the understory. **maps:** *AT* Blacksburg Ranger District; USGS Interior, Waiteville, Newport, Eggleston.

**starting out:** Facilities are extremely limited in the wilderness. Large signboards with maps and info at the trailheads are all you'll find. Water and restrooms are available at the White Rocks Campground, just N of the widerness. Water is available on the *AT* near the War Spur Shelter and on the *War Spur Trail*. Be sure to treat all surface water before you drink it.

For hiking the trails described below, the *AT* topo map is adequate, although its scale is rather small.

**activities:** Hiking, Camping

**hiking:** A 5-mile segment of the *Appalachian* Trail passes through the wilderness and provides the primary hiking opportunity. Highlights along this section of the trail include Wind Rock, an outcrop that affords superb views of Stony Creek Valley below Potts Mountain. The other trails in the wilderness—the *War Spur Trail* and *Chestnut Trail*—connect to the *AT* and also offer outstanding scenery. The two trails form a 2.5-mi loop, with scenic highlights that include magnificent views from an overlook on the *War Spur Trail* and cathedral-like stands of virgin hemlock, spruce, and fir trees. Hiking is easy to moderate on both trails; there are strenuous sections along the *AT* The trailheads are signed with distances to overlooks and other scenic attractions given. Only the *AT* is blazed, but all trails are easy to follow. Trail use is moderate to heavy.

**camping:** Primitive backcountry camping is permitted throughout the wilderness, except where posted otherwise. In practice, this means camping along the *AT*. The War Spur Shelter is located 5 miles from the trailhead described above.

The White Rocks primitive car campground lies N of the wilderness right next to the WV state line. 49 sites are widely spaced on a sparsely forested mountainside. Each site has a picnic table, grill, and lantern post. Privacy is adequate, and is improved by the small numbers of people who actually camp here. There are modern toilets and water in the campground, but no showers. Sites cost $4/night from May 1 to Sep 30; $2/night in Apr, Oct, Nov. To reach the White Rocks campground, from the jct of FR-722 and SR-635, take SR-635 E 3 mi to gravel SR-613. Turn R and go 0.7 mi to the campground entrance, L.

# Blacksburg Area

This is a long narrow area with two separate recreation areas—Pandapas Pond and Caldwell Fields. Between them lies the Eastern Continental Divide, elevation 2,220 feet. Caldwell Fields are a series of three fields that have been cleared of forest cover.

Two of the fields are landscaped and used for group camping. The largest of the three is left in a more natural state and is an excellent place to see wildflowers or observe wildlife, particulalry at dusk or dawn. Craig Creek, a stocked trout stream, runs behind the fields. On the other side of the Continental Divide is Pandapas Pond, an 8-acre, man-made impoundment that's a popular stop-off point for a morning or afternoon of fishing. Also in the are is a network of trails open to hiking and mountain biking. With a limited backcountry and camping opportunities, this part of the ranger district is best suited to a visit of half a day or a day.

Blacksburg (S) is the closest city.

**getting there:** From the jct of US-460 and US-460 BYPASS just N of Blacksburg, take US-460 N 2.8 mi to SR-621(Craig Creek Rd). Turn R and go (at 3.9 mi the pavement ends) 8.7 mi to Caldwell Fields, R. • Across US-460 from SR-621 is the entrance to the Pandapas Pond Rec Area.

**topography:** A pair of creeks flow E and W on either side of the continental divide. Above them to the N and E are 2 long mountain ridges—Sinking Creek Mtn and Brush Mtn. The mountain slopes are balnketed with a forest of southern Appalachian hardwoods with  rhododendron prominent in the understory. Elevations are between 2,100 and 3,200 ft. **maps:** USGS Newport, McDonalds Mill, Eggleston.

**starting out:** Facilities in the area are limited, so if you're going to stay a while, be sure to bring enough water with you. Pit toilets are located at the Pandapas Pond Rec Area.

Alcohol is not allowed in the rec area. Pets must be kept on a leash there.

**activities:** Fishing, Hiking, Camping, Mountain Biking

**fishing:** On the E side of US-460, Craig Creek begins on the Eastern Continental Divide and flows E in the shadow of Brush Mtn and Sinking Creek Mtn all the way to the James River near WV. A very small section—about 4 miles—is located on national forest land near Caldwell Fields and is stocked trout waters. At this point, Craig Creek is small with a mild gradient. Cover is good on both banks though it's a shallow creek with few deep pools. Access is from SR-621, which follows close beside the creek.

The other fishing opportunity in the area is on Pandapas Pond, a warm-water fishery with largemouth bass, crappie, and bluegill. Fishing is from the banks (unless you want to portage a canoe about 50 yds to put on the lake), where there are plenty of places from which to cast. A hiking trail circles the lake.

**hiking:** Although the *Appalachian Trail* passes along the N and E edges of this area, it isn't accessible from either Caldwell Fields or Pandapas Pond. If you want to hike it, follow the directions above to Caldwell Fields and proceed E on SR-621 to the trail access, about 6 miles. All of the other trails in the area are at Pandapas Pond. One trail here circles the pond and 2 others follow a combination of roadbeds and footpaths along Poverty Creek and across the mountain slopes. *Poverty Creek Trail* and *Gap Mountain Trail* are both multiple-use trails open to bikers and horseriders. Combined they cover 5 miles. Hiking on the trails is easy to moderate. Trail use is moderate to heavy. Access is from the parking area at Pandapas Pond.

**camping:** Without a large backcountry area and no developed campground, camping in the area is not particularly popular. The 2 group sites at Caldwell Fields are an exception, but they're reserved for organized groups. A couple of creekside sites can be found just down the road next to a small parking area. Backcountry camping is permitted along the trails at Pandapas Pond, but is not allowed in the rec area itself.

**mountain biking:** Riding in the area is on the trails and dirt roads in the Pandapas Pond Area. Combined, there are about 8 mile of ridable tracks, with a couple of short loop rides possible. Biking is easy to moderate in the area. Riding is not allowed within 300 ft of the pond.

# Pinnacles of Dan

Located east of the Blue Ridge near the headwaters of the Dan River, the Pinnacles of Dan area offers some of the most spectacular and dramatic mountain scenery in the Commonwealth. The area is unique among those covered in this book in that it's primary function is as a hydroelectric plant that supplies power to the City of Danville. The large and impressive backcountry is open to the public by the permission only of Danville. Hikers, anglers, and paddlers will all find a visit to the area amply rewarded. A hiking trail takes in the scenic highlights of the area, and the Dan River has stretches of wild trout waters and stocked waters. Below the power plant, it's a popular whitewater run with canoeists and kayakers.

Stuart (E) is the closest town.

**contact:** Pinnacles Hydroelectric Development, Danville, VA; 540/251-5141

**getting there:** From the jct of VA-8 and VA-58 in Stuart, take VA-8 S 4.1 mi to VA-103. Turn R and go 9 mi to SR-773. Turn R and go 1.4 mi to SR-648. Turn R and go 6.1 mi (at 3.1 mi the pavement ends; at 5.6 mi reach the entrance and info board) to the hydro plant.

**topography:** The terrain is defined by a deep gorge with steep walls rising almost vertically to a series of pinnacles. Elevations are between 1,600 and 2,700 ft. Hardwood forest covers most of the area. **maps:** USGS Meadows of Dan.

**starting out:** Before using the property, it is necessary to pick up a permit (free) from the hydro plant. Visitors should keep in mind that this area is a hydroelectric power station. Backcountry travel and outdoor activities are not primary management objectives, and the public is allowed here only with the permission of the City of Danville, which owns the plant. Access to the area is from 8 AM to 5 PM.

Alcohol is not allowed. No swimming in the river or lakes.

**activities:** Hiking, Canoeing/Kayaking, Fishing

**hiking:** 2 of the most rugged and precipitous trails in the state provide access to the magnificent pinnacles area, affording views of the gorge and surrounding countryside. Combined, the trails cover almost 6 miles between the hydro plant and Townes Dam. The trails are not blazed, but are not difficult to follow. Hiking, however, is strenuous. Access is at either the hydro plant or the dam. Back-tracking or a vehicle shuttle is necessary.

**canoeing/kayaking:** When the water level is up, the upper stretch of the Dan is a fun whitewater run. Water is almost continuous riffles and class II whitewater, with the biggest rapids up near the dam. The river is narrow here, less than 50 ft across in most places. The put-in is just outside the gate at the hydro station. Water flow depends on the hydro plant. The first easy takeout is 4 mi down SR-648 from the put-in.

**fishing:** The Dan River offers trout anglers 2 distinct fisheries. Above the dam, the 3-mile stretch of river is medium to large with an average gradient. This is a wild brook trout fishery, and catch-and-release is the rule. Access is by wading or from the hiking trail that follows the river. Below the power plant, the Dan is stocked trout waters. Here the river is medium to large also, but the water flow can be considerably greater than above the plant. Access is from SR-648, which runs beside the river. A couple points to keep in mind if fishing this part of the river: much of it passes through private property and canoeists and kayakers paddle it on weekends.

# Rocky Knob Recreation Area
## Blue Ridge Parkway

4,200-acre Rocky Knob is the southernmost rec area on the Blue Ridge Parkway in Virginia. Located on the eastern slope of the Blue Ridge is Patrick County, it features Rock Castle Gorge, a deep forested valley below the Blue Ridge. Mature hardwood forests with lush understories of mountain laurel and rhododendron provide habitat to wildlife that includes white-tailed deer, bobcat, and wild turkey. Outdoor recreation in the area centers around the *Rock Castle Gorge Trail*, a national scenic trail; a couple of cold mountain creeks that hold native stocks of brook trout; and camping in either the backcountry or at a large car campground. The Rocky Knob area is perfect for a daylong or weekend visit.

Floyd (N) and Stuart (SE) are the closest towns.

**contact:** Superintendent, Blue Ridge Parkway, 400 BB&T Building, 1 Pack Square, Asheville, NC 28801; 704/298-0398

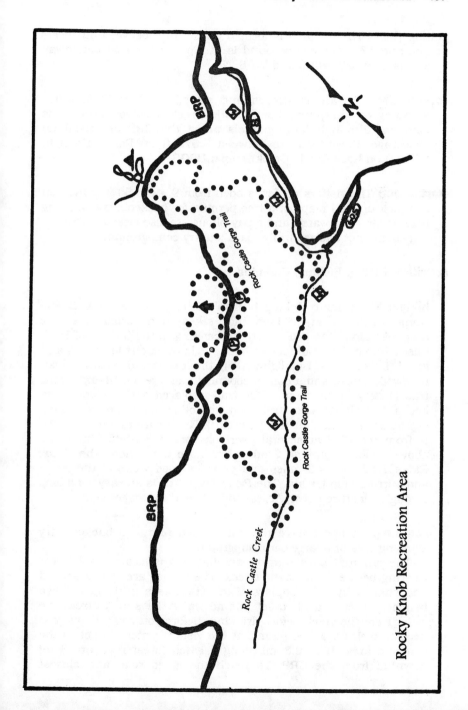

Rocky Knob Recreation Area

**getting there:** The rec area is located on the BRP between mileposts 166 and 173. The campground is at mp 167.1. Closest highway access is on US-58 (S) and VA-8 (N).

**topography:** Terrain is rugged and steep, with the Blue Ridge dropping off sharply to Rock Castle Creek. Most of the area is forested, although large parcels along the BRP are used for pasturage. Elevations are between 3,572 ft on Rocky Knob to 1,700 ft on Rock Castle Creek. **maps:** USGS

**starting out:** The visitors center is open from 9 AM to 5 PM daily. You can pick up trail maps and free permits for backcountry camping here. Restrooms, water, and a pay phone are also located there.

Pets are not allowed in the backcountry campground.

**activities:** Hiking, Fishing, Camping

**hiking:** The primary hiking trail in the area is the *Rock Castle Gorge Trail*, an 11-mi loop that takes in a series of scenic overlooks along the BRP before descending to the bottom of Rock Castle Gorge. The trail follows both single-track dirt footpaths and gated timber roads. Highlights along the trail include views, a lush hardwood forest, and a pair of cool mountain creeks. Hiking on the trail is easy to strenuous. The trail is blazed and moderate use keeps it well defined and easy to follow. A large trail map signboard is located at the 12 O'clock Knob parking area. Access is from the BRP at several overlooks or on SR-605 (directions above under *camping*). 2 other trails are worth note: the *Black Ridge Trail* covers 3 miles and provides good views of the gorge and surrounding terrain. The *Picnic Loop Trail* is an easy 1-mi loop through a mature forest. Access to both is at the visitor center.

**camping:** Campers have the option of a primitive backcountry camping area or a large car campground.

The primitive backcountry camping area is located in a forest clearing beside Rock Castle Creek. The 6 sites are widely spaced and shaded by lofty poplars. Each site has a grill, some have benches. There's a pit toilet but no water. Be sure to treat the water from the creek before drinking. Before you camp there, you need to pick up a free permit at the visitor center. To get to the camping area, hike 0.3 mi along a gated forest road or 3 mi downhill from the BRP. To reach the gated road and closest trailhead, leave the visitor center and go N on the BRP 3.8 mi to the jct with VA-8 at mp 365.1. Turn S onto VA-8 and go 3.6 to gravel SR-605. Turn R and go 0.6 mi to the trailhead and parking area.

The large car campground has 109 sites laid out in 4 large loops on a sparsely wooded hilly area with a dense understory of rhododendron. It's one of the nicer campgrounds on the BRP and in the state. The sites are large and well spaced; some offer a great deal of privacy, others not so much. Each site has a picnic table and grill. Restroom facilities (no showers) are centrally located. Sites cost $10/night. The campground is open from May 1 to Oct 31.

**fishing:** Rock Castle Creek is a native brook trout stream. It's a small to mid-sized creek that flows down a mild to average gradient. Forest cover on both banks is good, but not particularly dense. Access is via the gated fire road that is part of the *Rock Castle Gorge Trail*. It follows the creek for 3 miles. All parkway waters require single hook, artificial lures. Little Rock Castle Creek is small with an average gradient. Cover is very tight, making fly casting very difficult in most areas. Fishing is by wading, with access at the primitive camping area trailhead described above. NC or VA fishing licenses are valid on all BRP waters.

# New Castle Ranger District

## Jefferson National Forest

The New Castle Ranger District encompasses 139,314 acres in two major tracts and several smaller ones. The larger, more remote landholding is bounded by West Virginia (NW) and the Blacksburg Ranger District (W). The other district boundaries are formed by Johns Creek Mountain and Craig Creek (S). The other major parcel is long and narrow and encompasses a series of mountain ridges that form a line that runs northeast–southwest. Craig Creek forms the northern boundary of this area; the long southern boundary is formed by the limit of the national forest. Opportunities for outdoor recreation on the district are varied, with several trail networks, stocked and native trout streams for fishing, and developed recreation areas that include two campgrounds and three picnic areas. There are two designated wilderness areas, the remote, 3,570-acre Shawvers Run Wilderness and the 5,700-acre Barbours Creek Wilderness. Because the district is more isolated than other parts of the Jefferson National Forest, patterns of use are quite low, offering the backcountry traveler a chance to explore the natural environment away from the weekend crowds that are typical in other areas.

New Castle is the largest town on the district.

**contact:** New Castle Ranger District, State Route 615, Box 246, New Castle, VA 24127; 540/864-5195.

**getting there:** VA-311 provides the primary highway access to the district. All rec areas described below are located E of the highway. To get to the district ranger station, head NE out of New Castle on SR-615. Go 2.3 mi to the RS, L.

**topography:** The terrain throughout the district is mountainous, with the major ridges being Potts Mountain, North Mountain, and Price Mountain. Elevations reach 3,800 ft on Potts Mtn and on the border with WV. Most of the district is covered by hardwood forest, with hemlocks and other conifers also occuring. **maps:** USFS New Castle Ranger District; USGS topo maps are listed below under the separate headings.

**starting out:** Before coming to the Newcastle RD, make sure you have whatever supplies you're going to need. The district is located in a remote region of the state with only one small town close by. You can stop by the district ranger station and buy a district map or get up-to-date reports on local conditions. The office is open weekdays 8 AM to 4:30 PM. The USFS district map provides a good overview of the district, showing trails, rec areas, and stocked trout creeks. Don't try to use it for backcountry navigation, however, as the scale is too small to be of much use.

**activities:** Hiking, Fishing, Camping

**hiking:** There are 3 main trail networks on the district, covering a combined distance of approximately 60 miles. A handful of other, isolated trails brings the total mileage closer to 110. In addition to these, the *Appalachian Trail* passes through the district, though it's only on USFS lands for a short distance. Opportunities for backpacking trips are on North Mountain, in the Patterson Creek watershed, and at Roaring Run. Trail use throughout the district is light, with the large backcountry areas offering excellent opportunities for solitude. Most of the trails on the district are blazed. Trailheads are generally signed, though some only with a hiker icon. A good topo map is essential for hiking the backcountry.

**fishing:** 3 of the areas described below have stocked trout creeks running through them. While each of these creeks is exceptionally scenic and offers high-quality trout fishing, they each suffer from being shadowed by a road. There are no opportunities on the district for combination backpacking/fly-fishing trips.

**camping:** Backcountry camping is permitted on USFS lands throughout the district, except where posted. 3 of the areas described below have extensive backcountries, well suited to weekend backpacking trips.

Car campers can overnight at either of 3 developed car campgrounds on the district. Although they can be reached by vehicle, they are still primitive in character, and have limited facilities. Combined, they have 37 sites. Facilities are limited to pit toilets and hand water pumps (no water at Craig Creek). The Pines and Steel Bridge are both located beside stocked trout creeks.

# North Mountain Area

North Mountain is a long ridge that lies along a northeast–southwest axis in Craig Country near the border with the Blacksburg Ranger District. Except for a couple of forest roads, the area is undeveloped and affords a good opportunity to travel through some pretty remote backcountry. The *Appalachian Trail* passes nearby on Catawba Mountain, the next mountain ridge to the south. Backpackers wanting to combine travel in the North Mountain and on the *AT* can connect the two at the signed trailhead for Dragon's Tooth, just N of the trailhead on VA-311 described below. Because of the large backcountry and relative isolation, this is a good area for a weekend backpacking trip.

New Castle (N) is the closest town.

**getting there:** From I-81, take exit 140. Turn N onto VA-311 and go 1.2 mi to a jct. Turn L, continuing on VA-311. At 5.6 mi reach a parking area, L and access to the *AT*. At 9.3 mi is a small parking area. R and the W terminus of the *North Mountain Trail*. At 11.4 mi reach Wilderness Rd (FR-224), R. Several short spur trails run between the dirt road and the *N Mtn Trail*. • Access to the E end of the area is from New Castle. From SR-615 downtown, turn S onto SR-616 and go 1.2 mi to dirt and gravel SR-690. Turn R and go 0.9 mi to a fork. Turn R onto FR-5026 and go 1.2 mi to the end of the road and trailhead to the *Lick Branch Trail.*

**topography:** The upper slopes of North Mountain are rugged and steep. Terrain on the lower slopes and in the valleys is milder. Hardwood forests cover all of the upper elevations. Elevations on North Mtn reach 3,000 ft. Low point on Lick Branch is 1,350 ft. **maps:** USGS-FS Catawba, Looney.

**starting out:** There are no developed recreation facilities in this large backcountry area. Surface water is unavailable along most of the long *North Mountain Trail*, so preparations should be made to pack water in if you intend to camp. Lick Branch is the most convenient water source. Be sure to treat all surface water before drinking.

**activities:** Hiking, Camping.

**hiking:** The 13-mi *North Mountain Trail* is the major trail artery in the area. For most of its distance it follows the peaks of the mountain's summit ridge, providing good views of the surrounding countryside. 3 other trails provide access from the valley below on short (avg 1.5 miles), steep ascents. In all, there are about 25 miles of trails from which to choose. The trails are all connected, though loop options are limited to one. Most hikes, especially long ones, will involve backtracking or a car shuttle. Hiking on the trails is moderate to strenuous. Trail use is light. *Lick Branch Trail* begins on an old gated road bed at the end of FR-5026. Access to the connecting *Ferrier Trail* is 1 mile back up the road on another gated roadbed, but there's no parking there.

**camping:** Backcountry camping is permitted throughout the area on national forest lands, except where posted. Since the *North Mountain Trail* tracks far above water sources, you should plan on packing water in. There are no developed campgrounds in the area.

# Potts Creek Area

The defining physical feature of this area is Potts Creek, a cool, fast-flowing stream that is stocked with trout. It flows southwest out of West Virginia and crosses a large portion of the district before crossing into the adjacent Blacksburg Ranger District. With no real backcountry to speak of, the recreational center of this region is the primitive Steel Bridge Campground. Since there are no hiking or biking trails in this remote corner of Craig Co, most of the few visitors who venture here come for the trout fishing or simply for the remoteness itself. The campground is named for a bridge that used to span Potts Creek. The town of Paint Bank was named for the pigments that local Indians took from the creek's banks to color pottery, clothes, and cosmetics.

The closest town is New Castle (SE).

**getting there:** From the jct of VA-311 and VA-42 in New Castle, take VA-311 N 16.2 mi to the community of Paint Bank and VA-18. Turn R and go 2.8 mi to the Steel Bridge Rec Area.

**topography:** The topography surrounding the creek is rugged and imposing, though inaccessible to the hiker. Potts Creek flows through a narrow valley in the shadow of Peters Mountain, which forms the natural barrier between VA and WV. Elevation on Pots Creek is 1,800 ft. **maps:** USGS-FS Potts Creek.

**starting out:** Facilities in the area are very limited. There are pit toilets and a hand water pump at the campground, but that's about it. The area is open all year.

**activities:** Fishing, Camping.

**fishing:** Potts Creek is a beautiful, medium to large trout stream with a mild gradient. Its waters flow over a rocky bed, cascading over ledges and rock formations in places to create deep pools. Although the creek can be fished for about 25 miles, most of that length runs through private property. The best spot for anglers wanting a little quiet and isolation is at the campground. Access elsewhere is from a pair of roads: E of VA-311, VA-18 runs alongside the creek for about 3 miles. W of VA-311, SR-600/FR-17 provide access all the way to the Blacksburg RD, a distance of 12 miles. Potts Creek is stocked with rainbow trout.

**camping:** The 20 sites at Steel Bridge campground are spread out along a half-mile spur road on the south bank of Potts Creek. A canopy of pines and hardwoods provides shade and privacy, and most of the sites aren't even within view of each other. This is about as good as primitive car camping gets, with the one drawback that traffic from VA-18 can be heard. Fortunately, few cars use the road. Each site has a picnic table, grill, and lantern post. There are pit toilets and a hand water pump in the area. There is no fee to camp. Use is light, so finding a site is rarely a difficulty. The campground is open all year.

# Barbours Creek Wilderness Area

5,700-acre Barbours Creek Wilderness occupies the southeastern flank of Potts Mountain between its summit ridge and North Fork Barbours Creek. The wilderness is located in Craig Co, on the border with West Virginia. Although travel in the wilderness is limited, the area is remote and offers an excellent opportunity for backcountry solitude. The possiblity of observing wildlife in the area is high. The Pines Recreation Area, situated on the edge of the wilderness and on the north bank of Barbours Creek, provides primitive car camping in an otherwise remote region of the national forest. A single hiking trail passes through the wilderness to the top of Poots Mountain. Barbours Creek is a stocked trout stream.
New Castle (S) is the closest town.

**getting there:** From downtown New Castle, take VA-311 N 4.6 mi to SR-611. Turn R and go 5 mi to SR-617. Turn L and go 5 mi to The Pines primitive campground. • Another route is to go E on SR-615 out of downtown New Castle 0.5 mi to SR-617. Turn L and go (at 0.8 mi the pavement ends) 4.5 mi to paved SR-611. Turn L and go 1.1 mi to SR-617. Turn R and go 5 mi to the campground, L.

**topography:** Area terrain is rugged and mountainous. Elevations on the summit ridge reach 3,800 ft. The steep mountainsides are blanketed in a forest dominated by hardwoods, with hemlocks and pines also present. Lowest elevation in the area is on Barbours

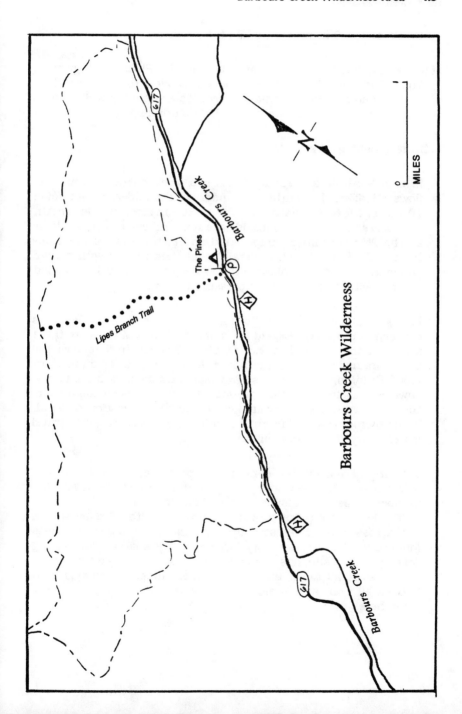

Creek, at 1,700 ft. **maps:** USGS-FS New Castle

**starting out:** Facilities in the area are at The Pines Campground. You'll find water (hand pump) and vault toilets there. Other than that, the area is entirely undeveloped. Water from Lipes Branch or Barbours Creek should be treated before drinking.

**activities:** Fishing, Hiking, Camping

**fishing:** North Fork Barbours Creek is a stocked trout stream that flows SW along the southern boundary of the wilderness for some 10 miles. SR-617 runs beside the creek for most of this length, with access at pullouts alongside the road. Access is also available at The Pines primitive campground and at the start of the *Lipes Branch Trail*. The creek is small to medium in size with a mild gradient. It's flow is shallow with few deep pools, but there's good cover on either bank. Fishing pressure is light.

**hiking:** A single trail (open to horses too) crosses the wilderness between Barbours Creek and the summit of Potts Mtn, where there are excellent views. The 2.3-mi *Lipes Branch Trail* follows the small drainage of the same name. Elevation gain is more than 2,000 ft; hiking is strenuous. The signed trailhead is 0.1 mi back down SR-617 from the campground. Or you can hike along a short connector trail from the campground to the *Lipes Branch Trail*. With no other connecting trails or other accesses, round-trip travel is necessary. Trail use is light.

**camping:** Backcountry camping is permitted throughout the wilderness. With only one trail providing access, however, the number of easily accessible sites is limited.

The Pines is a primitive car campground with 14 sites spread out across a large forested area on the lower slopes of Potts Mountain. The sites are very large and well spaced, maximizing privacy. Each site has a picnic table, grill, and lantern post. Facilities are pit toilets and a hand water pump. The campground is open all year, and is almost never crowded. There is no fee to camp here.

# Patterson Creek Area

Patterson Creek, the physical center of this area, flows between a pair of mountains: Patterson Mtn to the north and Price Mtn to the south. Located in Botetourt County near the eastern edge of the district, this is a remote, undeveloped area with access provided by a single dirt and gravel forest road. Although signs of logging are present and some areas have been clearcut, most of the backcountry is heavily forested. The summit of Patterson Mountain offers good views of the surrounding countryside. With low traffic volume and a fairly large trail network, this area is a good destination for a weekend camping trip. Evidence of logging in the area is abundant—lots of pine and thinned forest.

New Castle (W) is the closest town.

**getting there:** From downtown New Castle, take SR-615 E 6.5 mi to SR-606. Turn R and go 2.4 mi to SR-612. Turn L and go 0.3 mi to a fork. Bear R onto gravel FR-184. Trailheads are located along 7 miles and are signed with hiker icons. FR-184 makes 5 unimproved creek crossings better handled by 4WDs than other types ov vehicles. • Another access is from I-81. Take exit 150 and turn W onto US-220. Go 8.6 mi to SR-630. Turn L and go 0.3 mi to SR-606. Turn R and go 8.5 mi to SR-612 and access to the backcountry area.

**topography:** Elevations are between 2,250 ft on Patterson Mtn and 1,200 ft on Patterson Creek. The terrain is steep at the higher elevations, but levels out on the lower slopes. Forest cover is mixed, with pine and hardwood species present. **maps:** USGS-FS Oriskany.

**starting out:** This is an undeveloped backcountry area with no facilities. Water is plentiful in Little Patterson and Patterson Creeks and in the many smaller streams that drain into them. Be sure to treat all surface water before drinking.

**activities:** Hiking, Camping.

**hiking:** A network of almost 20 miles of trails blankets this area. 2 main trails—*Price Mtn Trail* and *Patterson Mtn Trail*—follow a pair of parallel summit ridges. Other trails connect at right angles and run between the mountains and Patterson Creek. Trail highlights include mountaintop views, creeks, and an isolated woodland setting. Hiking on the trails is moderate to strenuous. Trail use is light. Access to most trails is along FR-184, where there are several trailheads, and on SR-606, where an access to Price Mtn Trail is located. Trails are blazed with yellow bars.

**camping:** Backcountry camping is permitted throughout the area, except where posted otherwise. There are no developed campgrounds in the area. Some roadside campsites are located along FR-184.

# Roaring Run Area

Located in the extreme northeast corner of the district, the Roaring Run area is bounded by West Virginia and the scenic creek that gives the area its name. Most of the backcountry here occupies the summits and slopes of Deisher and Pine Mountains. A large picnic area is in the center of the area, with a small network of hiking trails and a stocked trout stream offering the main recreational activities. Of historical interest is the Roaring Run Furnace, an iron furnace from the nineteenth century that's listed on the National Register of Historic Places. Signs in the area explain its operation. Although the area requires some effort to get to, visitors are rewarded by remote solitude and natural beauty. The recreation area is open all year.

Eagle Rock (SE) is the closest town.

**getting there:** From I-64, take exit 21. Turn S onto SR-696 and go 0.3 mi to SR-616 (Rich Patch Rd). Turn R and go 5.4 mi to SR-621 (Roaring Run Rd). Turn L and go 3.2 mi to the rec area entrance, R.

**topography:** The mountain terrain in the area varies from lazy coves to steep summit slopes. Elevations are between 1,100 ft on roaring Run and 3,700 ft on Pine Mountain. Forest cover is predominantly hemlocks and hardwoods, with an understory of rhododendron **maps:** USGS-FS Collierstown, Longdale Furnace.

**starting out:** The only facilities in the area are pit toilets at the picnic area. Water must be packed in or taken from Roaring Run. Be sure to treat all surface water before drinking. The picnic area is open all year. Signboards with trailmaps are located at the trailheads.

**activities:** Hiking, Fishing, Camping

**hiking:** 3 interconnecting trails in the area cover a total distance of almost 14 miles. Scenic highlights along the trails include the iron furnace, an exceptionally scenic mountain creek and falls, and forested mountain slopes that offer good views in winter. In combination, the trails form a 3-legged national recreation trail. The entire loop can be hiked, or you can choose to hike only one trail or parts of trails. The loop trails are connected in a rough figure eight shape, with circuit hikes of 4 or 9 miles possible. Access is in the picnic area, with the trails spreading out to the SW. Hiking is easy along the lower loop, strenuous on the upper. The trails follow tram lines from the days when the iron furnace was in operation. Trails are blazed and easy to follow. Trailheads are clearly signed. Trail use is heavy near the picnic area, moderate on the upper loop. There are 2 trailheads; 1 is in the picnic area. To reach the other, leave the rec area and turn S onto SR-621. Go 0.9 mi to SR-615. Turn R and go 0.6 mi to a large parking area and trailhead, R.

**fishing:** Roaring Run is a small creek that flows over an average to steep gradient. It's an exceptionally attractive mountain creek, with a very rocky bed and dense cover of rhododendrons and hemlocks on both sides. Access is from the picnic area or from the hiking trail that follows it upstream. It's a stocked trout creek. It is fishable for about 2 miles between the picnic area and its mouth at Craig Creek. Access is from SR-621.

**camping:** Primitive backcountry camping is permitted throughout the area on national forest land, except where posted. It is not allowed in the rec area.

# Roanoke Mountain Recreation Area
## Blue Ridge Parkway

Located just south of the Roanoke city limits, this 1,100-acre area offers travelers on the Blue Ridge Parkway the diversion of a four-mile drive to the top of Roanoke Mountain with stunning views of the surrounding mountains and valleys. In addition to attracting photographers and nature lovers, the mountain is a popular launch site for hang gliders. The other attractions at this relatively small stopping point are a car campground and a five-mile hiking trail that winds through the forest that blankets the area's ridges and valleys. Whether you're driving the Blue Ridge Parkway looking for a place to stop for a picnic, want to spend the night, stretch your legs on a short hike, or just get a good overview of this part of Virginia, Roanoke Mountain is a good bet.

Roanoke (N) is the closest city

**contact:** Superintendent, Blue Ridge Parkway, 400 BB&T Building, 1 Pack Square, Asheville, NC 28801; 704/298-0398.

**getting there:** On the Blue Ridge Parkway, the access road that leads to the campground is at milepost 120.5. The Roanoke Mtn loop road is at mp 120.4. From I-81, take exit 143. Turn E onto I-581/US-220 and go 11.2 mi to the Blue Ridge Parkway. Turn N onto the BRP and go 1.2 mi to the rec area.

**topography:** The mountain ridges and narrow valleys of the Blue Ridge are forested with southern Appalachian hardwoods. The terrain is most rugged on Roanoke Mountain, where elevations exceed 2,200 ft. **maps:** USGS Garden City.

**starting out:** Facilities (restrooms, water) are in the campground. A pay phone is located at the entrance. A paved 4-mile loop road climbs Roanoke Mtn and offers outstanding views from several overlooks. The road is popular and is closed after sundown.

**activities:** Hiking, Camping

**hiking:** The main trail in the area is the 5.4-mi *Chestnut Ridge Loop Trail*, which circles the campground and winds up to the Blue Ridge after passing the eponymous ridge. The trail offers campers the chance to expore the local woodlands, but scenic highlights along the trail are few. Hiking on the trail is easy to moderate. Access is at the Chestnut Ridge overlook, where there's a large trail map, or at the Gum Spring overlook, where the trailhead is not signed. Equestrians also use the trail. Another short trail leads from the parking area atop Roanoke Mtn to the summit. The trail is heavily used and is improved with stone steps. It's less than a quarter-mile to the top.

**camping:** The large car campground is laid out in 2 main loops. The tent loop has 74 sites; the RV loop 31. The sites are large and widely spaced, offering a high level of privacy. A canopy of hardwoods provides shade and keeps the area cool. Each site has a picnic table, grill, and lantern post. Modern restroom facilities (no showers) are located in the middle of each loop. Sites cost $10/night. Sites are almost always available. The campground is open from May 1 to October 31.

# Peaks of Otter Recreation Area
## Blue Ridge Parkway

Located next to the Glenwood Ranger District of the Jefferson National Forest, the Peaks of Otter area is perched high atop the Blue Ridge northeast of Roanoke. It's a popular stopping-off point for folks driving the Blue Ridge Parkway and a popular destination as well. The Peaks of Otter Lodge is located here, offering overnight accomodations amidst natural mountain beauty. There are attractions for backcountry travelers as well, with an extensive network of hiking trails that affords spectacular views of the surrounding region and a car campground for overnight stays. A visitor center and a nineteenth century farm where living history demonstrations can be seen round out the amenities. Away from these features, steep mountain slopes are draped in hemlocks and hardwood species and cool mountain streams rush down rocky chutes. With no backcountry camping permitted, this area is perfect for a day or weekend visit, with the campground or lodge used as a base.

Bedford (SE) and Buchanan (NW) are the closest towns.

**contact:** Superintendent, Blue Ridge Parkway, 400 BB&T Building, 1 Pack Square, Asheville, NC 28801; 704/298-0398

**getting there:** The rec area and trails are located on the BRP between mileposts 83 and 86. Nearest highway access is from VA-43, which enters from the E at mp 86.

**topography:** Forest cover includes southern Appalachian hardwoods, hemlock, and dense slicks of rhododendron in the understory.

Areas around the lake and lodge have been cleared and landscaped. The mountainous terrain is rugged and steep. The elevation on Flat Top is 4,004 ft. **maps:** USGS Peaks of Otter

**starting out:** Stop by the visitor center before heading out onto the trails. You can pick up a trail map, brochures, or parkway guide there. They also have an extensive selection of guide books for sale. Restrooms, water, and a pay phone are all located on the premises. A service station is next door.

**activities:** Hiking, Camping

**hiking:** Hikers will find a wide range of trails at Peaks of Otter, from short, easy leg stretchers to strenuous climbs up the area's steep mountain slopes to scenic overlooks. One pair of trails—*Fallingwater Cascades Trail* and *Flat Top Trail*—has been designated a national recreation trail. Beginning at a common trailhead, one trail drops down into a lush forest beside a mountain creek that tumbles in a series of cascades over exposed rock faces. The other climbs to a cluster of rock outcrops. In all, 7 trails cover 15 miles of terrain that includes steep forested slopes and rolling meadows. A couple of trails offer exceptional views of the surrounding countryside. In general, trail use is heavy. Trails are improved with footbridges, steps, handrails, and benches. Hiking is moderate to strenuous on most trails, with the easiest hikes being around Abbott Lake and on the *Johnson Farm Trail.* Several of the trails can be connected to form loops, though back-tracking is also necessary on a couple of the trails.

**camping:** A 132-site car campground is located at Peaks of Otters. The large, well-spaced sites are arranged in 3 loops, with tent campers in a loop apart from the RV campers. The campground is located on a forested mountain slope where hardwoods provide shade and lend a high degree of privacy to the sites. Each site has a picnic table, grill, and lantern post. Sites cost $10/night. The campground is open from May 1 to Oct 31. Backcountry camping is not allowed along the Blue Ridge Parkway.

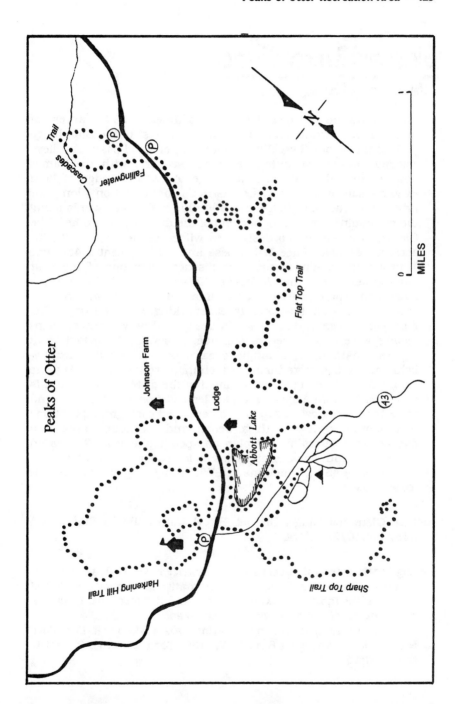

# Glenwood Ranger District

## Jefferson National Forest

The Glenwood Ranger District occupies 74,128 acres of mountainous terrain between the summit crest of the Blue Ridge (E) and the James River (W). It is a region of small pastoral valleys wedged between stunning mountain scenery, with the James flowing through a spectacular gorge. A narrow wedge of land extends southwest from the district's main section along the ridgeline of the Blue Ridge. The Blue Ridge Parkway winds along the mountain's spine from one end of the district to the other. The Glenwood contains two designated wilderness areas, the 8,900-acre James River Face Wilderness and the adjacent 2,450-acre Thunder Ridge Wilderness. The district offers one of the best environments on the Jefferson National Forest for outdoor recreation. The extensive, well-maintained trail network provides lots of options for high-quality backpacking or hiking trips. The high percentage of district lands designated as wilderness helps ensure a certain degree of solitude. A series of stocked trout waters clustered in a single area makes it possible for fly-fishermen to fish more than one mountain creek in a day. And the James River, forming a long segment of the district's boundary, is a magnet for both anglers and paddlers. Visitors wanting to spend more than a day can camp at two developed campgrounds. At one is a mountain lake with a beach and swimming area and bathhouse. Visitors should plan on spending at least 2 days on the district, with backcountry trips as long as a week possible.

Troutville (SW), Buchanan (SW), and Glasgow (N) are the closest towns.

**contact:** Glenwood Ranger District, Box 8, Natural Bridge Station, VA 24578; 540/291-2188.

**getting there:** Interstate access to the district is via I-81, which runs parallel to the NW. A more scenic alternative is to enter the district on the Blue Ridge Parkway. It runs the district's entire length, providing access to all trails and rec areas.

To get to the district ranger station, take I-81 to exit 175. Turn N onto US-11 and go 1.8 mi to VA-130. Turn R and go 2.1 mi to the district RS, L.

**topography:** Most of the district consists of the rugged, steep slopes of the Blue Ridge. Along the James River and in several small valleys the mountain slopes flatten out and the terrain is more level. Elevations are between 4224 on Apple Orchard Mtn and 700 ft on the James River.**maps:** USFS Glenwood Ranger District; USGS topo maps are given below under the individual headings.

**starting out:** District maps, brochures, and other info are available from 2 sources. A USFS info center is located in Natural Bridge at the jct of US-11 and VA-130 (exit 175 from I-81). The district RS is open 8 AM to 4:30 PM weekdays. The USFS district topo map provides an excellent overview of the Glenwood RD, showing all trails and rec areas. Its scale is too small, however, to use for backcountry navigation.

**activities:** Hiking, Fishing, Camping, Canoeing/Kayaking

**hiking:** The district lists 186 miles of trails on its inventory, including a 53-mi segment of the *Appalachian Trail*. Apart from the *AT*, which crosses the district from one end to the other, the trails are concentrated in large networks in two areas—the North Creek/Middle Creek Area and the James River Face/Thunder Ridge Wilderness Areas. These trails take in some of the most spectacular scenery on the JNF, including mountain vistas, scenic waterfalls, and the James River, which flows through a particularly attractive gorge. The trails are well maintained, with trailheads clearly signed. Even trails in the wilderness areas, which are left in a primitive state, are easy to locate and follow. The trail networks in both of the backcountry areas described below are large enough to accommodate multi-day backpacking trips. Using lengths of the *AT* in combination with these trails only increases the possibilities for long treks.

**fishing:** Anglers have the option of fishing for trout on several stocked mountain streams or going after warm-water species on the James. Fishing on the James is best done from a canoe. The trout creeks are accessible from roads which run beside them. Apart from float trips on the James, there really aren't any opportunities for backcountry fishing trips on the district.

**camping:** Campers on the district can choose between spending a night in the backcountry or overnighting at either of 2 primitive car campgrounds. Backcountry camping is permitted throughout the district on NF lands. The most popular areas are along the *AT* and in the 2 designated wilderness areas. The car campgrounds are both attractive, with a rustic, backcountry atmosphere.

Organized groups can camp at Hopper Creek Campground. Capacity is 50 and reservations are required. The fee is $10. Facilities include vault toilets and a campfire circle. The campground is available year round.

**canoeing/kayaking:** Paddling on the district is on the James River. See the next section below for details.

# James River

The James River is Virginia's largest. The waters that eventually form the James begin their descent high in the mountains of western Virginia and West Virginia. They form the Cowpasture, Calfpasture, Bullpasture, and Jackson Rivers before joining to create the James near Clifton Forge. From there, the James crosses the entire state, eventually emptying into the Chesapeake Bay at Hampton Roads. Along the way, the river passes through some of the most spectacular scenery in the Commonwealth. Between Buchanan and Glasgow, the river forms a boundary of the Jefferson National Forest. Here the mountains rise in great majestic sweeps from the river's edge and hold it in shadow for long periods of the day. Because of the scenery and easy access at both towns, this run of river is a popular day trip for canoests and kayakers. Anglers too enjoy the remote isolation that the national forest offers for most of this segment of river.

The towns of Buchanan and Glasgow are at opposite ends of this stretch of the James.

**getting there:** From I-81, take exit 162. Turn N onto US-11 and go 3.9 mi to Lowe St at the edge of Buchanan. Turn L and go 0.6 mi to a parking lot and river access. • To get to the take-out, from the jct of US-501 and VA-130 in Glasgow, take VA-130 W 0.4 mi to SR-684. Turn L and go 0.5 mi to the parking area beside the Maury River.

**topography:** The terrain on either side of the James is a combination of unimposing hills and impressive mountains. On the river's S bank, most of the land is forested. Elevations on the river are approximately 700 ft. **maps:** USFS Glenwood Ranger District; AT Glenwood–New Castle Ranger Districts; USGS-FS Buchanan, Arnold Valley, Snowden, Big Island.

**starting out:** You won't find any facilities on the river, so be sure to bring enough water for the trip. Either the USFS or the AT topo maps are sufficient for this section of the river. The USFS map has the advantage of showing river access points.

**activities:** Canoeing/Kayaking, Fishing, Camping.

**canoeing/kayaking:** Although it's the largest river in the state, up in the mountains it's a little less imposing. At the put-in, it's less than 100 yds across; at the take-out, it has widened somewhat, but not considerably. This segment of the river will appeal to paddlers mostly for its spectacular scenery. There's some whitewater, but most of the river is flat, with intermittent rapids that are class I-II. From Buchanan to the take-out at Glasgow is about an 18-mile float; plan on a full day on the water. Just beyond the take-out is the Balcony Falls Dam. The take-out is at the mouth of the Maury River, on its upstream bank. The portage to the parking area is about 200 ft.

**fishing:** Anglers on the James go after smallmouth bass, muskies, flathead catfish, and rock bass. Fishing is best done from a canoe. There are plenty of stretches of slow water on the river, making it pretty easy to fish and navigate at the same time.

**camping:** This segment of the river is perfect for a day trip. If you want to camp, however, it's permitted on national forest lands. This means the south, or right-hand bank. There are several locations suited to camping. One is the Locher Tract, which offers very primitive conditions in a developed setting not far from the river. It's located just before the start of the James River Face wilderness and is also accessible by car.

# North Creek and Middle Creek Recreation Areas

Occupying a large region in the middle of the district between the James River and the Blue Ridge Parkway, this area features two developed recreation areas, a handful of stocked trout creeks, and a selection of hiking trails that includes a long stretch of the *Appalachian Trail*. Although not as remote or scenic as the James River Face wilderness, this area offers outdoor enthusiasts a little more variety, particularly for shorter, less ambitious outings. The car campground, roadside access to all of the trout creeks, and several trail loops of less than 10 miles make daylong or weekend trips easy and enjoyable. Middle Creek picnic area has tables, grills, and a single shelter in a pleasant, easily-accessible creekside setting.

Buchanan (W) is the closest town.

**getting there:** From I-81, take exit 168. Turn E onto SR-614 and go 3.2 mi to gravel FR-59. Turn L and go 2.5 mi to the North Creek primitive campground. • To reach Middle Creek picnic area and access to the *AT*, instead of turning L onto FR-59, continue on SR-614 for 1.2 mi to a parking area and trailhead, L. The picnic area is ahead another 0.3 mi. • Another access to the area is from the Blue Ridge Parkway via FR-812 between mileposts 76 and 77.

**topography:** Elevations are between 4,200 ft on Apple Orchard Mtn and 800 ft on Jennings Creek. The terrain is rugged and steep, particularly on the upper slopes near the BRP. **maps:** USGS Arnold Valley, Buchanan, Peaks of Otter; AT Glenwood–New Castle Ranger Districts.

**starting out:** Facilities (water, pit toilets) are located at both North Creek and Middle Creek Rec Areas. Water sources are also plentiful in the backcountry. Remember to treat all surface water. Several secondary and forest roads provide access to most of this area. SR-614, the major access, is paved. The others are not.

**activities:** Fishing, Hiking, Camping.

**fishing:** 4 of the best creeks for trout fishing on the district run through this area and converge before emptying into the James River. Combined, McFall's Creek, Jennings Creek, Middle Creek, and North Creek offer anglers 10 miles of stocked trout waters. Access to all 4 is via the secondary and forest roads that wind through the area. FR-59 follows North Creek, while SR-618 and SR-614 follow the other 3. Jennings Creek is the major drainage, with the other 3 creeks emptying into it. Its size ranges from samll near its headwaters on the Blue Ridge to large below the mouth of North Creek. Its gradient also varies considerably, from steep near

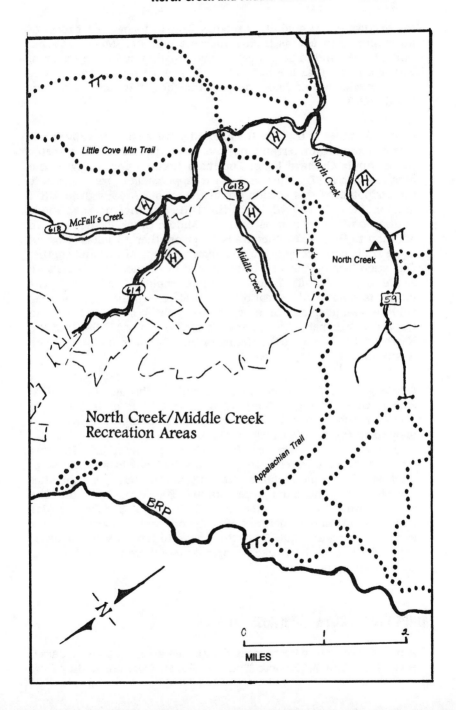

North Creek/Middle Creek
Recreation Areas

the headwaters to mild at its mouth. SR-614 follows it for most of its length, with access from numerous pullouts. McFalls Creek, North Creek, and Middle Creek are all small to mid-sized streams, with gradients that are mostly in the average range. Cover along these creeks is excellent, despite the fact that dirt roads run beside all 3.

**hiking:** 30 miles of trails in the area offer the chance to explore the forested mountain terrain, observe wildlife, and see the scenic 200-ft Apple Orchard Falls. The main hiking opportunity in the area is along a 17-mi segment of the *Appalachian Trail*. Access to the endpoints of this section are at the jct of VA-43 and the BRP; and on FR-812 100 yds S of the BRP. Another access, about midway on this section, is near the Middle Creek Picnic Area. In addition to the *AT*, 6 other trails cover another 13 miles. Most of these trails connect with the *AT*, allowing loops of various lengths. One such loop of 7 miles can be formed by connecting the *AT* with *Apple Orchard Falls Trail* and the *Cornelius Creek Trail*. The former is a national recreation trail that passes through a special wildlife management area where songbirds migrate from the tropics in summer. The trailhead is at the end of FR-59, N of the North Creek Campground. Hiking on most area trails is moderate to strenuous.

**camping:** Backcountry camping is permitted throughout the area, except where posted. Camping withing 300 ft of the primary access roads, however, is not permitted. Camping is also not allowed in the Middle Creek Picnic Area.

The car campground at North Creek rec area has 15 sites situated on North Creek. The sites are laid out in a single loop. Each site has a picnic table, fire ring, and lantern post. facilities are pit toilets and hand water pumps. The fee is $5/night. The campground is open all year. This is a pretty popular campground, and sometimes fills up on peak weekends. Arrive early in spring and fall. If you just have to have a warm shower, drive over to Cave Mtn Lake rec area, where there's a bathhouse at the swimming beach.

# James River Face Wilderness Area

A pair of adjacent wildernesses define this area: 8,900-acre James River Face and 2,450-acre Thunder Ridge. Combined, they form the largest tract of roadless backcountry on the district and offer the best opportunity on the district for exploring a large, pristine backcountry area. The area's natural boundaries are the James River, Arnold Valley, and the Blue Ridge. The region's scenery is exceptional, with views of the valley and James River Gorge from several of the hiking trails. A single secondary/forest road runs between the valley and the Blue Ridge Parkway and divides the 2 wilderness areas. The dirt and gravel road is actually the reason for there being two wilderness areas instead of only one: by definition, designated wildernesses must be roadless. The remote backcountry is prime wildlife habitat. Black bears, white-tailed deer, wild turkey, and ruffed grouse all inhabit the deep forests. The network of hiking trails, including a long segment of the *Appalachian Trail*, allows hikers and backpackers the chance to explore the different aspects and environments of the wilderness. Not far west of the James River Face Wilderness is Cave Mountain Lake Recreation Area, with facilities for camping, picnicking, and swimming on a supervised beach. While portions of the wilderness areas can be explored in a day, vast backcountry invites multi-day treks.

Glasgow (NW) is the closest town.

**getting there:** From I-81, take exit 175. Turn N onto US-11 and go 1.8 mi to VA-130. Turn R and go 3 mi to SR-759. Turn R and go 0.8 mi to SR-782. Turn L and go 1.8 mi (pavement ends after 1.1 mi) to a parking area at Locher Tract. Other parts of the area can be reached from SR-759. Instead of turning onto SR-782 to go to Locher Tract, continue on SR-759 2.4 mi to a 3-way jct. To the R on SR-781 it's 1.7 mi to the Cave Mtn Lake Rec Area. To the L on SR-781, go 1.4 mi to the *Belfast Trail*. At 1.5 mi the pavement ends and at 1.9 mi the road becomes FR-35. Reach the trailhead to the *Sulpher Spring Trail* at 3.1 mi and to the *AT* at 5.8 mi. The BRP (milepost 71) is less than 100 yds up the road.

**topography:** Rugged and mountainous, spectacular in many places where the mountains loom over Arnold Valley and the James River. The mountain ridges and valleys are blanketed in a dense hardwood forest. Elevations are between 700 ft on the James River and 4,200 ft at Apple Orchard Mtn. **maps:** USGS-FS Snowden; *AT* Glenwood–New Castle Ranger Districts

**starting out:** There are no facilities at all in the wilderness areas. Water sources are abundant in the wilderness, but all surface

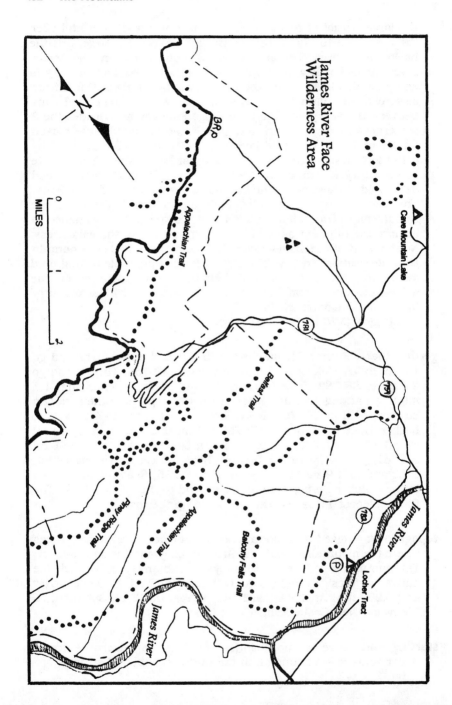

water should be treated before drinking. Restrooms and water are available at the Cave Mtn Lake Rec Area, located 3 miles W of the wilderness. The area is open May 1 to Nov 4. The parking fee for non-campers is $2/vehicle. Public use of alcohol in the rec areas is not allowed. The rec area gets very busy on summer weekends.

The USGS topo map has a larger scale and is better suited to serious orienteering, but the AT map does show both wilderness areas and is passable as a topo.

**activities:** Hiking, Camping

**hiking:** 38 mi of trails, including a 17-mi segment of the *Appalachian Trail*, provide access to all corners of the wilderness. Scenic highlights are views of the James River Gorge and Arnold Valley, Balcony Falls, remote forested mountains, and cool mountain creeks. Apart from the AT, which runs through the center of the wilderness, the other 5 trails fan out and connect to the secondary and forest roads that run along the wilderness boundaries. These trails are all between 3 and 7 miles long. With most trails connecting to the AT and such an extensive roadless backcountry, this area affords the best opportunity on the district for a multi-day backpacking trek. The only drawback is that the layout of the trails doesn't really permit loop hikes, except by using sections of road located at the edge of the wilderness. Hiking throughout the wilderness is moderate to strenuous, with trails left in a relatively primitive condition. Trail use is light throughout the area, with the AT receiving the heaviest use. Horses are allowed on the *Balcony Falls Trail*, *Sulphur Spring Trail*, and *Piney Ridge Trail*. All trailheads are signed. Access to the AT is at several points along the BRP and at the US-501 bridge across the James River. Trailhead to the *Balcony Falls Trail* is located at Locher Tract . A pair of other trailheads are located on SR-781/FR-35. See above for directions to all trailheads.

**camping:** Primitive backcountry camping is permitted throughout both wilderness areas.

Although there are no developed campgrounds in the wilderness areas, nearby Locher Tract offers primitive camping conditions. To get there, follow the directions above to the *Balcony Falls Trail*. In an open grassy field beside the James River are 4 sites identified by fire rings, which are the only alterations to the area. Mosquitoes can be abundant in the area.

A very attractive car campground is located at Cave Mountain

Lake Rec Area. The 42 sites are only average in size, but are spread out over a large area and isolated from each other by heavy forest cover. The sites offer a large measure of privacy. Each site has a picnic tabel, grill, and lantern post. Restrooms are located in the area, and showers are available at the nearby lake bathhouse. Sites cost $10/night. The campground is open May 1 to Nov 4.

# Otter Creek Recreation Area

## Blue Ridge Parkway

Unrolling north from the banks of the James River, the Otter Creek Recreation Area is located at the transition from mountains to piedmont. At only 650 feet above sea level, it's the lowest point on the parkway in either Virginia or North Carolina. Instead of the typical rugged mountain terrain encountered along the Blue Ridge, here you'll find gentle forested slopes and a meandering creek—all within sight of the James, the largest river in the Commonwealth. Covering just 552 acres in a long narrow profile, Otter Creek is the smallest rec area on the Virginia half of the BRP. Attractions here include a car campground, small network of hiking trails, visitor center, restaurant and gift shop, and a large picnic area on the shore of the James. The rec area is a good place for an overnight or to take a break for a couple hours from driving along the parkway.

Big Island (S) is the closest town.

**contact:** Superintendent, Blue Ridge Parkway, 400 BB&T Building, 1 Pack Square, Asheville, NC 28801; 704/298-0398

**getting there:** The rec area is located on the Blue Ridge Parkway between mileposts 60.6 (campground) and 63.6 (visitor center). Highway access is from VA-130 or US-501.

**topography:** Terrain at the rec area is unusually mild for the Blue Ridge. The uplands are gentle and rolling for the most part, similar to the piedmont. Except for large cleared and landscaped areas, hardwood forest is predominant. Elevations are between 650 and 850 ft. **maps:** USGS Big Island

**starting out:** You can pick up maps and brochures or buy from a small selection of guidebooks at the visitor center, which overlooks the James River. Restrooms, water, and pay phones are located there and at the restaurant next to the campground. The visitor center is open daily from 9 AM to 5 PM.

**activities:** Hiking, Camping, Fishing

**hiking:** The major hiking trail in the area is the 3.2-mi *Otter Creek Trail*. It parallels the BRP and Otter Creek between the visitor center and campground. Despite its proximity to the parkway, it has an atomosphere of remoteness, as it passes through a beautiful forest and follows Otter Creek. Creek crossings are on footbridges and the trail is easy to follow. Access to the trail is from the visitor center, the restaurant, or at Otter Lake. 2 shorter trails of interest begin at the visitor center. The half-mile *Canal Lock Trail* begins by crossing a footbridge that hangs suspended from the main parkway bridge across the James. A trail signboard is located next to the restaurant. The trail leads to a restored canal lock that was operational from 1851 to 1880. Placards beside it describe how the canal-lock system worked. The *Trail of the Trees* is another half-mile loop that begins at the visitor center. Signs identify area flora and scenic views of the river can be seen.

**camping:** The 69 sites at the car campground are arranged in 2 loops in an area shaded by hardwood forest beside Otter Creek. 45 of the sites are for tent campers; the others are for RVs and trailers. The sites are not particularly large, and they're pretty close to each other, but privacy is improved by the dense forest cover and by the light use—especially at the tent sites—that the campground receives. Each site has a picnic table, grill, and lantern post. There are modern restrooms, but no showers in the campground. Sites cost $10/night. Tent sites are usually available. The campground is open from May 1 to October 31.

**fishing:** Otter Lake is a small impoundment located at milepost 83 on the parkway. While it's no destination for a fishing expedition, it can provide an hour or two of fun fishing for largemouth bass and panfish. A 1-mi trail circles the lake. Only artificial lures can be used and a VA or NC fishing license is required.

# Lake Robertson State Recreation Area

This 581-acre park and backcountry area is located at the foot of the Allegheny Mountains in Rockbridge County west of historic Lexington. At its center is the eponymous 31-acre lake, a popular spot for both anglers and canoeists. Facilities around the shore are similar to those found in many state parks: a pool with bathhouse (open May 20 to Labor Day); large picnic area with shelter, tables, and grills; developed car campground; park office with fishing supplies for sale; and a network of trails that winds through the forested backcountry. Despite the recreational development, the area is a haven for wildlife, particularly migrating birds in fall and winter. In the backcountry, white-tailed deer and wild turkey roam the woods. The Lake Robertson SRA is perfect for families looking for an outdoor outing with the comforts of a large park. The campground makes weekend visits possible.

Lexington (E) is the closest town.

**contact:** Superintendent, Lake A. Willis Robertson, RFD 2, Box 251, Lexington, VA 24450; 540/463-4164

**getting there:** From downtown Lexington, take US-11BUS S 1 mi to VA-251. Go straight onto VA-251 and go 10 mi to SR-770. Turn L and go 2 mi to the rec area entrance, R.

**topography:** The lake and rec area are situated on the western edge of a broad valley that lies in the shadow of the Allegheny Mountains. Park terrain includes both gently rolling hills and the lower slopes of North Mtn. Except where land has been cleared to create a park setting, the terrain is heavily forested with southern hardwoods and northern evergreen species, including several species of cedar. **maps:** USGS Collierstown

**starting out:** Stop off at the visitor center before you take to the trails or lake. They can supply you with a trail map and park info there, as well as register you for a camp site. A pay phone is outside. Pit toilets are located by the boat ramp. In season, the pool bathhouse is open. Hunting takes place on the recreation area in fall and winter. If you plan to hike the trails during those times, be sure to wear blaze orange.

Alcohol is not allowed. Swimming in the lake is not permitted.

**activities:** Hiking, Fishing, Camping, Canoeing/Kayaking

**hiking:** An 8-mile network of of trails provides access to all corners of the backcountry. Beginning near the boat ramp, the trails fan out to the north and west, climbing the gentle lower slopes of North Mtn. The trails are well worn and easy to follow, but not blazed. They follow a combination of old seeded roadbeds and single-track footpaths. Hiking is easy to moderate. Trailheads are signed. A pair of shelters are located along the trails.

**fishing:** Anglers have the option of fishing from the shoreline, where there are numerous open spaces to facilitate casting as well as a fishing pier, or from a boat. Species caught are largemouth bass, walleye, and sunfish.

**camping:** An attractive car campground is nestled in an area sparsely forested with hardwoods and pines. Unfortunately, the 53 small sites are squeezed in pretty close to each other. Privacy is minimal when the campground is crowded, but that doesn't seem to be very often. Each site has a picnic table, grill, water, and electrical hookup. A Shower/restroom facility with hot water is located at the center of the campground. Sites cost $11/night, $15 with a trailer. Use is light to moderate. The campground is open from Mar 1 to Dec 1.

**canoeing/kayaking:** The lake's 31 acres offer a pleasant setting for a morning or afternoon paddle. Since there really isn't room for any kind of longer trip, it's best to combine some paddling with fishing. The lake's shoreline is attractive, with hardwoods and cedars making up most of the forest cover. Boat traffic is typically light, and is mainly canoes and jon boats. Boats with gasoline motors are not allowed on the lake. Put-in is at the boat ramp.

# James River Ranger District
## George Washington National Forest

Encompassing 164,260 acres in the Allegheny Highlands, the James River Ranger District is the home to Lake Moomaw and the headwaters of the James River, formed from the confluence of the

Jackson and Cowpasture Rivers. Almost all of the district's lands lie within Alleghany County; a small section at the south end is within Botetourt County. Boundaries are formed by West Virginia (W), the Jefferson National Forest (S), and the Warm Springs Ranger District (N). Douthat State Park also borders the district along its northern edge.

Outdoor recreation on the district is diverse and dispersed over three major backcountry areas and on the Jackson River, a popular whitewater run. Lake Moomaw is the best known and most popular. The southern half of the lake is located within the James River RD (the northern half belongs to the Warm Springs RD), where there are facilities on shore for camping, picnicking, fishing, boat launching and hiking. The recreation areas are open seasonally, usually from May to the end of September. Other backcountry areas are centered around Fore Mountain, the Rich Hole Wilderness (the district's lone designated wilderness), and the North Mountain Area, where there's another developed recreation area. Facilities there include a swimming beach on a small lake, bathhouse, picnic area, and hiking trails. The district recently created the Highland Scenic Tour, a 19-mile auto tour with 14 stations that describe the area's natural environment.

Covington and Clifton Forge are the largest towns on the district.

**contact:** James River Ranger District, U.S. Forest Service, 810-A Madison Ave, Covington, VA 24426; 540/962-2214.

**getting there:** I-64 bisects the district E–W and provides the primary highway access. US-220 and US-60 are the other major highways on the district.

To get to the district ranger station, take I-64 to exit 16. Turn W onto US-60/220 and go 0.1 mi to the entrance just before a large gas station, R.

**topography:** The Allegheny Mountains dominate the district's topography. These summits reach their peak in the district on Big Knob, which tops out at over 4,000 ft. Lake Moomaw is another prominent, and relatively new, physical feature. Major waterways are the Jackson River, the Cowpasture River, and the Headwaters of the James River at their confluence. USFS James River Ranger District; USGS topo maps are listed below under the separate headings.

**starting out:** A stop by the district ranger station is a good idea before planning your trip into the backcountry. They can supply you with district maps, trail pamphlets, brochures and other info. It's open weekdays from 8 AM to 4:30 PM. If you arrive on a weekend, most of the same info is available at the Gathright Dam Visitor Center, open weekends from noon to 4 PM (also open weekdays).

**activities:** Hiking, Canoeing/Kayaking, Fishing, Camping, Mountain Biking

**hiking:** Although there are only 80 miles of trails on the district, they pack a punch. There are 4 distinct trail networks on the district, with excellent opportunities for backpacking or day-hikes of almost any length. The trails that stand out for their scenic beauty and potential for backcountry travel are found in the Fore Mountain Area and the Rich Hole Wilderness Area. Trails in both areas combine exceptional scenery with backcountry isolation. Shorter trails are found in and around the district's rec areas. Trail use on the district is not heavy, and few of the trails are rated more than moderate to hike.

**canoeing/kayaking:** Paddlers can choose between the stunning scenery and flat-water of Lake Moomaw or the stunning scenery and whitewater of the Jackson River.

**fishing:** Anglers have their choice of a deep lake that holds almost every species of freshwater game fish found in the Comonwealth, a river quickly gaining a reputation as one of the best trout fisheries in the state, and a small, intimate mountain creek that's stocked with trout. These bodies of water are Lake Moomaw, the Jackson River below Gathright Dam, and Pounding Mill Run. Although there really aren't any opportunities for backpacking/fishing trips (unless you count a possible paddling/fishing/camping trip on Lake Moomaw), these waters all offer good potential for an enjoyable day on the water.

**camping:** Each of the areas described below offers the possibility for backcountry camping except for the Jackson River Area. Not that it isn't possible to camp along the river, but the land is privately owned and you'll have to seek the permission of the owners before making camp. You probably won't want to anyway, as the 18-miles segment of river is the perfect length for a day's paddle.

As for car campgrounds, there's only one. It's the Morris Hill Campground, located on Lake Moomaw. It's open from May 1 to Oct 31. A fee is charged.

**mountain biking:** Biking on the district is confined to forest roads in 2 of the areas below: Fore Mountain and Rich Hole Wilderness. "Confined" is probably the wrong word, since the first area offers a 12-mile ride that can be continued for at least another dozen miles on the roads and trails of the Warm Springs RD, and the second offers what is arguably the most outrageously scenic ride on the entire GWNF. In either case, riding conditions are quite good, since both roads are open to motor vehicles. Don't worry about traffic though, as there isn't likely to be any.

# Lake Moomaw Area

2,530-acre Lake Moomaw was created in 1981 when construction on the Gathright Dam was completed. The lake's remote location and beautiful mountain shoreline makes it one of the real treasures of outdoor recreation in the state's mountain region. No electricity is generated by the dam, it was built solely for flood control along the Jackson River. Divided between Alleghany and Bath Counties, the lake is also split between two national forest ranger districts: the James River and Warm Springs. The recreation areas along the south shore belong to the James River RD. They include three separate areas: Morris Hill Campground, Coles Mountain Recreation Area, and Fortney Branch Boat Launch. Recreation on the lake of course focuses on the water. Boating, fishing, swimming, and sunbathing are the most popular activities, and facilities for each are located at the recreation areas. Coles Mountain features a long sandy beach for swimming, a large picnic area with 80 sites, a boat ramp, and a bathhouse with hot-water showers. The area is open from May 1 to September 30 each year. At Fortney Branch there's another boat ramp, as well as access to the area's hiking trails. Finally, the Morris Hill Campground offers visitors a place to overnight nearby the lake. Whether you come to Lake Moomaw to canoe, kayak, fish, hike, or camp, plan on staying at least two days to absorb as much of the physical beauty and recreation potential that the lake offers.

Covington (S) is the closest town.

**getting there:** From I-64, take exit 16. Turn N onto US-220 and go 5.2 mi to SR-687. Turn L and go 3.2 mi to SR-641. Turn L and go 0.6 mi to SR-666. Continue straight on SR-666 and go 3.6 mi to the rec area entrance.

**topography:** Elevation on the lake is 1,582 ft above sea level. The terrain surrounding the lake is mountainous, with summits that reach elevations above 3,000 ft. Forest cover consists of both hardwoods and conifers. **maps:** USFS Lake Moomaw and Gathright Dam; USGS-FS Falling Spring, Mountain Grove.

**starting out:** The US Army Corps of Engineers maintains a visitor center at the dam. Inside, you can pick up brochures, trail maps, and other info. It's open weekdays from 8 AM to 4:30 PM, weekends noon to 4 PM. Restrooms, water, and a pay phone are located at the boat ramp and Coles Mtn Rec Area. The USFS topo map of the lake is the best guide to the area.

**activities:** Canoeing/Kayaking, Hiking, Fishing, Camping

**canoeing/kayaking:** Lake Moomaw offers one of the best large, flat-water paddling environments in the Virginia mountains. The lake offers plenty of room too, with a length of 12 miles and a shorline that extends for 43 miles. Although many types of watercraft can be seen on the water on summer weekends, including powerboats, sail boats, jet-skis, and water-skiiers, the lake's remote location seems to keep traffic to a tolerable minimum. Even with the other boats, you'll probably be so busy soaking in the amazing mountain scenery that you'll hardly notice they're there. The lakeshore is owned entirely by the USFS, which means that the only development is a couple of inconspicuous rec areas. You can put your canoe or kayak on the water at Cole Mountain Rec Area or Fortney Branch. Overnight trips are possible by using Morris Hill Campground as a base or camping in the backcountry along the lakeshore. There's one primitive campground on Greenwood Pt (see Warm Springs RD for details) or you can make your own no-trace camp anywhere along the lake's perimeter. Information on other boat ramps and rec areas is included in the Warm Springs RD.

**hiking:** 4 trails wind through the forested slopes and along the shoreline of Lake Moomaw, covering about 8 miles of mountain terrain. Most of the trails are designed for short hikes from the rec areas to the lake. Only the 5.3-mi *Oliver Mountain Trail* provides an opportunity for rugged hiking through the backcountry. It passes through a hardwood forest as it ascends the mountain on a steep footpath that begins at the Fortney Branch boat ramp. The trailhead is a little difficult to locate. As you enter the boat ramp parking area look for a break in the guard rail on the L. There's no sign, but you should see the bright yellow diamond blaze. Once you find the trail, it's easy to follow. The other trails begin in the campground or picnic area and are easy to locate. Hiking is moderate. Trail use is moderate.

**fishing:** Lake Moomaw counts 25 species of fish as inhabitants, making it a paradise for fishermen. These species include almost all of the warm-water and cold-water species that naturally occur in Virginia: brown, rainbow, and brook trout, largemouth, rock, and smallmouth bass, chain pickerel, yellow perch, black crappie, channel catfish, yellow bullhead, and several species of sunfish. Anglers can fish from either the shoreline or from a boat. There's plenty of room for bank-casting at Cole Mountain Rec Area and near the Fortney Branch boat ramp. Fishing from a canoe, however, will allow you to cover a lot more water. One obstacle to fly-fishermen is the lake's depth, which averages 80 ft. The coldwater species often hold far below the surface. For some outstanding fly-fishing for trout and smallmouth, check out the dam's tailrace on the Jackson River. This has become one of the most popular trout fisheries in the state. A full description is given below in the next section.

**camping:** Primitive backcountry camping is permitted anywhere on national forest lands except where posted. It is not allowed in or around the rec areas or boat ramps. One of the advantages of backcountry camping around Lake Moomaw is that you can backpack or paddle to a site.

Car campers can overnight at Morris Hill Campground on a forested slope above the lakeshore. The very attractive campground has 55 large sites spread out in a dense forest of hardwoods and pines. There's plenty of space between the sites and the level of privacy they offer is quite good. The campground is rarely crowded, which adds to it atmosphere of isolation. Each site has a pcinic table, grill, and lantern post. There are restrooms and showers with hot water. Sites cost $8/night. 15 of the sites can be reserved by calling 800/280-CAMP. The campground is open from May 1 to Oct 31.

# Jackson River Area

Flowing south out of the Allegheny Mountains, the Jackson River is one of the highlands' major drainages. In 1981 the completion of Gathright Dam—built for flood control on the river—created 2,530-acre Lake Moomaw and effectively divided the Jackson in half. The section below the dam offers some of the most superb scenery in this part of the state. Small farms line the banks and the rolling hills of the river's valley and stunning mountain summits crowd them on all sides. This setting has made the river a magnet for canoeists, kayakers, and fly-fishermen. The national forest has developed a handful of access points along the 19-mile segment of the river between the dam and the town of Covington. These are used by both paddlers and anglers. Most of the land on either side of the river is private property; be sure to respect the rights of the owners. You can't float past Covington, but you wouldn't want to. A monstrous Westvaco Plant is located on the river there that looks like it sprung from the imagination of Terry Gilliam.

Covington (S) is the closest town.

**getting there:** The first put-in on the river is located just below the dam that forms Lake Moomaw. From I-64, take exit 16. Turn N onto US-220 and go 5.2 mi to SR-687. Turn L and go 3.2 mi to SR-641. Turn L and go 0.6 mi to SR-666. Continue straight on SR-666 and go 3.6 mi to SR-605. Turn R and go 2.5 mi to Stilling Basin Rd. Turn R and go 0.8 mi to the end of the road and parking area beside the river. • To reach the last take-out before Clifton Forge: From I-64, take exit 16. Turn N onto US-220 and go 5.2 mi to SR-687. Turn L and go 0.9 mi to Mays Lane. Turn L and go 0.3 mi to a parking area and river access.

**topography:** The river flows through a narrow valley surrounded by a small band of farms and the forested mountain slopes. Elevation on the river is 1,400 ft. The mountains rise 2,500 ft from the river. **maps:** USGS Falling Spring, Covington.

**starting out:** Although there are no facilities on the river, those at the Lake Moomaw rec areas and the Gathright Dam Visitor Center are close by the put-in. There are restrooms, water, and pay phones at each of the areas. See above under "Lake Moomaw" for additional information. The district topo map shows all of the access points and is sufficient for navigating the river.

**activities:** Kayaking/Canoeing, Fishing

**kayaking/canoeing:** From the Gathright Dam at the S end of Lake Moomaw to the last take-out just above Covington, the Jackson River offers one of the most scenic whitewater runs in the state. Although the rapids are all in the class I-II range and there are long stretches of flat water, the mountain views more than make up for the lack of extreme whitewater thrills. This is not a river for novices, but paddlers with only intermediate skills should have little problem handling the Jackson's whitewater. By southern Appalachian standards, it's a pretty big river, with a width that averages about 100 ft. The banks are lined by both small farms and patches of hardwood forest. The distance between the first put-in and last take-out is 18 miles. There are 4 other access points along that stretch. The whole stretch of river here makes a good day-trip.

**fishing:** The section of the Jackson River below the Gathright Dam is stocked trout water. Special regulations are in effect, and all trout caught must be immediately released. The dam's tailrace has quickly become one of the hottest trout-fishing locations in Virginia. Almost any weekend day will find 10–20 flyfishermen casting into the rapids and long pools. (This book's front cover photo was shot on one such morning; thanks to the fly-fishermen who let me photograph them). To reach this area, follow the directions above to the first put-in just below the dam. In addition to that area, there are 5 other access points on the river. These all provide fishing access. Wading is necessary in most places, as the banks don't offer much open space. Another option is a combination float/fish trip. There are long stretches of flat-water on the river, punctuated by short, class I-II rapids. Perfect conditions for a canoe/fly-fishing trip. In addition to the trout, the river supports populations of smallmouth and rock bass.

# Fore Mountain Area

This large backcountry area extends northeast from the town of Covington all the way to the boundary with the Warm Springs Ranger District and Douthat State Park. It is a region of rugged, forested mountains, including Alleghany County's highest peak, Big Knob. The area is a haven for all kinds of wildlife; black bear, white-tailed deer, wild turkey, ruffed grouse, and many smaller mammals such as racoon and squirrel are seen. Backcountry travel and recreation are defined by two long hiking trails—the *Fore Mountain Trail* and the *Dry Run Trail*—and by Pounding Mill, a stocked trout creek. Although the area borders Covington on the south, there are no facilities at all in the backcountry. The area is well suited to a long day-hike or a weekend backpacking trip. Longer treks are possible by combining the backcountry areas of the ranger district and state park that are adjacent to the north.

Covington (S) is the closest town.

**getting there:** To reach the S terminus of the *Fore Mtn Trail*, take exit 16 from I-64. Turn E onto US-60 and go 0.2 mi to SR-797 and the entrance to the district work center. Turn L and go 0.3 mi to a parking area and trailhead. • To reach Pounding Mill, the *Dry Run Trail*, and the *Fore Mtn Trail*: From I-64, take exit 16. Turn W onto US-60/220 and go 1.3 mi to E Dolly Ann Dr (SR-625). Turn R and go 6.3 mi (at 1.9 mi the pavement ends and the road becomes FR-125) to an unsigned jct. Turn L and go 50 yds to a parking area and trail access.

**topography:** The major physical features of this area lie on a NE–SW axis. Elevations on Pounding Mill are as low as 1,400 ft. Elevations on Big Knob reach 4,000 ft. The mountain slopes are forested with southern Appalachian hardwoods, with some pines interspersed. **maps:** USGS-FS Covington, Clifton Forge, Healing Spring.

**starting out:** There are no facilities in this large backcountry area. Since it's S end borders the town of Covington, however, restrooms, water, food, lodging and NF info are close by. The district RS is located less than half a mile from the area's S access points. At the N end is Douthat SP, which can be used as a basecamp. Facilities there include restrooms, water, and pay phones, as well as a car campground and restaurant. If you're going to hike the 2 main trails in the area, pick up the pamphlet that gives a mile-by-mile description of them at the district RS. Surface water is abundant in the backcountry, but should be treated before drinking.

**activities:** Hiking, Mountain Biking, Fishing, Camping

**hiking:** 2 long trails define the hiking opportunites in this area. The 14-mi *Fore Mountain Trail* is the marquis trail in the area and on the district. A trail that is popular with hikers, backpackers, and equestrians, it's maintained by the Bordernieer Riding Club. The trail runs between the Dolly Anne Work Center in Covington and the border with the Warm Springs RD about 1 mi SW of Douthat SP. The trail follows a more-or-less straight line up the mountain on a combination of narrow footpaths and seeded roadbeds. Loop hikes are not possible, though connections can be made with the trails of the ranger district and state park to the N, or with the area's other major trail, the 9-mi *Dry Run Trail*. Both trails offer a good environment for backpacking or day-hikes. Hiking along each of the trails is moderate, though conditions and treadways vary considerably. The only downside to hiking the trails is that loops are not possible; backtracking or a vehicle shuttle are necessary. Highlights along the trails include solitude, mountain vistas, and the chance to see wildlife. Both trails are marked and easy to follow.

**mountain biking:** Opportunities for mountain biking in the area are limited to a single forest road open to motor vehicle (moderate traffic level) and a couple of side roads, both open and gated. FR-125 runs the length of the area from Covington to the Warm Springs RD, a distance of about 15 miles. You can ride this road one-way and then turn around or, when you reach the district line, just keep going and hook up with the network of roads and trails on the Warm Springs RD. The road is generally well maintained, with riding easy to moderate. In fall and winter it gets a little busy with hunters.

**fishing:** Although the area isn't a major destination among anglers, Pounding Mill provides 4 miles of stocked trout waters in a lush forest setting. The small drainage flows SW in the shadow of Fore Mountain. It has a very rocky bed and drops down over an average gradient. Cover on both sides is dense, with lots of rhododendron for fly-fishermen to contend with. Access is from FR-125, which follows the creek all the way upstream from Covington. There are numerous pullouts along the dirt and gravel road.

**camping:** Primitive backcountry camping is permitted anywhere in the area on national forest lands except where posted. Fore Mountain Trail and Dry Run Trail both offer good sites. If you want to car camp, there are sites along FR-125. The only drawback is the road's proximity to Covington, which seems to make it a late-night weekend magnet for young revelers.

# Rich Hole Wilderness Area

Although it doesn't receive as much attention or publicity as Lake Moomaw, this large, dispersed area may be the premiere backcountry area on the James River Ranger District. There are actually two components to the area, connected by the recently completed *Highland Scenic Tour*, a 19-mile auto tour that takes in some of the area's natural highlights. At one end is the Rich Hole Wilderness, a 6,450-acre roadless backcountry with old-growth hardwood forests, rich wildlife habitat, and excellent opportunities for backpacking solitude. At the other end is the Longdale Recreation Area and Top Drive. The recreation area provides facilities for swimming on a small lake (there's a bathhouse), picnicking, and hiking on a series of mountain trails. Top Drive is a dirt and gravel road with pullouts and side trails that simply offers some of the most spectacular mountian scenery in Virginia. Whether you travel the road by car or mountain bike, it should be included in any "don't miss" list of Virginia attractions. If the idea of traffic congestion similar to Skyline Drive comes to mind, forget it. This is a remote, unpaved road that requires some effort on suspension-jarring mountain roads to get to. Unless you come on a peak weekend, you'll probably have the road to yourself. With a road through the clouds and a roadless wilderness, this corner of the district offers the best of two worlds. Come for a weekend with a mountain bike and backpack and experience them both.

Clifton Forge (W) is the closest town.

**getting there:** From I-64, take exit 35. To reach the wilderness, turn NE onto SR-850 and go 1.4 mi to FR-108 just past a bridge. Turn L onto the dirt and gravel road and go 1.3 mi to a parking area R. Another access is to continue on SR-850 3.7 mi past FR-108 to a parking area and trailhead, L. • To reach Top Drive, take exit 43 and turn S onto dirt and gravel FR-447 (Top Drive). The road continues up the mtn 6.6 mi to SR-770. Turn R and go 4.1 mi to VA-269. L it's 1.7 mi to the Longdale Rec Area, L. This end of Top Drive and the rec area can be reached more easily from exit 35 on I-64.

**topography:** 2 long mountains—North and Brushy—are separated by the narrow valley through which I-64 passes. Brushy Mtn is slightly higher, with elevations that exceed 3,400 ft. North Mountain is rugged and steep, with numerous rock outcrops. Elevations in the valley are as low as 1,200 ft. Forest cover is

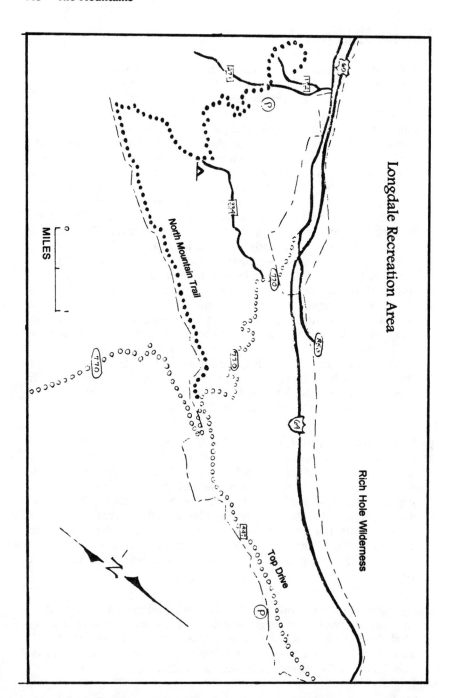

dense throughout the backcountry, with both hardwood and conifer species present. **maps:** USGS Collierstown, Longdale Furnace, Millboro, Nimrod Hall.

**starting out:** If it's open (May 15 to Sep 30), Longdale Rec Area is a good starting point. Facilities there include restrooms and water, and it's only a short drive from Top Drive. If you're taking the auto tour or biking up Top Drive, station #1 is at the N end of the drive, at exit 43 off of I-64. There's a large signboard with maps of the route available. If the holder is empty, you can get a guide at the district RS in Covington.

Groups larger than 10 people are not allowed in the wilderness.

**activities:** Hiking, Mountain Biking, Camping

**hiking:** Ther are 2 distinct trail networks in the area. In the Rich Hole Wilderness Area 2 trails cover a total distance of 11 miles in the wilderness and just outside it. These trails offer a good oppotunity for long day-hikes or for a single overnight backpacking trip. Highlights along the trails are lush, old-growth forests and wilderness solitude. The chances of seeing wildlife are high. The 2 trails connect, but loop hikes are not possible. Backtracking or a vehicle shuttle are necessary. The signed trailheads are located on FR-108 and SR-850. Directions are given above. In keeping with the wilderness ethic, the trails are left in a primitive state. Hiking along them is moderate.

The other trail network begins in the Longdale Rec Area and consists of 3 trails, a short loop trail, a short trail that ends at an overlook, and the 12.5-mi *North Mrn Trail*. The last begins in the rec area and climbs the mountain to Top Drive (FR-447) which it joins for 3 miles before ending at the start of the short *Cocks Comb Trail*. If you want to earn the spectacular views that Top Drive and the trail afford, then hiking up North Mtn is the way to go. The trail is steep and the hiking strenuous. Trail use in both areas is moderate.

**mountain biking:** If you're only going to take one mountain biking trip on the James River RD, it should be on Top Drive. The combination of a well-maintained forest road, spectacular views on both sides, and little or no traffic most days, makes this one of the outstanding rides on the GWNF. You can start your ride at the N end of the drive or at the bottom of Collierstown Rd (it's actually better to start 2 miles away at the Longdale Rec Area, since there's parking). Either way, the ride is 11 miles long and unforgettable. Riding ranges from easy to strenuous, with the climb up Collierstown Rd (SR-770) the steepest section. (You can avoid it by riding in the opposite direction). This route makes the ideal day-trip. Give yourself plenty of time to stop at the numerous overlooks and don't forget to bring a camera.

**camping:** Primitive backcountry camping is permitted throughout the area on NF lands except where posted. The Rich Hole Wilderness offers the best opportunity for backpacking in a remote, isolated setting. *North Mountain Trail* is also suitable for backpacking.

# Douthat State Park

With national forest land on either side offering a wealth of outdoor recreation, the decision to put a state park right in the middle of it all might at first seem a little strange. The reason it works, however, is that 4,493-acre Doutaht State Park complements the large backcountry areas that surround it, rather than simply offering a little more of the same. The park provides numerous facilities geared toward family recreation, while the surrounding national forest is primarily undeveloped backcountry. At the center of the park is 50-acre Douthat Lake, a scenic impoundment surrounded by wooded mountain slopes. Visitors can boat, fish, swim on the lake, or have a picnic at one of the large picnic areas that line its shores. Also overlooking the lake is the visitor center/restaurant complex, housed in one of the original CCC buildings left over from the park's earliest days. Nearby is a large car campground and cabins for rent. And if you tire of all the development, you can take to one of twenty-four trails that seem to cover every inch of the backcountry. Finally, if it's pristine, isolated backcountry you desire after all, simply hike one of the trails out of the park and connect with the trails of the national forest.

Clifton Forge (S) is the closest town.

**contact:** Douthat State Park, Route 1, Box 212, Millboro, VA 24460; 540/862-8100

**getting there:** From I-64, take exit 27 and turn N onto SR-629. Go 2.8 mi to the park entrance. At 5.5 mi come to the fee shack.

**topography:** Park terrain is defined by uplands forested with hardwood and pine species and numerous small streams that feed Wilson Creek, the park's major drainage. Mountain slopes are steepest along the park's W edge. **maps:** USGS Healing Springs.

**starting out:** Entance fee to the park is $1/vehicle weekdays, $2 on weekends. Pick up a trail map or park brochure in the park office. Facilities (restrooms, water, pay phone) are at the park office and lake. Crowds tend to concentrate in the lake area, while the trails are often relatively uncrowded.

Public use or display of alcohol is not allowed. Pets must be kept on a leash.

**activities:** Hiking, Canoeing/Kayaking, Fishing, Camping

**hiking:** Although most park activity centers around the lake, the real prize here is the 40-mile network of trails that seem to cover every corner of the backcountry. The trails cross and recross each other so many times and in so many combinations that the potential for hikes of varying length and terrain is dizzying. Scenic highlights along the trails are mountain views, cool forests, and small mountain creeks with a couple of waterfalls. Signed trailheads are located at several parking areas along the main park road and near the lake. The trails are blazed and easy to follow. Trail conditions cover the full range from easy to moderate. The park trail guide (available free at the park office) indicates the difficulty level of each trail and provides a map to help sort out the 24 trails. Trail use is moderate to heavy. For longer treks, including backpacking trips of more than a day, you can hook up with the national forest trails that runs N and S just beyond the W border of Douthat SP. For more info, see the sections on the Warm Springs and James River Ranger Districts.

**canoeing/kayaking:** 50-acre Douthat Lake is very popular with paddlers and other boaters. The park rents rowboats and paddle boats; on nice weekends at least a dozen boaters can usually be found drifting around the small lake or casting for fish. Serious backcountry paddlers will be disappointed by the lake's small size and frequently crowded conditions, though it is quite attractive. It's best suited to anglers looking to spend an afternoon on the water or to families introducing children to water sports.

**fishing:** Anglers have the option of fishing Douthat Lake or Wilson Creek. Both are fee-fishing waters from the end of March to September 30. A daily fishing permit must be purchased to fish during that period. If you decide to fish the lake, you can cast from the shore or put a boat on the water. Both methods are popular and the fishing pressure is often heavy. The lake is stocked with trout twice a week, and also holds populations of largemouth bass, chain pickerel, bluegill, and catfish. After Sep 30 the lake is normal stocked trout water.

Wilson Creek is medium sized with a mild gradient that provides about 4 miles of fishable water. The creek has recently been added to the park's fee-fishing program. Forest cover is pretty good on both banks, with hemlocks prominent. Access is from park roads or hiking trails. The dam's tailrace has been put aside as a fishing area reserved for children under 12.

**camping:** The large car campground has 98 sites laid out in 3 loops that are in effect 3 small campgrounds. Unfortunately, the sites are small and squeezed toghether pretty tightly. If the campground is crowded, forget about any privacy. Each site has a picnic table, grill, and lantern post. Scattered hardwoods and pines provide shade. Some sites are beside the lake. In each loop the sites are located in a sparsely wooded area. A shower/restroom facility is located at the center of each loop. Sites cost $12/night, $17 if you want to be on the water. Pets are $3 extra. The campground is open from mar 1 to Dec 1. You can reserve sites by calling 800/933-PARK

The park also has camping facilities for organized groups.

# Gathwright Wildlife Management Area

This 13,428-acre primitive backcountry area is part of a large complex of publicly-owned land surrounding Lake Moomaw. The land immediately around the lake is managed by the U.S. Forest Service; past that is a buffer zone managed by the Department of Game & Inland Fisheries. The Gathright WMA occupies two tracts on either side of the lake's narrow, northern branch. The larger parcel encompasses the eastern slope of Allegheny Mountain and borders West Virginia. All backcountry recreation is limited to this tract. The area is known best to hunters, who come in fall and winter to pursue white-tailed deer, wild turkey, and ruffed grouse. The old roadbeds they follow into the backcountry can be used by hikers and backpackers at other times of year. Also on the tract is Mill Creek, a small stream that flows into Lake Moomaw and supports a native population of rainbow trout. Perhaps the best recreational opportunity in the area is found on FR-55 (High Top Drive), an unpaved forest road that follows the ridge crest of Allegheny Mountain for twenty-five miles. For mountain bikers, the road is a dream come true. The Gathright WMA provides a more rugged and primitive backcountry experience than the developed recreation areas at Lake Moomaw. It will appeal to those looking for a challenge and to meet nature on its own terms.

Warm Springs (E) is the closest town.

**contact:** Gathright WMA, P.O. Box 996, Verona, VA 24482; 540/248-9360

**getting there:** From the jct of US-220 and VA-39 E of Warm Springs, take VA-39 W 11.3 mi to SR-600. Turn L and go 2.5 mi to the start of the WMA. Parking areas and signed trail accesses are located along the R side of the road for the 5 miles between the High Top Fire Trail and Lake Moomaw.

**topography:** The WMA occupies the E slope of Allegheny Mtn. The mountainous terrain is blanketed with a forest of hardwoods and conifers. Elevations are between 3,500 ft on the mountain and 1,582 ft on Lake Moomaw. **maps:** USGS Falling Spring, Mountain Grove.

**starting out:** There is no ranger station or office on the WMA. Nor are there any facilities. These can be found nearby on Lake Moomaw, however, where there are several developed recreation areas with restrooms, water, and pay phones. Surface water is abundant in the WMA backcountry except at the highest elevations. All water should be treated before drinking. Hunting takes place on the WMA in fall and winter. If you come during those times, be sure to wear blaze orange.

**activities:** Hiking, Mountain Biking, Camping, Fishing

**hiking:** There is no formal network of hiking trails on the WMA. Nevertheless, the backcountry is not entirely inaccessible. A series of gated roadbeds follow small drainages up the mountain from SR-600. There are small parking areas at each of these access points and they are clearly marked. None of the roads connects, so backtracking is necessary. Each of the trail offers about 1.5 miles of hiking one-way. The roadbeds are not blazed, but they are not difficult to follow. Hiking is moderate. Trail use is light, except during hunting season.

**mountain biking:** The best mountain biking in the area is on FR-55, also known as High Top Rd. The dirt and gravel logging road follows a high ridge along the WV state line for 25 miles. The road is rarely traveled, except by occasional logging trucks and hunters. It offers riding in a mountaintop environment, with superb views throughout in winter and from a few overlooks year round. Riding is easy to moderate. To reach FR-55, leave the WMA and turn W onto VA-39 from its jct with SR-600. Go 6.2 mi to the WV state line and FR-55. Turn L onto the road. You can park at any of numerous pullouts or drive to the N end of the High Top Fire Trail, 6 mi S.

**camping:** Primitive backcountry camping is permitted throughout the area, except where posted otherwise.

**fishing:** Trout anglers can try their luck in Mill Creek, a small stream that supports a native population of rainbow trout. The creek flows over a rocky bed with a mild gradient. Cover is mixed, with some areas along the banks forested and others meadow. The river can be fished for about 3 miles above Lake Moomaw, into which it flows. Access is from pullouts along SR-600.

# Warm Springs Ranger District
## George Washington National Forest

Occupying 171,526 acres in Bath and Highland Counties, the Warm Springs Ranger District is a remote region of deep forests and pastoral valleys. The combined human population of the two counties is less than 10,000, and the region is known principally as the home of the world-famous Homestead Resort, as well as for its unsurpassed scenery and opportunities for outdoor recreation. The western border of the district is formed by West Virginia and the Monongahela National Forest; to the south is the James River District of the GWNF. Also in Bath County are the Gathright Wildlife Management Area and Douthat State Park, furthering the potential for backcountry recreation.

The major developed recreation area on the district is Bolar Mountain and Bolar Flats, located on the western shore of Lake Moomaw, a 2,530-acre impoundment completed in 1981 to assist in flood control of the Jackson River. The lake's alpine setting makes it an area of rare beauty, and there are facilities for camping, picnicking, swimming, fishing, and boat launching. Backcountry recreation on the rest of the district is more dispersed. There are several excellent networks of hiking trails, some outstanding trout fishing on a couple of large rivers, mountain biking, and camping at four primtive car campgrounds or in the vast undeveloped backcountry.

There are no major towns or cities on the district. Clifton Forge (S) and Covington (S) are the closest.

**contact:** Warm Springs Ranger District, U.S. Forest Service, Hwy 220 South, Route 2, Box 30, Hot Springs, VA 24445; 540/839-2521.

**getting there:** I-64 runs just S of the district and provides the primary access. US-220 runs N–S through the district, while US-250 provides the easiest access to its NW extremity.

The district ranger station is located on US-220 S of the resort town of Hot Springs.

**topography:** The district is firmly situated in the area of western VA known as the Allegheny Highlands. The mountains here sit on an elevated plateau that is 1,600 ft above sea level. Mountain summits generally do not exceed 4,000 ft, with an orientation that runs NE-SW. The major rivers—the Jackson and Cowpasture—are aligned in the same direction. Forest types are a mix here, with Appalachian and northern hardwood and conifer species both present. **maps:** USFS Warm Springs Ranger District; see below under each heading for USGS topo maps.

**starting out:** Before heading out into the backcountry to hike, bike, or paddle, a stop by the district RS is worthwhile. They can provide you with trail maps and brochures, or sell you a district map. The

RS is open weekdays from 8 AM to 4:30 PM. The district's center of activity is Lake Moomaw. Although the term "crowd" is relative in a county with only 7,000 residents, it does get a little busy on summer weekends.

**activities:** Hiking,    Fishing,   Mountain Biking,   Camping, Canoeing/Kayaking.

**hiking:** There are 124 miles of hiking trails on the district. Trails range in length from short spurs and fishermen's trails around Lake Moomaw to longer trails that follow rivers and mountain ridges. Although the district lacks a single long-distance "name" trail such as the *Appalachian Trail*, it does boast extensive trail networks at the Locust Springs Rec Area, in Hidden Valley, and in the Wilson Creek Area. Any one of these locations is ideal for a multi-day backpacking trip. The district's trails generally in good shape, with trailheads clearly signed and treadways blazed and easy to follow. Trail use throughout the district is moderate, except at Lake Moomaw, where the few short trails can get pretty crowded during the peak summer season.

**fishing:** A variety of fisheries and conditions await anglers who come to the district. Most noted is Lake Moomaw, which is host to a wide cross-section of warmwater and coldwater species. Travelers dedicated to non-motorized boats can get at the fish from a canoe. Just be sure to bring tackle that can go deep, as that's where many of the fish are, trout expecially. Trout anglers look to combine hiking or backpacking with fishing will find some of the biggest troutwater tucked away in the highland backcountry. The prime locations are Locust Springs and Hidden Valley, both of which have a major drainage flowing right through their hearts, with trail access in gorgeous settings. Pads Creek in the Rough Mountain Wilderness Area offers trout angling on more intimate waters.

**mountain biking:** The 2 main riding areas on the district are Hidden Valley and the Wilson Creek Area. They offer different conditions with one thing in common: miles of trails and unpaved roads. Although the district maintains none of its trails primarily for mountain bike use, many of the hiking trails follow old roadbeds that are perfectly suited to off-road riding. And riders looking for more of a challenge can tackle virtually any of the district's trails, since only a few are closed to bikes. Riding on most of the trails and roads described below is moderate. Traffic—even on forest roads open to motor vehicles—is almost universally light.

**camping:** Each of the 5 areas described below offers ample opportunity for backcountry camping. At Lake Moomaw you can hike or paddle to your campsite; at the other 4 areas it's hike only, with backcountries perfectly sized for weekend backpacking trips.

In addition to the backcountry, there are 5 car campgrounds on the district. Bolar Mountain Campground at Lake Moomaw is the only one that is fully developed with electrical hookups. The other 4 are small and primitive, with facilities limited to hand water pumps and pit toilets. These areas offer a nice compromise between large, crowded car campgrounds and backpacking.

**canoeing/kayaking:** For paddlers coming to the Allegheny Highlands in search of flat water, Lake Moomaw is the destination. The lake offers a scenic alpine setting in a remote location that is one of the real treasures of western Virginia.

# Lake Moomaw Area

Lake Moomaw is divided between two national forest ranger districts; the southern half belongs to the James River RD, the northern half to the Warm Springs RD. Situated in a remote corner of the state and surrounded by the graceful swells of the Alleghenies, the 2,500-acre lake is one of the jewels of outdoor recreation in the Commonwealth. Although recreation inevitably focuses on the water, where there's ample opportunity for anglers and boaters of all stripes to indulge their enthusiasms, the lake's 43-mile shoreline features several developed recreation areas with campgrounds and picnic areas with tables, grills, and shelters. There's also a fairly substantial trail network and the large backcountry of the Gathright Wildlife Management Area, which occupies 13,500 acres between the lake and the West Virginia state line. With so much to do and such spectacular scenery, it's best to reserve at least a weekend for your visit.

Warm Springs (NE) and Hot Springs (NE) are the closest towns.

**getting there:** From the jct of US-220 and VA-39 E of Warm Springs, take VA-39 W 11.1 mi to SR-600. Turn L and go 7.1 mi through the Gathright WMA to the lake entrance. At 7.5 mi come to a jct: R is the campground, L is the boat ramp.

**topography:** Elevation on the lake at its normal level is 1,582 ft. The mountain ridges that surround the lake are blanketed with a dense cover of hardwoods and conifers. Elevations reach 3,000 ft on Coles Mtn and Allegheney Mtn. **maps:** USFS Lake Moomaw–Gathright Dam Area; USGS Falling Spring, Mountain Grove.

**starting out:** If you need information or supplies before heading out into the backcountry or onto the lake, stop by the Lakeside Outfitters convenience store next to the boat ramp. Inside they sell fishing and camping supplies as well as snack food. A pay phone is located outside and restrooms and water are nearby in the picnic area.

**activities:** Canoeing/Kayaking, Fishing, Hiking, Camping

**canoeing/kayaking:** Although the lake is popular with all kinds of watercraft—power boats, sailboats, jet-skis, and water-skiers are all encountered—its remote setting and stunning scenery make it perfect for paddling a canoe or kayak. Since it's far off the beaten path, it doesn't ever really get crowded, a blessing for paddlers hoping to avoid the whine of outboards. The lake's profile is a round mid-section with 2 long branches that extend N and S. Total length of the lake is 12 miles—just long enough for a full day's paddle. The scenic lakeshore is entirely publicly owned; the only developments are the dam (located near the S end), marina, and several NF campgrounds and picnic grounds. Overnight paddling excursions are possible by using one of the developed campgrounds as a base (all are located on the water) or pulling up on some isolated spot along the shore and making your own camp.

**fishing:** 25 species of fish inhabit Lake Moomaw. Of these, more than a dozen are game fish, representing the full range of freshwater fish found in the commonwealth. Species commonly caught are largemouth, smallmouth, and rock bass; brown, rainbow, and brook trout; chain pickerel; bluegill; black crappie; yellow bullhead; channel catfish; yellow perch; northern pike; and several species of sunfish. Fishing from the shoreline is possible at the rec areas, but it doesn't really compare to getting a boat out on the water. The average lake depth is 80 ft, and coldwater fish are typically taken at the lower depths.

**hiking:** 10 miles of trails wind through the wooded uplands and drop down to the shoreline along Lake Moomaw. The longest of these is 3.3-mi Greenwood Point Trail, which ends at a primitive lakeshore campground that can only be reached on foot or in a boat. The other 5 trails in the area range in length from 0.1 to 2 miles, and run around and through the rec areas that line the lakeshore at Bolar Mtn. Trailheads are located at various points along the Bolar Mountain access road and rec area parking lots. They are mostly signed and easy to locate. Hiking is easy. Trail use is heavy during the summer season. For backpackers and hikers wanting a more challenging and rugged backcountry experience, the trails of the adjacent Gathright WMA are a perfect bet. See the separate entry for descriptions and trailheads.

**camping:** Primitive backcountry camping is permitted on NF lands except where prohibited. In practice, this means that if you're in a canoe or kayak you can camp pretty much anywhere around the lake you want—except near the rec areas and dam, of course. Backpackers will want to head into the more extensive backcountry of the Gathright WMA (located next door to the N), as opportunities on NF land are very limited around the N half of the lake.

Car camping is popular with families at Lake Moomaw, and the Bolar Mtn Campground has 90 sites in 3 different locations along the lakeshore. These are fully developed campgrounds, with sites that have electrical hookups and shower/restroom facilities with hot water. The mid-sized sites are located in a heavily wooded area that adds somewhat to privacy, but with summer crowds, this is not the place to come looking for rustic solitude. Each site has a picnic table, grill, and lantern post. Some of the sites offer outstanding views out over the lake. Sites cost $10/night, $12 with hookup. The campground is open from May 1 to Nov 30. Use is moderate to heavy. Arrive early to get a site during summer weekends.

# Hidden Valley Area

With a broad pastoral valley that is home to a restored antebellum mansion that is on the National Register of Historic Places and proximity to the world-famous Homestead Resort, Hidden Valley is the most distinctive area on the George Washington National Forest. Visitors to the region will find one of western Virginia's

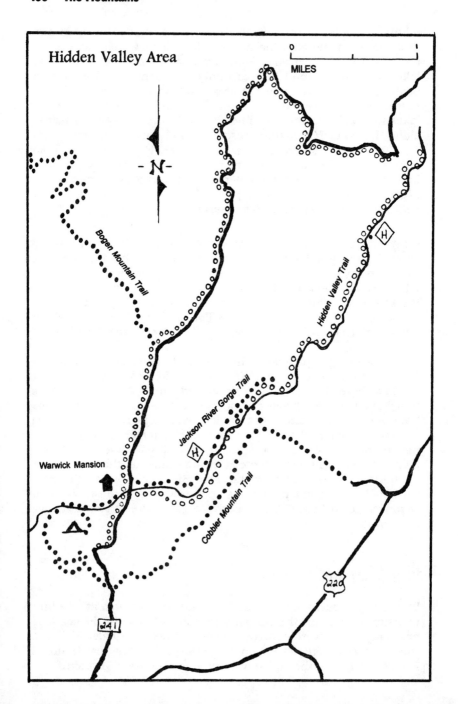

most attractive rivers flowing through a pastoral valley that lies at the feet of the Warwick Mansion, a stuning example of the Greek Revival style of architecture. The entire region evokes a time and place from a past century. That atmosphere has not been lost on Hollywood. In 1992 Sommersby was filmed here, starring Richard Gere and Jodie Foster. The mansion, now run as a B&B, remains just about the only development in the valley. The Hidden Valley recreation Area, with facilities for primitive camping and picnicking, is located at the valley's southern entrance. An extenisve network of trails allows visitors to explore the valley and surrounding forested mountains on foot or bike. Fly-fishermen come to try their luck in the Jackson River. Just across the highway is the Blowing Springs Campground and Back Creek Gorge, providing additional opportunities for camping, hiking, and trout fishing. No tour of the Virginia backcountry would be complete without a visit to the Hidden Valley Area. If you come, give yourself at least a weekend to explore its enchanting environs.

Warm Springs (SE) is the closest town.

**getting there:** From the jct of US-220 and VA-39 E of Warm Springs, take VA-39 W 3.2 mi to SR-621. Turn R and go 1 mi to Hidden Valley Rd (FR-241). Keep L and go 1.5 mi to the campground, L. The trailhead and parking area for the *Hidden Valley Trail* is located 0.5 mi ahead. • To reach the Blowing Springs Campground, continue W on VA-39 past the turn for Hidden Valley and go 6.4 mi to the entrance, L.

**topography:** National forest lands here occupy the broad, pastoral Jackson River Valley and Back Creek Mountain to the W. Elevation on the river is 1,600 ft at the Warwick Mansion; the mountain rises as much as 2,000 ft from the valley floor. The mountains are forested, while the valley is mostly small, scenic farms. **maps:** USGS-FS Warm Springs, Sunrise

**starting out:** You can use either Blowing Springs of Hidden Valley Campgrounds as a basecamp for exploring this area. Facilities at both include hand water pumps and pit toilets. It's a good idea to bring whatever you think you'll need with you, as there are no large towns in the immediate vicinity and services are extremely limited. At the parking area for the Hidden Valley Trail and Jackson River there's a large signboard with a trailmap brochure available. This provides a good overview of the trail network but should not be substituted for a topo map.

**activities:** Hiking, Mountain Biking, Fishing, Camping

**hiking:** Approximately 21 miles of trails fan out NE and NW from the Hidden Valley Campground. Some of the most appealing trails on the district, they povide access to the all of the area's diverse habitats: hardwood and conifer forests, riparian corridors, agricultural fields, meadows, and mountain ridges. Trailheads are clearly marked and are at 2 locations, in the campground and at a large parking area just across the Jackson River from the Warwick Mansion. Most of the trails connect and can be reached from either trailhead, but in general if you want to hike upstream along the Jackson River it's best to start from the Warwick Mansion Access. Plus you'll get a good view of the antebellum manor from there. The manor is now run as a B&B and its grounds are closed to the public. Access to the trails in the campground is from a large parking area across from site #28. *Lost Woman Trail* begins here. The trails in this area follow a combination of old roadbeds and single-tracks. Some are blazed and all are easy to follow. Hiking is easy to moderate. Trail use moderate except on the Hidden Valley Trail below the swinging bridge, where it's heavy. All trails are open to bikes, many are open to horses. The former are popular, particularly on the Jackson River trails.

**mountain biking:** Hidden Valley is without doubt one of the most scenic and charming areas in the Commonwealth to explore by mountain bike. Whether you choose to ride on paved roads, dirt and gravel forest roads, or the area's extensive trail network, the combinations of little traffic, good road and trail conditions, and exceptional scenery are bound to please. All of the area's trails are open to bikes, and better yet, most have treadways that are well maintained and easy to ride. The *Hidden Valley Trail* and the trails areound the campground are especially ideal for riding. They can be used in combination with FR-241 to create long loops. Although backcountry bike/camp trips are certainly possible here, it probably makes more sense to use the Hidden Valley Campground as a base from which to explore the area, as it provides more flexibility. Riding on the roads and trails in the valley is easy. As you move upstream or onto the mountain ridges, riding becomes moderate. See above under "hiking" for trailheads and a fuller description of the trails.

**fishing:** By the standards of Virginia trout waters, the Jackson River is big water. No fly-fisherman will want to complete a trip to the area without fishing this gorgeous river. Flowing down out of Highland Co, it's one of the major drainages of the Allegheny Highlands. Where it flows through Hidden Valley it's a large river with a mild gradient and shallow flow. Cover varies considerably. In some places the river flows through open fields, elsewhere there's forest cover. Access to the river is from either the *River Loop Trail*, which begins in the campground, or from the *Hidden Valley Trail*. The latter is preferred, as it permits easy access upstream for 5 miles. Regulations on the river are single-hook, artificial lures only. It's stocked trout waters. Fishing pressure is moderate.

On the other side of VA-39 is another trout creek well known by Virginia's fly-fishing afficionados. Like the Jackson, Back Creek is a relatively large stream. It flows over a mild gradient and a very rocky bed that forms some large pools. The cover varies, with large sections of the banks open and grassy or lined with rock formations. Back Creek is stocked trout waters. Access is from the Blowing Springs Rec Area on SR-600 and from *Back Creek Gorge Trail*, which begins at the back of the campground. Fishing pressure is moderate.

**camping:** Primitive backcountry camping is permitted on national forest lands except where posted. In addition to the backcountry, there are 2 primitive car campgrounds in the area—Blowing Springs and Hidden Valley.

The Hidden Valley Campground has 30 sites on a level, sparsely forested area not far from the Jackson River. Sites are large and well spaced, offering a good amount of privacy. Each site has a picnic table, grill, and lantern post. There are pit toilets and water spigots in the campground. Sites cost $4/night. Use is light to moderate. The campground is open from Mar 15 to Jan 1.

Blowing Springs has 23 sites in a large 2-level clearing beside Back Creek. The sites are large and well spaced. Privacy is quite good here, particularly because the campground is frequently empty. Each site has a picnic table and grill. There are pit toilets and a hand water pump in the area. Sites cost $4/night. The campground is open from Mar 15 to Jan 1.

# Beards Mountain Area

The Beards Mountain Area occupies a large rectangular tract of national forest land north of Douthat State Park and south of VA-39. The Cowpasture River forms a natural boundary to the east and US-220 runs parallel to the area to the west. Also forming part of the southern boundary is the James River Ranger District. Apart from the Rough Mountain Wilderness, the extensive backcountry here offers the best opportunity for wilderness solitude. The roads that cross through the area see little traffic and most of the hikers who come to the region are content to wander the trails of Douthat State Park. That leaves the door open to backpackers looking for an overnight trip through forested uplands. Of course day trips are possible too. Equally appealing is to explore the area from a mountain bike. The isolated, unpaved roads seem ready-made for bikers looking for the challenge of semi-mountainous terrain without the difficulties of single-track trails not groomed for bike traffic. Longer trips are possible by crossing into the park or forest lands adjacent to the south of the area.

Clifton Forge (S) is the closest city. Limited services are available in Warm Springs (NW), Hot Springs (W), and Millboro Springs (E).

**getting there:** There are numerous access points to this area. VA-39 forms the N boudary. From its jct with US-220 E of Warm Springs, go E 4.2 mi to gated FR-364 (a hiking or biking access), R. Continue ahead on VA-39 2.2 mi to SR-683. Turn R onto the dirt and gravel road and go 0.6 mi to a jct with FR-1745 and a trailhead. Or go 1.4 mi further E on VA-39 to SR-629 (Douthat Park Rd). Turn R and go 1.3 mi to FR-194, a good starting point for mountain biking trips in the area. E on VA-39 from the turn onto SR-629 it's 5.1 mi to VA-42 and the crossroads town of Millboro Springs.

**topography:** The mountainous terrain here lacks a single defining feature. Instead there are a series of smaller summits: Little Mare Mtn, Brushy Ridge, Beards Mtn, and Middle Mtn. The terrain is relatively mild in most areas, with elevations between 4,000 and 1,600 ft. Hardwood forest covers most of the acreage. **maps:** USGS–FS Healing Spring, Warm Springs, Nimrod Hall, Bathalum.

**starting out:** This is a large backcountry area with no facilities. The campground in Douthat State Park on the area's S perimeter makes an excellent basecamp for those who want to explore the area, but would rather not backpack. Facilities in the park include restrooms, water, pay phones, and a restaurant.

**activities:** Hiking, Mountain Biking, Camping

**hiking:** A network of 9 trails covers 32 miles of forested mountain terrain. The trails connect with the 40-mi trail network in Douthat State Park and the Fore Mtn Area on the James River RD. Hikes of almost any lenght up to 50 miles are easily planned by combining several trails in 2 or 3 of these areas. Where trail connections do not exist, they can often be created by hiking along abandoned or open roads that see little or no vehicle traffic. Highlights along the trails in the NF are the scenic views from overlooks and the remote forested setting. The chance of observing wildlife is good. There are numerous trailheads in the area. You can use one of those described above or start your trek in Douthat SP. Whatever you decide, be sure to bring a good topographic map of the area. Most of the trails are easy to locate and follow, though there are some obscure sections and jcts with hunter's trails and old roadbeds can make matters confusing. Hiking is moderate to strenuous. Trail use is light to moderate.

**mountain biking:** There are outstanding opportunities throughout the backcountry here for mountain biking, on trails and open and gated forest roads. The main artery is FR-194, a dirt and gravel road that parallels paved SR-629. It connects with a number of trails and gated roads, and, after a short connection on SR-629, with FR-125, another unpaved road that crosses into the James River RD and runs S all the way to Covington. None of the trails in the area are officially closed to mountain biking; nevertheless, most are unsuitable for one reason or another. 2 exceptions are the Beards Mtn and Beards Mtn Spur Trails. Together they cover 8 miles of mountainous terrain from a trailhead on SR-629. In all, there are more than 30 miles of trails and roads suitable to riding in the area. Riding is easy to moderate. Use is light, by both bikes and motor vehicles. The trails in Douthat SP are closed to bikes.

**camping:** Primitive backcountry camping is permitted throughout the area on national forest lands except where posted. Most of the trails in the are are suitable for backpacking trips.

# Rough Mountain Wilderness Area

This are encompasses two large rectangles on national forest land, the 9,300-acre designated wilderness and a slightly larger tract adjacent to the southeast. Although the small town of Millboro is located at the northeastern entrance to the area, this large backcountry area is almost completely devoid of human impact. An unpaved road and a RR line rund through its interior and there's a small recreation area used by picnickers and campers, but the rest of the area is forested mountains and small creeks. Thae situation is ideal for the area's wildlife. Among the inhabitant's here are black bear, white-tailed deer, and wild turkey. For outdoor recreation, there's hiking, biking, camping, and fishing. Despite the variety, there really isn't a whole lot of any one activity. There's a single short hiking trail, a primitive camping area with just 3 sites, a small trout creek, and about a dozen miles of forest roads for mountain biking. Maybe it's best to come to this area with a field guide or a camera with zoom lens and study the wildlife that makes its home in the undisturbed backcountry.

Millboro (NE) and Clifton Forge (SW) are the closest towns.

**getting there:** From I-64, take exit 43. Turn W onto SR-780/850 and go 0.3 mi to SR-850. Turn L and go 0.8 mi to SR-780. Turn R and go 1.8 mi to dirt and gravel SR-633. Turn L and go 4.1 mi to FR-129. Turn L and go 1 mi to the Bubbling Springs Rec Area. Ahead on FR-129 it's 5.1 mi to the signed trailhead to the *Crane Trail*, R. Parking is very limited. • From the jct of VA-39 and VA-42: go S on VA-42 50 yds to SR-633. Turn L and go 5.8 mi (at 5.1 mi the pavement ends) through downtown Millboro Springs to FR-129. Turn R and go 1 mi to the rec area entrance, L.

**topography:** Although the elevations here are hardly exceptions, Rough Mountain is aptly named. The upper mountain slopes are rugged and steep. Forest cover includes both conifers and hardwood species. Elevations are between 1,500 ft on Pads Creek and 2,900 ft along the mountain's summit. **maps:** USGS–FS Nimrod Hall

**starting out:** The Bubbling Springs Rec Area makes a nice, primitive basecamp for exporing the wilderness. The picnic/camping area is almost always empty, and there's a hand water pump and pit toilet there.

Group size in the wilderness is limited to 10.

**activities:** Hiking, Camping, Mountain Biking, Fishing

**hiking:** The single hiking trail in the area is the 3-mi *Crane Trail*. After following a RR line from its trailhead on FR-129, it turns NW and climbs steeply up to the summit of Rough Mtn where there are good views. From there it drops down the other side of the mtn to VA-42. Hiking on the trail is moderate to strenuous. Trail use is light.

**camping:** Campers in the area have several options. For the most primitive camping, hike into the wilderness and make camp along the Crane Trail. No-trace camping is permitted throughout the wilderness.

If you arrive too late to backpack in or just can't bear to part with your car, there are still a couple of options. Primitive car camping is permitted at Bubbling Springs, although it isn't technically a campground. There are 3 sites at the edge of a clearing there, each with a picnic table and grill. A pit toilet and hand water pump are located in the area. There's no fee to camp there are it's open all year. Another option for car campers is to park at one of the roadside pullouts along FR-129 and make camp along Pads Creek. There are no designated sites or facilities here, but the understory is mostly open and finding a site is not difficult. This area is also a good bet for mountain bikers who want to camp.

**mountain biking:** Riding in this area is on a pair of forest roads, one of which is maintained, one of which is not. FR-129 can be ridden for almost 8 miles between SR-633 and the railroad tracks. At the tracks the road dead ends at SR-630, which follows the tracks SW to VA-42, a distance of 4 miles. Conditions along most of this road are very rugged and challenging, although the road is quite level. Riding throughout the area is easy to moderate. Bikes are not allowed in the Rough Mountain Wilderness. This is an O.K. area for a short ride, but not much more.

**fishing:** Trout anglers who come to the area will want to try their luck in Pads Creek. The smallish creek meanders SW over a very rocky bed and large rock ledges that produce a mild to average gradient with some nice pools. The forest cover of both banks is quite dense. The creek is stocked for the fishable portion along FR-129, a distance of 8 miles. Access is from the road, which has numerous pullouts.

# Locust Springs Recreation Area

Located at the end of Virginia is Highland County, Locust Springs is the most out-of-the-way backcountry area on the George Washington National Forest. Its remote location is fitting, as its backcountry seems to belong to another world anyway. The highland forest is dominated by tree species unusual for Virginia, including red spruce, hemlock, beech, birch, cherry, and maple. Cool mountain streams flow through the open understory, dropping down out of the mounatins to feed Laurel Fork, the area's major drainage and one of the creeks that feeds the Potomac River, whose headwaters are here. This is an area designed for hikers and backpackers. The extensive backcountry is criss-crossed by linear clearings left by the trams that once hauled timber from the area. Today these tramlines have been converted into a large network of hiking trails that extends into all corners of the area. Wildlife in the area is abundant and frequently seen. Beavers are particularly numerous. White-tailed deer, black bear, snowshore rabbit, mink, and muskrat are also present. The Locust Springs Area is ideally suited to a weekend trip, though longer visits won't disappoint.

Bartow, WV (SW) and Monterey, VA (SE) are the closest towns.

**getting there:** From the jct of US-220 and US-250 in Monterey, take US-250 W 20.5 mi (at 13.7 mi enter WV) to WV-28. Turn R and go 6.7 mi to FR-106. Turn R and go 1.2 mi to the rec area and parking lot.

**topography:** Elevations in the area are between 2,700 and 4,100 ft. Part of the Allegheney Highlands, an upland mountain plateau. The mountain slopes in the area are varied, with some steep sections but mostly milder grades. Numerous small drainages meander through the forests of northern conifers and hardwoods. **maps:** USGS Thornwood, Snowy Mountain.

**starting out:** Be sure to bring whatever you need with you, as the closest large town is 30 miles away. Facilities in this remote area are limited, but you'll find a hand water pump and pit toilet in the picnic area.

**activities:** Hiking, Camping, Fishing

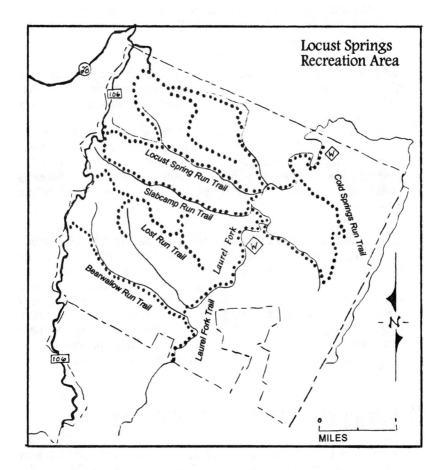

**hiking:** The outstanding trail network here covers 28 miles, extending into all areas of the backcountry and permitting exploration of the full range of this magnificent environment. The trails mostly follow old tram lines, which means they take the path of least resistance. Since water does the same, most of the trails follow one of the many streams that drain the area. Access to all trails is from the main parking area. From there, the trails fan out to the E and S. Most trails run E-W; the *Laurel Fork Run Trail*, which crosses the area from S to N, is the major exception. Trail connections are numerous, and loop hikes of almost any length are imaginable. Most trails are blazed and easy to follow. The main trailhead and trail jcts are signed. Hiking is easy to moderate. Trail use is moderate.

**camping:** Primitive car camping is possible at the parking area, where there are scattered tables and grills. Also there is an AT-style shelter. A hand water pump and pit toilet are the only facilities in the area.

To really experience the wonders of the area, however, it's best to leave your car behind and venture into the backcountry. Low-impact camping is permitted throughout the area, and the generally open understory makes finding a site easy. Water is abundant along most of the trails, but should be treated before drinking.

**fishing:** Laurel Fork is a native brook trout fishery. The large creek runs through the area for 7 miles from S to N before eventually joining the Potomac River. The stream is exceptionally scenic, with a rocky bed, deep pools, and a mild to average gradient. Cover varies, with sections of the banks forested and others grassy meadow. Access from a hiking trail which follows it for its entire length. Getting to Laurel Fork requires a 3-mi hike from the main trailhead described above. This is one of the best opportunities to fish a remote, wild trout stream in all of Virginia.

# Highland Wildlife Management Area

Located in remote, isolated Highland County, this 14,283 acre preserve encompasses part of the fertile Bullpasture River valley and the Allegheny Mountain ridges and summits that surround it. The management area is split between two major landholdings, one on each side of the river. A short section of the river—the beautiful Bullpasture River Gorge—actually flows along the southern boundary of one of the tracts. The river provides anglers with some of the most exciting fishing in the Allegheny Highlands. Hunters know the area too. The backcountry is managed to provide habitat for game species such as black bear, white-tailed deer, and wild turkey. Backcountry travelers will appreciate the network of seeded roadbeds and hiking trails that criss-cross the area. The roads can be traveled on foot or mountain bike; the trails are only suitable for hiking. With so many acres to explore, a backpacking trip is a good way to get on familiar terms with some of the more remote spots on the WMA. With no facilities and a backcountry that gets left in a pretty primitive state, this area is best suited to those who like their outdoor trips to be just a little bit challenging.

McDowell is the closest town.

**contact:** Highland WMA, P.O. Box 996, Verona, VA 24482; 540/248-9360

**getting there:** There are several access points to the 2 parts of the WMA. To reach the NW section: from US-250 in McDowell, turn S onto SR-678 and go 2.7 mi to SR-615. Turn R and go 1.7 mi to a parking area and gated road. To reach the SE section: continue S on SR-678 3.2 mi to SR-612. Turn L and 0.3 mi to a river ford. Park there beside the road (or with 4WD cross and park at a gated road, R). To reach the main access to the SE section, continue S on SR-678 5.6 mi past SR-612 to a large parking area at a swinging bridge across the Bullpasture River, L.

**topography:** Terrain on the WMA combines the almost-flat bottomland of the Bullpasture River with the mountain ridges and coves of the Alleghenies. The mountain topography includes areas of both mild and steep slopes. Forest cover is a mixture of southern and northern hardwood and conifer species. Elevations are between 1,800 ft and 4,390 ft on Sounding Knob. **maps:** USGS Williamsville, Monterey Southeast.

**starting out:** This is a large backcountry area with no facilities. Surface water is abundant in the backcountry, but should be treated before drinking. Hunting takes place here in the fall and winter. If you come during those seasons, wear blaze orange.

**activities:** Hiking, Fishing, Camping, Mountain Biking

**hiking:** There are plenty of trails and gated roadbeds that provide access to the heart of the management area. None of them is signed or blazed, however, so you'll need to approach hiking on them with an intedpendent mind. Despite the lack of markings, the trails really aren't that difficult to located and follow. In fact, with a good map you should have no difficulty in navigating the area. In any event, it's worth the effort, as the WMA provides some of the most scenic country in the Allegheny Highlands. Trail highlights include the Bullpasture Gorge, dense hardwood forests, and the pastoral valley. It's hard to guage the number of miles of roads and trails, but in all there's probably at least 30 miles to explore. Hiking is easy to moderate. Trail use is light, except during hunting season.

**fishing:** Anglers have the option of trout fishing on big water or small. By any reckoning the Bullpasture River is a beautiful body of water where it passes through Bullpasture Gorge. 20 to 50 feet across and flowing beneath rock walls and towering hemlocks, the river features both rapids and long, deep pools. This is big trout water that should excite even the most jaded fly-fisherman. The only drawback to this stretch of the river is that SR-678 follows closely along one bank. Of course the road makes access very easy. There's a parking area at the swinging bridge. From there you can follow the river by wading or hiking along the bank. The river's gradient is mild and pooling is outstanding. There are about 4 miles of fishable water on public land. The river is stocked. Fishing pressure is moderate.

In the NW section of the WMA, Davis Run is a small stream with an average gradient, rocky bed, and thick forest cover. One of the WMA roads (open to motor vehicles) runs beside the creek for about a mile, providing access. From there. you can wade upstream for another mile or two. This is a native brook trout fishery with tight casting conditions. Fishing pressure is light.

**camping:** Primitive backcountry camping is permitted anywhere on the WMA except where posted. Finding a site is not difficult in most areas.

**mountain biking:** A mountain bike is the perfect vehicle for exploring the WMA's 20 miles of gated and open roads. Riding conditions vary with the surface; in general conditions are good, but with a few unimproved river crossings. Riding in the NW section is moderate; in the SE section it's easy. The layout of the roads doesn't really lend itself to loop rides; some backtracking is inevitable. If you get tired of riding on the dirt and gravel roads of the WMA, SR-678 is a paved road that runs the length of the Bullpasture River between McDowell and Williamsville in Bath Co. The valley is exceptionally scenic and the winding road doesn't see much traffic. It's about a 5-mile ride from on section of the WMA to the other.

# Deerfield Ranger District

## George Washington National Forest

The Deerfield Ranger District encompasses 164,183 acres of mountain uplands and river valleys in the Alllegany Mountains. District lands form a rough rectangle in Highland, Augusta, and Rockbridge Counties. The scenic Calfpasture River, which mostly flows through a narrow valley of private farm land, divides the district in half. The Deerfield is a region of remote mountain summits covered in thick forests. At the northern end is the 6,519-acre Ramsey's Draft Wilderness, the district's only designated wilderness. The mountains and coves provide habitat for a wide range of wildlife, including white-tailed deer, black bear, and wild turkey. Opportunities for outdoor recreation are excellent, with long hiking and backpacking trips particularly well favored by the extensive trail network. There's lots of room for backcountry solitude on the trails, with some outstanding mountain scenery along several of the ridge trails. Fly-fisherman can pursue native trout on Ramsey's Draft, a beautiful mountain stream that runs through the wilderness of the same name. Without a developed campground on the district, campers take to the trails. The Deerfield Ranger District's combination of vast backcountry acreage and primitive conditions makes it perfect for a weekend or extended backpacking trip.

Monterey (W), Staunton (E), and Harrisonburg (NE) are the closest cities.

**contact:** Deerfield Ranger District, U.S. Forest Service, Route 6, Box 419, Staunton, VA 24401; 540/885-8028.

**getting there:** US-250 crosses the district in its N half. US-220 runs parallel to the W, while I-81 and VA-42 parallel it to the E. The district RS is located on VA-254 on the E edge of Staunton (exit 222 off I-81).

**topography:** A pair of lofty mountain ridges separated by the narrow Calfpasture River Valley describes the district topography. Elevations are higher on the E half, where Elliot Knob reaches 4,463 ft, the district's highest point. **maps:** USFS Deerfield Ranger District; USGS topo maps are listed below under the separate headings.

**starting out:** You can pick up district maps, trail maps, and brochures at the district RS in Staunton. They're open from 8 AM to 4:30 PM weekdays.

**activities:** Hiking, Mountain Biking, Camping, Fishing, Canoeing

**hiking:** Hiking is the area of outdoor recreation where the Deerfield RD really shines. Each of the 3 areas described below features an extensive trail network that beckons both day-hikers and backpackers. Of the 124 miles of trails listed in the district inventory, a little more than 100 are about evenly divided among these 3 areas. Conditions throughout the district are primitive.

**mountain biking:** Both the Shenandoah Mountain Area and the North Mountain Area offer bikers plenty of miles to cover. On the former area, riding is on a combination of trails and forest roads, with long challenging rides possible by connecting the two. On the latter area, riding is confined to the roads, but the rugged mountain terrain keeps the riding anything but tame.

**camping:** Each of the 3 areas described below offers excellent opportunities for primitive backcountry camping. Backpacking trips of 2 days to a week are possible at each. Ramsey's Draft Wilderness is the most popular area.
Deerfield is the only district on the GWNF that doesn't have a developed campground.

**fishing:** Opportunities for angling on the district are limited. Backcountry fly-fishermen will enjoy fishing for native brook trout in a remote wilderness setting on Ramsey's Draft. At the other end of the spectrum, Braley Pond offers no-sweat fishing on a small impoundment that's just a short walk from the parking area.

**canoeing:** Braley Pond offers the only navigable water in the areas described below. Unfortunately its only a small impoundment used mostly be local fishermen.

# Shenandoah Mountain Area

Apart from the mountain that's the dominant physical feature of the area, the defining feature of this area is the *Shenandoah Mountain Trail*. Following the mountain's crest ridge for the entire length of the district, the trail provides access to a large backcountry area that encompasses a third of the district's total acreage. A pair of valleys—Cowpasture to the west and Deerfield to the east—lie at the moutain's bottom and define the area. US-250 forms the area's northern limit, providing access to the trail and a historical site. In 1862 Confederate soldiers dug a series of breastworks into the mountain. Still visible today as shallow ditches, you can see them from a short loop trail with interpretive placards. Apart from military history, the area's main attraction is the chance to take a muti-day trek into remote wilderness. The long, multi-use trail makes it possible to hike, bike, or ride into the remote backcountry on Shenandoah Mountain. With no facilities and few visitors, this is the place to come if you're looking for solitude and the challenges vast backcountry.

Staunton (E) is the closest city.

**getting there:** Easiest highway access to the trail is from US-250. From Staunton (exit 222 off I-81) take US-250 W approximately 26 mi to a parking area at the Confederate Breastworks (2 mi W of the Mountain House Rec Area) and trail access. • To reach the S terminus: from the jct of VA-39 and VA-42, take VA-39 W 7.9 mi to Millboro Springs and SR-633 (Pig Run Rd). Turn R and go 7.7 mi (at 4.3 mi the pavement ends) to paved SR-629. Turn R and go 1.2 mi to dirt and gravel SR-627 (Scotchtown Draft). Turn L and go 2.5 mi to the trailhead and small parking area, R.

**topography:** Terrain on Shenandoah Mountain is steep and rugged is most places, with numerous areas of exposed rock and cliff faces. The forest cover consists of both hardwoods and conifers, with northern and souther species represented. Elevations on the mountain reach 3,800 ft. **maps:** USGS McDowell, Deerfield, Williamsville, Green Valley.

**starting out:** Facilities along the trail and in the backcountry are very limited. There are pit toilets at the confederate breastworks and water 2 mi E of there at Mountain House Rec Area. Surface water is available along the trail, but it should be treated before drinking.

**activities:** Hiking, Camping. Mountain Biking

**hiking:** This area is defined by a single, multi-use trail—the 31-mile *Shenandoah Mountain Trail*. The trail runs in a straight line along the ridgetops of the eponymous mountain between SR-627 to the south and the Dry Run RD to the north. US-250 bisects the trail near the Ramsey's Draft Wilderness and provides the easiest access. The trail follows a combination of paths, including seeded roadbeds and single-track. In addition to offering backpackers the best chance in the area for a multi-day hike, the trail is open to equestrians and mountain bikes. Highlights along the trail, which is the longest on the district, are scenic vistas to the west and east and remote solitude. Although there are easy and moderate stretches along the trail, the rugged mountain terrain it passes through makes hiking generally strenuous. The trail is blazed with yellow diamonds at regular intervals and is not difficult to follow. Trailheads are signed. Use is moderate. If you're hiking S from the Confederate Breastworks on US-250, the trail begins 100 yds E on gated FR-396. Before hiking the Shenandoah Mtn Trail, check out the short *Confederate Breastworks Trail* that begins at the small parking area.

**camping:** Primitive backcountry camping is permitted throughout the area, except where posted otherwise. The Shenandoah Mountain Trail and the primitive roads that cross and parallel it offer plenty of opportunity for backpack or mountain bike camping.

**mountain biking:** With miles of gated roadbeds, rarely traveled forest roads, and the S section of the *Shenandoah Mountain Trail* (24 miles), this is the best area on the district for mountain biking. Conditions vary considerably depending on the surface, but one factor is constant: mountainous terrain. At the easier end of the scale are the forest roads that are open to motor vehicles. Most of these are near the S end of the area. The longest is FR-394, a twisting dirt and gravel road that parallels the trail for its lower 12 mi. For more arduous conditions—including sections where dismountaing is necessary—you can ride the *Shenandoah Mountain Trail* itself. The trail follows sections of road, old roadbeds, and single-track, creating a variety of challenging riding conditions. Short connector trails make it possible to ride both the trail and the forest roads, with several loop rides possible. The best starting point for riding the Shenandoah Mountain Area is on

SR-627, at either the S terminus of the trail or at the jct with FR-394. Avoid using the district topo map for navigating the roads, as it isn't particularly accurate. The GWNF road map is better, but it isn't a topo.

# Ramsey's Draft Wilderness Area

Located between US-250 and the Dry River Ranger District, Ramsey's Draft Wilderness takes its name from the drainage that flows south off of Shenandoah Mountain and empties into the Calfpasture River. The lone designated wilderness on the district, it covers 6,519 acres of forested mountain terrain that is a refuge for backpackers, fly-fishermen, nature photographers, hikers, and wildlife. Among the diverse species of flora and fauna that inhabit the ridges and coves are black bear, wild turkey, and white-tailed deer. Also present is a large tract of virgin timber, with hemlocks and hardwoods more than 300 years old. The wilderness offers the best opportunity on the district to encounter the natural world in its most unaltered state. Outside the wilderness but still in the general vicinity is Braley Pond, a small impoundment stocked with trout. A picnic area there has tables, grills, water, and a pit toilet. Immediately outside the wilderness in Mountain House, another small picnic area. Its scraggly appearance and location right beside US-250 make it rather unappealing, but it does have a hand water pump and pit toilet. Ramsey's Draft Wilderness is ideal for a weekend backpacking trip.

Staunton (E) is the closest city.

**getting there:** From Staunton, take US-250 W approximately 24 mi to FR-68 and the Mountain House Rec Area and access to the wilderness via hiking trail. Turn R and go 0.1 mi to the parking area and trailhead. Another access is from the Braley Pond Rec Area, located 4 miles E of the wilderness. To reach it, take US-250 W from Staunton 19 mi to SR-715. Turn R and go 0.4 mi to FR-348.1. Turn L and go 0.6 mi to the rec area entrance, L.

**topography:** The mountain terrain throughout the wilderness is rugged and steep. Forest cover is predominatly northern hardwood species, with some conifers present, particularly along the major drainages. Elevations are between 2,200 ft on Ramsey's Draft and 4,282 on Hardscrabble Knob. **maps:** USFS Ramsey's Draft Wilderness; USGS West Augusta, Palo Alto.

**starting out:** Facilities are located just outside the wilderness at the Mountain House Rec Area. There are pit toilets there and a hand water pump. The same facilities are also at the Braley Pond Rec Area. A signboard with a wilderness map is located at the wilderness entrance.

Group size in the wilderness cannot exceed 10. Swimming in Braley Pond is prohibited.

**activities:** Hiking, Fishing, Camping, Canoeing

**hiking:** A 32-mile network of trails crisscrosses the wilderness, allowing hikers and backpackers to explore all of its corners. Trails range in length from short connectors to the 8-mi Bald Ridge Trail and 7-mi Ramsey's Draft Trail. Most of the trails connect, but the few loop hikes that are possible are quite long. Day-hikes along most routes will inevitably involve backtracking. On the other hand, with connections to trail networks on the Dry River RD and the *Shenandoah Mountain Trail*, hikes of several days to a week are possible. Trail highlights in the wilderness include the primitive conditions, lush hardwood and conifer forests, and a good chance to observe wildlife. Creek crossings are not improved and must be done by rock hopping or wading. At high water this may be difficult or impossible. The main trailhead is just N of the Mountain House Rec Area. Other access points are along the *Shenandoah Mountain Trail* and *Wild Oak Trail*, both of which skirt the wilderness. Hiking ranges from easy to strenuous, depending on elevations and number or water crossings. Trail use is light to moderate.

**fishing:** Ramsey's Draft supports a native population of brook trout. Although the creek flows through pristine wilderness, its course and channel have been radically altered over the past 50 years by a series of floods associated with tropical storms. The size of the stream varies considerably depending on the time of year and water level. In summer it is often a small creek that happens to flow down a very wide channel; In late winter and early spring it is a large river that is impossible to cross in many places. Despite these fluctuations, Ramsey's Draft offers the opportunity to fish for wild brook trout in a beautiful wilderness setting. Access to the stream is via the *Ramsey's Draft Trail*, which follows it upstream for almost 10 miles. Only artificial lures with single hooks can be used.

Braley Pond offers a less rugged and more easily accessible

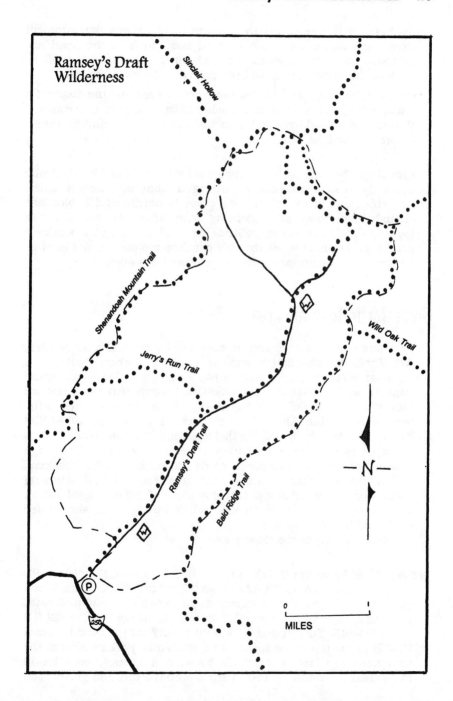

Ramsey's Draft
Wilderness

Sinclair Hollow

Shenandoah Mountain Trail

Jerry's Run Trail

Ramsey's Draft Trail

Bald Ridge Trail

Wild Oak Trail

—N—

0                    1
MILES

fishing experience. You can fish the small, scenic impoudment from the shoreline or from a small boat. Fish in the pond are rainbow trout, largemouth bass, channel catfish, and sunfish. Underwater structures have been placed to improve fish habitat.

**camping:** Ramsey's Draft is the most popular area on the district for backpacking trips. Primitive backcountry camping is permitted throughout the wilderness. It is not allowed in the Mountain House or Braley Pond Rec Areas.

**canoeing:** The only paddling opportunity is on Braley Pond. Really the only reason to bother putting a boat on such a small impoundment is to fish it. The pond is scenic and a pleasant enough place to spend a morning or an afternoon, but if you're looking for backcountry solitude or a place to get a workout paddling, this isn't it. Boats with gasoline motors are not allowed on the lake. The portage from the parking lot is about 100 yds.

# Great North Mountain Area

This large backcountry area is bounded by the Calfpasture River (W), VA-42 (E), US-250 (N), and the district's southern limit. It is a mountainous area dominated by two long ridges that lie along the familiar northeast–southwest axis: Great North Mtn and Crawford Mtn. Both are part of the Alleghenies, a large chain that lies to the west of the Blue Ridge. The district's highest summit—Elliot Knob—is found on Great North Mountain. Outdoor recreation in the area is focused on primitive backcountry travel. The large network of trails and unpaved roads attract hikers, backpackers, and mountain bikers. Nature photographers will find sweeping vistas and the possibility of catching some of the area's wildlife on film. Black bears, wild turkey, white-tailed deer, and ruffed grouse all inhabit the area.

Craigsville (E) is the closest town.

**getting there:** From the N: take VA-254 W 7.1 mi from the district RS to VA-42. Bear L onto VA-42 and go 0.7 mi to SR-688. Turn R and go 4 mi (at 0.6 mi the pavement ends) to the trailhead and small parking area. • To reach another access, continue S on VA-42 8.2 mi to SR-845. Turn R and go 4.8 mi (at 0.7 mi the road becomes FR-82) to the top of the mountain and a small parking area at the trail crossing.• From the S: Take VA-42 N from its jct with VA-39 in Goshen 6.1 mi to SR-687. Turn L onto the dirt and gravel road and go 2.6 mi to the S terminus of the North Mtn Trail, R. Or continue N on VA-42 6.1 mi to SR-845. Follow directions above to the trailhead and parking area.

**topography:** The terrain is a combination of rugged, steep upper slopes and much milder lower slopes where mountain and valley meet. Forest cover consists of northern and southern species of hardwoods, with some conifers also present. Elevation reaches 4,463 ft on Elliot Knob. Low point is about 1,600 ft. **maps:** USGS-FS Elliott Knob, Craigsville, W Augusta, Stokesville.

**starting out:** This is a large backcountry area with no facilities. Services are available in the small towns along VA-42. Surface water is not readily available along the major trails. Plan on bringing enough with you or hiking down a side trail until you reach a water source. Surface water should be treated before drinking.

**activities:** Hiking, Mountain Biking, Camping

**hiking:** A 32-mile trail network is anchored by a pair of trails laid end to end, forming a single long trail. The 14.4-mi *North Mountain Trail* and the 8-mi *Crawford Mountain Trail* together span the entire area from US-250 to the Rockbridge Co line. Side trails branch off, connecting the main artery with various roads in the area. While this layout makes loop hikes more or less impossible, it does provide the opportunity to enter deep into remote, mountainous backcountry. Add to that the fact that this is the least visited area on the district, and the potential for a high-quality backcountry trip is high. Along with the remoteness, several vantage points offer spectacular vistas. The trails follow both narrow footpaths and old roadbeds. Blazes exist, but the trails are generally not well marked. The same goes for trailheads, most of which are not signed. Hiking is moderate to strenuous. Trail use is light. Trail maps with descriptions of these trails are available from the district RS

**mountain biking:** A series of forest roads that cross Great North Mountain and wind along its lower slopes makes this one of the better areas on the district for riding. Riding is moderate to strenuous. Long loop rides are possible by using sections of VA-42 or SR-600 and SR-629, all of which are paved. The forest roads are all maintained, though conditions are primitive and traffic virtually nonexistent. The terrain is mountainous (except on the paved roads that run through valleys) and riding is moderate to strenuous. Avoid using the district map for backcountry navigation. Its accuracy leaves much to be desired. The 3 trail access points described above are all good places to begin rides.

**camping:** Primitive backcountry camping is permitted throughout the area on national forest lands, except where posted. Sites should be at least 100 ft from roads and trails.

# Goshen–Little North Mountain WMA

Covering more than 33,500 acres of upland terrain at the eastern edge of the Allegheny Mountains, Goshen–Little North Mountain is the largest wildlife management area in the state. The national park of national forest proportions make it a paradise for backcountry travelers. Its lands spread out in two main parcels, with the rugged and scenic Maury River flowing between them. The eastern half has a long, narrow profile on the summit ridge and slopes of the eponymous mountain. The other tract is squarish in shap, and occupies a series of small, steep mountains. Forest cover is consistent across the WMA, and consists primarily of hardwoods. Although the areas is managed primarily for wildlife habitat—white-tailed deer, black bear, and wild turkey are all present—hikers, backpackers, anglers, and mountain bikers will find plenty to occupy their time. An extensive network of gated roads and foot trails provides access to all parts of the WMA. There are numerous access points, and backcountry trips of almost any length can be pieced together. There are is maintained in a primitive state, and there are no facilities such as visitor centers or campgrounds to draw crowds. Except during hunting season, the magnificent backcountry is practically deserted. This is a good destination for weekend backpacking, fishing, or mountain biking trips.

Goshen (NW) and Staunton (NE) are the closest towns.

**contact:** Goshen–Little North Mountain WMA, P.O. Box 996, Verona, VA 24482; 540/248-9360.

**getting there:** There are 3 access points for the SW section of the WMA. From the jct of US-11 and VA-39 NE of Lexington, turn NW onto VA-39. Go 13.5 mi to the Laurel Run Access, L or 17 mi to the Guys Run Access, also L. Or continue straight ahead 1.4 mi to SR-780. Turn L and go 4.2 mi to the Gochenour Branch Access, L. • There are several access points along the long, narrow NE section of the WMA. From the jct of VA-39 and VA-42 in the community of Goshen, take VA-42 N 9.4 mi to SR-687. Turn R and go 0.1 mi to SR-684. Turn L and go 2.8 mi to SR-601. Turn L and go 3.2 mi to a gated road and small parking area, R. Or continue N on VA-42 from the jct with SR-687 in Craigsville to other access points at 5.9 mi and 7.3 mi. Both are gated roads with small parking areas, R.nd go 2.6 mi to a gated road and small parking area, L.

**topography:** Much of the WMA terrain consists of a narrow ridge of forested mountain slopes between fertile valleys given over to agriculture. Elevations are between 3,400 ft and 1,300 ft on the Maury River. **maps:** USGS Augusta Springs, Elliott Knob, Goshen, Millboro.

**starting out:** This is a vast backcountry area with no facilities and no development of any kind. A map of the area showing trails and access points is available by calling or writing the address above. Water is abundant in the backcountry, but all surface water should be treated before drinking. Hunting takes place in the fall and winter. Visitors should wear blaze orange during that period.

**activities:** Hiking, Mountain Biking, Camping, Fishing

**hiking/mountain biking:** The WMA is laced by a network of gated roads well suited to both hiking and riding. Because of the WMA's shape and the layout of the roads, loops are not really an option, so some backtracking is inevitable. You probably won't mind though, since that means you'll simply get to take in the scenery twice. The roads are well defined and easy to locate and follow. Access points are all clearly signed (directions given above). The main highlights on the trails are the lush forest setting and the opportunity to observe wildlife. There are approximately 25 miles of trails in all.

**camping:** Primitive backcountry camping is permitted throughout the WMA, except where posted. The whole area offers excellent opportunities for backcountry travel.

**fishing:** Anglers have their choice of fishing big trout water or small trout water. The Maury River is the area's major drainage, and one of the primary rivers in the state's mountain regions. By Virginia standards, therefore, it qualifies as big water. The 7-mi segment that flows through the WMA is exceptionally scenic, with a boulder-strewn bed and steep forested slopes rising from its banks. VA-39 follows close beside the river, but is often out of site. The gradient is mild to average. Fishing is by wading, with numerous access points along the highway. The river is stocked.

On the other side of VA-39 are a pair of small mountain streams that empty into the Maury: Laurel Run and Guys Run. Both are exceptionally scenic creeks, flowing over rocky beds through a lush hardwood forest. Together, they offer about 7 miles of fishing on native trout waters. Access is from the gated roads that run beside them. Guys Run, the longer of the two, is a nice destination for a backpacking/fly-fishing trip.

# Goshen Pass Natural Area

The Goshen Pass Natural Area covers 936 acres along the beautiful Maury River and Goshen Pass. The lands are adjacent to those of the 33,500-acre Goshen—Little North Mountain Wildlife Management Area. There are no facilities or developments at either area, and for the backcountry enthusiast, the two areas combined offer one vast outdoor playground. The natural area unwinds along the river and VA-39, which runs beside it. There are numerous pullouts along the road for photographing the gorge and a parking lot is located at a swinging bridge across the river. Outdoor recreation here is focused on the river, with fly-fishing and whitewater paddling both popular activities. Hiking and backpacking are possible on the extensive network of trails and gated roadbeds that run through the adjacent WMA.

Goshen (W) and Lexington (S) are the closest towns.

**contact:** Goshen Pass Natural Area, Virginia Department of Conservation and Recreation, 203 Governor St, Suite 302, Richmond, VA 23219; 804/786-1712

**getting there:** From Lexington, turn N onto US-11. Go 2.3 mi to VA-39. Turn L and go 15.3 mi to an unsigned dirt road, R. Turn onto the road and go 0.1 mi to a parking area at a swinging bridge across the river.

**topography:** The Maury River drops through a gorge where steep, forested slopes tower over the river below. There are numerous expsed cliff faces and rock outcrops. Elevation on the river is approximately 1,300 ft. **maps:** USGS Goshen

**starting out:** The natural area is a primitive backcountry area with no developed facilities. There are numerous pullouts along VA-39 from which to observe the gorge and river. A few scattered picnic tables and grills are located at some of the pullouts.

**activities:** Fishing, Kayaking/Canoeing, Hiking, Camping

**fishing:** The Maury River offers fly-fishermen the chance to fish for trout on a big, beautiful river. The mountain scenery is unsurpassed—not even the highway that follows the river detracts very much—and the river drops down a boulder-strewn bed with a mild to average gradient. Access is from pullouts on VA-39 or from the parking area at the swinging bridge. The river is stocked trout waters. Fishing pressure is heavy in spring. Water levels drop considerably in summer.

**kayaking/canoeing:** For expert paddlers, this is one of the fines, most outrageously scenic stretches of whitewater in the state. The 6-mile stretch of river between the put-in at the swinging bridge and the bottom of Goshen Pass is an almost contnuous run of class II-IV whitewater through the sheer cliffs and precipitous slopes of a towering gorge. The river is large, with a width that averages at least 100 ft across. The best times to run the river are in late winter and spring, when the water is up. By July and August water levels are usually too low.The take-out is at a bridge on VA-39 just above Rockbridge Baths.

**hiking:** A network of trails begins at the swinging bridge on the Maury River. Although a short segment of the trails is on the Goshen Pass Natural Area, the trails soon enter the Goshen—Little North Mountain WMA, where there is an extensive network ideal for long day-hikes or backpacking trips. See the separate entry above for more details.

**camping:** Primitive backcountry camping is permitted throughout the adjacent WMA. It is not allowed at the roadside pullouts and picnic areas along VA-39. See the separate WMA entry above for more information.

# Pedlar Ranger District

## George Washington National Forest

The 144,906 acres of the Pedlar Ranger District form an elongated rectangle that follows the ridges and slopes of the Blue Ridge Mountains between the James River (S) and Rockfish Gap and the start of the Shenandoah National Park(N). The Blue Ridge Parkway and the *Appalachian Trail* trace the district's highest elevations from one end to the other, offering vehicle and foot access to the large backcountry. There is a single designated wilderness on the district, the 9,835-acre St. Mary's Wilderness. Although the Pedlar is the smallest ranger district on the George Washington National Forest, it's extensive backcountry areas and scenic highlights offer a diversity of outdoor recreation potential. Hiking and backpacking are probably the most popular activities on the district, due to the extensive trail networks on three of the areas described below. The *Appalachian Trail* is of course a perennial favorite as well. Anglers can fish for trout on the ponds at the Sherando Recreation Area or on cool mountain creeks that harbor both stocked and native populations. Sherando Lake is the only developed recreation area on the Pedlar; it offers swimming on a small lake with a beach and bathhouse, an extensive picnic grounds, and an attractive car campground. This part of the district is most popular with families. The district's backcountry is extensive enough to support backpacking trips of a weekend or a week.

The closest cities are Lexington (SW), Buena Vista (SW), Staunton (NW), and Waynesboro (N).

**contact:** Pedlar Ranger District, U.S. Forest Service, 2424 Magnolia Ave, Buena Vista, VA 24416; 540/261-6105.

**getting there:** I-81 runs close beside the length of the district's W boundary, providing the major interstate access. A more scenic approach is on the Blue Ridge Parkway, which bisects the district from north to south. Highway access from the N is on I-64; from the S on US-501.

To reach the district ranger station, from I-81 take exit 188. Turn E on US-60 and go 3.4 mi to downtown Buena Vista. • From the Blue Ridge Parkway, exit at milepost 45.5 onto US-60. Turn W and go 4.4 miles to downtown Buena Vista. The ranger station is on the corner of Magnolia Ave and 24th St.

**topography:** The terrain throughout the district is mountainous, though in many places it is not exceptionally rugged or steep. On some of the lower slopes it is even mild. Elevations on the district are between 700 ft on the James River and 4,071 ft on Mt Pleasant. **maps:** USFS Pedlar Ranger District; see below under separate heading for USGS topo maps.

**starting out:** Before heading out into the backcountry, you can stop by the district RS to pick up maps, brochures, other info, or to check on current conditions. It's open weekdays from 8 AM to 4:30 PM. The USFS district map provides a good overview of the district and is useful as a roadmap, but for backcountry travel, it's scale is too small to be of much use.

**activities:** Hiking, Camping, Fishing

**hiking:** The district claims 170 miles of trails, including a 58-mi segment of the *Appalachian Trail*, which runs through the district from end to end. The AT roughly parallels the Blue Ridge Parkway, making it possible to park and hike short sections of the trail or to take longer trips and use 2 cars or a vehicle shuttle. The trail passes through some stunning mountain scenery along its route through the Pedlar. It is blazed with white bars and all trail access points are signed. Connections can be made with the trails at the Mt Pleasant Scenic Area and the Crabtree Falls Area to create long loop hikes or to take in scenic attractions off the *AT*. The other 2 major trail networks are in the St Mary's Wilderness and the Sherando Lake Rec Area. The former offers the more primitive and isolated conditions. The trails at these 2 areas actually run into each other, allowing longer hikes. Trails throughout the district are well-maintained; trailheads are clearly signed and most trails are blazed. Trail use varies from light to heavy depending on the area. Crabtree Falls is by far the busiest and seems to always draw a crowd.

**camping:** Most people who camp on the Pedlar choose to

backpack. No-trace backcountry camping is permitted anywhere on NF lands, except where posted. In general, it is not allowed near recreation areas or along roads. The only developed campground on the district is at Sherano Lake. It is very scenic, and offers facilities for swimming, picnicking, fishing, and hiking. It is the most popular area on the district with families.

**fishing:** Not counting the James River, which is described under the Glenwood Ranger District, fishing on the Pedlar means fishing for trout. There are a pair of small, stocked lakes at the Lake Sherando Rec Area. There's also a pair of stocked trout creeks. Elsewhere on the district there are a small handful of stocked trout creeks, although they aren't located in the backcountry areas described below. Access to these mountain streams is via the secondary and forest roads that run beside them. If you want to fish them, pick up a copy of the district topo map; it highlights each of them. Wild trout waters are found in the St Mary's Wilderness, which offers the best opportunity on the district for a backpacking/fly-fishing expedition.

# Mt Pleasant Scenic Area

The 7,580-acre Mt. Pleasant Scenic Area was designated by Congress in 1994, one of only seven national scenic areas in the nation. It occupies a broad swath of mountain slopes and ridges on the eastern slope Blue Ridge Mountains. As its name suggests, it is an area of exceptional scenic beauty, with exposed ridges and summits providing spectacular mountain views. One of the more remote areas on the Pedlar Ranger District, its chief attractions are hiking and backpacking trips through a large, rarely visited backcountry area. The *Appalachian Trail* passes through, connecting it with other parts of the ranger district and with the Blue Ridge Parkway, which is to the west. Scattered fields are a good place to observe the wildlife that frequents the area, white-tailed deer in particular.

Beuna Vista (W) is the closest town.

**getting there:** From I-81, take exit 188. Turn E onto US-60 and go 12.2 mi to SR-634 (at 3.4 mi reach US-501 and downtown Buena Vista; at 7.9 mi reach the BRP). Turn L and go 1.7 mi to dirt and gravel SR-755. Turn R and go 2.7 mi (at 1.7 mi the road becomes

FR-48) to a parking area at an *AT* crossing. Or continue ahead 0.3 mi to FR-51. Turn R and go 50 yds to a parking area and trailheads.

**topography:** The majority of the area's mountainous terrain is blanketed with a forest of oaks and hickories. A few areas, however, are grassy meadow. Elevations reach their peak on Mt Pleasant (4,071 ft). **maps:** USGS-FS Forks of Buffalo, Montebello.

**starting out:** This is a large primitive area with no facilities. Water is available along most of the trails, but surface water should be treated before drinking.

**activities:** Hiking, Camping

**hiking:** 3 trails comprise the hiking and backpacking opportunities in the area. The main footpath is the *Appalachian Trail*, which passes through the area from S to N. A pair of other trails, the 6-mi *Henry Lanum Loop Trail* and the 4-mi *Hotel Trail*, connect to the *AT*, making loop hikes of several different lengths possible. Highlights along the trails are mountain vistas, good campsites in mountain meadows, and the remote location. The odds of observing wildlife in the area are good. Trailheads are signed and the trails are blazed and well maintained. Hiking is moderate. Use is light to moderate, depending on the time of year. The *AT* is the most popular trail.

**camping:** Primitive backcountry camping is permitted throughout the area, except where posted. An *AT* shelter is located 1.5 mi S of the vehicle access on the loop hike formed with the *Hotel Trail*. One popular camping area is the large meadow on the N side of FR-48 where the *AT* crosses the road.

# St Mary's Wilderness

At 9,835 acres, the St Mary's Wilderness is the largest roadless backcountry area on the Pedlar Ranger District and its only designated wilderness. Located on the mountain slopes west of the Blue Ridge and east of the Shenandoah Valley, it is a remote region of hardwood forests, rugged mountain slopes, and cool cascading streams. The St Mary's River, which crosses most of the wilderness, is the area's major drainage. The St Mary's gorge and falls are a popular scenic attraction in the area. The area is popular with both backpackers and fly-fishermen; on peak-season weekends the trails and backcountry can become fairly congested. If you can, try to plan your visit for a weekday or the off-season, when you'll likely have the place to yourself.

Staunton (N), Waynesboro (NE), and Buena Vista (SW) are the closest large towns.

**getting there:** The wilderness can be reached from either I-81 or the Blue Ridge Parkway. From I-81, take exit 205. Turn E onto SR-606 and go 1.5 mi to US-11. Turn L and go 0.1 mi to VA-56. Turn R and go 1 mi to SR-608. Turn L and go 2.2 mi to A fork. Bear R, continuing on SR-608. Go 0.3 mi to FR-41. Turn R and go 0.6 mi to FR-42 (at 0.2 mi the pavement ends). L it's 1.2 mi on FR-42 to a trailhead, R. Ahead on FR-41, it's 0.8 mi to the end of the road and a parking area and the *St Mary's Trail*. • Access from the Blue Ridge Parkway is to the SE end of the wilderness. The trailhead is located at milepost 23 across the road from Fork Mtn Overlook.

**topography:** Mountainous, but not very high in elevation. The wilderness is located on the western slope of the Blue Ridge. The Shenandoah Valley is to the west. Elevations are between 1,800 ft on the St Mary's River and 3,300 on Mineback Mtn and the BRP. **maps:** USFS St Mary's Wilderness; USGS-FS Big Levels, Vesuvius.

**starting out:** There are no facilities in the wilderness. Signboards with maps and wilderness regulations are located at the trailheads on the Shenandoah Valley side of the wilderness. Surface water is available along most of the trails, but should be treated before drinking. The wilderness is a popular backpacking spot and can get pretty crowded on peak season weekends.

Group size is limited to 10 in the wilderness.

**activities:** Hiking, Fishing, Camping

**hiking:** 13 miles of trails allow hikers to enter the heart of the wilderness. The longest of these, the 6.5-mi *St Mary's Trail*, follows the St Mary's River across the width of the wilderness and is popular with fly-fishermen and backpackers. A short spur trail leads to a scenic falls on the river. Another connecting trail leads to the Blue Ridge Parkway. With most of the trail mileage deep within the hardwood forest that covers the summits, ridges, and coves within the wilderness, the main attraction here is the remote wilderness atmosphere. A couple of loop hikes can be formed by combining trails with segments of FR-162, a dirt road that runs along much of the wilderness boundary. In keeping with the wilderness ethic, trails are not blazed and creek crossings are by wading or rock-hopping. Hiking is moderate to strenuous. Access is from the trailheads described above.

**fishing:** There was a time when the St Mary's River was highly regarded by trout anglers. Increased levels of acid in the water, however, have killed off a high percentage of the fish and altered the fishery. Where once rainbow trout were the dominant species, they have mostly died out and been replaced by brook trout. The St. Mary's River is a small to medium creek with an average gradient that can be fished for about 4 miles in the wilderness. Access is from the *St Mary's Trail*, which runs beside it. The St Mary's is wild trout water, but with special regs in effect. Only single-hook lures can be used.

**camping:** Backcountry camping is one of the most popular activities in the wilderness. It is permitted in all locations, except where posted. Currently, camping is not allowed on the lower sections along the St Mary's River.

# Sherando Lake Recreation Area

The Sherando Lake rec area—the most popular spot on the Pedlar Ranger District—combines family-oriented outdoor activities with an extensive backcountry that can be reached by half a dozen hiking trails. 24-acre Sherando Lake—constructed by the CCC in the 1930s—is at the center of the rec area proper. A swimming beach is the focal point of the area and can get quite busy on summer weekends. Other facilities include a bathhouse with warm showers, a large picnic grounds with dozens of tables and grills, and an attractive car campground. Sherando Lake and smaller Upper Lake are both stocked trout waters, as are two of the creeks that flow down off the Blue Ridge through the area. Away from the developed rec area the large backcountry is defined by a pair of mountain ridges and is bounded by the Blue Ridge Parkway and the St Mary's Wilderness. There are at least half a dozen routes for day hikes of less than ten miles here, with possibilities for longer treks by combining the trails of the St Mary's Wilderness. Most rec area facilities are open from April 1 to October 31.

Waynesboro (NE) and Buena Vista (SW) are the closest towns.

**getting there:** From the BRP, exit at milepost 16.2 onto SR-814. Go S 4.4 mi to FR-91 and the rec area entrance, L. • Trail access is possible from the Blue Ridge Parkway, where there are trailheads at the Slacks Overlook (mp 19.8) and Bald Mountain Overlook (mp 22.3).

**topography:** The campground and lake are nestled in a narrow slot valley between Torry Ridge and the Blue Ridge. The terrain is mountainous, but not particularly rugged. Mountain slopes are covered with hardwood tree species. Elevations are between 3,300 ft near the BRP and 1,700 ft on Back Creek. **maps:** USGS-FS Big Levels, Sherando.

**starting out:** Before you can enter the rec area, you have to pay a $5/vehicle parking fee. Once there, stop by the visitor center at the beach pavilion to pick up trail maps, brochures, or check on current conditions. Facilities (restrooms, water, pay phone) are all located nearby. The visitor center and facilities are open from Apr 1 to Oct 31.

Public use of alcohol is not allowed in the rec area. Pets are allowed, but must be kept on a leash.

**activities:** Hiking, Camping, Fishing, Canoeing

**hiking:** Almost 20 miles of hiking trails wind through and around Sherando Lake and environs. Several short trails circle Sherando Lake, while 3 longer trails follow the ridges and creeks up to the Blue Ridge Parkway. Loops of varyious lengths from 1 to 15 miles can be formed by combining 2 or more trails. Scenic highlights along the trails include views of the 2 lakes, lush hardwood forests, cold mountain creeks, a gorge with waterfalls, and scenic vistas from the Blue Ridge Parkway. With trail access at both the rec area and at 2 overlooks on the BRP, one-way hikes with 2 cars or a vehicle shuttle are possible. From the rec area to the BRP is about a 5-mi hike. The trails in this area are all blazed and trailheads are signed. Heavy use keeps the treadways well defined and easy to follow. The trails that wind through the rec area receive the most use; The *Torry Ridge Trail* and *Mills Creek Trail* are more remote and less traveled. Hiking in the rec area is generally easy; on the longer trails, grades are moderate to

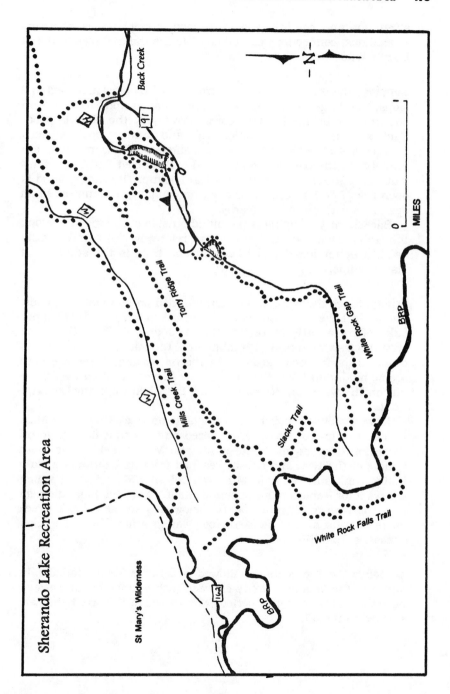

Sherando Lake Recreation Area

strenuous and conditions more rugged. For longer backpacking expeditions, connections can be made to the trail network in the St Mary's Wilderness.

**camping:** The attractive car campground has 64 sites arranged in 3 loops. The large, well spaced sites are shaded and isolated from one another by thick forest cover. Privacy at the sites is good. Each site has a picnic table, grill, and lantern post. Modern restrooms are located in the area and showers with warm water are available in the bathhouse at the lake. Sites cost $10/night for a tent site, $15 for a site with electrical hookup. The campground is open from Apr 1 to Oct 31. Off-season camping is permitted in an open area with pit toilets nearby.

Backcountry camping is permitted outside of the rec area along the trails. Since the trails here are relatively short and heavily used, a better location for backpacking trips is the adjacent St Mary's Wilderness.

**fishing:** Since the rec area is often crowded on summer weekends, Sherando Lake is a poor choice for backcountry anglers. Upper Lake offers a little more isolation and doesn't have the same crowds of swimmers and sunbathers, though it's by no means deserted during peak season. In the off season, these are both scenic mountain lakes that invite bank fishermen. A canoe can be put on the water on Sherando Lake. Both lakes are stocked with trout.

More remote trout fishing is available on Back Creek and Mills Creek, a couple of small to mid-sized streams that flow down off the Blue Ridge on moderate gradients. Mills Creek is the more remote of the two, and can be reached from its headwaters via a hiking trail (start at Bald Mtn Overlook at BRP mp 22.3) which follows it for 4 miles to an impoundement. Above the impoundment it's a native brook trout fishery; below, it's stocked. Back Creek offers about a mile of stocked trout waters below Sherando Lake. Access is from FR-91.

**canoeing:** Car-top boats are allowed on 24-acre Sherando Lake. In summer, the lake gets pretty crowded with swimmers. Off season, however, a canoe is the perfect way to get to the trout that are stocked in the lake.

# Crabtree Falls Area

For outdoor photographers and lovers of nature at its most dramatic, Crabtree Falls is the highlight of the Pedlar Ranger District. In fact, it's the number one stop for outdoor enthusiasts of all stripes. The reason is the series of cascades on Crabtree Creek that plunge a total of 1,200 feet in five major drops over massive rock formations. From the parking lot, the hike to the first series of cascades is only 700 feet, meaning that even the relatively sedentary get the chance to view the falls. For the more ambitious the trail continues three miles to the upper falls and Crabtree Meadows, where there's a connection to the *Appalachian Trail*. The falls are located on the eastern side of the Blue Ridge in Nelson Country above the South Fork Tye River. The area is perfect both for a short stopover to snap some pictures or merely gaze at the falls, as well as for longer treks into the backcountry.

Buena Vista (SW) and Waynesboro (NE) are the closest towns.

**getting there:** From the BRP, exit at milepost 27 onto VA-56 and go E 6.5 mi to the trailhead and small parking area, R.

**topography:** The terrain around the falls is rugged, mountainous, and steep. Exposed rock faces and massive boulders form much of the creekbed. The surrounding forest is predominantly hardwoods and hemlocks. Elevations are between 1,500 and 3,100 ft. **maps:** USGS-FS Massies Mill

**starting out:** There's a large parking lot at the lower trailhead. On weekends, it can get pretty busy there. Facilities at the trailhead are pit toilets and across the arched footbridge a pay phone and water pump. Water levels are highest, and the falls most spectacular, during late winter and early spring, though they won't disappoint at other times of year either. NOTE: A couple of dozen people have died climbing on the slippery rocks around the falls. Be careful!

**activities:** Hiking, Camping

**hiking:** The single trail in the area is the 2.9-mi *Crabtree Falls Trail*. Most visitors hike it to the first series of cascades and then turn around and head back to their cars. The lower sections of the trail are improved with a cool arched footbridge across the South

Fork Tye River and a series of steps and platforms with benches. The trail is worth hiking past the first falls, however. If passes through a mature hardwood forest and has several other overlooks for viewing the falls. After 2.9 miles it reaches Crabtree Meadows. From there, you can either return to the trailhead or hike 0.5 mi up a forest road to connect with the *Appalachian Trail*. From there, you can hike to Georgia or Maine, depending on your mood and level of ambition. Hiking on the *Crabtree Falls Trail* is moderate to strenuous. Trail use is very heavy.

**camping:** Although backcountry camping is permitted in the area, it isn't allowed along the *Crabtree Falls Trail*. That mean that you have to hike up to the *AT*—or start out at the upper end of the trail in Crabtree Meadows.

# Dry River Ranger District

## George Washington National Forest

With more than 227,000 acres in Virginia and West Virginia, the Dry River Ranger District is the largest on the George Washington National Forest. It is roughly rectangular in shape, with lands on three counties: Augusta and Rockingham in VA, and Pedleton in WV. Most of the land holdings are on the summit ridge and eastern slope of Shenandoah Mountain, a part of the Alleghenies. Boundaries are formed by the Deerfield Ranger District (S) and the Lee Ranger District and WV state line (N). The district's major waterways are the North, Dry, and North Fork Shenandoah. All three flow in a generally easterly direction off of the slopes of Shenandoah Mtn.

Despite the vastness of the district's backcountry, outdoor recreation (in VA at least) is mostly confined to the district's southeast corner. The three areas described below—North River, Little River, and Hone Quarry—are arrayed one next to the other on a large, continuous tract of national forest land. While this concentrates visitors to the district in a single locale, it also facilitates backcountry expeditions of several days or longer. Although much of the activity is centered around small lakes and picnic areas, backcountry travelers will be more interested in the extensive network of hiking trails and seldom-traveled roads that make perfect mountain bike tracks. The developed facilities on the district include 5 campgrounds (3 in VA), 4 picnic grounds, and 2 small lakes with boat ramps. Fly-fishermen will find cool mountain creeks stocked with trout in each of the areas described below. In addition to these, Dry River and the North Fork Shenandoah River are also stocked with trout.

Bridgewater (E) and Harrisonburg (E) are the closest towns.

**contact:** Dry River Ranger District, U.S. Forest Service, 112 North River Road, Bridgewater, VA 22812; 540/828-2591.

**getting there:** US-33 is the only major highway that runs through the district. I-81 is parallel to the east and provides access from all parts of the state. To reach the district RS, leave I-81 at exit 240. Turn W onto VA-257 and go 3.3 mi to VA-42 in downtown Bridgewater. The district RS is located on N River Rd..

**topography:** Elevations on Shenandoah Mountain exceed 4,000 ft on the WV border. At the base of the mountains they drop to about 1,600 ft. The terrain is mountainous, but not exceptionally steep or rugged. Forest cover is extensive, and consist of hardwoods, pines, and northern conifer species. **maps:** USFS Dry River Ranger District; for USGS topo maps see below under individual listings.

**starting out:** A stop by the district RS is worthwhile before heading out into the backcountry. Available there are maps and guidebooks for sale, as well as a number of free brochures and trail guides. You can also get info on current conditions. The busiest part of the district is the area around Todd Lake and North River.

**activities:** Hiking, Mountain Biking, Fishing, Camping, Canoeing/Kayaking

**hiking:** The district trail inventory lists 163 miles of trails. Of these, 75 miles are included in the 3 areas described below. Trails range in length from the 26-mile *Wild Oak Trail*, a national recreation trail that circles the North River Area, to short leg-stretchers and fishermen's loops around the district's small lakes. Hiking on most of the district's trails is moderate; the terrain is mountainous, but not exceptionally steep or rugged. Most trailheads are clearly signed and easy to locate, and a majority of the trails are blazed, most with a yellow diamond. Trail use is moderate, except in the immediate vicinity of the more popular rec areas, where it often heavy heavy during the summer season. Hikers and backpackers should be aware that hunting takes place on the district in fall and winter. Blaze orange is required If you're going to be in the backcountry during this time.

**mountain biking:** Bikers coming to the district will find plenty of opportunity for riding, on both open roads and on the district's trails. The conditions encountered on each are strikingly different. The majority of the backcountry roads, though dirt and gravel, are well maintained and provide a level, easy riding surface. The terrain is mountainous, so riding is moderate, with some strenuous segments. Once you get off the roads and onto the trails, however, the conditions become significantly more challenging. None of the district trails are maintained for bike riding, though many follow old road beds. Obstacles encountered include very rocky treadways, steep sections impossible to ridge, and paths that scramble over boulders where dismonting is essential. Add to that unimproved river crossings and bikers who venture off the beaten path face riding conditions that are frequently difficult and strenuous. With one or two exceptions, bikes are permitted on all district trails.

**fishing:** Although the district is not a major angling destination, backcountry fly-fishermen will find a handful of cool mountain streams stocked with trout on which to practice their art. The most popular area is probably North River and Elkhorn Lake, both of which offer quality trout fishing in a scenic alpine setting.

**camping:** No-trace backcountry camping is permitted on NF lands except where posted. In practice, this generally means that anywhere outside of designated rec areas and away from roads is acceptable. The large trail system on the E slope of Shenandoah Mountain offers plenty of options for backpacking trips of 2 or 3 days.

Car campers have their choice of 3 campgrounds—2 in the North River area and 1 at Hone Quarry. These are all primitive areas with limited facilities and a rustic feel. The campground at Todd Lake is the most developed and the only one that offers showers. A fee is charged at each campground. They're open all year.

**canoeing/kayaking:** Opportunities for paddling on the district are extremely limited. Only a couple of small impoundments have boat access, and these are primarily for the benefit of fishermen. In fact, if you're not going to be fishing from your canoe or kayak, you may as well leave it at home or look elsewhere for paddling opportunities.

# North River Area

The North River Multiple Use Area is a 25,000-acre portion of the George Washington National Forest managed for timber production, hunting, fishing, outdoor recreation, scenic beauty, water production, and flood control. The area is located in Augusta County, with boundaries formed by West Virginia (W), the Deerfield Ranger District (S) and the Little River Area (N). With 2 campgrounds, a recreational lake with a small fishing beach, another lake stocked with trout, and a 40-mile network of hiking trails, this is the premiere backcountry area on the Dry River Ranger District. Most of the recreation facilities are clustered in the foothills at the eastern edge of the area; to the west, the backcountry extends up the forested slopes of Shenandoah Mountain and the border with West Virginia. These wooded slopes and ravines are home to many species of wildlife, including black bear, white-tailed deer, wild turkey, and ruffed grouse. The large picnic grounds and swimming beach at Todd Lake are the center of the bustling summer season. Another, smaller picnic area is located at the Staunton Dam on the North River. For families looking for an outdoor recreation area that's easy to get to and offers lots of variety, the North River Area is a good bet. It's even better for backpackers looking to take a 2- or 3-day hike.

Bridgewater (E) is the closest town.

**getting there:** From Bridgewater (exit 240 from I-81) take VA-42 W 3.7 mi to SR-747. Turn R and go 6.8 mi to SR-730. Keep straight on SR-730 and go 1.3 mi to SR-718. Keep straight and go 1.1 mi to dirt and gravel FR-95. Turn L and go 0.1 mi to the trialhead to the *White Oak Trail*. Continueing on FR-95 go 0.7 or 1.1 mi to a parking spur and a trailhead to the North Gorge Trail. At 3.1 mi is FR-523 and the entrance to the Todd Lake Rec Area. The pavement ends past the rec area. 1.4 mi past the Todd Lake entrance come to a jct with FR-95B. L it's 0.9 mi to the North River campground, 2 mi to a picnic ground at the dam across the river.

R it's 1.7 mi to FR-533, L and Elkhorn Lake.

**topography:** Because of its location in the Allegheney Foothills, the mountain terrain in the area is not particularly rugged or steep. Mountain slopes are forested with hardwoods and pines. Elevations are between 1,500 on the North River and 4,351 ft on Little Bald Knob W of the rec areas. **maps:** USGS-FS Stokesville, Reddish Knob, W Augusta, Palo Alto

**starting out:** The main centers of activity are the rec area at Todd Lake and the campground at North River. A parking fee at Todd Lake Rec Area of $4/vehicle is charged. The area is open from Memorial Day to Labor Day. Facilities there are restrooms, water, and changing rooms. There are water and pit toilets at the North River Campground, and pit toilets at Elkhorn Lake. Either of the campgrounds makes a good base for exploring the area. Expect crowds in the rec area during the summer months.

Alcohol is not allowed in day-use areas.

**activities:** Hiking, Mountain Biking, Camping, Fishing, Canoeing/Kayaking

**hiking:** The major hiking trail in the area is the 26-mi *Wild Oak Trail*, a national recreation trail. The long loop trail forms a circle around the entire area, forming connections with a handful of other shorter trails. The well-maintained trail follows a combination of single-track and old roadbeds through forested terrain that mostly follows mountain ridges. Highlights along the trail include the remote setting and scenic vistas from numerous overlooks and rock outcrops, the most spectacular of which is Little Bald Knob. The trail is blazed with a whitish-silver diamond. Trailheads are clearly signed. Hiking on the trail is moderate to strenuous. Side trails account for an additional 13 miles of hiking in the area. The most popular is the 4.2-mi *North River Gorge Trail*, an exceptionally scenic trail that passes through a lush hardwood forest beside the river. River crossings are not improved and can be difficult or impossible during high water. Trailheads are on FR-95 and in the North River Campground. Brochures describing both of these trails in detail are available at the district RS. For longer treks, hike the Wild Oak Trail to Ramsey's Draft Wilderness, where it connects with the full network of trails there (see separate listing above). Trail use is moderate to heavy.

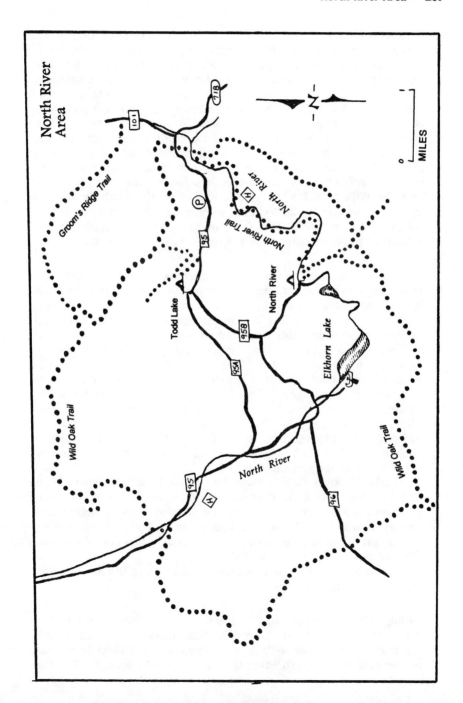

**mountain biking:** Bikers will find the North River backcountry an excellent area to explore. FR-95 is the major road in the area. It's a well-maintained dirt and gravel road that receives very little traffic beyond the rec areas and Elkhorn Lake. From there, it ascends Shenandoah Mtn to the WV state line. Several other roads intersect, including FR-85, which follows the state line past the Shenandoah Picnic Area to a jct with SR-924 and access to the Hone Quarry Area (or a return to the area on FR-101 for about a 50-mi trip). In short, there are enough miles of road to keep even an ambitious rider staisfied. In addition to the roads open to motor vehicles, several of the area trails are also suitable to bike riding (not the *Wild Oak Trail* through). Riding on the roads is easy to moderate, on the trails it's more strenuous. You can park at the trailhead to the *Wild Oak Trail*, or to begin in a more remote setting, at the North River Campground or at Elkhorn Lake.

**camping:** Campers coming to the area have plenty of options. Primitive backcountry camping is permitted throughout the area on national forest land, except where posted otherwise. It is not allowed in or around any of the rec areas. The *Wild Oak Trail* provides a popular 3-day backpacking trip.

There are 2 primitive car campgrounds in the area. Teaberry Campground is located at the Todd Lake Rec Area. 20 large, well-spaced sites are situated in a heavily wooded area above the lake. The sites offer a degree of privacy that is exceptional for a car campground. Each site has a picnic table, grill, and lantern post. The fee is $10/night. There are 2 Restrooms with showers. Although the campground is developed, it still has a primitive backcountry feel. Use is heavy during peak season, light during the off-season. It's open all year.

The North River Campground has 10 smallish sites spread out in a loop in a forest clearing with shade provided by pines. Each site has a picnic table and grill. The sites are close together and privacy is minimal, due to the lack of forest cover. There are pit toilets and a hand water pump in the area. Sites cost $5/night. The campground is open all year.

Low-impact car camping is also possible along the forest roads that run through the area.

**fishing:** Visitors coming to fish the area have a couple of options. North River, which flows down off of Shenandoah Mtn is the area's major drainage. It offers 13 miles of stocked trout water from near its headwaters to North River Gap and the NF boundary. It's size and gradient varies considerably along its length, due to a couple of dams and impoundments. Its flow is also liable to seasonal change. The 7-mi stretch above Elkhorn Lake is medium to large with a very rocky bed. Access here is from FR-95, which parallels the river. Elkhorn Lake is also stocked with trout, and it supports populations of largemouth bass, channel catfish, and bluegill. Fishing can be done from the lakeshore, from 1 of 3 fishing platforms, or from a boat. Below Lake Elkhorn and a second small impoundment, North River becomes a small to medium-sized creek that flows through an exceptionally scenic gorge. The cover here is excellent and access if by hiking trail only.

**canoeing/kayaking:** There's a boat launch onto Elkhorn Lake, but the only reason to put a boat on the 54-acre lake would be to fish, since it's too small for any kind of paddling trip.

# Little River Area

This is a small area wedged in between the Hone Quarry Recreation Area to the north and the North River Multiple-Use Area to the south. It extends from the national forest boundary at the bottom of the Allegheney Mountains west to the summit crest of Shenandoah Mountain and the West Virginia line. The area is most frequently used by hunters. Local game species are black bear, white-tailed deer, wild turkey, and ruffed grouse, as well as a host of smaller mammals. Hikers and backpackers use the trails that follow the long ridges to the top of the mountain, where the arduous climb is rewarded with panoramic vistas. Hearthstone Lake, built for flood control on the Little River, is stocked with rainbow trout. The area is well-suite for a daytrip or in combination with longer trips to the adjacent areas.

Bridgewater (E) and Harrisonburg (E) are the closest cities.

**getting there:** From Bridgewater (exit 240 from I-81) take VA-42 W 3.7 mi to SR-747. Turn R and go 6.8 mi to SR-730. Keep straight on SR-730 and go 1.3 mi to SR-718. Keep straight and go 1.1 mi to a jct with FR-95, L. Bear R where the road becomes dirt and gravel FR-101 and go 0.8 mi to a small parking area R and access to the *Grooms Ridge Trail,* L. At 1.8 mi come to a forest road and a sign for Little River. Turn L onto the steep, rugged road and go 0.7 mi to the end of the road at Hearthstone Lake.

**topography:** Little River flows SE off of Shenandoah Mtn into Hearthstone Lake, an artificial impoundment at the bottom of the Allegheney foothills. Highest elevations in the area (4,000 ft) are on Reddish Knob at the border with WV. Low point is 1,600 ft. **maps:** USGS-FS Reddish Knob,

**starting out:** There aren't any facilities in this area. A short drive N or S, however, and you'll be at the Hone Quarry Rec Area or the Todd Lake Rec Area. Water and restrooms can be found at both areas. The lack of developed rec areas here results in fewer visitors and a chance to travel through more isolated backcountry.

**activities:** Hiking, Mountain Biking, Camping

**hiking:** 3 trails cover a total distance of 9 miles. Each of the 2 mian trails in the area starts on FR-101 and climbs to Reddish Knob, where there are spectacular views of VA and WV. The trails follow a more-or-less straight line up the mountain; backtracking or a vehicle shuttle on FR-85 is necessary. The signed trailhead to the trails is located on FR-101 0.6 mi N of the turn for Hearthstone Lake. The trails follow a combination of old roadbeds and footpaths. They're blazed with yellow diamonds.

**mountain biking:** Although biking in the area is limitied to FR-101, the road forms part of a long loop that passes through isolated backcountry and follow the crest of Shenandoah Mountain, where there are superb views. The loop is formed by riding FR-101 S to FR-95. FR-95 is then followed all the way up the mountain to FR-85. Turn R there and follow the mountain and the state line to SR-924. Turn R and descend the mountain past Briery Lake and to a jct with FR-101. Turn R and return to the starting point. The loop covers about 50 miles. The roads are well-maintained, but don't see much traffic outside of the rec areas. Riding is easy to strenuous.

**camping:** Primitive backcountry camping is permitted throughout the area on national forest lands, except where prohibited.

Although there's no developed car campground in the area, there are plenty of roadside sites along FR-101.

# Hone Quarry Recreation Area

Located at the southern end of Rockingham County, the Hone Quarry Area is the northernmost of the three backcountry areas that occupy coninuous national forest lands. While the picnic area makes this a suitable place for daytrips—particularly for families with young children—the extensive backcountry beckons backpackers with ambitions of multi-day treks. Hone Quarry Campground is an attractive small primitive car campground that can serve as a basecamps for such trips. In the picnic area are a shelter, tables, and grills beside Hone Quarry Run. That creek and Briery Branch are both stocked trout waters, good for a morning or afternoon of fly-fishing. As with the two areas to the south, Hone Quarry is set on the eastern slope of Shenandoah Mountain, a part of the Allegheney range.

Bridgewater (E) and Harrisonburg (E) are the closest cities.

**getting there:** From I-81, take exit 247 (Harrisonburg). Turn W onto US-33 and go 0.3 mi to VA-42. Turn L and go 5.6 mi to VA-257. Turn R and go 11.1 mi to dirt and gravel FR-62. Turn R and go 1.7 mi to the campground entrance.

**topography:** Highest elevations in the area are on Shenandoah Mtn, on the WV border, where they exceed 4,000 ft. At the confluence of Hone Quarry Run and Briery Creek, they've dropped to 1,600 ft. Forest cover consists of hardwoods and conifers. **maps:** USGS-FS Reddish Knob, Briery Branch, Brandywine

**starting out:** Faciliites are located in the picnic area, where there are pit toilets and a hand water pump. This area is the center of activity, with 23 picnic sites that are popular with families during the summer months. Pit toilets can also be found at Briery Lake.

**activities:** Hiking, Fishing, Camping

**hiking:** The trail network that fans out NW from the Hone Quarry Rec Area features 7 trails that cover 25 miles in all. The trails are similar in nature and most connect with each other, allowing hikes of various length. The basic trail orientation is NW-SE, with trails following ridgelines, creeks, and hollows. Some of the trails offer panoramic views of the mountains; their main appeal, however, is their location in remote, forested backcountry and the possibility they offer for weekend backpacking trips. The trails follow a combination of treadways, including old roadbeds and rocky single-tracks. Hiking is mostly moderate, with some strenuous stretches. Use is light to moderate. Trailheads are located at various points along FR-62, including at the rec area. Most trails are blazed with yellow diamonds.

**fishing:** Trout anglers have their choice of tw cold mountain streams that run down the E slope of Shenandoah Mtn. Briery Branch is a medium-sized stream with an average gradient that flows through lush forest cover. Its bed is rocky and numerous ledges create excellent pooling action. The creek offers almost 3 miles of fishable water below Briery Lake, a small impoundment. Access is from paved SR-924, which parallels the creek and has several pullouts and parking at the lake. Both creek and lake are stocked trout waters. Fishing on the lake is from the shoreline, which is mostly open.

Hone Quarry Run is a smaller creek with a mild to average gradient that runs parallel to Briery Branch. It too offers about 3 miles of fishable water, beginning below a small impoundment. Access is from dirt and gravel FR-62, which runs beside the creek. Parking is available alongside the road or at the Hone Quarry Rec Area. The creek is stocked.

**camping:** Primitive, low-impact backcountry camping is permitted throughout the area on NF lands, except where posted. It is not allowed in the picnic grounds.

The primitive car campground features 10 sites in an attractive grove of hemlocks beside Hone Quarry Run. Each of the large, well-spaced sites has a picnic table, grill, and lantern post. The degree of privacy in the campground is high, and the remote setting adds to the atmosphere. There are pit toilets in the campground, but no water source. Sites cost $5/night. The campground is open all year.

# Lee Ranger District

## George Washington National Forest

With land holdings on either side of the Shenandoah Valley southwest of Front Royal, the Lee is the northernmost district on the GW National Forest. Located only an hour west of Washington, D.C., its backcountry is a popular destination among urbanites looking for a weekend retreat. The district encompasses almost 190,000 acres in the counties of Shenandoah, Frederick, Page, and Warren. A part of the district is located in Hampshire and Hardy Counties in West Virginia. The major physical feature of the district is Massanutten Mountain, a 50-mile-long ridge that rises 2,000 feet from the broad valleys to its east and west. A fork of the Shenandoah River flows north along each side of its base. The mountain was formed from sandstone, limestone, and shale about 350 million years ago. Although the mountain is the district's most prominent feature, the highest peaks are located to the west, along the WV state line.

Outdoor recreation on the district is centered around Massanutten Mtn and the South Fork Shenandoah River. The latter is one of the most popular destinations for river trips in the entire state. The forested ridges and hollows of the mountain are laced with hiking trails, making the area a magnet for backpackers. Cool mountain streams stocked with trout provide fly-fishermen with miles of fishable water. Although access is easy enough to make daytrips fesible, at least a weekend is required to adequately sample the pleasures that the Lee Ranger District has to offer.

Closest large towns are Harrisonburg (SW), Elkton (SE), Shenandoah (SE), Luray (E), Front Royal (NE); New Market, Edinburg, Woodstock, and Strasburg lie between the district's 2 major sections.

**contact:** Lee Ranger District, U.S. Forest Service, 109 Molineu Rd, Edinburg, VA 22824; 540/984-4101.

**getting there:** I-81 runs between the 2 sections of the district and provides the major vehicle access.

To reach the district ranger station: From I-81, take exit 279. Turn E onto VA-185/SR-675 and go 0.2 mi to Windsor Knit Rd. Turn L and go 0.2 mi to Molineu Rd. Turn L and go 0.2 mi to the RS parking lot. • To reach the Massanutten Visitor Center: from I-81, turn E onto US-211 and go 4.2 mi to the entrance, R.

**topography:** The dominant physical feature of the district's E half is Massanutten Mtn, a long, narrow spine that rises 2,000 ft between the 2 forks of the Shenandoah River. The upper slopes of the mountain are steep and rugged, with numerous exposed rock faces. W of broad Shenandoah Valley are the district's other land holdings. In VA, these encompass Little North and Little Sluice Mtns. The highest elevations on the district (3,200 ft) are found here. **maps:** USFS Lee Ranger District. See below under the separate headings for USGS topo maps.

**starting out:** Before heading out, you can pick up maps, guidebooks, or check on current conditions at one of two places: the district ranger station or the Massanutten Visitor Center. The district RS is open weekdays from 8 AM to 4:30 PM. The visitor center is open Apr 1 to Oct 31 from 9 AM to 5 PM daily. The district topo maps gives a good overview of the district and shows the location of the major rec areas, but for backcountry travel its scale is too small. It's also not entirely accurate in showing road and trail locations.

**activities:** Hiking, Mountain Biking, Camping, Fishing, Canoeing/Kayaking

**hiking:** With 294 miles of trails, the Lee RD is a major destination for hikers and backpackers. No other national forest district in Virginia can boast of more trail mileage; only the Mt Rogers NRA and Shenandoah NP offer hikers greater variety and distance. Better still, just about all of the trails on and around Massanutten Mtn can be connected in one way or another, making backcountry trips of days or even weeks possible. In covering so much territory, the district's trails utilize a wide array of pathways—gated roads, seeded roadbeds, single-track rocky paths, paved footpaths, and a rope-guided trail for the visually impaired. All of this without a mile of the *Appalachian Trail*, which parralels district lands on the other side of Page Valley in Shenandoah NP. Trail highlights on the Lee are undoubtedly the views from Massanutten Mountain, which take in breathtaking scenery in all four directions. Getting at these views is at least one of the goals of most hikers that come to the district. Overlooks can be reached by short, leisurely strolls, or arduous long-distance treks.

**mountain biking:** The Massanutten Mountain Area is a mountain biker's paradise. With dozens of miles of dirt and gravel as well as paved roads, a mountain bike is the perfect means for covering a lot of ground in a short period. Add the numerous trails that follow old roadbeds and are open to bikes to the vehicular roads, and there's enough challenging terrain to keep bikers busy for days. The most extensive riding opportunities are on the S half of Massanutten Mtn, although exploring Fort Valley on its series of paved roads makes for an enjoyable, if somewhat tame, trip.

**camping:** The Lee RD is one of the best on the GW for extended backpacking trips. Almost all of the backcountry is open to primitive camping, and the district has the largest network on trails on the GWNF. Since just about all of the trails on Massanutten can be connected one way or another, hikes of up to a week are easily planned.

Developed campgrounds on the district include 4 designed for car access and 2 for canoe or kayak access on the S Fork Shenandoah River. All of the car campgrounds have an imtimate, rugged character that is a nice compromise between backcountry camping and the ease of vehicle access.

**fishing:** Trout and smallmouth bass are the game species that lure anglers to the Lee RD. The S Fork Shenandoah River is one of the state's real hot spots for smallmouth bass. With easy canoe access, this is one of the best mountain rivers for multi-day fishing expeditions. Trout anglers will find a handful of intimate creeks in the backcountry of Massanutten Mtn. Most of these are stocked and can be reached from a road.

**canoeing/kayaking:** The S Fork Shenandoah River offers a 50-mile float through some of the most majestic mountain scenery in the southern Appalachians. Water is mostly flat and class I-II. The attraction here really isn't the intensity of the rapids (intermediate paddlers should be able to handle it with no problems), but the unforgettable setting. Trips of 1 to 3 days are very popular on the river in the warm months.

# Massanutten Mountain Area (South)

The southern half of the long, narrow spine of Massanutten Mountain is the defining geographical feature of this area. Seen from a distance, the mountain seems isolated in a broad valley between mountain ranges to the east and west. National forest lands here are also defined by the mountain ridge, encompassing the summit and flanks, but no more. US-211 forms the boundary on the northern side, but it's a somewhat arbitrary one: national forest lands continue north the entire length of Massanutten Mtn. This area affords a good opportunity for extended backcountry trips, whether on foot or on bike. With no developed recreation areas except for the New Market Picnic Area on US-211, the number of visitors to the region stays pretty low. Trails and dirt roads follow a straight northeast-southwest line through the area, mostly on the summit of the mountain at the bottom of its eastern slope. The Shenandoah River parallels national forest lands to the east. From overlooks on top of the mountain, you can see the Shenandoah River and the soaring peaks of Shenandoah National Park beyond.

Shenandoah (E), Elkton (SE), and New Market (NW) are the closest towns.

**getting there:** To reach the S access: from I-81 take exit 247 and turn E onto US-33. Go 12.1 mi to SR-602. Turn L and go 4.7 mi to SR-636. Turn L and go 2.3 mi (at 1.1 mi the pavement ends) to the start of the NF, where the road becomes FR-65. There are trailheads and fishing access along a 10-mi stretch of the road N to FR-375. • From Skyline Dr, turn E onto US-33 and go 11 mi to SR-602. Turn R and follow directions above. • To reach the N access: From I-81, take exit 264 (New Market). Turn E onto US-211 and go 4.2 mi to the visitor center, R, or 4.8 mi to the New Market Gap picnic area, also R. There are trailheads at both locations.

**topography:** The upper reaches of Massanutten Mtn are steep and rugged, with lower slopes that have a much milder grade. Forest cover is dense and is predominantly hardwoods. Elevations are between 1,400 ft in the valley and 3,000 ft on Morgan Knob. **maps:** USGS-FS Tenth Legion, Hamburg, Stanley, Elkton W.

**starting out:** Facilities are limited in the backcountry here. There are pit toilets at the New Market Gap Picnic Area on US-211, and water and restrooms at the visitor center just up the road from there. They also sell a good selection of guide books and maps.

**activities:** Hiking, Mountain Biking, Fishing, Camping

**hiking:** 30 miles of trails follow the high ridge line of Massanutten Mtn and drop down on short, steep spurs to Cub Run Rd (FR-65). At 24.5 miles, *Massanutten Mtn South Trail* is the longest in the area. Starting from the New Market Picnic Area, it follows a straight line S along the crest of the mountain on a combination of old road beds and narrow footpaths. Overlooks along the route provide exceptional views of Page Valley and the Blue Ridge Mtns of

Shenandoah NP to the E. The trail is blazed and easy to follow. Hiking is moderate. The trail ends near the S end of Cub Run Rd. Water is available only intermittently along the trail. If starting from the visitor center, take the *Wildflower Trail* to the picnic area and connect with the *Massanutten Mtn S Trail*. With little possiblity for loop hikes in this area, most trips will involve either backtracking or a vehicle shuttle. Connections with trails N of US-211 are also possible, allowing for extended expeditions.

**mountain biking:** The combination of an almost-empty backcountry area and access on a well-maintained dirt and gravel road make this an excellent area for mountain biking. In addition to Cub Run Road (FR-65), which runs in a straight line from near the area's S end to Catherine Furnace (a 10-mi trip), there are another 10 to 15 miles of dirt roads and old road beds open to bikes. The N section of the Massaunutten Mtn South Trail follows one such road bed that provides scenic vistas and challenging conditions. Riding on FR-65 or the other vehicular roads is easy to moderate, with mostly level terrain. This is a good area for a day trip or a weekdend bike/camp trip.

**fishing:** Two streams that run through the backcountry here are stocked trout waters. Boone's Creek flows through the lush valley between First and Second Mountain at the S end of this area. It's a medium-sized creek with a mild to average gradient and a very rocky bed. The cover on both banks is outstanding and pooling is good. Access is from SR-636 where it first enters national forest land. There are pullouts along the road and you can wade or hike upstream. The creek can be fished for about a mile.

Cub Run is a longer stretch of water that flows N to Catherine Furnace before turing E and eventually emptying into the Shenandoah. It's a small to medium stream with an average gradient and a very rocky bed. The attractive creek has good cover and some small pools. Access is from FR-65, which follows beside it for almost its entire length. Cub Run can be fished for about 5 miles. There are good campsites along the creek for overnight angling trips.

**camping:** Backcountry camping is permitted throughout the area on national forest land, except where posted otherwise. Mountain bikers and fly fishermen looking for campsites will find plenty beside FR-65 and Cub Run.

# Wolf Gap Recreation Area

Wolf Gap is the only area on the Virginia side of the district that is not on Massanutten Mountain. In fact, it's located on the other side of Shenandoah Valley on the border with West Virginia. The mountains here are smaller and less striking than Massanutten, with names that even evoke their diminished stature: Little North and Little Sluice. The upside is that the backcountry is more remote and gets less notice and fewer visitors than the recreation areas on Massanutten. At its southern edge is the recreation area, with a small car campground and picnic grounds that include tables and grills. The backcountry is served by a small network of hiking trails, and mountain bikers will find several trails and dirt roads for riding. The area offers a good alternative to the peak-season crowds on other parts of the district.

Woodstock (E) is the closest town.

**getting there:** From I-81, take exit 283 (Woodstock). Turn W onto VA-42 and go 5.6 mi to SR-675. Turn R and go 3.1 mi to a jct with SR-717. Keep R on SR-675 and go 5.1 mi to the rec area entrance, R.

**topography:** The terrain is mountainous, with generally mild slopes and a few steep, rugged areas. Forest cover is predominantly pines and hardwoods, with most of the forest relatively young. Elevations are between 1,500 and 3,000 ft. **maps:** USGS Wolf Gap, Orkney Springs, Woodstock, Lost City.

**starting out:** facilities are at the rec area, where you'll find a hand water pump and pit toilets.

**activities:** Hiking, Mountain Biking, Camping

**hiking:** Hiking in the area is limited to a few one-way trails, with the possibility of connecting 2 of the trails into a single long hike. In all there are about 15 miles of trails in the area. Trailheads are signed with hiker icons. Access to the *Big Schloss Trail* and *Tibbet Knob Trail* is at the campground. Access to a segment of the *Big Blue Trail* is on SR-600. Highlights along the trails are scenic overlooks and the remote woodland setting. The trails follow a combination of old roadbeds and narrow footpaths. Hiking is moderate and trail use is light to moderate.

**mountain biking:** bikers will find the dirt and gravel roads that lace the backcountry a good way to explore the area. Although the mileage is somewhat limited, a lack of traffic helps to compensate. You can use the campground at Wolf Gap as a parking area or base camp for exporing the region. Riding is moderate, except on some of the trails, where it's strenuous. This area is best for a daytrip.

**camping:** Primitive backcountry camping is permitted throughout the area on NF lands excepted where posted otherwise.

The primitive car campground at Wolf Gap has 10 sites set in a heavily wooded area on the WV border. Each of the large sites has a picnic table, grill, and lantern post. Privacy is good at the sites. Facilities are limited to pit toilets and a hand water pump. There is no fee to camp here. The campground is open all year. Use is light.

# Camp Roosevelt Recreation Area

Bounded by US-211 to the south and the Little Fort and Elezabeth Furnace Areas to the north, this smallish area occupies the summit ridges of Kerns and Massanutten Mountains and the narrow valley that separates them. At the north of the area is Camp Roosevelt, located on the site of the first CCC camp, operated from 1933 to 1942. North of the campground and picnic area at Camp Roosevelt, national forest lands split around fort valley. Trails and roads connect the Camp Roosevelt Area with the two backcountry areas described below on either side of the valley. This permits extended bike, car touring, or backpacking trips. The Massanutten Mountain Area (South) is also adjacent, just across US-211. The campground at Camp Roosevelt provides a good base for exploring the entire Massanutten Mountain Area. Families looking to spend a couple of relaxing hours outdoors can take advantage of the picnic facilities next door. There are shelters, tables, and grills in an attractive woodland setting. In the backcountry there are long and short hiking trails with a few overlook that afford magnificent views of Page Valley and the majestic peaks of Shenandoah National Park. Mountain bikers can ride the well-maintained dirt road that runs through the heart of the area, and connect to other roads (both paved and unpaved) that wind through the mountains and valley. And anglers can try their luck in Passage Creek, a stocked trout stream.

**getting there:** From I-81, take exit 264. Turn E onto US-211 and go 4.2 mi to Lee Highway, L and the Massanutten Visitor Center, R. Turn L onto Lee Highway and go 9 mi (at 1.5 mi come to the *Massanutten Story Trail*, R and the end of the pavement; at 8 mi is the trailhead to the *Lion's Tale Trail*, L) to paved SR-675. Turn R and go 0.2 mi to the rec area.

**topography:** Upland terrain varies between relatively mild and extremely steep and rugged, with exposed rock faces at the highest elevations. Forest cover is consistent throughout the area, and is predominantly hardwoods and pines. Elevations are between 2,822 ft on Catback Mtn and 1,300 ft near the base of Kerns Mtn. **maps:** USGS-FS Hamburg

**starting out:** Facilities are at either end of the backcountry area here. At the visitor center on US-211, yoiu'll find a good selection of guide books and maps for sale. There are also restrooms and water there. It's open daily from 9 AM to 5 PM between Apr and Oct. You'll find pit toilets and water at the Camp Roosevelt Picnic Area.

**activities:** Hiking, Mountain Biking, Fishing, Camping

**hiking:** As with the other parts of the Massanutten Mtn Area, hikers will find the trails around Camp Roosevelt one of the area's major draws. Although this area is smaller than the others, and has only about 15 miles of trails, connections with trails on the areas adjacent to the N and S permit uninterupted hikes of more than 100 miles. The 9-mi *Duncan Hollow Trail* is the main artery in the area. It follows a small drainage in a narrow seam between two high ridgelines. The trail begins 0.1 mi past the campground on SR-675. The trailhead is signed and the trail blazed. It ends on US-211 E of the New Market Picnic Area. Hiking is moderate to strenuous. A couple of other short trails connect the *Duncan Hollow Trail* with the Lee Highway. If you want to hike N from the area, one option is to begin at the the S terminus of the *Massanutten Mtn Trail*, located on SR-675, 0.4 mi E of the Camp Roosevelt Rec Area. The trail runs N along the mountain ridge 24 miles to the Elizabeth Furnace Rec Area

2 short trails in the area deserve special note. One is the *Massanutten Story Trail*. It begins on a curved boardwalk and follows a quarter-mile pave path to an overlook with spectacular views to the east. Along the route, placards tell the story of the history and geology of Massanutten Mountain. The trailhead is on

history and geology of Massanutten Mountain. The trailhead is on Lee Hwy, 1.5 mi N from US-211. The other is the *Lion's Tale Trail*, a national recreation trail. Designed for the visually impaired, the 0.5-mi loop trail allows the sightless to experience the sensations of a mountain woodland setting. Placards in Braille (and type) describe the environs from the point of view of a mountain lion. It is a project of the Lions Club. Hiking on both these trails is easy.

**mountain biking:** Mountain bikers in the area have 2 main arteries to choose from. The easier is the 10 miles of Lee Hwy between US-211 and SR-675. The well-maintained road is open to motor vehicles, but receives very little traffic. It's paved for the first 1.5 miles N from US-211, then it's smooth dirt and gravel. Riding is easy. To complete a 20-mi loop, hook up with the *Duncan Hollow Trail* just E of the campground and ride it S along the small drainage that gives the trail its name. The trail follows a combination of old roadbed and single-track. Riding is moderate to strenuous. For longer trips, you can ride N into Fort Valley on paved roads through scenic farmland, or cross US-211 S and connect with the trails described above in the previous section.

**fishing:** Trout anglers in the area can try their luck in Passage Creek, a small with a mild to average gradient and a very rocky bed. The creek flows N along dirt and gravel Lee Highway, which provides access from numerous pullouts. The forest cover along the stream is very good, creating a very scenic setting and tight conditions that will frustrate fly-fishermen in places. Passage Creek is stocked trout waters. cover.

**camping:** Backcountry camping is permitted throughout the are on national forest land, except where posted otherwise. The Duncan Hollow Trail offers the best opportunity for a backpacking trip.

The Camp Roosevelt Campground has 10 sites located in a heavily wooded area. The large sites are placed far from each other, assuring a maximum degree of privacy for campers. Each site has a picnic table, grill, and lantern post. There are modern restrooms and water spigots in the campground. Sites cost $8/night. The campground is open all year. Use is light to moderate, depending on the time of year.

# Little Fort Recreation Area

Occupying a long, narrow strip of mountain ridges and long valleys, the Little Fort Area overlooks Fort Valley to the east and the deep bends of the North Fork Shenandoah River to the west. At the center of the area is a primitive car campground and the Woodstock Observation Tower, a CCC-era project that affords magnificent sweeping vistas of the surrounding countryside. Although most visitors simply drive up winding, gravel SR-758 to see the sights from the tower, the area offers more intrepid backcountry travelers plenty of highlights. For backpackers, there's a long hiking trail that crosses the area's entire length, and for fly-fishermen, a stocked trout creek runs out of backcountry that can only be reached on foot or a mountain bike. The area is perfect for a day trip or short overnight, with longer trips possible by combining other parts of Massanutten Mountain.

Woodstock (W) is the closest town.

**getting there:** From US-11 in the town of Woodstock (exit 283 off I-81), take SR-758 E 8 mi (after 4.5 mi the pavement ends and the road becomes a winding, steep dirt and gravel road) to the Woodstock Observation observation tower. The rec area is located 1.3 mi E of there on SR-758.

**topography:** A series of long, narrow mountains—Green, Powell, and Three Top Mtns—are separated by very narrow valleys. The uplands are rugged and steep. Elevations are between 1,000 ft in Fort Valley and 2,687 ft. **maps:** USGS-FS Rileyville, Edinburg, Toms Brook, Strasburg.

**starting out:** SR-758 is the center of this area, splitting it into 2 almost equal halves. Along the road are the major destinations in the area: the Woodstock Observation Tower and the Little Fort Rec Area. The road also connects the town of Woodstock with Fort Valley. Limited facilities are available at the campground, where you'll find pit toilets.

**activities:** Hiking, Fishing, Camping

**hiking:** As with the other 3 areas on Massanutten Mtn described here, hiking in the Little Fort Area is dominated by a single long trail that runs in a straight line along the NE–SW orientation of the mountain. The *Massanutten Mtn West Trail* covers 17 miles between Signal Knob and SR-675 in Edinburg Gap. The trail offers the best opportunity in the area for backpacking expeditions (for longer trips connect with the trails of the Elizabeth Furnace Area, described below), with highlights that include scenic vistas from several overlooks and remote backcountry. Vehicle access is at Edinburg Gap (S terminus), at the Little Fort Rec Area or from the Woodstock Observation Tower. These last 2 accesses are near the trail's midpoint. It's N terminus can only be reached on foot. The trailheads are signed and the trail is blazed. Hiking is moderate to strenuous.

**fishing:** Trout anglers can try their luck on Peter's Mill Run, a gorgeous creek that flows down off of Powell Mountain and into Fort Valley and Passage Creek, the area's major drainage. It's small to medium in size with an average to steep gradient that descends over ledges and a very rocky bed.. The forest cover is thick on either side, although a fairly open understory allows for relatively easy fly-casting. Access is from SR-758 along a short distance or from a gated roadbed that follows the creek upstream. Peter's Mill Run is stocked trout waters for about 2 miles. Above that it supports native populations.

**camping:** Primitive backcountry camping is permitted throughout the area on national forest land except where posted otherwise. There's plenty of opportunity for backpacking trips on the *Massanutten Mtn Trail.*

The primitive car campground at Little Fort has 10 sites in a wooded area. The sites are large and spread out over a large area. Each site has a picnic table, grill, and lantern post. There are pit toilets. Privacy is good, though the campground is not exceptionally attractive. Nevertheless, it makes a good base camp for exploring the area. Use is light to moderate. It's open year round. There's no fee to camp there.

# Elizabeth Furnace Recreation Area

Located at the northeast end of Massanutten Mountain, this is the closest national forest area to Washington, D.C. It's named for an iron furnace that dates from the nineteenth century. Today the area is designated the Passage Creek Day-Use Area, with facilities for camping and picnicking. In the backcountry, the major attractions are a large network of trails and a stocked trout creek. Massanutten Mountain, the area's dominant physical feature, is a long, narrow spine that rises abruptly between the broad valleys of the north and south forks of the Shenandoah River. The south fork once served as a transportation artery for shipments of pig iron that were produced in the local furnace. Hike to one of the overlooks on the area's trails and you can see them unwind for miles beneath the shadow of the mountain. With easily-accessible day-use facilities and an extensive backcountry that offers impressive natural scenery, this is the most popular area on the ranger district.

Strasburg (NW) and Front Royal (NE) are the closest towns.

**getting there:** From I-81, take exit 296. Turn S onto VA-55 and go 1.5 mi to a jct with US-11. Turn R and go 0.2 mi on US-11/VA-55 to another jct. Turn R onto VA-55 and go 5.1 mi to SR-678 (Fort Valley Rd). Turn R and go 3.9 mi to the picnic area, L. The campground is ahead another 0.5 mi, also L.

**topography:** The long, narrow spine of Massanutten Mtn rises steeply from valleys to the E and W. The mountain terrain is heavily forested in most areas, with hardwoods and pines predominant. Elevations are between 2,100 and 500 ft. **maps:** USGS-FS Strasburg, Rileyville, Bentonville.

**starting out:** The Elizabeth Furnace Rec Area can be used as a base camp or as a convenient starting-out place. Water and restrooms are located in the picnic area.

Alcohol is not allowed in the Passage Creek Day-Use Area.

**activities:** Hiking, Fishing, Camping

**hiking:** The trail grid here consists of a single trail that follows the long, narrow ridgeline of Massanutten Mtn and a network of shorter trails at the N end of the area. The *Massanutten Mtn East Trail* runs almost arrow-straight for 23 miles between the rec areas at Elizabeth Furnace and Camp Roosevelt. Signed trailheads are located at each area. Aside from the remote mountain setting, the main highlights along the trail are the superb long-range views from several overlooks. for most of its length the trail follows a narrow footpath that's blazed with orange. Hiking is moderate to strenuous. Trail connections can be made with the *Duncan Hollow Trail* in Camp Roosevelt or with any of half a dozen other trails around Elizabeth Furnace. These trails fan out to the W and E of the rec area, winding through steep, mountainous terrain. 2 of the trails, the *Signal Knob Trail* and *Bear Wallow Trail*, connect to the *Massanutten Mtn West Trail*, which follows the W side of the mountain ridge (see Little Fort Rec Area for a description). In all these trails offer hikers another 13 miles to explore, including several loop options which can be done in a day. Trail highlights include rock outcrops that afford views of the surrounding valleys. These trails can be reached from a parking area on SR-678 0.6 mi N of the picnic grounds. The trails are blazed and easy to follow. Use is moderate.

**fishing:** The only opportunity for fishing in the area is on Passage Creek. The major drainage for Fort Valley, it flows through the valley for its entire length. On private property for most of its course, by the time it reenters national forest land near Elizabeth Furnace, its a fairly large creek flowing over a mild to average gradient on a rocky bed. Cover is only average, and poor in places due to the presence of SR-678 at its side. The road makes access easy, but of course diminishes the attractiveness of the creek and the pleasures of fishing it. It can be fished for 4 miles on NF land. It's stocked trout waters.

**camping:** Primitive backcountry camping is permitted on NF lands, but not within the Passage Creek Day-Use Area. Despite this restriction, the area offers ample opportunity for backpacking trips, particularly along the Massanutten Mtn East Trail, where there's a trail shelter at Veach Gap, 8 mi S of the trailhead.

Car campers can overnight at one of the 30 sites in the Elizabeth Furnace Campground. The sites are situated in an attractive wooded area beside Passage Creek. Each of the moderated-sized sites has a picnic table, grill, and lantern post. Privacy is adequate, though not outstanding. There's a Shower/restroom facility as well as pit toilets. Sites cost $11/night. Use is moderate to heavy. The campground is open all year.

Group campsites are available in the area by reservation only. Call the district RS for information.

# South Fork Shenandoah River

Seen from on of the peaks of Massanutten Mountain to the west or the Blue Ridge Mountains to the east, the South Fork Shenandoah River looks like a long, watery snake. Every couple of miles between Luray and Front Royal the river doubles back on itself in long graceful curves. Although that sort of profile is more customarily found on slow-moving coastal rivers, the Shenandoah offers one of the most popular whitewater canoeing and kayaking runs in the entire state. And the mountain scenery is unrivalled, with long mountain summits that rise thousands of feet on either side on Page Valley. The valley itself is home to small, scenic farms that seem to evoke earlier centuries. From Luray to Front Royal, the river unwinds for 50 miles of some of the prettiest mountain scenery in the Commonwealth. This is the perfect place to introduce yourself to whitewater paddling, or, if you're an old hand, to experience an unforgettable river that is rich in history. When you come, be sure to bring your fishing gear, as the river rates very high among smallmouth bass fisheries in the state.

Luray (S) and Front Royal (NE) are the closest towns.

**getting there:** More than 10 river accesses along this stretch of the river. To reach the first put-in, take I-81 to exit 264 (New Market). Turn E onto US-211 and go 9.9 mi to SR-646 just across a bridge. Turn L and go o.1 to the river access. • To get to the take-out: from I-66, take exit 6. Turn S onto US-340. Go 4.1 mi to a traffic light at Kriser Rd. Turn R and go 0.5 mi to Luray St. Turn L and go 0.2 mi to the river and parking area.

**topography:** The river is located at the W edge of a braod valley, backed up by the precipitous slopes of Massanutten Mtn. Elevation on the river is approximately 750 ft. **maps:** USGS Elkton W, Tenth Legion, Stanley, Hamburg, Luray, Rileyville, Bentonville, Front Royal.

**starting out:** Facilities on the river are very limited. In short, bring what you need, and leave home what you can't afford to lose. If you're planning on specding more than a day on the river, make sure to bring an adequate supply of water. Pit toilets are located at High Cliff Rec Area.

**activities:** Canoeing/Kayaking, Fishing, Camping

**canoeing/kayaking:** As the Shenandoah winds is way N from Luray to Front Royal, it presents paddlers with a variety of water conditions. The large majority of the water is flat, with rapids that are mostly class I-II and up to class III coming at fairly long intervals. There are 2 low-water bridges that should be portaged on this section. To paddle the entire section from the boat access W of Luray to Front Royal is a 3-day trip. Shorter trips are possible by launching or taking out at any of 9 other river access points. The W bank of the river is followed by a series of secondary roads with easy access to the boat ramps. Sections of the W bank are also on national forest land, with 2 developed canoe camps for multi-day river trips. Although conditions are the river are not difficult, inexperienced paddlers should seek instruction or take a guided trip before attempting to paddle the river alone. See appendix A for a list of area outfitters.

**fishing:** The S Fork Shenandoah is known far and wide as one of the best rivers for smallmouth bass fishing in Virginia. Other species of game fish in the river are largemouth and rock bass, muskellunge, bluegill, and channel catfish. Conditions on the river include long deep pools, shallow riffles, and rock ledges. With easy canoe access at almost a dozen points between Luray and Front Royal, the Shenandoah is an outstanding destination for daylong or multi-day float/fish trips.

**camping:** Paddlers taking multi-day trips down the S Fork Shenandoah will find varying camping conditions. All of the E bank and most of the W bank is privately owned. When camping on private property, always ask the permission of the landowners first. On the W bank between Foster's Landing and the former site of the Hazard Mill Rec Area almost all of land is on the GW National Forest. Primitive backcountry camping is permitted anywhere on NF land except where posted. In addition, High Cliff is a developed canoe camp with 8 sites. Each site has a picnic table and grill. This is a minimally developed area with facilities are limited to pit toilets. The campground has vehicle access too. These campgrounds are open all year. NOTE: District maps show a second canoe camp named Hazard Mill. Hurricane Fran destroyed the area in September, 1996. As this book went to press there were no immediate plans to rebuild it.

# Shenandoah National Park

In the beginning decades of this century, the area that is now Shenandoah National Park was heavily settled and the land had suffered from years of overuse. In 1926 Congress authorized the establishment of the park and the purchase of lands and removal of settlers began. The park was dedicated in 1936. Since then, the forests have regenerated themselves and the land has healed. Once barren mountainsides now harbor white-tailed deer, black bear, bobcat, wild turkey, ruffed grouse, and other wildlife. 100 species of trees make up the dense forest cover that blankets almost all corners of the park. The park encompasses more than 195,000 acres on the ridges, slopes, and coves of the Blue Ridge Mountains. But that land is not all wilderness. Since its earliest days, the park has been a place where people and nature met. Skyline Drive traverses the Blue Ridge for 109 miles from Rockfish Gap to Front Royal. Along the route are restaurants, gas stations, waysides, campgrounds, and visitor centers. None of these are commercial establishments, but are run by the park for the comfort and convenience of its visitors. And most visitors are content to experience the park from their cars while driving along Skyline Drive. While the road is unquestionablyone of the nation's most scenic, it's only in the backcountry that you can get a true sense of the magical world of Shenandoah National Park. A good way to start is to hike a stretch of the *Appalachian Trail*. It follows the same route as Skyline Drive, but seems to travel through a different world. Away from the traffic and the amenities is the hush of forest glades, the whisper of waterfalls slipping into pools, the rustle of white-tailed deer in the grass. A vast network of hiking trails serves the Shenandoah backcountry. You can hike a mile or hike a hundred miles. Or five hundred. And the entire backcountry is open to backpacking and primitive camping. If you bring a fly rod, you can fish any of dozens of cool mountain streams. The park is one of the largest native brook fisheries still remaining on the east coast. In short, Shenandoah National Park offers the best opportunity to explore the natural habitats of the southern Appalachians. Visits of any length are guaranteed to be rewarding.

From S to N, major towns near the park are Waynesboro (S), Charlottesville (SE), Luray (W), and Front Royal (N). There are dozens of other smaller towns within a fifteen minute drive of the park.

**contact:** Superintendent, Shenandoah National Park, Route 3 Box 348, Luray, VA 22835-9051; 703/999-2266

**getting there:** The park is easy to reach from any direction. In the north, I-66 passes within 5 miles of the Front Royal access, while I-64 provides access to Skyline Dr at the Rockfish Gap access in the south. I-81 parallels the park to the W. There are 4 entrance stations.

**topography:** Such a large park inevitably has drastic variations in terrain. Although the park is mountainous throughout, it is not consistently so: steep, rugged ridges exist side by side with rolling meadows or forest glades. 95% of the park is forested, with 100 tree species represented. The highest elevation on Skyline Drive is 3,680 ft. Highest elevation in the park is 4,051 ft on Hawksbill Mtn. **maps:** Trails Illustrated Shenandoah NP; PATC and USGS topo maps are listed below under individual headings

**starting out:** Entrance fees (good for 7 days) are $5/vehicle, $3 if you enter on bicycle. An annual pass costs $15. Information is available at several visitor centers and waysides, described below under each section. When you enter the park you'll receive a park map and brochure. The map provides a good overview of the park and facilities. The best maps to use for navigating the backcountry are the PATC topo maps. They're for sale at the visitor centers. Speed limit on Skyline Drive is 35 mph.

Dogs are allowed in the backcountry, but must be leashed at all times. Campfires are not allowed in the backcountry.

**activities:** Hiking, Fishing, Camping

**hiking:** There are more than 500 miles of trails in the park. These trails range in length from short roadside leg-stretchers to strenuous backcountry treks. The scenery along the trails is often breathtaking, with mountain vistas, frequent wildlife sightings, waterfalls, and lush forests with a diversity of hardwood and conifers all part of the appeal. The park's longest trail is the *Appalachian Trail*, which crosses the park from one end to the other, a distance of 107 miles. The trail roughly parallels the route of Skyline Drive, crossing and recrossing it numerous times. The *AT* is perhaps the most lovingly maintained hiking trail in the world. It is certainly the most famous. Trail access points are located at frequent intervals along Skyline Drive. The trail is blazed with white bars. The *AT* intersects with many of the park's other trails, offering a tantalizing array of short and long hikes. Almost of every corner of the park's backcountry is served by one trail or another. Heavy trail use and frequent maintenance keeps the treadways clearly defined and easy to follow. Trailheads are jcts are signed. Foot trails are blazed in light blue, horse trails in yellow. No one should visit Shenadoah without spending at least some time hiking it trails through the backcountry.

**fishing:** The mountains of Shenandoah NP are laced with dozens of native trout waters. Because park lands are primarily on the upper slopes of the Blue Ridge Mountain, most of these are headwater streams that often begin as little more than trickles. As they flow down the mountains many quickly gather size, however, so that they are large enough to support populations of brook trout. These creeks are among the most scenic in all of Virginia. Most flow over rocky beds though beautiful forests. Because of the elevation the gradients are generally moderate to steep. All waters within the park are open to catch-and-release fishing. Harvesting is permitted on some streams with populations large enough to sustain the pressure from takings. A list of these creeks is available from visitor centers. A Virginia fishing license is required to fish in the park. Only a single-hook artificial lure can be used. Fishing is permitted all year.

**camping:** Primitive backcountry camping is permitted anywhere in the park except where posted. A free permit is required to camp. You can pick one up at one of the entry stations or visitor centers.

Car campers have 3 campgrounds to choose from: Big Meadows, Lewis Mountain, and Loft Mountain. All 3 are located in the S half of the park. Lewis Mountain is the smallest and most appealing. The other 2 are massive operations meant to accommodate the maximum number of visitors. The campgrounds have different dates of operation, but some camping is usually available from Mar to Dec. Since campground opening dates change every year, you should not rely on the dates given below, but should only use them for general reference. Reservations are accepted at Big Meadows.

# Rockfish Gap to Swift Run Gap

The park's southern third is bounded by Waynesboro and I-64 (S) and US-33 (N). This is a relatively undeveloped part of the park, with only the campground at Loft Mountain and the Dundo Group Camp. Most of the accessible backcountry here is west of Skyline Drive, where there are two large wilderness areas separated by the thin line of Madison Run and the gated road that runs beside it. Opportunities for backcountry solitude are outstanding here. A handful of native brook trout waters flow through the wildernesses and they are served by an extensive network of hiking trails.

Waynesboro (S), Charlottesville (SE), Elkton (NW), and Stanardsville (NE) are the closest towns.

**getting there:** Access to the S third of the park is at Rockfish Gap or Swift Run Gap. US-33 provides access to the latter. To reach Rockfish Gap take from I-64 to exit 99.

**topography:** Terrain is mountainous. Forest cover is consistent throughout the area. Elevations reach their peak on Hightop (3,587 ft). **maps:** PATC #11; USGS Grimora, Browns Cove, McGaheysville, Swift Run Gap.

**starting out:** Information and facilities (restrooms, water, pay phone) are available at the Loft Mountain Wayside (milepost 79.5). It's open from May 15 to Oct 31.

**activities:** Hiking, Camping, Fishing

**hiking:** The *Appalachian Trail* enters the park from the S and crosses Skyline Drive no fewer than 15 times before reaching Swift Run Gap. The main trail network is W of both the *AT* and Skyline Drive, in a pair of adjacent wilderness areas. Most trails intersect with the AT and follow streams or ridges down the slopes of the Blue Rige toward the S Fork Shenandoah River. More than a dozen different loop hikes are possible by combining various trails. Access is from parking areas along Skyline Drive. Hiking ranges from easy to strenuous.

**camping:** Primitive backcountry camping is permitted throughout the park. A free permit, available at the visitor centers and ranger stations, is required.

Loft Mountain Campground has 175 sites arranged in a series of adjacent loops. The sites are small and closely spaced, minimizing privacy. The are has been mostly cleared of tree cover. Each site has a picnic table and grill. restrooms are centrally located, and showers are available at the campstore. The fee is $12/night. The campground is open from May 15 to Oct 31.

**fishing:** 5 of the trails in this section of the park follow creeks that flow W down the slope of the Blue Ridge and feed into the S Fork Shenandoah River. Another stream, Madison Run, is followed by an old gated road. Fishing on all of these creeks is somewhat similar in that all are small headwater streams that drop down over fairly steep gradients and offer about 2or 3 miles of fishable water. Since all are located within wilderness areas, the potential for a fly-fishing/backpacking trip is outstanding. Fishing is not permitted on One Mile Run.

# Swift Run Gap to Thornton Gap

The large middle section of the park is also the busiest. On this section are located two campgrounds, three restaurants, cabins, and a visitor center. There's also a large picnic area at South River. The area is bounded by the two highways that provide access: US-33 (S) and US-211 (N). In the backcountry there are adjacent wilderness areas that are served by a comprehensive network of hiking trails. Also in the area is Old Rag Mountain, a granite-domed peak that is one of the most visually arresting and popular highlights in the park. Although this part of the park is inevitably the most crowded, it's still possible to escape deep into the backcountry.

Luray (NW), Elkton (SW), and Stanardsville (SE) are the closest towns.

**getting there:** S access: on US-33 between Elkton (W) and Stanrdsville (E). N access: on US-211 between Luray (W) and the jct with US-522 (E).

**topography:** This section of the park contains its most varied geography. The granite dome of Old Rag Mtn is here, as are the Big Meadows, the largest open area in the park. The park's highest peak is also here: 4,051 ft on Hawksbill Mtn. **maps:** PATC #10; USGS Big Meadowns, Old Rag Mtn, Fletcher, Elkton E, Luray,

Thornton Gap.

**starting out:** Infromation and facilities (restroom, water, pay phone) are available at 3 locations. The Big Meadows Wayside (milepost 51) is open from Mar 31 to Dec 1. The Byrd Visitor Center is at the same location. Skyland Lodge (milepost 42) is open from Mar 31 to Dec 1. The Panorama (milepost 31.5) is open from Apr 1 to Nov 1.

**activities:** Hiking, Camping, Fishing

**hiking:** The park's wide, busy mid-section also contains the greatest concentration of hiking trails. Unlike the southern section, most of the trails here are located on the eastern side of Skyline Drive and the Blue Ridge. The major network is located E of Skyland and NE of Big Meadows in a large wilderness area. Old Rag Mountain is the dominant geographic and scenic feature. Loop hikes of almost any distance are possible by combining two or more trails in the area. The *AT* provides the major throughway and offers connections to many of the area's trails. Hiking ranges from easy to strenuous. Trail use is heavier here than in other regions of the park. Access to trails is from parking areas on Skyline Drive and from the *AT*.

**camping:** Primitive backcountry camping is permitted throughout the park, except where posted. A free permit, available at the visitor centers and entrance stations, is required.

Car camping is available at 2 campgrounds. Lewis Mountain Campground has 31 sites arranged in a large loop. The attractive grounds are sparsely wooded. The sites are only small to average in size; privacy is correspondingly limited, especially when the campground fills up. Each site has a picnic table and grill. Restrooms are centrally located. Showers are available at the campstore, as is a small selection of supplies. The campground is located at milepost 57.5. It's open from May 1 to Nov 1.

The Meadows Campground has a whopping 238 sites. The small sites are arranged in a series of adjacent loops. The lack of tree cover and the proximity of the sites to one another diminishes privacy to a minimum. Each site has a picnic table and grill. There are restrooms located throughout and a large shower facility. Sites cost $14/night. In summer and fall the campground is often full. The Meadows is open from Apr 1 to Oct 31. Reservations are available from Memorial Day to Oct 31 by calling 800/365-CAMP.

**fishing:** A few of the trails the drop down the E slope of the Blue Ridge follow mountain streams that harbor trout, though most of the trout waters in this section are not accessbile by hiking trail. At the S end of the area there's trail access to the Conway River and the Rapidan WMA. Trout waters in the area are mostly small headwater creeks that flow over very rocky beds that have a moderate to steep gradient. Aside from the chance to fish a native brook trout fishery, the wilderness areas offer excellent opportunities for multi-day fishing expeditions.

# Thornton Gap to Front Royal

Although most Washingtonians enter the park at Front Royal, this is a relatively quiet section of the park. There's no developed campground, so few people remain in the region after sundown. When (and if) the Matthews Arm Campground reopens, that will probably change, but for now the only developed facilities in the area are the Dickey Ridge Visitor Center and the Elkwallow Wayside and Picnic Area. Opportunities for long hiking trips, backcountry camping, and fly-fishing for native brookies are excellent in this part of the park, particularly at the southern end where there are large areas of wilderness.

Front Royal (N) and Luray (SW) are the closest towns.

**getting there:** S access: on US-211 between Luray (W) and the jct with US-522 (E). N access: from I-66, take exit 6. Turn S onto US-340 and go 4.3 mi to the park entrance, L.

**topography:** The vast majority of the terrain here is forested with hardwoods. Terrain is mountainous, with the grades of slopes and ridges varying considerably. Elevations top out at 3,474 ft on Hogback Mtn. **maps:** PATC #9; USGS Chester Gap, Bentonville, Thornton Gap, Luray, Front Royal.

**starting out:** Information and facilities (restrooms, water, pay phone) are available at 2 locations. The Dickey Ridge Visitor Center (milepost 4.6) is open from Apr 1 to Nov 1. The Elkwallow Wayside (milepost 24.1) is open from Apr 1 to Nov 1.

**activities:** Hiking, Camping, Fishing

**hiking:** The *Appalachian Trail* closesly parallels Skyline Drive until milepost 10, when it veers to the NE and leaves the park. The *Dickey Ridge Trail* follows the road from there to its enpoint at the Front Royal Entrance Station. Apart from the linear corridor followed by those two trails, there are a pair of trail networks near the section's S end. They are concentrated in a pair of wilderness areas, one on each side of Skyline Drive. The network that begins at the Elkwallow Picnic Area is the more extensive of the two. It offers several long loop hikes and excellent opportunities for backpacking trips. Trailheads to all trails are at parking areas along Skyline Drive and on the *AT*. Hiking in the area is easy to strenuous. Trail use is moderate.

**camping:** Primitive backcountry camping is permitted throughout the NP except where posted. A free permit is required to camp in the backcountry.

There is no developed campground in this part of the park.

**fishing:** Hiking trails follow 3 trout streams in this section of the park. Jeremy's Run is the longest of these, offering about 5 miles of fishable water. Piney River and the N Fork Thornton River are the other two. As with the creeks throughout the park, these are small headwaters that harbor native brook trout. The stream gradients are generally moderate to steep and the creeks have very rocky beds. The woodland setting on all these creeks makes them among the most delightful of fishing environments in all of Virginia. Jeremy's Run is particularly well suited to a backpacking/fly-fishing trip.

# Rapidan Wildlife Management Area

The Rapidan WMA is named for the river that has long been regarded as the best trout fishery in Virginia. Although a massive flood in 1995 has altered the situation for the time being, the WMA's 10,326 acres of rich, forested mountain ridges and coves still make it one of the best backcountry destinations in the mountain province. Part of the reason is its location. The two largest WMA tracts are surrounded by lands that belong to Shenandoah National Park. The effect is a vast backcountry where the distinction between park and management area is unfelt by the hiker, backpacker, or fly-fisherman. As you hike up into the upper reaches of the Rapidan, you'll be surrounded by a forest of towering hemlocks and hardwoods. The sparkling river twists and drops over ledges and around boulders. Even with the effects of the flood still working their way through the ecosystem, the area is worth a visit simply to enjoy its scenic beauty.

Stanardsville (S) is the closest town.

**contact:** Rapidan River WMA, 1320 Belman Rd, Fredericksburg, VA 24482; 540/248-9360.

**getting there:** From the jct of Skyline Drive and US-33, turn E onto US-33 and go 8.9 mi to VA-230. Turn L and go 3 mi to SR-667. (L the road follows the Conway River upstream. it's ? mi to the start of the WMA.). Continue straight on VA-230 4.2 mi to SR-662. (at 5.5 mi the pavement ends)

**topography:** The mountainous terrain is rugged and steep. Lush hardwood and conifer forests cover most of the acreage. Elevations are between 900 and 3,500 ft. **maps:** USGS Fletcher, Madison.

**starting out:** The WMA is a large, undeveloped backcountry area with no developed facilities. If you're coming to hike or camp, there's no shortage of water, but be sure to treat all surface water before drinking.

**activities:** Fishing, Hiking, Camping

**fishing:** The 2 main tracts of the WMA offer 2 different fisheries. In the N tract is the Rapidan River, which is joined by the Staunton River below the WMA on Shenandoah NP lands. These are both designated as fish-for-fun trout waters. All fish caught must be immediately released. Both creeks are wild trout waters. This watershed was devastated by a flood in 1995, with drastic consequences for the fisheries. As this book went to press, the lower sections of the streams remained closed. The upper reaches of the Rapidan, where flood damage was relatively minor, could still be fished. At these upper stretches the Rapidan is a small, quiet mountain creek flowing over a mild to steep gradient. It is exceptionally beautiful and still offers one of the best backcountry fishing experiences in the state. Summer flows are generally low. Access is from SR-662, which follows the length of the river here.

On the WMA's S tract is the Conway River, a trout creek with characteristics similar to the Rapidan. Only the river's upper reaches are on the WMA . Here the river is a native brook trout fishery, with some native browns toward the lower end of the WMA. Access is from SR-667, which parallels the river.

**hiking:** Although most visitors to the WMA come to fish, it's location amidst lands belonging to the Shenandoah NP offers hikers the opportunity to take trips short or long. Trails can be accessed from either the Rapidan Tract or the Conway River Tract. In keeping with NP standards the trails are well maintained, blazed, and easy to follow. Hiking is moderate to strenuous, with significant elevations gains as the trails follow mountain ridges up to Skyline Drive. One trail follows the Staunton River and is easier to hike.

**camping:** Primitive backcountry camping is permitted on the WMA and in Shenandoah NP. If you're going to camp in the NP, you must first obtain a free permit from one of the visitor centers.

# The Piedmont

# Piedmont Region Key Map

1. Fairy Stone SP
2. Philpott Lake
3. Smith Mountain Lake SP
4. White Oak Mountain WMA
5. Holliday Lake SP
6. Buckingham-Appomattox SF
7. James River WMA
8. Horsepen Lake WMA
9. Hardware River WMA
10. Staunton River SP
11. Occoneechee SP
12. Twin Lakes SP
13. Twin Lakes SP
14. Prince Edward-Gallion SF

15. Cumberland SF
16. Bear Creek Lake SP
17. Amelia WMA
18. Powhatan WMA
19. Pocahontas SP
20. Lake Anna SP
21. C.F. Phelps WMA
22. Prince William Forest Park
23. Sky Meadows SP
24. G.R. Thompson WMA
25. Bull Run Regional Park
26. Fountainhead Regional Park
27. Huntley Meadows Park
28. Riverbend Park
29. Great Falls Park

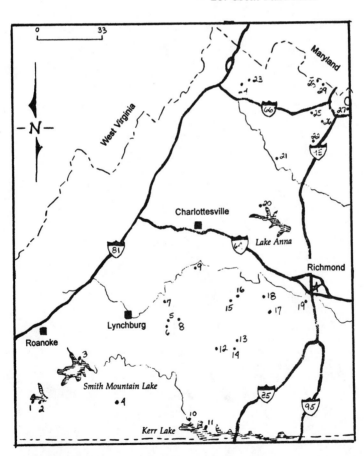

# Introduction

The piedmont refers to the broad band of gently rolling hills that runs the length of the state between the mountains and the coastal plain. Virginia's piedmont is part of a much larger geographical configuration that runs from southern New York to eastern Alabama. Literally meaning "at the foot of the mountain," the long, rolling piedmont lies pressed up against the Appalachian Mountains for its entire length. Its eastern limit is determined by the flat, low-lying lands of the Atlantic coastal plain. In Virginia's northern region, the piedmont is relatively narrow, as the mountains move northeast and the Potomac River flows out of the northwest. In truth, until the Potomac empties into the Cheasapeake Bay, there isn't really much of a coastal plain at all; the piedmont extends almost to water's edge. As you move south, however, the piedmont widens as the mountains continue veering to the southwest and the coastal plain extends no farther west than an imaginary line that runs from Washinton, D.C. to Richmond and continues south through the Carolinas, which have a similar geographical configuration of coast–piedmont–mountains.

Like the coastal plain, the appearance of the piedmont has been radically altered by human settlement and exploitation over the past three centuries. In its natural state, the piedmont was once home to a vast deciduous forest that covered the entire middle section of Virginia. European settlers quickly realized the potential of the fertile soil for growing crops and pasturing animals, and cleared increasingly large areas of forest cover until by the end of the nineteenth century more than 90% of the tree cover had been removed. This condition persists more or less unchanged into the present, and partly accounts for the limited opportunities for backcountry recreation in the area. Put simply, there just isn't that much backcountry left. The large majority of the land is privately owned; most of it is still agricultural, though in the twentieth century increasing population and the demands it places on natural resources have also begun to take their toll. Fortunately, concern about this process and the consequences of eliminating natural habitats has resulted in significant parcels of land being set aside for wildlife conservation and outdoor recreation.

On the piedmont, these areas include the wildlife management areas, state parks, and state forests which make up the bulk of this chapter. On them the hardwood forests of oak, poplar, maple, and sweetgum are being allowed to regenerate themselves on the region's gentle slopes and in the rich bottomlands along the river floodplains. These areas are again becoming a haven for wildlife, with native species such as white-tailed deer, beaver, river otters, wild turkey, pheasant, ruffed grouse, and wood ducks occuring in increased numbers.

The other remaining areas for outdoor recreation are located on the large lakes that punctuate the rolling countryside of the piedmont. These areas too are a result of the demands of human populations in the twentieth century, but in a less direct manner. Activities such as canoeing, kayaking, and fishing are the result of these large lakes being created, not the reason for them. All of the large lakes in the middle of Virginia are man-made. All were created when dams were constructed across the state's major rivers for a variety of reasons, hydro-electric power generation and flood control being the primary two.

Outdoor recreation on the piedmont is something of a challenge. Most of the backcountry areas are rather small, and though many have well-maintained trail networks and attractive campgrounds, there simply isn't enough acreage in most places to allow for long-distance treks. There are a few notable exceptions of course, but adventuring in the middle of the state is on a more modest scale than in the mountains or on the coast. The best times of year for outdoor activity here are the spring and fall. Summer days are often hot and humid, with temperatures frequently in the 90s. On these days, most people prefer the refreshment of the beach or the cooler temperatures of the mountains. The parks and forests of the piedmont are well suited to short visits, or for families who want to take advantage of the amenities not found in the more rugged backcountry areas of the state.

# Fairy Stone State Park

Located at the western end of Philpott Lake, on an adjacent but separate lake, this 4,868-acre park provides a popular summertime swimming area as well as an extensive backcountry and the serene waters of Fairy Stone Lake. The park takes its name from a legend associated with the cross-shaped stones that are unique to the area. According to the legend, the stones are the crystallized tears of the wood fairies who wept when they heard the news of Christ's death. Facilities at the popular park are numerous, and include a swimming beach, food concession, bathhouse, picnic grounds with shelters, tables, and grills, car campground, and boat rentals. During the summer months, the beach draws large crowds. Away from the beach, however, is an extensive backcountry, with a large network of hiking trails. These forested slopes are home to a variety of wildlife, including white-tailed deer, woodchuck, raccoon, wild turkey, and several species of duck. The park is best-suited for a daylong visit, with many amenities for families.

Collinsville (SE) and Martinsville (SE) are the closest towns.

**contact:** Fairy Stone State Park, Route 2, Box 723, Stuart, VA 24171; 540/930-2424

**getting there:** From the Blue Ridge Parkway, exit onto VA-8 at milepost 365.1. Go E on VA-8 12.5 mi to VA-57. Turn L and go 7.8 mi to VA-346. Turn L and go 1 mi to the park entrance.

**topography:** The rolling piedmont that surrounds Fairy Stone Lake is covered by a hardwood forest with an understory in which rhododendron is prominent. Large areas have been cleared to facilitate the park-like setting. Elevation on the lake is 1,000 ft. **maps:** USGS Philpott Reservoir.

**starting out:** Entrance fee to the park is $2/vehicle on weekends, $1 on weekdays. Before heading out onto the trails or lake, pick up a park map at the park office. Most facilities (restrooms, water, pay phone) are located near the swimming beach.

The public use or display of alcohol is not allowed. Pets must be kept on a leash.

**activities:** Hiking, Camping, Canoeing/Kayaking, Fishing

**hiking:** 2 separate trail networks provide access to the park's extensive woodland backcountry. The main trail network covers just over 10 miles of short trails. Since most of the trails connect with one another, you can string together loops of different lengths. A second trail network is located across the lake from the main part of the park. 4 trails cover 3.5 miles, with several loops possible. Most of the trails in the park are similar, winding along upland ridges through hardwood forest. There are some vantage points that offer views out over the lake, but the real attraction is the forest setting. Although not all trails are blazed, heavy use keeps them clearly defined and easy to follow. Hiking is easy to moderate. Footbridges cross wet areas. Trailheads are signed. To reach the trailhead to the smaller trail network, follow directions below to the boat ramp, continuing past it 0.1 mi to the trailhead parking area, L.

**camping:** The car campground has 51 sites spread out over a heavily forested hillside. Although the setting is pleasant, the sites are small and crowded together, reducing privacy to a minimum. Each site has a picnic table and grill. The sites cost $15/night. There's one centrally located shower/restroom facility. The campground is pretty popular, and can get crowded on peak weekends. It's open from Mar 1 to Dec 1. Reservations are available by calling 800/933-PARK.

A 4-site primitive backcountry camping area offers a more isolated setting. A 1.5-mi hike is necessary to reach the sites. A permit is required to camp in the area.

**canoeing/kayaking:** 168-acre Fairy Stone Lake provides a quiet setting for a half-day or day on the water. With gasoline powered motors prohibited from the lake, boat traffic is kept to a minimum. Apart from the busy area at the park's beach, the serene shoreline is blanketed with a forest of hardwoods. Since the lake is fairly small, a short paddle or a fishing trip are ideal excursions. The park rents paddle boats and rowboats during the summer. To reach the park boat ramp, leave the main park entrance and go 0.5 mi on VA-346 to SR-346. Turn R and go 0.8 mi to the boat ramp, R.

**fishing:** With the much larger and better-known Philpott Lake next door, Fairy Stone Lake doesn't receive much attention from area anglers. Nevertheless, it supports populations of largemouth bass, walleye, crappie, and bluegill. Fishing from a canoe is the best bet. A few open areas along the shoreline provide a second option.

# Philpott Lake

One of the most beautiful lakes in central Virginia, man-made Philpott Lake sprawls across three counties in the shadow of the Blue Ridge Mountains. The lake was created in the years after World War II when the U.S. Army Corps of Engineers constructed a dam across the Smith River to provide flood control and power generation. The deep 2,880-acre lake—it has a shoreline of more than 100 miles—unwinds its 15-mile length in a long, narrow profile. 6,500 acres of the surrounding land is publicly owned, so that the lake sits nestled among the forested foothills of the western piedmont. Twelve recreation areas that provide boat access, campgrounds, swimming beaches, and hiking trails are the only development you'll find along the lake's shoreline. Although the lake offers outdoor enthusiasts of all stripes a vast watery playground, it offers the most to canoeists and kayakers. Aside from many secluded inlets and coves to explore, the lake provides one of the best opportunities for multi-day paddling trips away from the coast. Deer Island and Mize Point both feature campgrounds that can only be reached by boat. Although sailboats, powerboats, jet-skis all share the lake, its 15-mile length helps keep the traffic spread out. Come during the week or off-season, and you'll find hardly anyone at all on the water.

Collinsville (SE) and Martinsville (SE) are the closest towns.

**contact:** U.S Army Corps of Engineers, Project Manager's Office, Philpott Lake, Route 6, Box 140, Bassett, VA 24055; 540/629-2703

**getting there:** From the jct of VA-8 and VA-57, take VA-57 N 14.5 mi to Philpott Dam Rd (SR-904). Turn L and go 1 mi to the management center. There are numerous other access points around the lake, including six with boat ramps.

**topography:** Philpott Lake lies at an elevation of 1,000 ft in the shadow of the Blue Ridge Mountains. The terrain surrounding the lake is dominated by the characteristic hills of the piedmont, but this close to the mountains they are more truly foothills. Forest cover is general except in the park areas; hardwoods and pines are both present. **maps:** USGS Philpott Reservoir.

**starting out:** Reservoir maps, brochures, and other info are available at the management center next to the dam. The center is open weekdays from 8 AM to 4 PM. An overlook there provides excellent views out over most of the lake.

**activities:** Kayaking/Canoeing, Fishing, Camping

**kayaking/canoeing:** Among large lakes in the Commonwealth, Philpott is unsurpassed for scenic beauty. Its location in the shadow of the Blue Ridge Mountains means a shoreline of heavily forested foothills. In spring and autumn, the displays of color are spectacular. The only drawback to paddling is the popularity of the lake with all types of watercraft. Sailboats, bass boats, jet-skis, and power boats pulling water skiiers are all encountered. Fortunately, the lake's long, narrow profile helps keep the boats spread out. And there are plenty of fingers and coves to escape into. Nearby Smith Mountain Lake helps draw much of the power boat traffic away, but if you come during peak season with visions of an empty lake set in pristine wilderness, you'll be disappointed. In addition to the boat ramp described above, there are half a dozen other access points located all around the lake.

**fishing:** The lake boasts a large selection of game fish, including species that are both native and non-native species. Both warm-water and cold-water species are taken. Largemouth and smallmouth bass, brown and rainbow trout, walleye, black crappie are all abundant. Coho salmon and lake trout are also present. The lake is deep and the shoreline drop-off steep, presenting a challenge to anglers fishing from a canoe or kayak. Most anglers find success fishing deep.

**camping:** Canoeists and kayakers can choose from 2 primitive backcountry camping areas on the lake that can only be reached by boat. Mize Point is located within a mile of the dam and the put-in at Philpott Park. It's part of the mainland, but there's no vehicle access. Each of the 12 campsites in the area has a picnic table, grill, and tent pad. There are pit toilets and drinking water in the area. Sites cost $8/night. Deer Island is more remote, but still only a short paddle from the Philpott Park put-in (not quite 2 miles).

There are 29 sites on the island. Each site has a picnic table and grill. Pit toilets and drinking water are available. The sites cost $8/night. Campgrounds are open all year.

In addition to these areas, there are 5 more rec areas with developed car campgrounds. Some of these have sites that are on the water. Sites at these campgrounds cost $8/night, $12/night for sites on the water. Facilities include modern restrooms and showers. Some offer camping year round, others are only open between Apr 1 and Oct 1.

# Smith Mountain Lake State Park

The 1,506-acre park is located on the north shore of the vast lake that gives the park its name. The man-made lake was created when a dam was constructed on the Roanoke River in 1966. The primary purpose of the project was electricity production. Outdoor recreation on the lake has been a related and popular benefit. Park facilities are designed to take advantage of these recreational possibilities. Most park visitors come to launch there boats or to sunbathe and swim in the beach area. The backcountry area is rather limited, and with so many people enjoying the water on summer weekends, this is not the place to come to seek wilderness isolation. Not that there's a lack of less austere outdoor recreation available. With the largest lake entirely within Virginia on its doorstep, the park offers anglers, canoeists, and kayakers easy access to its possibilities. Facilities on land include a car campground, boat ramp, beach with bathhouse, visitor center, boat rentals, and small network of hiking trails. The park is ideal for families looking to spend some time outdoors with a minimum of planning and effort. Sea kayakers wanting to cover a considerable distance without going to the ocean will appreciate the sheer size of Smith Mountain Lake. The park is open all year.

Roanoke (NW) is the closest city.

**contact:** Smith Mountain Lake State Park, Route 1, Box 41, Huddleston, VA 24104; 540/297-6066

**getting there:** From the jct of US-29 and VA-43, turn W onto VA-43 and go 12.7 mi to SR-626. Turn L and go 11.8 mi to the park entrance, R.

**topography:** The terrain surrounding the lake is typical of the western piedmont: Forested uplands undulate in gentle, rolling hills. Some areas have been cleared and landscaped to foster a park-like setting. Lake elevation is 795 ft. **maps:** USGS Smith Mountain Dam, Moneta SW.

**starting out:** The parking fee is $2/vehicle on weekdays, $3 on weekends. Additional fees are charged for boat launches and using the swimming beach. Facilities (restrooms, pay phones, water) are located at the boat ramp. Park maps and brochures are available at the visitor center or from the park office.

The public use of alcohol is not permitted. Pets must be leashed. Swimming in the lake is only allowed in designated areas.

**activities:** Canoeing/Kayaking, Fishing, Hiking, Camping

**canoeing/kayaking:** With a length of 40 miles and 500 miles of shoreline, Smith Mountain Lake is almost a small inland sea. There's no shortage of room to paddle, nor of coves and inlets to explore. Paddlers should keep in mind, however, that you will not be the only ones on the lake (at least not on peak-season weekends). Water-skiers, jet-skiers, sailboats, bass boats, and power boats are all a presence—a sometimes noisy and unwelcome one too. Also, such a large body of water is susceptible to conditions that vary considerably. The lake's surface can be mirror-still with not a breath of wind to be felt, or there can be choppy, windy conditions that challenge even experienced paddlers. The lakeshore is generally scenic, though most of it is privately owned with at least some development, though there is little unattractive commercial development. In addition to the boat ramp in the park, there are more than a dozen access points around the lake, which make it possible to take one-way trips with a vehicle shuttle. Camping is possible on the lakeshore at any of a number of campgrounds or on the parts of the shoreline that are publicly-owned. Since there are no designated backcountry sites on the lake, the best rule of thumb is to be as discreet as possible an to avoid areas that are obviously privately owned, such as golf courses and resorts. A $2 fee is charged to put in at the boat ramp in the state park.

**fishing:** Smith Mountain Lake is one of the most highly regarded spots for striped bass fishing in Virginia. Because of the lake's vast size, anglers utilizing specialized electronic fish-finding equipment and power boats that can cover a lot of water have a distinct advantage over those who fish from the shore or from a canoe or kayak. Still, fishing can add another element of excitement to paddling trips. In addition to stripers, the lake holds populations of largemouth and white bass, channel catfish, crappie, and sunfish. For land-bound anglers, there's plenty of open space on the shoreline to cast from, and a fishing pier is located next to the boat ramp.

**hiking:** With only 4 short trails, the state park is not a major hiking destination. The trails are not intended to compete with the more popular water-based activities in the park, but they do add another dimension for visitors interested in the ecology of the land that surrounds the lake. Combined, the trails cover about 4.5 miles. The major attractions along the trails are the forested uplands and lakeside vistas. The 1.3-mi *Turtle Island Trail* is a nature interpretive loop trail with a guide available at the trailhead. Hiking on all park trails is easy. Signed trailheads are located on the main park road.

**camping:** The park's car campground has 50 sites located in a semi-forested area. The sites are rather small and not very well spaced, which minimizes privacy. Each site has a picnic table, grill, and lantern post. There are modern restrooms and a cold water outdoor shower. The sites cost $8/night, $3 more if you bring a pet.

# White Oak Mountain WMA

Covering 2,700 acres of forested and open piedmont terrain that barely qualify as hilly, the White Oak Mountain Wildlife Management Area belies its name. The WMA is located in the southwestern piedmont in Pittsylvania County; the western boundary is formed by the Banister river. The area is best known to hunters, who pursue white-tailed deer, wild turkey, and small mammals in the area's forests and fields. Anglers come to fish the five small ponds, which harbor several warm-water species. For the outdoor enthuusiast or nature photographer, White Oak Mountain offers the chance to travel through upland and bottomland forests in various stages of succession, to observe wildlife, or to camp out in the backcountry. The area is intensively managed to improve wildlife habitat, but conditions are primitive, and except during hunting season, the area is likely to be just about deserted.

Chatham (W) is the closest town.

**contact:** White Oak Mountain WMA, Route 6, Box 410, Forest, VA 24551-9806; 804/525-7522.

**getting there:** From US-29 in Chatham, take the SR-832 exit. Turn E onto SR-832 and go 4.1 mi to SR-649. Turn R and go 2.5 mi to SR-640. Turn R and go 0.9 mi to gravel SR-706. Turn R and go 1.2 mi to SR-707. Turn L and go 0.1 mi to an information board and the entrance to the WMA.

**topography:** The rolling countryside typical of the piedmont supprts a variety of plant communities. A mixed hardwood–pine forest covers the majority of the preserve, but there are also large open areas maintained for wildlife habitat. Elevations are between 550 and 900 ft. **maps:** USGS Spring Garden.

**starting out:** Facilities on the WMA are very limited. There's an information board with a WMA map at the entrance described above, but that's about it. You can get a map that shows the location of the ponds and most of the trails from the address above. Hunting occurs on the WMA in fall and winter. If you go during that time, wear at least one article of blaze.

**activities:** Hiking, Camping, Fishing, Mountain Biking, Canoeing

**hiking:** As on most of the other WMAs in Virginia, the trail network consists mainly of old gated roadbeds and narrow footpaths used perennially by hunters and anglers. These unsigned, unblazed trails extend into all corners of the WMA and cover a total distance of about 10 miles. Hiking is not difficult, nor is locating or following the trails, but conditions are somewhat different from those hikers and backpackers are accustomed to in parks and forests. The main highlights along the trails are the chance to observe wildlife and to travel through the native woodlands that once covered almost all of the piedmont. Access to the trails is at numerous small parking areas at the start of the gated roads. Trail use is light, except during hunting season, when non-hunters

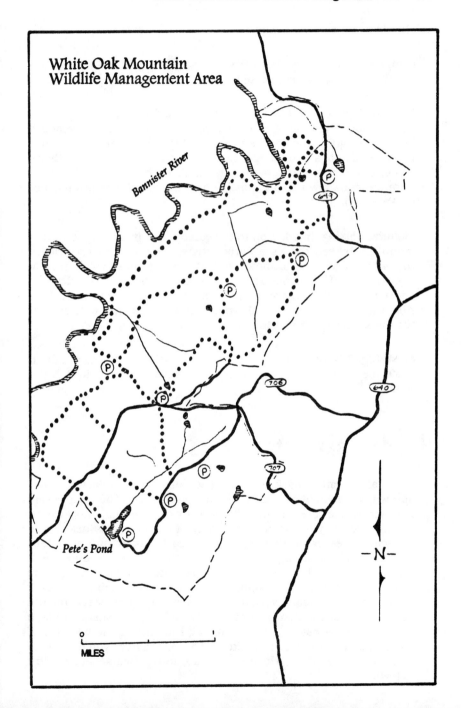

White Oak Mountain
Wildlife Management Area

Bannister River

706

640

707

Pete's Pond

-N-

0          1
MILES

should avoid the backcountry.

**camping:** Primitive backcountry camping is permitted throughout the WMA, except where posted.

**fishing:** 5 ponds on the WMA are open to fishing. Of these, only Pete's Pond, the largest, is named on the WMA map. Largemouth bass, bluegill, and catfish are all taken from its waters. Largemouth bass and bluegill can be caught in each of the other 4 lakes, too. Grass Carp in the lake can't be harvested. Fishing is from the banks, which are mostly open. It's possible to put a canoe on Pete's Pond.

**mountain biking:** In addition to the gated roads (which are closed to mountain bikes), there's a fairly extensive network of unsurfaced roads that are open to motor vehicles. Since these roads receive almost no traffic (some are closed seasonally), they are ideal for short rides. While there simply isn't enough mileage for a long ride, the roads offer a nice alternative to hiking as a way to explore the backcountry. Riding is easy.

**canoeing:** It's possible to put a canoe on Pete's Pond, although since it's so small the only reason to do so would be to fish the pond.

# Holliday Lake State Park

This rather small park is located within the boundaries of the sprawling Appomattox-Buckingham State Forest. The park covers 250 acres, the forest almost 20,000. In combination, they afford the backcountry visitor a nice variety of outdoor activities. While the state forest is particularly well suited to hiking and mountain biking trips, the state park offers a developed campground which can be used as a base for exploring the area, as well as a 115-acre lake which accomodates boating, fishing, and swimming. The park is geared toward family visits, with a white sand beach on the lake, a lifeguard station and diving platform, picnic shelters, and a bathhouse/concession stand. A hiking trail circles the lake, but if you're looking for a real backcountry experience, you'll have to venture outside the park into the state forest (see separate entry below).

Appomattox (W) and Farmville (E) are the closest towns

**contact:** Holliday Lake State Park, Route 2, Box 622, Appomattox, VA 24522; 804/248-6308.

**getting there:** From the jct of US-460 and VA-24 in Appomattox, go E on VA-24 7.8 mi to SR-626. Turn R and go 3.3 mi to SR-640. Turn L and go 0.2 mi to SR-692. Turn R and go 2 mi to the park entrance. The entire route is signed.

**topography:** Gently rolling piedmont terrain is covered with a forest of pines and hardwoods. Some areas around the lake have been cleared. Elevation on the lake is 500 ft. **maps:** USGS Holliday Lake.

**starting out:** An entrance fee of $1/vehicle is charged. Facilities (restrooms, water, pay phone) are at the visitor center and bathhouse complex. You can pick up a park map and brochure at the former. Peak season crowds congregate at the beach.

Alcohol is not permitted in the park. Pets must be leashed.

**activities:** Canoeing/Kayaking, Fishing, Hiking, Camping

**canoeing/kayaking:** Holliday lake offers a pleasant woodland setting for a short paddle or for fishing from a canoe. Drawbacks to the lake are its small size and the presence of the popular beach. There's a boat ramp in the park. You can launch your own boat from there, or rent a canoe from the park. Rental rates are $16/day Rentals are available between May and Sep. All boats must be off the lake by dark. Boats with gasoline engines are not permitted on the lake.

**fishing:** If you bring rod and reel, you can fish for a good variety of game species that inhabit the lake: northern pike, crappie, channel catfish, largemouth bass and sunfish. The best method is probably to bring or rent a canoe, though there are places along the shore from which it's possible to cast.

**hiking:** The only hiking trail to speak of in the park is the 5-mi *Lakeshore Trail*. As its name suggests, it circles the lake, passing through the forest that crowds its shoreline. The signed trailhead is behind the bathhouse. Trail improvements include wildlife observation decks built over the lake. Hiking on the trail is easy.

**camping:** The park's car campground has been recently refurbished. 30 sites are laid out in a double loop in a sparsely wooded area. The proximity of the sites to one another diminishes privacy. Each site has a picnic table, grill and lantern post on a platform of crushed cinders. There's a shower/restroom facility (hot water). Fee is $11/night; $15/night with hookup. If you bring a pet, you must pay an extra $3/night. Campground is open Mar 1 to Dec 1.

# Appomattox-Buckingham State Forest

19,706 acres of managed woodland sprawl across the two counties that give this forest its name. Although outdoor recreation is only one of the forest's several management objectives, and not really a high priority, Appomattox-Buckingham offers the backcountry traveler a rather enticing environment, particularly by piedmont standards. White-tailed deer, wild turkey, ruffed grouse, and quail inhabit the area, and four small natural areas preserve forest types typical of the piedmont. The main recreation attraction here is the large network of dirt state roads and gated forest roads. With a minimum of automobile traffic—and in some cases none at all—on dozens of miles of roads, hikers and mountain bikers are free to roam at will. And since this isn't a major destination on the outdoor circuit, odds are good that you'll have the place pretty much to youself. Except perhaps in fall and winter, when hunting takes place. Without any facilities to speak of or marked trails, this area is probably best for those looking for a bit of a challenge. Since camping is prohibited on the forest, trips longer than a day should be based out of Holliday Lake State Park (see separate listing above), located within the state forest's boundaries.

Appomattox (W) and Farmville (E) are the closest towns

**contact:** Appomattox-Buckingham State Forest, Route 3, Box 133, Dillwyn, VA 23936; 804/983-2175

**getting there:** Numerous state roads provide access to the forest. From Appomattox, take VA-24 E 6 mi where it reaches the forest and skirts its N boundary. Side roads SR-616, SR-626, and SR-636 all enter into the heart of the forest. Another option is to follow directions below to Holliday Lake SP, which lies within the state forest at its SE end.

**topography:** Piedmont tableland is covered in pine and hardwood forests in various stages of succession. The forest is managed for timber production; age and species of tree vary accordingly. Elevations are between 500 and 700 ft. **maps:** USGS Holiday Lake, Andersonville.

**starting out:** There are no facilities in the forest. A map that shows the forest roads is available at Holliday Lake SP or by contacting the forest at the above address. Visitors to the forest should wear blaze orange during hunting season, which occurs in the fall and winter.

Camping is not allowed in the state forest outside of Holliday Lake SP.

**activities:** Hiking, Mountain Biking.

**hiking/mountain biking:** Although there are no designated, signed, or blazed trails in the forest, there is no shortage of opportunity for hiking or riding through the forest. The numerous roads that criss-cross forest lands are all open to non-motorized travel. Most are open to motor vehicles as well, though traffic is very light. With a map and a little imagination, a hike or ride of almost any length can be put together. The forest roads are mostly level and in good shape. Travel on foot or bike is easy.

# James River Wildlife Management Area

The James River WMA encompasses 1,200 acres of river bottomland and rolling piedmont upland on the north bank of the James River. It's located in Nelson County in one of the least developed areas on the piedmont. A trip down the river on either side of the WMA reveals a stretch of small farms, with little or no other development, that seems to go on forever. Access to the James, Virginia's largest river, is one of the main benefits of the refuge. The other is active management to provide habitat for a diversity of wildlife species. While an emphasis is place on game species of interest to hunters, the WMA is also one of Virginia's Watchable Wildlife areas. Visitors frequently see white-tailed deer, rabbits, and other small mammals. Wild turkey, bobwhite quail, river otter, and beaver are also present, but are less frequently seen. Waterfowl species such as Canada geese and wood duck can be seen on the freshwater marsh near the river. Nature photographers and birders will both find the James River WMA a rewarding location.

Buckingham (SE) is the closest town.

**contact:** James River WMA, Route 6, Box 410, Forest, VA 24551-9806; 804/525-7522.

**getting there:** From downtown Scottsville, take VA-6 W 2.8 mi to SR-626. Turn L and go 16.2 mi to gravel SR-743. Turn L and go 0.3 mi to a fork. Bear L and go 0.8 mi to the river and boat ramp. • From US-60 1.5 mi W of Buckingham, turn W onto VA-56 and go 13 mi to SR-626 and go 0.8 mi to SR-743. Follow directions above to the boat ramp and river.

**topography:** Uplands on the WMA are the gently rolling hills that characterize the piedmont. The one-time agricultural fields have mostly reverted to forest, with some areas maintained in an open state to provide wildlife habitat. The forests are still relatively young, with pines the predominant species. Elevations are between 350 and 500 ft. **maps:** USGS Howardsville.

**starting out:** There are no developed facilities on the refuge. If you're going to stay awhile or paddle the river, bring as much water with you as you'll need. Hunting takes place on the WMA in fall and winter. It's a good idea to wear blaze orange during this period.

**activities:** Canoeing/Kayaking, Camping, Hiking, Fishing

**canoeing/kayaking:** Where the James River passes through the WMA it has already flattened out from its whitewater descent from the mountains. Most of this stretch of the river is flatwater, with a few riffles interspersed. The river is wide here and most of the land on either bank is open, as this is farm country. If you're putting in upstream of the WMA, it's about a 15-mile float from the put-in at Bent Creek off US-60. Downstream, it's a 9-mile float to the next boat ramp at Howardsville. Of course, much longer trips are possible, as the James crosses the entire state. One such 2-day trip is from the James River WMA to the Hardware River WMA, a 25-mile float.

**camping:** Primitive backcountry camping is permitted anywhere on the WMA except where posted. Canoe or kayak camping is a possiblity, as there's plenty of open space along the shore of the James.

**hiking:** Hiking on the WMA is fairly limited and is not particularly rewarding. Because the land has recently been agricultural and is managed to optimize wildlife habitat, the scenery along the trails is a scraggly hodge-podge of meadows, planted fields, and immature pine forests. While this combination may not be very visually appealing, it does afford a good chance to view wildlife. About 5 miles of gated roadbeds and foot trails criss-cross the WMA, providing access to all its various habitats. None of the trails are signed or named, though locating and following them is not difficult. In fact, because large parts of the refuge are cleared, cross-country travel is quite simple. Hiking throughout the WMA is easy. Trails are reached from several parking areas on the main WMA road.

**fishing:** Fishing on the James River is possible from the banks or from a canoe. With the current here usually slow, a day spent on the river fishing from a canoe can be quite rewarding. Smallmouth bass is the main sportfish that anglers go after here, with muskellunge, channel catfish and sunfish also present.

# Horsepen Lake Wildlife Management Area

Like most of the wildlife management areas on the piedmont, Horsepen Lake encompasses a variety of habitats—pine/hardwood upland forests, former agricultural fields reverting to forest, large clearings, and bottomland hardwood forest—managed to accommodate local wildlife. Mammals that inhabit the preserve include white-tailed deer, river otter, mink, opossum, fox, and muskrat. Doves and wild turkey the major bird species present. At the center of the WMA is an 18-acre lake that offers area anglers the chance to fish for warm-water game species in a farm-pond setting. Although most visitors to Horsepen Lake WMA are hunters or fishermen, the 3,065-acre preserve also attracts nature photographers, hikers, campers, and paddlers. Except during hunting season, the WMA is never very crowded; during summer the lake is the busiest area. Unless you're a hunter, it's best to avoid the area during deer gun season.

Buckingham (N) is the closest town.

**contact:** Horsepen Lake Wildlife Management Area, Route 6, Box 410, VA 24551-9806; 804/525-7522.

**getting there:** From US-60 in the small community of Buckingham, turn S onto SR-638 and go 3 mi to the WMA entrance, L. Ahead it's 1.1 mi to the boat ramp.

**topography:** A large majority of the rolling hills that cover the WMA are blanketed by a pine/hardwood forest, slowly regenerating after years of agriculture. Wildlife clearings and bottomland hardwood forest are also present. Average elevation is 500 ft. **maps:** USGS Buckingham, Andersonville.

**starting out:** There are no facilities on the WMA. You can get a map that shows trails and roads from the address above. Hunting takes place on the WMA in fall and winter. If you visit during periods of hunting activity, wear at least one article of blaze orange.

**activities:** Canoeing, Fishing, Hiking, Camping

**canoeing:** 18-acre Horsepen Lake is the perfect size for spending a lazy afternoon drifting on the water or angling for bass from a canoe. Although boats with motors are also allowed on the lake, most boaters come for the fishing, so there's not a lot of actual motoring going on. The lakeshore is scenic, with a combination of forest and meadow. There's a boat ramp at the N end of the lake.

**fishing:** Game species in Horsepen Lake include largemouth bass, black crappie, northern pike, bluegill, and channel catfish. The best way to fish the lake is from a canoe, though there's also room along the shoreline for landbound anglers to cast from.

**hiking:** A network of maintained trails and gated roadbeds extend into all reaches of the WMA. Although these trails are used primarily by hunters, they provide hikers and backpackers the chance to explore the local natural environment or simply take a pleasant walk in the woods. The trails are not blazed or signed, but they are not difficult to locate or follow, as most begin at gated roads that are reached from the main roads that provide ingress to the WMA. Hiking on the trails is easy. Trail use is light, except during hunting season.

**camping:** Primitive backcountry camping is allowed anywhere on the WMA except where posted otherwise.

# Hardware River Wildlife Management Area

Although it sits on the banks of the James River, the Hardware River WMA is named for the smaller river that forms a part of its boundary and runs through its interior. The 1,034-acre preserve is located on the central piedmont in Fluvanna County, about half way between the mountains and the coast. Combining the floodplain of the James and rolling uplands forested with a combination of harwood and pine species, the WMA offers habitat for wildlife that uncommon for a part of the state that is predominantly agricultural. The main activities on the WMA are hunting, fishing, and canoeing the James. Commonly seen wildlife species include white-tailed deer and wild turkey, with numerous other small mammals present. Although the majority of visitors to the refuge are hunters, hikers, backpackers, nature photographers, and birders should not overlook the area's offerings. The boat ramp allows canoeists and kayakers to explore as much as the James River as they want. One drawback to the backcountry setting of the preserve is the active set of railroad tracks that run beside the river. As many as ten trains pass through each day. The refuge is open all year, with the heaviest concentration of visitors coming during hunting season. Nonhunters should probably avoid the area during deer gun season.

Scottsville (NW) is the closest town.

**contact:** Hardware River Wildlife Management Area, 1320 Belman Rd, Fredericksburg, VA 24482; 540/248-9360.

**getting there:** From the jct of VA-6 and VA-20 in downtown Scottsville, turn E on VA-6 and go 3.7 mi to SR-611. One access to to turn R and go 2.5 mi (at 1.6 mi the pavement ends) to the end of the road at a gated roadbed that enters the WMA interior. The reach the other access and boat ramp continue straight on VA-6 and go 2.7 mi to SR-646. Turn R and go 3.6 mi to the parking area on the James River

**topography:** The broad flood plain of the James is flat. Uplands rise and fall in gentle swells. Formerly agricultural, much of the area is now covered by a young forest in various stages of succession. Wildlife clearings are also prevalent. Elevations are between 250 and 450 ft. **maps:** USGS Scottsville, Diana Mills.

**starting out:** There are no facilities on the WMA. If you're going to stay a while or heading out for a trip on the river, bring enough water with you. Hunting takes place in the fall and winter. If you're going to visit during those times, wear at least one article of blaze orange.

**activities:** Canoeing/Kayaking, Fishing, Camping, Hiking

**canoeing/kayaking:** Paddlers can use the WMA's boat ramp on the James as a put-in or take-out spot. This section of the river is mostly flat-water and class I riffles, with one or two class II rapids downstream. As far as piedmont rivers go, the James is wide here, befitting the state's largest river. The scenery is mostly of small farms that line either side of the river. The closest upstream put-in is at Scottsville, 6 river miles away. Downstream, its a scenic, 7-mi float to the boat ramp at New Canton under the US-15 bridge. Multi-day trips of almost any length are possible on the river, which can be run all the way from the mountains to the sea. Campers along the river should be sure to only camp on public land—such as the WMA—or to seek the permission of landowners before making camp on their property.

**fishing:** Both the Hardware and James Rivers support populations of game fish. Smallmouth bass, channel catfish, crappie, and sunfish are the main catches. Fishing can be done from the bank of either river, or, for a more remote, adventurous outing, from a canoe on the James. The water upstream from the WMA is flatter and easier to fish from a canoe.

**camping:** Backcountry camping is permitted on WMA lands except where posted. Canoeists and kayakers using the WMA as a stopover point will find plenty of space beside the banks to make camp. One drawback to camping there, however, is the proximity to the trains that seem to rumble through all night long.

**hiking:** Although the WMA is not a main hiking destination by any means, a small network of gated roadbeds and trails does allow on-foot exploration of the backcountry. Except during hunting season, the trails are virtually deserted, meaning you'll probably have a good chance of spotting wildlife. The trailheads are not signed and the trails themselves are not blazed, though finding and following them is easy. Just look for parking areas along the main WMA roads at any of several gated roadbeds. Park your car, bring a map and compass, and start exploring.

# Staunton River State Park

Staunton River State Park covers 1,597 acres on Kerr Reservoir at the confluence of the Roanoke and Dan Rivers. The reservoir—known in the Commonwealth as Buggs Island Lake—straddles the Virginia/North Carolina state line. It is one of the most popular recreational lakes in either state, and on late spring and summer days draws a crowd of watersports afficionadoes to its 50,000 acres. Sailboats, bass boats, power boats pulling water skiers, and jet skis can all be seen plying its waters. Staunton River SP is but one of more than a dozen developed recreation areas in the two states that dot the lake's 800-mile shoreline (see Occoneechee SP below and *North Carolina: A Guide to Backcountry Travel & Adventure*). Predictably, the focus at each is on boating, fishing, and camping. Stuanton River features facilities for each of these activities, with a boat ramp, car campground, and plenty of room along its extensive shoreline to drop a line in the water. Other facilities in the park include a swimming pool, two large and scenic picnic areas, rental cabins, and a pair of tennis courts. Although there's little here to appeal to the ardent backcountry traveler, if you're in the area and want to spend a day on the water, the park is a convenient destination.

South Boston (W) is the closest town.

**contact:** Staunton River State Park, Route 2, Box 295, Scottsburg, VA 24589; 804/572-4623

**getting there:** From the jct of US-501 and US-360/US-58 outside of South Boston, take US-360/US-58 E 0.7 mi to where US-360 and US-58 split. Turn L onto US-360 and go 8.2 mi to VA-344. Turn R and go E 10.1 mi to the signed park entrance.

**topography:** The terrain rises from the lake in gentle swells and folds.

While most of the land outside the park is agricultural, the majority park lands are forested, except where open spaces have been maintained for park development. Forest cover is mostly pines, with a mixture of hardwoods in many places. Elevations on the lake is 300 ft **maps:** USGS Buffalo Springs.

**starting out:** Parking fees are $1/vehicle on weekdays, $2 on weekends. A park map and brochure are available from the park office, where there's also a pay phone. Water and restrooms are at the pool bathhouse, in the picnic areas, and beside the boat ramp. Park activity centers around the boathouse, and, to a lesser degree, the picnic areas. Much of the rest of the park is empty most days. Many facilities close seasonally.

Public use of alcohol is not allowed. Pets must be kept on a leash. Swimming in the lake from the shoreline is prohibited.

**activities:** Hiking, Camping, Canoeing/Kayaking, Fishing.

**hiking:** The park has a single long trail and 5 short spurs that cover a combined distance of 10 miles. While the trails offer a nice way to stretch your legs or get away from the main park activity areas, they don't offer much in the way of scenery or natural attractions. The longest trail, 7.5-mi *River Bank Trail*, loops around the park, following the shoreline for most of its langth. Views of the lake and the chance to see some wildlife are the main draws. The trail is not very well maintained. Access is at the picnic areas, campground, or on the main park road. Trail use is light.

**camping:** The car campground has 46 sites laid out in 2 loops. The sites are in a pleasant area of scattered pines and hardwoods, with denser forest in the surrounding region. Unfortunately, the sites themselves are not very attractive, with a gravel spur and dissheveled appearance. Each site has a picnic table and grill, and there's a centrally-located bathhouse with showers and flush toilets. Privacy would be minimal when the campground filled, but it rarely does. Sites cost $11/night, $15 with hookup. The campground is open from mar 1 to Dec 1.

**fishing:** There are plenty of places along the shoreline from which it's possible to cast, and bank fishing is a popular activity in the park, particularly among local anglers. The most popular spots are at the picnic areas, where there's plenty of room. Another option is to fish from a canoe or kayak, but keep in mind that Kerr Lake is huge and fish tend to be concentrated in limited areas. Without the ability to cover a lot of water, you could be in for a long, frustrating day. Largemouth, white, and striped bass, black and white crappie, and bluegill all inhabit the lake.

**canoeing/kayaking:** There's no denying that Buggs Island Lake isn't a first choice for backcountry paddlers. With only average scenery, and seasonally heavy traffic from power boats, jet skis, water-skiers, and sailboats, the lake can get pretty crowded and noisy. Still, it does offer a seemingly endless shoreline, and there are plenty of branches and coves to disappear into, if only briefly. Also, it's possible to camp almost anywhere along the shoreline, as long as you stick to the low-impact ethic. Off season, when the bass boaters and water-skiers are all home watching sports on TV, the lake can be downright peaceful.

# Occoneechee State Park

Named for the Indians who flourished in the area for more than 400 years until they were driven out in 1676, Occoneechee State Park occupies 2,690 acres on the north shore of Kerr Reservoir. The 50,000 acre man-made reservoir—known in Virginia as Buggs Island Lake—is the largest lake in the Commonwealth. Its 800 miles of shoreline are lined with numerous recreation areas, in both Virginia and North Carolina. The state park has a small network of hiking trails, a picnic grounds with shelters, tables, and grills, and a car campground. But probably the major attraction in the park is its access to the lake. There are numerous places along the banks from which it's possible to fish, and 2 boat ramps make it easy to get out on the water. In summer, the lake attracts anglers, water- and jet-skiers, sailboats and motorboats in large numbers. On land, remnants of the nineteenth-century plantation house and gardens of William Townes are visible along one of the trails.

Clarsville (W) is the closest town.

**contact:** Occoneechee State Park, Route 2, Box 3, Clarksville, VA 23927; 804/374-2210

**getting there:** From downtown Clarksville, take US-58 E 1.6 mi to the signed park entrance, R.

**topography:** The piedmont plateau that rolls upward from the Kerr Lake is home to both young hardwoo–pine forests and large grassy clearings. Elevation on Kerr Lake is 298 ft. **maps:** USGS Clarsville N, Clarsville S, Tungsten.

**starting out:** A park entrance fee of $1/vehicle is charged. Facilities (restrooms, water) are found at the large picnic area and at the boat ramp. A pay phone and vending machines are located at the park office. Stop by to pick up a copy of a park map and brochure before roaming the park's trails. The park closes at 10 PM.

Alcohol is not allowed. Pets must be kept on a leash. Swimming is not allowed from the park.

**activities:** Canoeing/Kayaking, Fishing, Hiking, Camping.

**canoeing/kayaking:** With 50,000 acres of lake, there is certainly no end of water to paddle. The problem for canoeists and kayakers is that the lake is geared toward (and very popular among) powerboaters. This problem is compounded by the fact that the state park sits on a main channel with very few coves in the immediate vicinity. On the positive side, the lake is so vast and elsewhere there are so many coves and inlets that it really isn't hard to find a quiet spot. Since primitive camping is permitted on lands surrounding the lake, a multi-day trip is no problem. In short, figure on about a 3- to 5-mi paddle from the park (in either direction) to reach a pleasant, scenic part of the lake. Or, if you prefer, use one of the dozens of other boat ramps outside the SP. If you put in at on of the park's 3 boat ramps, you have to pay a $3 launch fee. NOTE: the park is adjacent to a sea-plane landing area.

**fishing:** Kerr Lake supports populations of striped bass, largemouth bass, bluegill, chain pickerel, and crappie. There are plenty of places to fish from along the banks, or you can launch a boat from the park. With such a large body of water, however, finding fish can be difficult, especially if you're limited to a relatively small area. Nevertheless, it's hard to pass up the temptation to try a lake renowned among sportsmen for its fishing.

**camping:** The large car campground has 95 sites in 3 loops. The large sites are well spaced and forest cover adds to privacy, which is generally quite good. Each site includes a picnic table and grill. 2 of the loops have a central shower/restroom facility (hot water). Sites cost $12/night, $17 with hookup. If you bring a pet, it costs an extra $3. The campground is open Mar through Nov, though opening dates can vary significantly from year to year.

**hiking:** Hiking in the park is rather limited. In all, there are about 3 mi of trails in the park on 5 trails with lengths between 0.2 mi and 1.2 mi. The highlight is the *Plantation Trail*, which winds through the former grounds of the Occoneechee Plantation, where signs of the garden and buildings can still be seen. Placards along the trail describe some of the features of the plantation grounds. The plantation burned to the ground on Christmas, 1898. Trailheads are mostly signed and easy to locate. Trails are not blazed, but are not difficult to follow. Hiking is easy.

# Briery Creek Wildlife Management Area

The centerpiece of this 3,164-acre wildlife management area is 845-acre Briery Creek Lake, an impoundment formed by the damming of two creeks. Lake and upland forest combine to provide a variety of habitats that are managed primarily for the hunting and fishing opportunities they afford. Established in 1989, the land is just beginning to return to a natural state after having been exploited for timber and agricultural uses. As a result, some of the recent farmland remains cleared, providing fertile feeding grounds for white-tailed deer, wild turkey, and quail. The forest too is young, with stands of pure pine in some areas. On the lake, wood ducks, mallards, and other waterfowl are seen in fall and winter. Recreational facilities at Briery Creek are limited, with only a boat ramp, fishing pier, and hiking trail. As a result, it's one of the more interesting and natural backcountry areas on the piedmont to explore. Visitors should be aware that hunting occurs in the fall and winter.

Farmville (N) is the closest town.

**contact:** Briery Creek Wildlife Management Area, Route 6, Box 410, Forest, VA 24551; 804/525-7522.

**getting there:** From Farmville, take US-15 S 7 mi to Rt 790, the WMA access road. Turn R onto the road. At 0.4 mi is a parking area, L; at 0.6 mi reach the trailhead to the *Briery Creek Lake Nature Trail*, L; and at 0.7 mi come to the boat ramp, L.

**topography:** The rolling piedmont terrain rises gradually from the lake. Plant cover is a mixture of pine–hardwood forest and wildlife clearings. Average elevation is 450 ft. **maps:** USGS Hampden Sydney.

**starting out:** The only facility at the WMA is a toilet near the boat ramp. You can pick up maps of the WMA and other info at the VDGIF office at 1700 S Main St (in the Farm Credit Service Bldg) at the S end of Farmville. Although not a topo, their free single-sheet map provides a sufficient overview of the area, showing major trails . Hunting takes place on the WMA in fall and winter. Be sure to wear blaze orange if you visit during that period.

**activities:** Canoeing/Kayaking, Fishing, Camping, Hiking

**canoeing/kayaking:** Surrounded by relict farmland and regenerating forests, Briery Creek Lake offers a very scenic natural setting for a half-day or day-long paddle. Canoeists and kayakers should note that the WMA is primarily a fishing destination, with most anglers fishing from motor boats (10 HP or less only). Nevertheless, the general atmosphere is one of quiet and serenity. Since primitive camping is allowed, an overnight paddling trip is even possible. Put-in is at the boat ramp.

**fishing:** The most popular activity at Briery Creek Lake is fishing. Even in winter, anglers can be spotted on the banks and in boats out on the water. Species taken from the lake include largemouth bass, chain pickerel, channel catfish, crappie, and bluegill. Unlike many of the piedmont lakes, Briery Creek is small enough to give bank casters and canoe-based anglers a chance at getting over some fish without high-tech electronic equipment.

**camping:** Primitive backcountry camping is permitted on the WMA for up to 7 consecutive days. Campsites should not be within 100 yds of the lake. Open fires are not allowed.

**hiking:** The 0.5 mi *Briery Creek Lake Nature Trail* is the lone designated trail in the area. It follows both a gated and seeded road bed and a single-track dirt footpath on a loop through a mixed forest where pines predominate. The blazed trail is easy to follow and hike. Other hiking opportunities are found on the several gated hunting roads and tracks that lace the area. Most lead from one of the several roads the enter the WMA and end at the lake.

# Twin Lakes State Park

A pair of small lakes—Goodwin and Prince Edward—give this park its name. Located on the southeast edge of Prince Edward–Gallion State Forest in Prince Edward County, the park encompasses 425 acres of rolling piedmont. Although the park is geared more toward casual outdoor recreation—a swimming beach and picnic grounds are popular areas in summer—than serious backcountry travel, a network of trails for hikers and bikers and the proximity of the 7,000-acre forest are two reasons to visit. The park also offers a developed campground as well as fishing or paddling on the lakes. Wildlife seen in the park includes beavers, red fox, white-tailed deer, quail, and wild turkey. The majority of park land is covered with a second growth forest of pines and hardwoods. The park is open year round.

Farmville (NW) and Crewe (E) are the closest towns.

**contact:** Twin Lakes State Park, Route 2, Box 70, Green Bay, VA 23942; 804/392-3435

**getting there:** From the jct of Main St and US-460 in downtown Farmville, take US-460 E 3.8 mi to Rt 696. Turn R and go 5.2 mi to Rt 612. Turn L and go 1.7 to Rt 613. Turn R and go 2.8 mi (at 1.3 mi is an entrance to Prince Edward–Gallion SF, R) to the park entrance, L. The entire route is signed.

**topography:** The rolling piedmont terrain is blanketed by a young pine-hardwood forest. Average elevation is 500 ft. **maps:** USGS Green Bay.

**starting out:** A parking fee of $1-2/vehicle is charged. Once inside, stop by the park office to pick up a trail map and park brochure. A pay phone and vending machines are there too. Restrooms and water are near the picnic area, with a bathhouse and concession stand (open seasonally) beside the lake. A small fee is also charged for swimming. The swimming beach is inevitably the busiest part of the park in summer. The park closes at dusk.

Alcohol is not allowed. Pets must be kept on a leash.

**activities:** Hiking, Camping, Fishing, Canoeing/Kayaking, Mountain Biking.

**hiking:** 3 park trails cover a total distance of 7 mi. The 2 longest trails—they cover a combined length of 5.5 mi—circle the 2 park lakes. The trails wind in and out of the forested slopes above the lakes. Open areas provide the chance to spy wildlife. The blazed trails are signed and easy to follow. Improvements include boardwalks over wet areas. Trailheads can be reached from either of the 2 large parking areas. Connections can be made with the larger system of gated and open dirt and gravel roads that criss-cross the adjacent state forest. Trail use is moderate.

**camping:** The park's car campground consists of 33 sites spread out in 2 loops in an area lightly forested with pines and hardwoods. Each site includes a picnic table and grill. The sites are not particularly large and are fairly close to one another, minimizing privacy. A single restroom/shower facility is located at the center of the main loop. Sites cost $15/night Mar–Oct; $13/night in Nov. A pet fee of $3/night is charged. The campground is open Mar through Nov. The campground is rarely crowded, filling up only on holiday weekends.

Camping outside the designated campground is not allowed.

**fishing:** Fishing is a popular activity on both park lakes. Although fishing from a canoe is the preferred method, there are also enough open spaces along the shore of each lake to allow for bank casting. Species taken from the lakes are channel catfish, largemouth bass, sunfish and crappie.

**canoeing/kayaking:** The 2 small park lakes offer a place to take maybe an hour's or two paddle. You have the option of bringing your own boat or renting a canoe in the park. Both lakes have a boat ramp; rental canoes are limited to Goodwin Lake. The setting on the lakes is generally on of quiet woodlands, with 2 exceptions: the beach on Goodwin Lake and the Cedar Crest Conference Center compound on Prince Edward Lake. Prince Edward Lake is the quieter and more remote of the two.

**mountain biking:** Although riding in the park is limited to a single short road, that road connects to the larger network of gated and secondary roads in the Prince Edward–Gallion SF (see separate entry below). Riding in both park and forest is easy to moderate, with most roads level and clear. You can rent a bike from the park.

# Prince Edward-Gallion State Forest

At 6,970 acres, Prince Edward–Gallion is the smallest of the four piedmont state forests. The pine–hardwood forests that cover its rolling piedmont terrain are managed for wildlife habitat, resource protection, timber sales, and outdoor recreation. Although lacking facilities and improvements typical of many areas used by outdoor enthusiasts, the forest offers some interesting attractions to the serious backcountry traveler. First of these is the large network of gated and dirt secondary roads. While none of these are maintained as trails per se, all are open to foot and mountain bike travel. With a good map and a little imagination, you can put together hikes or rides of many different lengths. In planning a route, however, keep in mind that camping is not allowed on the forest. The car campground in the adjacent Twin Lakes State Park can be used as a base camp if you want to stay more than a day. Scenery in the forest is a mixed bag, with many stages of forest succession visible due to management practices and logging. Wildlife encountered includes squirrels, raccoon, muskrat, white-tailed deer, wild turkey, and quail.

Crewe (E) and Farmville (NW) are the nearest sizable towns.

**contact:** c/o Appomattox-Buckingham State Forest, Route 3, Box 133, Dillwyn, VA 23936; 804/492-4121.

**getting there:** From the jct of Main St and US-460 in downtown Farmville, take US-460 E 3.8 mi to Rt 696. Turn R and go 5.2 mi to Rt 612. Turn L and go 1.7 to Rt 613. Turn R and go 2.8 mi (at

1.3 mi is an entrance to Prince Edward–Gallion SF, R

**topography:** Average elevation in the forest is 500 ft. Forest cover is predominantly pine plantations, with the old growth having been logged long ago. Areas of hardwood forest also exist. **maps:** USGS Hampden Sydney, Green Bay.

**starting out:** There are no facilites at all in the forest. Information is available at the adjacent Twin Lakes SP, as are facilities (water, restrooms, pay phone). Hunting occurs during fall and winter. Although it's not easy to get seriously lost in the forest, having the USGS topos will help you make sense of the many criss-crossing roads.

**activities:** Hiking, Mountain Biking.

hiking/**mountain biking:** All hiking or riding in the forest is on roads. Some of these are secondary roads open to automobiles, many others are gated forest roads. Surfaces vary, but are mostly dirt or gravel. There's a single 2-mi designated bike trail loop that passes through both the forest and Twin Lakes SP. The park is probably the best place to begin a trip anyway, since there's a large parking area. Riding throughout the forest is generally easy to moderate, due to the mild topography, with slightly more difficult conditions on the gated roads. Best of all, you'll probably have the roads to yourself.

# Cumberland State Forest

Cumberland State Forest encompasses 16,242 acres of mature bottomland hardwood forest, second-growth upland pine-hardwood forests, and pine plantations. The Willis River runs through a small section of the forest and then along its northwest edge for almost ten miles. Four small lakes break the woodlands and provide water-based recreation. Four small (16–38 acres) protected natural areas preserve forest types native to the piedmont. Wildlife present in the forest includes wild turkey, quail, ruffed grouse, white-tailed deer, albino squirrels, raccoon and other small mammals found throughout the piedmont region. Forest management is focused on outdoor recreation, resource preservation, and for-profit logging, not necessarily in that order.

Recreation is centered on the river and lakes and on the splendid *Willis River Trail*. The forest is set up for day trips only, with camping only permitted in Bear Creek Lake State Park (see separate entry below), which is encompassed by the state forest. Hunting takes place on the forest in fall and winter.

Farmville (S) is the closest large town.

**contact:** Cumberland State Forest, Route 1, Box 250, Cumberland, VA 23040; 804/492-4121.

**getting there:** From the jct of US-60 and VA-45 N of Farmville, take VA-45 N 3 mi (at 2 mi reach the town of Cumberland) to Trent Mills Rd (SR-622). Turn L and go 3.2 mi to Oak Hill Rd (SR-629). Turn L and go 0.8 mi to a fork and jct with Bear Creek Lake Rd (SR-666), L. Keep R on SR-629 for 0.9 mi to Forest View Rd (SR-628), L and the signed entrance to the forest headquarters, R

**topography:** Rolling piedmont upland is covered in a mixed pine–hardwood forest in various stages of succession, with some plantations of pure pine. The Willis River, the area's major drainage, runs along the NW edge of the forest. Elevations are between 200 and 450 ft. **maps:** USGS Gold Hill, Whiteville, Hillcrest.

**starting out:** A stop at the forest headquarters is worthwhile before heading out into the backcountry. Not only can the rangers provide you with maps and other info, but they're willing to share their intimate knowledge of the forest. While there, pick up a copy of the *Guide to Virginia's Piedmont Forests*, which has good maps of the 4 state forests in the piedmont. Camping is not allowed on the SF; a car campground is located in Bear Creek Lake SP.

**activities:** Hiking, Canoeing/Kayaking, Fishing, Mountain Biking.

**hiking:** The centerpiece of the area is the 16-mi *Willis River Trail*, which follows a single-track dirt path from one end of the forest to the other. Despite its name, the trail doesn't really run beside the river, though it does come in contact with it several times and roughly parallels it at a distance of 1 to 2 miles. Hiking is through hardwood bottomland forest and upland forests in various stages of growth. The trail is blazed and generally easy to follow. To reach the S trailhead, leave the forestry center and turn R onto gravel

Oak Hill Rd. Go 1.2 mi to a sign for Winston Lake, with parking areas on both sides of the road. The trail begins on the L at a large signboard below the lake. The trail crosses a forest road every mile or two, providing plenty of access points. The N terminus is at a swinging bridge across the Willis River, 1 mi N of a crossing at SR-615. Hiking along the trail is easy.

Other hiking in the forest is on the gated and secondary dirt and gravel roads that lace the area. Unlike at the other piedmont state forests, this is not a particularly appealing option, even less so with the *Willis River Trail* as an alternative.

**canoeing/kayaking:** The Willis River is a slow-moving river that rises to the southwest in Appomattox–Buckingham SF and flows in a northeasterly direction through Cumberland SF before emptying into the James River just above Cartersville. Although not very well known outside of local circles as a paddling destination, the 10-mi stretch through Cumberland SF offers a remote, scenic river trip through bottomland hardwood forest. The put-in is on Arrowhead FR, 1 mi W of the forest headquarters. Take-out is on SR-608 at Trenton Mills. Another option is to continue downstream to the James, a distance of about 10 mi. There's a boat ramp on VA-45 in Carterville.

Another option for paddlers is to explore the intimate waters of Winston and Arrowhead Lakes. Both lakes are quite small (5–10 acres), but offer a serene setting for fishing or just taking it easy. Both have boat ramps that will accommodate small craft.

**fishing:** The smallmouth bass fishing in the Willis River is reputed to be quite good. Largemouth bass and northern pike are also taken from the river. Fishing is either from a boat or by wading. The river is large—about 50 ft across—with a current that is usually slow. In addition to the river, there are small lakes on the forest that harbor largemouth bass, northern pike, and bluegill. All have open space along the banks from which to cast, and all can accommodate small boats.

**mountain biking:** As in the other piedmont state forests, mountain biking is permitted on both secondary roads (most of which are dirt and gravel) and on gated roads closed to vehicles. The drawback here is that the secondary roads do receive a fair amount of traffic; and that the patchwork layout of forest land makes it difficult to put together long rides without leaving the SF at least briefly. That said, there are some nice, fairly remote roads for riding, particularly in the southern section of the forest near Winston Lake. A good map is necessary to navigate these routes, unless you're wholly unconcerned about getting lost. Riding is easy to moderate.

# Bear Creek Lake State Park

The centerpiece of this 326-acre park is a small lake (40 acres) with facilities for swimming, boating, and fishing. The park is completed surrounded by the 16,500 acre Cumberland State Forest, substanitally increasing opportunities for backcountry travel. The park itself is geared mostly toward families and day visitors. Between Memorial Day and Labor Day, when the swimming beach is open, the area gets pretty crowded with sunbathers and water lovers. Park amenities include a car campground, bathhouse with concession stand, and picnic area with shelters, tables, and grills. Off season, the lake provides a serene locale for a short paddle or a day's fishing. And there's a lakeshore trail that affords the chance to view wildlife in the park's aquatic and woodland habitats. Ducks, quail, and white-tailed can be seen in the area. Since there's no camping in the state forest, the park makes a good basecamp for multi-day trips on area trails or lakes.

Farmville (S) is the closest town.

**contact:** Bear Creek Lake State Park, Route 1, Box 253, Cumberland, VA 23040; 804/492-4410.

**getting there:** From the jct of US-60 and VA-45 N of Farmville, take VA-45 N 3 mi (at 2 mi reach the town of Cumberland) to Trent Mills Rd (SR-622). Turn L and go 3.2 mi to Oak Hill Rd (SR-629). Turn L and go 0.8 mi to a fork and jct with Bear Creek Lake Rd (SR-666), L. Keep L and enter the state park. The route is signed.

**topography:** The rolling piedmont terrain that surrounds the lake is forested with second-growth pines and hardwoods. Elevation on the lake is approximately 300 ft. **maps:** USGS Gold Hill.

**starting out:** There's a parking fee of $1/car on weekdays, $1.50/car on weekends. The park office can supply you with maps and brochures for the park and Cumberland SF, including a map of the *Willis River Trail*. Facilities (restrooms, water, pay phone) are at the swimming beach.

Alcohol is prohibited in the park. Pets must be kept on a leash.

**activities:** Hiking, Canoeing/Kayaking, Fishing, Camping.

**hiking:** A small network of 5 trails in the park covers almost 7 miles of terrain. The longest trail is the 3-mi *Circumferential Trail*, which, as its name suggests, circles the lake. In addition to the park trails, there is also access to the 16-mi *Willis River Trail*, which more or less parallels the river in Cumberland SF. The trailhead to the park trails is located near the bathhouse. Trailheads are signed and trails are blazed and easy to follow. Trail improvements include footbridges across wet areas. Hiking on all park trails is easy.

**camping:** The car campground has 45 sites in 4 different areas. The large, well-spaced sited are shaded by trees. Sites afford a good amount of privacy. Each site has a picnic table and grill. Shower/restroom facilities are located in the center of two of the loops. Sites cost $11/night; $15/night with hookup. If you bring a pet, it costs $3/night extra. The campground is open Mar 1 to Nov 1. Group camping is also available.

**canoeing/kayaking:** The small lake offers a pleasant setting for a short, leisurely paddle. You can bring your own boat or rent a canoe in the park. Rentals are available between Memorial Day and Labor Day. If you go during a peak season weekend, you'll have company on the water. Boats with gasoline motors are not allowed on the lake.

**fishing:** Fishing in the park is either from a long pier, from the shoreline, or from a boat. A boat is the best bet, though there are plenty of open spaces along the shore. Game species taken from the lake are northern pike, largemouth bass, crappie, channel catfish and sunfish.

# Amelia Wildlife Management Area

The forested hills and large meadows of this area are managed primarily for outdoor recreation centered around hunting and fishing. The area encompasses 2,217 acres of upland piedmont and bottomland hardwood forest on the south bank of the Appomattox River in Amelia County. Established in 1969, the management area's lands were, like the surrounding countryside, once given over to agriculture. Near its western edge is a 105-acre lake, with a boat ramp and several species of game fish. Wildlife encountered in the forest and meadows include white-tailed deer, wild turkey, rabbits, and doves; wood ducks are often seen along the river. Hunting takes place on the WMA in fall and winter. The area is best avoided during this time, as the number of hunters is fairly large.

**contact:** Amelia Wildlife Management Area, Route 6, Box 410, Forest, VA 24551-9806; 804/525-7522.

**getting there:** From the jct of US-60 and VA-13 in the town of Powhatan, take VA-13 S 3.9 mi to SR-609. Turn L and go 5.9 mi to a fork. Bear L, continuing on SR-609 3.1 mi to SR-352. Turn L and go 0.9 mi to the first parking area, R, with access to 2 trails. At 2.5 mi reach a fork in the road. The boat ramp and parking area are L.

**topography:** The terrain in the WMA is characterized by gently rolling hills covered in predominantly hardwood forest. Some unforested areas that are maintained as meadows are also present. Elevations are between 200 and 300 ft. **maps:** USGS Chula.

**starting out:** As this area is maintained primarily for hunting and fishing, it is largely primitive backcountry with few facilities. Aside from the boat ramp, there's a rifle range, archery range, and clay–bird shotgun range. If you're going to stay a while, be sure to bring enough water. Since the terrain is relatively mild, the only map you should need is the free WMA map, available from the above address or from the WMA headquarters in Farmville (see Briery Creek WMA for directions).

**activities:** Hiking, Canoeing/Kayaking, Fishing, Camping.

**hiking:** Hiking in the WMA more closely approximates true primitive conditions than at many of the other outdoor areas in the state. None of the trails are signed or blazed. In all, there are about

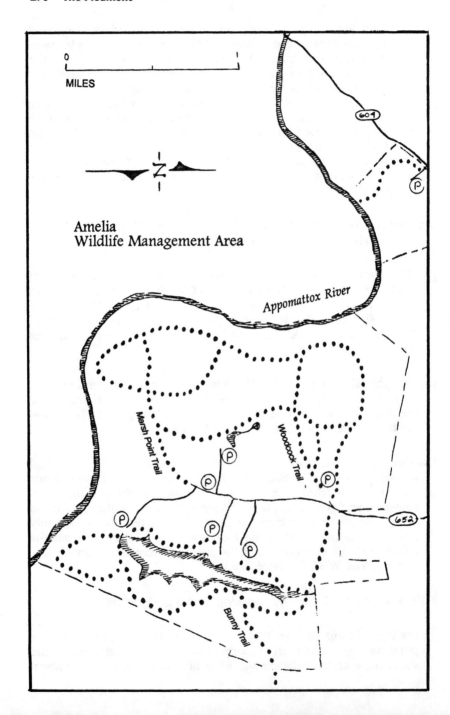

8 mi of trails, most of which interconnect, allowing for loops of varying length. The trails follow gated relict roadbeds or paths that have been beaten into place by hunters and fisherman. Although the refuge isn't so large that getting lost will likely be a problem, it's a good idea to bring a compass along.

**canoeing/kayaking:** Paddlers have their choice of either the 105-acre lake, or on the Appomattox River. The lake offers a small, scenic setting for a leisurely couple hours' paddle or fishing trip. The put-in is at the boat ramp. The Appomattox River, on the other hand is only accessible from outside the WMA, although it forms its N and E boundaries. The river, a tributary of the James, is a wide, slow-moving body of water in the vicinity Lake Amelia. Ther's nothing here to cause problems for even a novice paddler. Although there aren't any boat ramps in the area just upstream from the WMA, there are several informal put-ins at secondary road crossings. The same holds true for downstream, where the nearest ramp is down near Lake Chesdin.

**fishing:** Fishing on the lake can be done from either land or boat. On land, there's plenty of open space along the banks, and a handicapped-accessible fishing pier has been built beside the boat ramp. Good open areas along the shore for casting. Species taken from the lake are largemouth bass, walleye, crappie, channel catfish, and bluegill.

The Appomattox River—accessible only from a boat—contains largemouth bass, chain pickerel, catfish, crappie, and walleye.

**camping:** Primitive backcountry camping is permitted anywere on the WMA except within 100 yds of Amelia Lake and Sunders Pond. There are no camping facilities.

# Powhatan Wildlife Management Area

Like most of the surrounding countryside, the 4,500 acres of the Powhatan WMA were once farmland. Today, they are preserved and managed for outdoor recreation and wildlife preservation. In order to facilitate the creation of habitats hospitable to wildlife, the land is being maintained is a number of different forms. mixed pine-hardwood forest, bottomland hardwoods, wetlands, large meadows, and a series of ponds and creeks are all present.

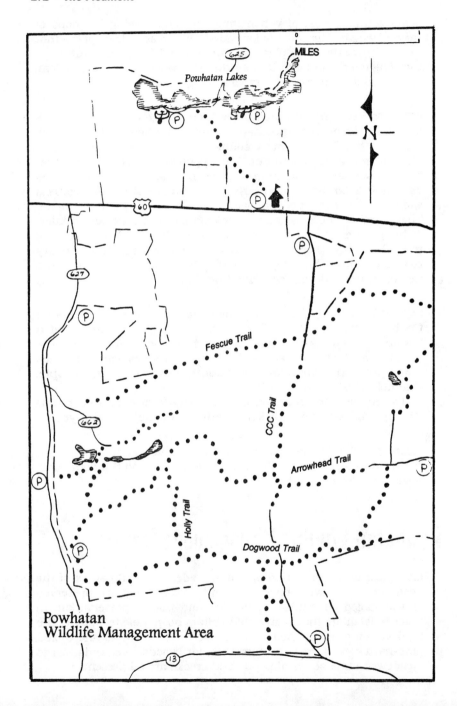

Powhatan Lakes

645

MILES

0

P

P

P

—N—

60

627

P

Fescue Trail

CCC Trail

663

P

Arrowhead Trail

P

Holly Trail

P

Dogwood Trail

P

Powhatan
Wildlife Management Area

P

13

Wildlife that frequents the area includes white-tailed deer, wild turkey, quail, doves, and numerous smaller mammals typical of the piedmont. Although the WMA stresses hunting and fishing as primary activities, there are also opportunities for hiking, camping, and canoeing or kayaking on one of four small lakes and ponds. Powhatan WMA is located 25 miles west of Richmond.

Powhatan (E) is the closest town.

**contact:** Powhatan Wildlife Management Area, 1320 Belman Rd, Fredericksburg, VA 22401; 540/899-4169.

**getting there:** The field office is located on US-60 4 mi W of Powhatan. Several roads provide access to various parts of the WMA. To reach the main access, from the field office, turn R onto US-60. Go 1.5 mi to Ridge Rd (SR-627). Go 1.3 mi to SR-662. Turn L and go 0.5 mi to a large parking area. (0.6 mi S of SR-662 on SR-627 is another trail access and small parking area. At 1.1 mi is another access. • To reach the lakes in the N half of the WMA., leave the field office and go E on US-60 0.9 mi to SR-684 (Bell Rd). Turn L and go 1.8 mi to SR-625 (Powhatan Lakes Rd). Turn L and go (at 1.2 mi the pavement ends) 1.5 mi to a fork in the road and access to both lakes.

**topography:** The gently rolling terrain of the eastern piedmont is alternately forested and maintained as grassy meadow. Several small creeks drain the area. Elevations are between 200 and 350 ft. **maps:** USGS Trenholm, Powhatan

**starting out:** Facilities are very limited. A stop by the field office is wothwhile before heading out into the backcountry. The rangers can supply you with a decent map of the area and answer questions about current conditions. Hunting takes place in fall and winter. Since the activity level can get pretty high on some days, non-hunters are better off visiting at other times.

Swimming in the lakes is not permitted.

**hiking:** A dozen miles of trails lace the S half of the WMA. The term "trails" is used loosely, as most of the paths follow gated roads or have simply been worn into place by anglers and hunters. There are no signed or blazed trails, such as you might find in a state park or national forest. Although many of these trails are quite easy to walk, hikers should be prepared for rugged conditions, including unimproved creek crossings. Bring along the topo sheets and a sense of adventure. The trails cross one another and interconnect, making loops of varying length possible. Although there are several trailheads located around the perimeter of the WMA, the main access road is as good a place to start as any. Because of the open nature of much of the countryside, there's a good chance of observing wildlife along the trails.

**fishing:** Anglers have their choice of 2 lakes in the N half, or 4 "farm" ponds in the S half. Species in both are the same: largemouth bass, chain pickerel, channel catfish, black crappies, and bluegills. All of these waters are relatively small, ranging in size from 2 to 32 acres. Both lakes and 3 of the ponds have easy vehicle access. One of the ponds requires a short hike to reach. Bank fishing is possible on the lakes and ponds; boats can be launched on the 2 lakes and on the 2 larger ponds. Lakes are open for fishing year round from one half-hour before sunrise to 11 PM.

**camping:** Primitive backcountry camping is allowed anywhere on the WMA except within 100 yds of a lake or creek.

**canoeing/kayaking:** Boats are allowed on the 2 lakes and on the 2 largest ponds in the S section of the WMA. With the largest lake only 32 acres, any paddling trip is necessarily short. Most boaters are there for the fishing. The 2 lakes in the N part of the WMA adjoin private land in a residential area. The ponds in the S section are more remote and offer greater seclusion. Despite the small size of the lakes and ponds, all offer an attractive setting for a trip. Since camping is permitted, overnight paddling trips are possible. Located near historic Chester

Chesterfield is the closest town.

# Pocahontas State Park

Less than a half-hour drive from Richmond, Pocahontas State Park is a woodland oasis on the edge of urban and suburban sprawl. With more than 7,600 acres of forested upland and wetland areas, the park is the largest in the state park system. Like several of the other piedmont state parks, Pocahantas was once a relatively small parkland set in a much larger state forest. In 1989, park and forest were combined, resulting in a vast woodland managed with outdoor recreation as a primary focus. The park layout still recalls the earlier arrangement, however, with most facilities concentrated within the original park boundaries. At the center of the area are two scenic impoundments—Beaver Lake (24 acres) and Swift Creek (150 acres)—that attract waterflow, wading birds, nature photographers, anglers, and canoeists. Also in the area are a car campground; large picnic area with shelters, tables, and grills; the largest public swimming pool in the state; a visitor center; boat rentals; and cabins. A network of more than 30 miles of multi-use trails sprawls across most of the park's acreage. The park is open year-round.

Richmond (NE), Chester (E), and Petersburg (SE) are the closest cities.

**contact:** Pocahontas State Park, 10301 State Park Rd, Chesterfield, VA 23838-4713; 804/796-4255

**getting there:** From the jct of US-360 and VA-288, take VA-288 S 6.7 mi to VA-10 (Iron Bridge Rd). Exit R and go 1.2 mi to SR-655 (Beach Rd). Turn R and go 4.1 mi to the park entrance, R. • From I-95 take exit 61. Go W on VA-10 7 mi to Beach Rd. Turn L and go 4.1 mi to the park entrance.

**topography:** The eastern piedmont location means that park terrain is nearly level, with shallow valleys cut by the small creeks that flow through the area. Apart from a few small areas that have been cleared and landscaped, parklands are forested with hardwoods and pines. **maps:** USGS Chesterfield, Beach.

**starting out:** Parking fees are $3/vehicle on weekdays, $4 on weekends. Facilities (restrooms, water, pay phone) are at the large picnic grounds/swimming pool area.

Pets must be kept on a leash. Public use of alcohol is prohibited. Swimming in the lakes is not allowed.

**activities:** Mountain Biking, Hiking, Camping, Canoeing/Kayaking, Fishing

**mountain biking:** The park's 25-mi network of old logging roads open to mountain biking provides one of the best opportunities for backcountry bike travel in the piedmont. Unlike many other areas where finding abandoned roads to ride on is often a matter of luck

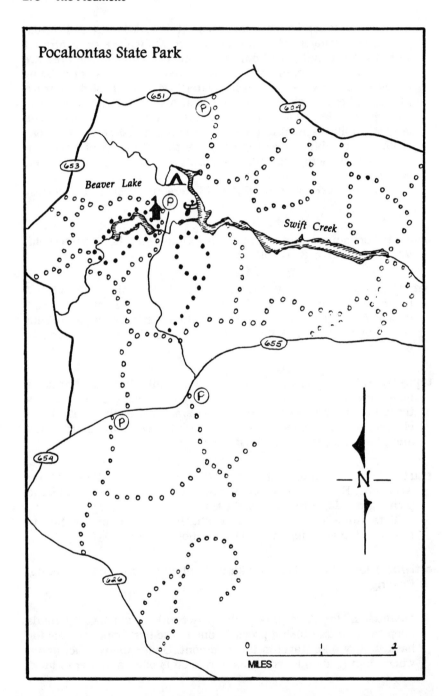

Pocahontas State Park

and persistence, the trails here have all been designated for bike riding. Trailheads are signed and there's a decent trail map available from the park office. Major access points are from within the park and along Beach Rd (SR-655) near the park office. All of the trails interconnect in one way or another; it's possible to create loop rides that combine as many as 5 or 10 trails. The trails follow a combination of well-maintained wide dirt paths and relict forest double-tracks that recievie little, if any, attention. The terrain is mostly level, making riding fairly easy, though some of the rougher trails do offer a more challenging ride. With trails extending into every corner of the park's 7,600 acres of piedmont forest and wetland habitat, a bike is the only way to explore all of it in a day.

**hiking:** In addition to the impressive network of biking trails (open to hikers too), another 7 miles of trails are open to hikers only. These trails are all located near the two main park lake's. The *Beaver Lake Trail* is the standout in the group. The 2.5-mi trail circles the scenic lake, where a carpet of water lilies cover the water's surface and herons and egrets wade the shallow water. Numbered stations along the route correspond to an interpretive trail guide. Other trails wind through the park's extensive forests. The trails are clearly marked and well maintained. Signed trailheads are located near the park entrance and at the visitor center.

**camping:** The 34-site car campground is located on two levels beside Swift Creek. The lower level is on the dammed creek's flood plain, and during heavy rains the water rises and inundates the sites. When they're above water, however, the sites are large and well-spaced, as are the sites on the upper level. Hardwoods provide shade and a measure of privacy. Each site has a picnic table and grill. Restrooms and showers are located in the upper loop. Sites cost $11/night, $15 with hookup. The campground is open from Mar 1 to Dec 1.

**canoeing/kayaking:** Paddling in the park is on Swift Creek, which in the park is actually a 150-acre impoundment created by a small dam. The lake doesn't offer a whole lot of room to paddle, but it is exceptionally scenic, and is a quiet, pleasant location for wildlife watching or fishing. It's a perfect location for beginning paddlers or for families wanting an easy way to spend a couple of hours on the water. Boats with gasoline motors are not allowed on the lake.

**fishing:** Swift Creek holds populations of largemouth bass, catfish, crappie, and bluegill. There are places along the shore from which it's possible to fish, but angling from a boat is preferred. That way, you can get away from the busy area around the boat ramp/picnic area/pool complex and find some of the lake's quieter spots. Fishing on Swift Creek is catch and release only.

# Lake Anna State Park

Lake Anna State Park occupies 2,058 acres and almost six miles of shoreline on 13,000-acre Lake Anna, a man-made impoundment created when a dam was constructed across the North Anna River. The popular park and recreational lake are located in Spotsylvania and Louisa Counties, southwest of Fredericksburg. The North Anna Nuclear Power Plant sits on the lake's western shore. The area was formerly a gold-mining center, and the park now offers summertime panning-for-gold programs. Outdoor recreation in the park centers around the lake, which is a popular destination for boaters and anglers. On land the park has a network of hiking trails, a beach with swimming area and bathhouse, a large picnic area with table, grills, and shelters, and a boat ramp. The lake and woodlands provide refuge for a variety of wildlife species, including beaver, muskrat, and white-tailed deer. Birders can observe raptors, waterfowl, wading birds, and songbirds, all present at various times of year. With its many amenities and programs, the park is a nice place for families to spend a summer day. Travelers in search of backcountry solitude can paddle the lake's numerous coves and inlets in a canoe or kayak.

Orange (NW) and Fredericksburg (NE) are the closest towns.

**contact:** Lake Anna State Park, Spotsylvania, VA 22553; 703/854-5503

**getting there:** From the jct of US-522 and VA-208 in Wares Crossroads, turn E onton VA-208 and go 8 mi to SR-601. Turn L and go 3.2 mi to the park entrance, L.

**topography:** Lake elevation is approximately 250 ft. Gently rolling hills rise from the lake on all sides. Large tracts of hardwood and pine forests alternate with agricultural land and some development. **maps:** USGS Lake Anna West, Belmont.

**starting out:** The entrance fee is $3/vehicle on weekends, $2 on weekdays. Stop by the visitor center to pick up a trail map and brochures before heading out into the backcountry. Inside are exhibits on local history and ecology. Facilities (restrooms, water, pay phone) are also here, as well as at the beach bathhouse.

The public use of alcohol is not allowed. Pets must be kept on a leash in the park.

**activities:** Canoeing/Kayaking, Fishing, Hiking

**canoeing/kayaking:** With 13,000 acres of surface area, there's no shortage of room to paddle on Lake Anna. The lake's long, narrow configuration, with numerous fingers stretching out from the main channel, only increases the opportunity for exploration. Countering the lake's natural characteristics, however, is its popularity with all kinds of watercraft. Come on a summer weekend and you'll have to share the water with power boats, sailboats, jet-skis, and water-skiers. The lake's shoreline is attractive in most locations, with minimal development and large tracts of forest of farmland. Access is from the boat ramp in the park. There are about 8 more boat ramps at various locations around the lake.

**fishing:** Lake Anna is a warm-water fishery that supports populations of largemouth and striped bass, walleye, chain pickerel, black crappie, bluegill, white and yellow perch, and channel catfish. You can fish from the shoreline in the park, but the odds of success are low. Even from a canoe, there's an awful lot of water to cover. Fish shelters have been constructed at various points around the lake to improve habitat. Still, fishing on such a large body of water without the benefit of a power boat or electronic equipment is always a hit-or-miss proposition.

**hiking:** 6 miles of hiking trails wind through the park's forests and fields and along the lakeshore. Highlights along the trails include scenic vistas, the ruins of an old plantation, and the chance to observe wildlife. The trails can be connected to form loops of varying length or to hike them all in sequence. Access is from a parking area on the main park road or from the visitor center. The trails are blazed and easy to follow. Hiking is easy. Trail use is heavy.

# C.F. Phelps Wildlife Management Area

The C.F. Phelps WMA covers more than 4,500 acres of floodplain and uplands on the eastern bank of the Rappahanock River. The area is managed primarily for wildlife habitat, which means that ground cover is a combination of forest and field. White-tailed deer, wild turkey, small mammals, and waterfowl on the river are the most frequently seen fauna. The WMA fronts the river for seven miles south of Kelly's Ford and northwest of Fredericksburg and its confluence with the Rapidan River. Although hunting is the number one outdoor activity on the preserve, there's plenty for non-hunters to do too. The preserve is kept in a primitve state, offering challenging conditions and an opportunity for backcountry solitude. Wildlife photographers will be particularly well rewarded. There's a large network of gated roadbeds to use for exploring the backcountry, but they're not blazed or signed, and a good map and sense of direction are necessary. On the river, canoeists and kayakers can paddle dowstream through the rolling piedmont all the way to Fredericksburg. One of the main appeals on the WMA is the lack of rules: you can hike off-trail if you want and make camp anywhere you like. The area is a good destination for outdoor enthusiasts looking for no crowds and something of a challenge.

Culpeper (W) is the closest town.

**contact:** C.F. Phelps WMA, 1320 Belman Rd, Fredericksburg, VA 22401; 540/899-4169.

**getting there:** From US-17 in Morrisville, go W on SR-634 1.3 mi to a jct with SR-637. Bear L onton SR-637 and go and go 1.5 mi to SR-651. Turn L onto SR-651 to parking areas at 0.6 mi and 1.1 mi. Or continue S to SR-631 and turn R to additional parking areas. The boat ramp is located on SR-672 on the W bank of the Rappahannock.

**topography:** The WMA encompasses rolling piedmont and sandy bottomland floodplain. The ground cover records some of the area's past, when logging and agriculture shaped the land. Although large open areas remain, most of the land is covered by a young pine/hardwood forest. **maps:** USGS Germanna Bridge, Richardsville.

**starting out:** The WMA is a primitive backcountry area with no facilities. Hunting takes place in fall and winter. Be sure to wear blaze orange if you visit during this period.

**activities:** Canoeing/Kayaking, Camping, Hiking, Fishing

**canoeing/kayaking:** The Rapidan has been designated a state scenic river. From Kelly's Ford downstream to its confluence with the Rapidan, the river passes through the fields and forests of the eastern piedmont. Long segments of flat water are punctuated by frequent low-grade rapids in the Class I-II range. For day-trips or overnight expeditions, this is one of the nicest, most manageable floats, on the piedmont. Below the WMA, most of the land along the river is private; if you're camping, be sure to ask permission from the landowners. The take-out is in Motts Run Park, 25 miles downriver

**camping:** Primitive backcountry camping is permitted throughout the WMA, except where posted. Canoe camping on the banks of the Rappahannock is popular.

**hiking:** Hiking in the WMA is primarily along gated roads, with some short foot trails also present. These trails are used mostly by hunters; at other times of year, they're virtually deserted. The trails all connect, allowing for numerous loop hikes and trips of almost any distance. There are approximately 15 miles of trails on the WMA. Hiking is easy. Finding and locating the trails is not difficult, even though they aren't signed or blazed. Highlights are the woodland setting, a good possibility of observing wildlife, and the remoteness of the area.

**fishing:** Anglers can fish the Rappahannock River or a small pond on the WMA. Fishing the river is best done from a canoe, although there are places along the banks from which it's possible to cast. The river is a warm-water fishery that supports populations of largemouth bass, black crappie, white perch, and bluegill. The river is well-known for its channel catfish; the current record holder was caught in the river. The 3-acre pond holds populations of largemouth bass, bluegill, and sunfish.

# Prince William Forest Park

Covering more than 17,000 acres of heavily wooded upland and bottomland floodplain, Prince William Forest Park is the largest preserve in the intensely developed northeast corner of the state and a welcome oasis at the edge of urban and suburban sprawl. The park is run by the National Park Service; outdoor recreation and wildlife habitat conservation are the main management objectives. Among a broad diversity of flora and fauna, the park is home to white-tailed deer, beaver, wild turkey, eastern box turtles, and opossum. After being logged almost from the beginning of colonial settlement, 50 years of protection have restored the forest to a lush habitat that filters sun away from the cool, moist floor. A network of hiking and biking trails criss-crosses most of the park, inviting visitors to leave their cars and spend a day in the wilds. While the trails are the main attraction, the park also offers a developed car campround, primitive backcountry camping, picnic grounds with tables and grills, CCC-built cabin camps, and a visitor center with exhibits and information. Open year-round, the park is especially magical after a winter snowstorm, when the park roads and bike trails become popular cross-country skiing tracks. The park is open all year during daylight hours.

Triangle (E), Dumfries (E), and Woodbridge (NE) are the closest towns.

**contact:** Superintendent, Prince William Forest Park, P.O. Box 209, Triangle, VA 22172-0209; 703/221-7181

**getting there:** From I-95, take exit 150. Turn W onto SR-619 (Joplin Rd) and go 0.2 mi to the park entrance, R.

**topography:** Rolling forested piedmont is laced with small creeks and drainages. Tree species in the upper story are predominantly hardwoods, with lush growths of ferns, mosses, and wildflowers on the forest floor. Elevations are between 100 and 300 ft. **maps:** USGS Quantico, Occoquan, Joplin, Independent Hill.

**starting out:** Entry fees (good for 7 days) are $4/vehicle, $2 if you enter on foot or a bike. Restrooms, water, and pay phone are at the visitor center. While there, pick up a park map of info on camping, fishing, biking, and other park activities.

Pets must be kept on a leash. They are not allowed in the

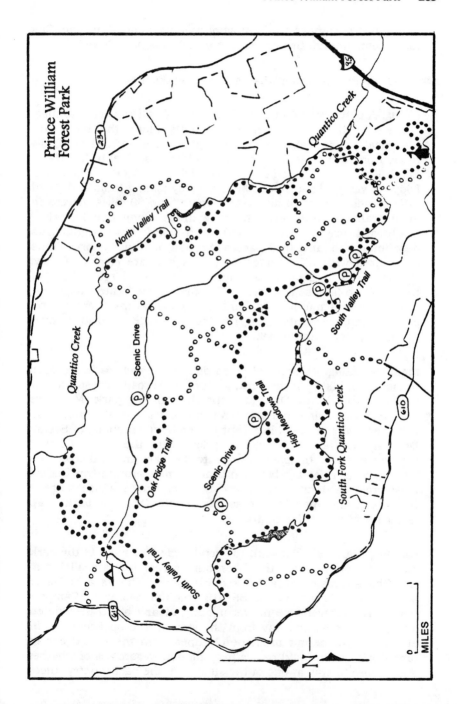

Prince William Forest Park

backcountry campground. Alcohol is only allowed in the Oak Ridge campground. Swimming in park lakes is not allowed.

**activities:** Hiking, Mountain Biking, Camping, Fishing

**hiking:** A network of 46 miles of hiking trails offers access to most corners of the park. Scenic highlights along the trails are historical sites, lush woodlands, and creeks and lakes. Trails range from short interpretive trails (guides available) to the 15-mi *South Valley Trail*, which closely parallels S Fork Quantico Creek. Loops of varing distance can be formed by joining trails and gated forest roads. One such loop covers more than 30 miles. Access to most trails is at lettered parking areas along Scenic Drive. Trailheads are clearly marked, and many have signboards describing habitat a trail passes through or local history. Trails are blazed with different colored bars and are easy to follow. Hiking ranges from easy to strenuous, though the large majority of trail mileage falls somewhere in the easy to moderate categories. Trails are well maintained, and heavy use keeps them clearly defined. Improvements along the trails include footbridges over wet areas, steps, and benches.

**mountain biking:** 16 miles of gated dirt and gravel roads are open to mountain biking in the park. Most of these roads are spurs that begin on the Scenic Dr that loops through the park. Most are dead-ends, meaning that you have to backtrack at the end. Loop rides really aren't possible except by combining sections of Scenic Dr, and even then there are few options. Still, the bike trails offer a good way to see the park or to get to the lakes and and creeks for fishing. Most rides are between 2 and 4 miles round-trip. Riding is generally moderate, with a few steep sections. Trailheads are at the designated parking areas on Scenic Dr. The park map (available at the visitor center).

**camping:** Campers who want to spend a night or more in the park have two options. Primitive backcountry camping is available at the Chopawamsic Creek Backcountry Area. This is a 400-acre parcel of land located across SR-619 from the main park. Campers here can choose between overnighting at any of 10 designated sites, or of camping away from the sites in the backcountry. In either case, a permit must be obtained from the visitor center (open 8:30 AM to 5 PM) before heading out. Regardless of whether you choose to stay at one of the sites or in the backcountry, there are no facilities in the area. Water must be packed in or surface water must be treated. The hike in to the sites is between 0.25 and 1 mi. There is no fee to camp at Chopawamsic Creek. The area is open from Feb 1 to Oct 15. Use is light year-round.

Oak Ridge, an 80-site car campground, offers a considerably less rugged camping experience. The medium-sized sites are spread out across a heavily wooded area. All the tree cover helps with privacy, although the sites are pretty close together. What helps even more is that the campground seems never to be crowded. Each site has a table, grill, and lantern post. Modern restrooms (no showers) are at the center of each of the 2 loops. Sites cost $7/night. The campground is open all year.

**fishing:** Although the park is not a major fishing destination, it's backcountry creeks, ponds, and small lakes hold populations of largemouth bass, chain pickerel, black crappie, catfish, and bluegill. Since there's no vehicle access and fishing pressure is generally quite light, these waters are good for a hiking/fishing trip. All fishing is from the banks or by wading. Access is via hiking or biking trail. Stop by the visitor center and pick up a copy of the park fishing pamphlet (it gives current closures) before heading out with road and reel.

# Sky Meadows State Park

1,862-acre Sky Meadows State Park has the kind of scenery that makes you want to take pictures. Located about an hour west of Washington, D.C. on the eastern edge of the Blue Ridge Mountains, the park sits just high enough on the mountain slope to provide panoramas of the surrounding countryside: rolling hills dotted with small farms where hand-split rail fences pen grazing cows. Farming here dates back to the 18th century, and the visitor center is housed in a stone farm house that was built a century later. Its owner gave it the evocative name Mount Bleak. Cows still graze on fields in the park, although the majority of uplands are blanketed with a mature hardwood forest. Backcountry creeks and springs add to the scenery. The best way to see the park is to hike its extensive trail network, which includes a 3-mile segment of the *Appalachian Trail*. Visitors wanting to spend more than a day can pitch a tent in the designated backcountry camping area. Other facilities include an attractive picnic area beside the farm buildings in an open grassy area with pleasant views. Extended trips are possible by hiking into the adjacent G. Richard Thompson WMA. The park is open all year from 8 AM to dusk.

Front Royal (SW) and Winchester (NW) are the closest towns.

**contact:** Sky Meadows State Park, 11012 Edmonds Lane, Delaplane, VA 20144; 540/592-3556

**getting there:** From I-66, take exit 23. Turn N onto SR-731 and go 0.5 mi to US-17 Turn L and go 5.8 mi to SR-710 (Edmonds Lane). • Another approach is from the jct of US-50 and US-17 in Faquier Co: take US-17 S 1.3 mi to SR-710 (Edmonds Lane) and the park entrance, R.

**topography:** Sitting in the transition zone where piedmont meets mountains, the park offers a little of both. The E part of the park is rolling countryside cleared for pasturage. Further W, the hills become steeper and are forested. Elevations are between 640 and 1,800 ft. **maps:** USGS Upperville, Linden

**starting out:** Entry fees are $1/vehicle on weekdays, $2 on weekends. Restrooms, water, and a vending machine are located at the park office. Pick up a park trail map inside.

Pets must be kept on a leash. Public use of alcohol is not allowed.

**activities:** Hiking, Camping.

**hiking:** The park has 2 different trail networks, located on opposite sides of US-17. W of the highway is the park's main trail network, with 10 miles of trails that meander through pasture and hardwood forest to the crest of the Blue Ridge. Included in the trails is 3.6 miles of the *AT*; it's located near the park's W border at the highest park elevations. The trails follow a combination of old roadbeds and narrow footpaths. Scenery along most of the trails is superb. *Snowden Trail* is a nature interpretive trail. All trails are blazed and easy to follow. Trailheads are signed, as are trail jcts. Improvements include footbridges, benches, and steps. Access is at the main parking area. Across the road is a second network of 4 miles. The main trail here is the 3-mi *Lost Mtn Bridle Trail*. Although it's open to horses, often there are none to be found. Views of the surrounding countryside are outstanding. Access is from US-17, 0.8 mi N of the park entrance.

**camping:** Camping in the park is at a 12-site primitive backcountry area. The sites are large and well-spaced, affording a good deal of privacy. The short hike to the sites is 0.75 miles along one of the park's historic roadbeds. A longer hike follows a footpath about 1.5 miles. Each of the sites has a picnic table, fire ring, and tent pad. One shelter is in the area. The campground is mostly wooded, and is quite attractive. Non-potable water is available from a pump; drinking water must be packed in. A pit toilet is centrally located. Sites cost $8/night. You can register at the park office or at the sites. registration station. If no sites are available—they sometimes fill up in spring and fall—you can hike or drive to the adjacent G.R. Thompson WMA, where backcountry camping is permitted throughout. The park campsites are open all year.

# G. R. Thompson Wildlife Management Area

Located only an hour west of Washington, D.C., the G. Richard Thompson WMA is a 4,000-acre upland preserve that is home to white-tailed deer, wild turkey, and ruffed grouse. Tucked into the northwest corner of Faquier County, the WMA straddles the transition zone where the piedmont rises up and becomes the Blue Ridge Mountains. Although the area is popular during the cooler months with hunters, non-hunters know it just as well, primarily because a seven-mile segment of the *Appalchian Trail* runs along its spine. In spring, visitors come to admire and photograph the impressive displays of large-flowered trillium. Or simply to enjoy the solitude of the expansive backcountry and to hike the large network of trails. In fall, several species of hawks can be seen migrating south for the winter. A small pond, stocked with trout, is another attraction. Since the preserve has no facilities at all and requires a certain amount of effort to explore, crowds stay away, making it a good place to visit for solitude seekers. Sky Meadows State Park is next door, increasing the opportunities for extended backcountry trips.

Front Royal (W) is the closest large town.

**contact:** G.R. Thompson Wildlife Management Area, 1320 Belman Rd, Fredericksburg, VA 22401; 540/899-4169

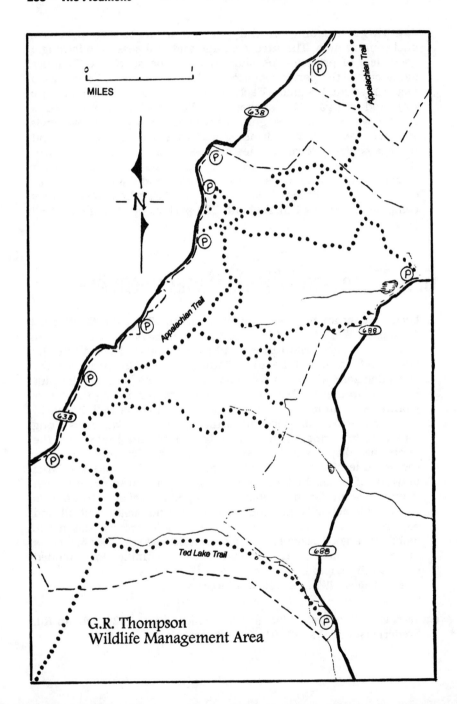

MILES

-N-

Appalachian Trail

638

Appalachian Trail

688

638

688

Ted Lake Trail

G.R. Thompson
Wildlife Management Area

**getting there:** Access to the WMA is on either the E or W side. On the E: from I-66, take exit 18 Turn N onto SR-688 (Leeds Manor Rd) and go 1.2 mi to parking area #2, L. From the N, take US-17 S 1.9 mi from its jct with US-50 in Faquier Co to SR-688 (Leeds Manor Rd). Turn R and go 5.5 mi to parking area #2, R. • On the W: take I-66 to exit 18. Go 0.1 mi S to US-55. Turn R and go 4.2 mi to SR-638 (Freezeland Rd). Turn R and go 3.4 mi to the end of the pavement. For the next 6 mi numbered parking areas 4-11 are located on the R side of the road.

**topography:** Located at the E edge of the Blue Ridge Mountains, the WMA terrain is somewhere between rolling piedmont and rugged mountain. Most of the land is forested with hardwoods, with intermittent wildlife clearings. Elevations are between 700 and 2,200 ft. **maps:** USGS Linden Upperville.

**starting out:** There are no facilities on the WMA. Although a few small creeks drain the area, water is scarce along the ridges. Be sure to bring enough with you. Hunting takes place on the WMA in fall and winter. Be sure to wear blaze orange during that time.

**activities:** Hiking, Camping, Fishing

**hiking:** The primary hiking artery on the WMA is the *Appalachian Trail.* It runs for 7 miles along a summit crest of the Blue Ridge the entire length of the preserve. Access is from many of the parking areas on the gated logging roads that run into the WMA's interior from SR-688 and SR-638. There's access from either road, but the hike from points along SR-638 is much shorter—less than a mile along most routes. Using a topo map and the gated roads, it's possible to form loops of many different lengths. In all, there are more than 20 miles of trails in the area. Using the *AT*, it's possible to hike N into the adjacent Sky Meadown SP and connect with the network of trails there. Hiking is easy to moderate. Except during hunting season (when you might want to avoid the area anyway—unless you're hunting) trail use is light. Trailheads are at most of the parking areas. Parking areas #2 and #4 provide access to opposite ends of the *Ted Lake Trail*, one of the few named trails in the WMA. Parking area #6 provides easy access to the *AT.* Scenic highlights along the trails include panoramas, wildflowers, and wildlife.

**camping:** Primitive backcountry camping is permitted throughout the WMA except where posted. Numerous clearings throughout the area offer good, scenic sites. Camping is not allowed at any of the parking areas.

**fishing:** Fishing on the WMA is limited to Lake Thompson, a 10-acre pond fed by a small creek. The pond is stocked with trout, and contains populations of smallmouth bass and catfish. Anglers can fish from the banks; there's no boat access. The lake is located just off SR-688, about 1.5 mi from its N end at US-17.

# Bull Run Regional Park

Although not really covered under any definition of backcountry, this large park merits inclusion in this guide because it is the northern terminus of the splendid, 17.5-mile *Bull Run–Occoquan Trail*, which follows the peaceful, meandering river corridor all the way to Fountainhead Park (see separate entry below). Mostly the park is given over to large ball fields, extensive picnic grounds (11 shelters), a pool, frisbee golf course, and the Bull Run Shooting Center. Of more interest to outdoor travelers is the large car campground. In addition to its scenic qualities and ecological importance, Bull Run played a considerable strategic role in the Civil War. Two major battles were fought nearby over control of the creek. It was during the first that Stonewall Jackson received his nickname, for refusing to retreat in the face of a seemingly assured Union victory. The rebel yell was born here too, when he urged his troops to "yell like Furies" during the Confederate counter-offensive. Today Bull Run meanders through hardwood forests that harbor wildlife: white-tailed deer, beaver, opossum, wild turkey, hawks, and great blue herons all inhabit the area. The park is open between the middle of March and end of November.

Mannassas Park (S) is the closest town.

**contact:** Bull Run Regional Park, 7700 Bull Run Dr, Centreville, VA 22020; 703/631-0550.

**getting there:** From I-66, take exit 53 and go S on VA-28 0.6 mi to Lee Highway (US-29). Turn R and go 3.1 mi to Bull Run Post Office Rd (SR-621). Turn L and go 1.1 mi to SR-2548. Turn R and go 0.8 mi to the park entrance.

**topography:** Park terrain is practically level. Large areas have been cleared and are maintained as playing fields and park-like settings. The rest of the acreage is covered by a hardwood forest. **maps:** USGS Manassas.

**starting out:** The entrance fee is $4/vehicle. Facilities (restrooms, pay phone, vending machines) are at the campground store. Maps and brochures are available there too. With the shooting range located within the park, the sound of gunfire is a constant presence.
Alcohol is prohibited in the park.

**activities:** Hiking, Fishing, Camping.

**hiking:** The only trail in the area is the 17.5-mi *Bull Run–Occoquan Trail.* It closely follows Bull Run between Bull Run and Fountainhead Regional Parks. Although the entire trail can be hiked in a single day, there are numerous access points along its route permitting hikes of various length. The trail map produced by REI (available at the campground store) shows access points and mileage. The trailhead is signed (next to the campground entrance) and the trail is blazed with blue rectangles. Hiking is easy. Creek crossings are on footbridges. Equestrians use the trail too. Trail use is light to moderate.

**camping:** The large car campground in the park has 150 sites spread out over a large forested area. A pair of shower/restroom facilities are centrally located. Most of the sites offer considerable privacy, due to the dense vegetation. Each site comes with a picnic table and grill. The fee is $12/night, $14 with hookup.

**fishing:** The hiking trail parallels Bull Run, Occoquan River and Occoquan Lake for its entire route, providing anglers with the chance to fish several different types of water. The best fishing is on the latter two bodies of water, where game species include striped and largemouth bass, flathead catfish, perch, and crappie. Fishing is from the banks or from a boat (except on Bull Run). A boat ramp is located at Fountainhead Regional Park.

# Fountainhead Regional Park

Located just south of the urban sprawl of northeastern Virginia, Fountainhead Park is a welcome oasis of rolling woodlands and deep blue water. Situated on the north shore of 2,100 acre Occoquan Reservoir, this park features both water-and land-based activities. On water, the lake's long narrow channel and forest setting offer a quiet paddling environment. Beneath the surface, nearly a dozen species of sport fish lurk. On land, the park is at one end of the 17.5-mile *Bull Run–Occoquan* Trail. It follows the lakeshore and meandering Bull Run to its northeastern terminus at Bull Run Regional Park (see separate entry above). Other park attractions include facilities not so oriented toward backcountry travel: a miniature golf course and archery range. Fountainhead Park is a pleasant place to spend a quiet weekend day, whether on water or land. The park is open March to November from dawn to dusk.

Woodbridge (SE) and W Springfield (NE) are the closest towns.

**contact:** Fountainhead Regional Park, 10875 Hampton Rd, Fairfax Station, VA 22039; 703/250-9124

**getting there:** From the jct of US-29 and VA-123 (Chain Bridge Rd), take VA-123 S 11 mi to Hampton Rd (SR-647). Turn R and go 3.1 mi (at 0.9 mi bear R at a fork) to the park entrance, L.

**topography:** Rolling piedmont above the Occoquan Reservoir. The majority of the park is covered by a hardwood forest with scattered groves of pine trees, with several cleared and landscaped areas. **maps:** USGS Occoquan.

**starting out:** A pamphlet that shows the park's trails is available at the marina concession stand. Facilities (restrooms, water, and vending machines) are at the marina. Other facilities include a concession stand and picnic area with tables, grills, and a shelter.

Alcohol is prohibited in the park. Neither swimming nor water-skiing is allowed.

**activities:** Hiking, Canoeing/Kayaking, Fishing.

**hiking:** Hiking within the park is on a pair of short nature trails.

Combined, they cover 3.5 mi. The trails, which wind through a second-growth forest with occasional lake views, are blazed and easy to follow. Hiking is easy to moderate. Trail access is at the picnic area parking lot. Also in the park is the S trailhead to the splendid, 17.5-mi *Bull Run–Occoquan Trail*, which follows the lake and Bull Run NW through serene woodlands to Bull Run Regional Park. There are several other access points along the trail, allowing for hikes of various lengths. The area along the trail's N end is of historical interest, as Bull Run played a strategic role in the Civil War and was the site of two of that war's bloodiest, most famed battles. A good trail map produced by REI is available at the marina. Hiking on the trail is easy. The trail is used by equestrians as well as hikers; traffic is light to moderate. Access in the park is at the large picnic area parking lot.

**canoeing/kayaking:** The 2,100-acre Occoquan Reservoir provides a surprisingly serene paddling environment at the edge of world-class urban and suburban sprawl. The man-made reservoir was formed when the Occoquan River was dammed. The lake spreads out in a serpentine shape amidst forested hillsides, with numerous small coves and branches. Because of its shape, there is easily enough water for a full day's paddle. The boat ramp is located beside the marina, with a launch fee of $4 charged. Boats with motors with more than 10 hp are not allowed, keeping traffic and noise to a minimum. The park rents rowboats.

**fishing:** Occoquan Reservoir holds largemouth bass, northern pike, walleye, channel and flathead catfish, crappie, and bluegill. The lake produced the state record flathead catfish. Fishing is done from a boat or from land. A small fishing pier is located adjacent to the marina. Fishing from land elsewhere is difficult, since most of the shoreline is forested.

# Huntley Meadows Park

Situated in the midst of the urban and suburban sprawl that is northeast Virginia, the 1,261 acres of this park provide a remarkable oasis. Although much of the park is given over to forest and field, the main attraction is the extensive wetland area that is the remnant of a former course of the Potomac. The park has made access to this rare natural habitat easy with the construction of a system of boardwalks and observation decks. Wildlife observed includes beavers, ducks, herons, frogs, snakes, and more than 200 species of birds at varying times of year. Although the park is not really set up for backcountry travel, the nature interpretive trails make it a required destination for anyone interested in experiencing the crucial—and increasingly rare—environment that is a wetland. The park is open year round dawn to dusk.

The park is located amidst suburban sprawl S of Alexandia.

**contact:** Huntley Meadows Park, 3701 Lockheed Blvd, Alexandria, VA 22306; 703/768-2525.

**getting there:** There are 2 entrances to the park. To reach the main entrance, from I-495 take exit 1. Go S on US-1 3.1 mi to Lockheed Blvd. Turn R and go 0.6 mi to Harrison Lane and the park entrance, L. • To reach the other entrance, from I-495 take US-1 S 1.5 mi to King's Highway. Turn R and go 2.5 mi to the small parking lot and trailhead, L.

**topography:** Terrain in the park is relatively level and low-lying, with elevations less than 100 ft above sea level. Major habitats are hardwood forest, wetland, and meadow. **maps:** USGS Alexandria, Mount Vernon.

**starting out:** Facilities in this very busy park are located at the visitor center. Inside are information and park exhibits, as well as restrooms, water, and pay phones. Hours are 9 AM to 5 PM daily except Tuesday; shorter hours in winter. The park offers a full schedule of nature classes.

Alcohol is not allowed.

**activities:** Hiking, Mountain Biking.

**hiking:** 5 short trails cover a combined distance of just over 3 miles. Although the trails are short, they wind through some of the most fascinating natural habitats in the state. The trails are all easy to hike, following wide paths of crushed stone and cinders, as well as an extensive boardwalk system over a vast wetland. This latter qualifies as one of the most well-constructed and magnificent trails in the commonwealth. The trail and its several observation platforms offer an unsurpassed opportunity to study a wetland habitat up close. Access to the trails is at either of the access points described above. Trail use is very heavy.

**mountain biking:** The 1.2-mi *Hike-bike trail* is the only park trail open to bikes. It follows a paved path from the trailhead and access on S Kings Highway to its terminus at the perimeter of the wetland area. Riding is easy on this level trail.

# Riverbend Park

As its name suggests, 409-acre Riverbend Park is located on the banks of a river—the Potomac. Along with Great Falls Park, adjacent to the south, the park is part of a long stretch of riverfront given over to outdoor recreation. Hiking trails, a boat ramp, a nature center, and riverside picnic area can all be found in the park. The park's woodlands and fields are home to quite a few species of birds and mammals. White-tailed deer are plentiful; Canada geese, osprey, and bald eagles can be seen at different times. Located less than fifteen minutes from Washington, D.C., Riverbend Park is perfect for a short outing, particularly for families with young children who will appreciate the nature center and interpretive trail. The park is open daily until 5:30.

Reston (S) and Sterling (SW) are the closest towns.

**contact:** Riverbend Park, 8800 Potomac Hills St, Great Falls, VA 22066; 703/759-9018.

**getting there:** From the jct of I-495 and the Georgetown Pike (VA-193) NW of McLean, take exit 13 and go W on Georgetown Pike 4.6 mi to River Bend Rd (SR-603). Turn R and go 2.3 mi to Jeffrey Rd (SR-1268). Turn R and go 0.8 mi to Potomac Hills St and the entrance to the park, R.

**topography:** Park terrain includes the low hills and shallow valleys common to the piedmont and a narrow band of river floodplain. The uplands are mostly forested, while the bottomland is a conbination of open areas, sandy shoreline, and hardwood forest. Elevations reach 150 ft above sea level. **maps:** USGS Seneca, Rockville.

**starting out:** You can begin a park visit at the visitor center. Inside you'll find exhibits on local flora, fauna, and history, information, and park maps and brochures. Restrooms, water, and a pay phone are there too. The visitor center is open weekdays 9 AM to 5 PM; weekends 12 AM to 5 PM; closed Tuesdays.

Alcohol is not allowed in the park. Pets must be kept on a leash. Swimming or wading in the river are not allowed.

**activities:** Hiking, Fishing.

**hiking:** A 10-mile trail network all visitors to explore all corners of the park. Most trails are short, but several can be connected to create longer hikes. Habitats encountered along the trails include the riverfront, forested uplands, and a grassy meadow where wildlife sightings are common. Also in the park are the remains of an old homesite. The *Paw Paw Passage* is an interpretive trail (guide available) that begins and ends at the nature center. Park trails are well-designed, well-maintained. Improvements include footbridges and boardwalks over wet areas. Access to the trails is from the main parking area. The *Potomac Heritage Trail* connects to the extensive trail system Great Falls Park, adjacent to the south.

**fishing:** 2 miles of river frontage give anglers plenty of room from which to cast. The park isn't a major fishing destination, but if you're looking to simply get a line in the water for a couple of hours, it provides a nice setting to do so. Fish most often caught are largemouthbass, smallmouth bass, and catfish.

# Great Falls Park

Situated on a high bluff overlooking the Potomac River, this 800-acre park is noteworthy for its rugged scenic grandeur and its significant historical role in colonial America. The Potomac River begins as an unimposing creek in WV. By the time it reaches Great Falls it is a major waterway that was once a primary artery of trade between the nation's capital and points west. At the falls, the broad expanse of water is forced over huge jagged rock formations into the narrow chute of Mather Gorge. The hydraulic effect creates one of the most impressive ongoing displays of nature's raw power in the East. By the end of the eighteenth century, American engineers were determined to render the falls navigable to river traffic by constructing a series of canals, the nation's first. The canals were built between 1785 and 1802 by the Patowmack Company, founded by George Washington. Although the canals soon were made obsolete by the advent of the railroad, their remains can still be seen in the park. Other park attractions are the network of hiking, biking, and horse trails; extensive picnic grounds and fields; scenic vantages overlooking the falls; and rock climbing on the soaring cliffs that face the river. The park is open every day except Christmas until dark. With so much of interest to explore and proximity to Washington, D.C., the park is often crowded. Riverbend Park (see separate entry above) is adjacent to the north.

Reston (W) and McLean (SE) are the closest towns.

**contact:** Great Falls Park, P.O. Box 66, Great Falls, VA 22066; 703/285-2966

**getting there:** From the jct of I-495 and the Georgetown Pike (VA-193) NW of McLean, take exit 13 and go W on Georgetown Pike 4.3 mi to Old Dominion Dr at a traffic signal. Turn R and go 1 mi to the park entrance.

**topography:** The park sits atop a rocky escarpment above the Potomac River. Sheer cliffs, rock outcropings, narrow strips of sandy beach and rolling piedmont are all encountered. Plant communities include hardwood–pine forests, swamps, and open fields. maps: USGS Falls Church, Vienna, Rockville, Seneca.

**starting out:** Entrance fees (valid for 7 days) are $4/vehicle, $2/person on foot or bike. The large, modern visitor center features exhibits on the history and ecology of the river and surrounding area. A variety of maps and brochures are available for free. Restrooms, water, pay phone, and a snack bar (open seasonally) are all there. Open weekdays 10 AM to 4 PM, weekends 10 AM to 5 PM.

The park prohibits alcohol. No wading or swimming. Pets must be kept on a leash.

**activities:** Hiking, Mountain Biking, Fishing

**hiking:** The network of 6 trails cover a total distance of 16 miles.

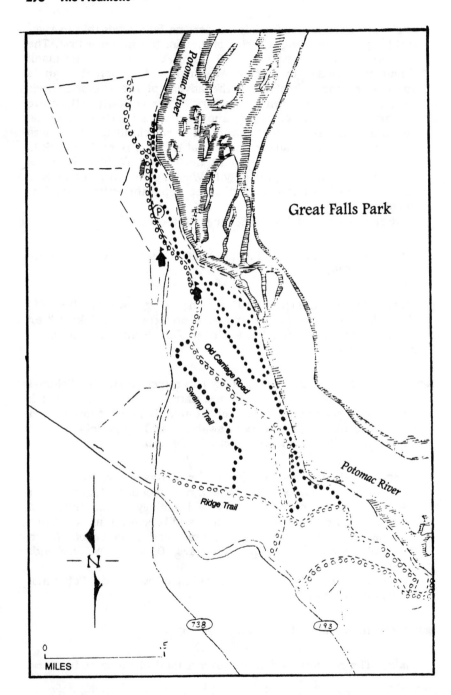

Potomac River

Great Falls Park

Old Carriage Road

Swamp Trail

Ridge Trail

Potomac River

N

738

193

0

MILES

All of the trails interconnect, making possible loop hikes of varying distances. The trails pass by the park's historical sites, cling to rocky ledges above the river (extreme caution is advised, especially with children), and wind through rolling piedmont forested with hardwoods and pines. Trails follow a mix of carriage roads and single-track dirt paths, with improvements that include footbridges and elaborate systems of steps up and down some of the rocky crags. Hiking is mostly easy to moderate, with cliffside trails demanding care and a nimble step, due to the lack of handrails. The trails are blazed, with trailheads and junctions signed. Equestrians and mountain bikers use some of the trails. Trail use is very heavy.

**mountain biking:** 6 miles of trails are open to mountain bikes. The major route is the *Old Carriage Road*, which runs along the spine of the park from one end to the other. It can be combined with the trails in riverbend park—it connects at two points—for longer rides. Several other trails also connect with the carriage road; the longest is 3-mi *Ridge Trail*. Riding along the trails is generally easy, with a few moderate stretches. The trails are often quite busy with hikers, equestrians, and other mountain bikers. Access is at the visitor center.

**fishing:** There are a few places in the southern part of the park (well below the falls) that afford access to the Potomac River. Game fish are largemouth and smallmouth bass, and catfish.

# The Tidewater & Eastern Shore

# The Tidewater & Eastern Shore Region Key Map

1. Accotink Bay WR
2. Pohick Bay Regional Park
3. Mason Neck NWR
4. Mason Neck SP
5. Leesylvania SP
6. Caldeon Natural Area
7. Westmoreland SP
8. Beaverdam Park
9. York River SP
10. Waller Mill Park
11. Newport News Park
12. Grandview Beach Preserve
13. Chippokes Plantation SP

14. Hog Island WMA
15. Ragged Island WMA
16. Lone Star Lakes Park
17. Kiptopeke SP
18. Eastern Shore of Virginia NWR
19. Mockhorn Island WMA
20. Saxis WMA
21. Chincoteague NWR
22. Seashore SP
23. Great Dismal Swamp NWR
24. Northwest River Park
25. Back Bay NWR
26. False Cape SP

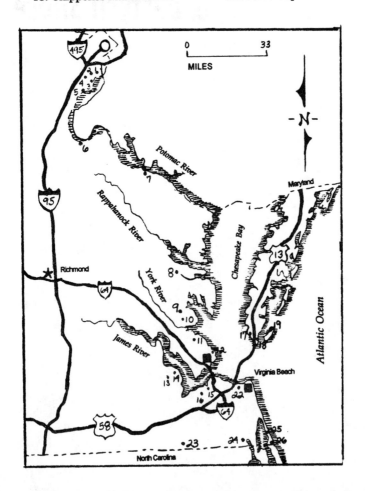

# Introduction

Virginia's tidewater and eastern shore are broad, low-lying areas of sandy bottomland and rich soil defined by large bodies of saltwater, brackish water, and fresh water. The coastal plain is widest at the southern end of the state, where it extends from Emporia to the Atlantic Ocean. An imaginary line running north and south through Richmond marks the western extent of the coastal plain. As you move north along that line, the coastal plain narrows, as the Cheasapeake Bay and then the Potomac River, rather than the Atlantic Ocean, define Virginia's eastern border. At the state's northeast corner, the coastal plain practically vanishes altogther, and piedmont uplands meet the Potomac River without an intervening region of low-lying plain. The eastern shore is located at the southern tip of the Delmarva Peninsula—its name is formed from Delaware, Maryland, and Virginia, the three states that share its lands—and is detatched from the rest of the state.

The region's diversity of coastal habitats translates into an immense ecological diversity. The Cheaspeake Bay is the largest estuary in North America. Its waters and shallow marshlands nurture and support a vast array of aquatic and land-based wildlife. The broad tidal rivers that empty into it—the James, York, Rappahannock, and Potomac—are no less important. Together these tidal waters form a system that is central to the coastal region's complex ecosystem. It's no coincidence that almost all of the national wildlife refuges in Virginia on situated on the bay or rivers that feed it. Those few that aren't—the Great Dismal Swamp, Back Bay, Chincoteage, and Eastern Shore of Virginia—are all located in close proximity, on the Atlantic Ocean or just inland. These wilderness preserves exist primarily to safeguard habitat used by the hundreds of species of birds that are permanent residents in eastern Virginia or migrate through every year along the Atlantic Flyway.

Virginia's Atlantic coastline consists of two components: a long, sandy beach that runs from Virginia Beach and the mouth of Cheasapeake Bay south to North Carolina, and a series of barrier islands backed by tidal marsh and salt flats on the eastern shore. Apart from the heavily developed areas in Virginia Beach, most of the ocean front exists in a pristine state. A long segment of the beach south of Virginia Beach is controlled by a state park and national wildlife refuge. Most of the barrier islands on the eastern shore are publicly owned or held by the Nature Conservancy. The eastern shore's isolation from the rest of the state has helped maintain that region's largely undeveloped state. Elsewhere on the coastal plain Virginia offers a contrast. Pockets of intense urban development coexist with large natural areas and extensive farmlands that have changed little in the past couple hundred years. Although the coastal plain is home to Virginia's three largest metropolitan areas, much of the region retains a pastoral, if not quite pristine, aspect.

Most opportunities for outdoor recreation in the tidewater and eastern shore focus on the water in one way or another. The fishing is of course world-famous. Anglers come to Virginia from all over to fish for saltwater species in the Atlantic surf and Cheasapeake, or to fish for freshwater species in the upper sections of the tidal rivers. And the Cheasapeake is rightly renowned for its crabs. For those wanting to explore large portions of the region, a canoe or kayak is the ideal vessel. Sea kayaks in particular seem ready-made for exploring the fragile coastal environments, spying on wildlife, and managing the wind and currents that are almost always factors out on the water. Multi-day paddling trips are possible in some of the more remote regions, and boat launches are ubiquitous throughout the region. On land the most popular activity is probably birding. The fall and winter migration periods are the best times for observing the hundreds of species of waterfowl, raptors, wading birds, shore birds, and song birds that pass through the region. The Potomac also provides habitat to a substantial population of bald eagles. Many of the wildlife refuges and parks have trail networks that permit visitors to explore the coastal forests and marsh lands. And there are campgrounds too, making it possible to set up base camp for longer trips or explorations.

Although the coastal region has the state's mildest climate, the best times to visit for backcountry enthusiasts are still spring and fall. Summer brings droves of tourists to the beaches and resort communities, and winter is chilly, with a few days where temperatures drop below freezing. Visitors should be prepared for severe storms at all times of year. Though rare, hurricanes and tropical storms can lash the coast from May to November, and winter is the season of nor'easters. The warm months are also the season of biting insects. Repellent is an essential during those times.

# Accotink Bay Wildlife Refuge

Situated on the grounds of the U.S. Army's Fort Belvoir, the Accotink Bay Wildlife Refuge is a 1,315-acre natural oasis preserved amidst the heavy residential and industrial development of northeastern Virginia. Visitors to the refuge encounter wetlands, marshes, streams, beaver ponds, and gentle slopes forested with climax hardwood species such as American beech, river birch, sweet gum, yellow poplar, oak, and hickory. Dogwood and mountain laurel are prominent in the understory. The diversity of habitats translates into a diversity of wildlife as well. More than 200 species of birds, including the bald eagle, great blue heron, great egret, wood duck, bufflehead, and wild turkey, have been observed on the refuge. Beaver are abundant, and white-tailed deer are sometimes seen in the woodlands and clearings. A well-designed trail network brings visitors in proximity to the habitats that nurture these wildlife species. Since the primary mission of the refuge is wildlife habitat conservation, outdoor recreation is limited to low-impact travel only. Nature photographers and birders will find the area particularly rewarding. The refuge is open all year during daylight hours.

Woodbrige (W) and Mount Vernon (E) are the closest towns.

**contact:** Environmental and Natural Resource Division, US Army Garrison Ft Belvoir, 9430 Jackson Loop, Bldg 1442, Ft Belvoir, VA 22060; 703/806-4007

**getting there:** From I-95, take exit 166. Turn S onto Backlick Rd and go 3.5 mi to US-1. Cross the highway onto Pohick Rd and go 0.7 mi to the refuge parking lot and trailheads, R.

**topography:** Wooded uplands, sandy bottomland, tidal marsh, and shoreline are all encountered on the refuge. The upland terrain rolls in gradual swells and is interlaced by small, slow-moving streams. Elevations do not exceed 50 ft. **maps:** USGS Fort Belvoir.

**starting out:** Facilities on the refuge are very limited. There are pit toilets at the trailhead parking area and a large map board with a holder for refuge maps, bird lists, and brochures. Other facilities are nearby on the army base and town.

Alcohol is not allowed on the refuge. Pets are permitted, but must be leashed.

**activities:** Hiking

**hiking:** A 5-mile trail network provides access to all parts of the refuge. Starting from the single trailhead described above, 9 trails fan out along the shore of Accotink Bay and Accotink Creek, and through wetlands and forested uplands. With such a diversity of habitats encountered, the trail network provides an excellent way to experience different aspects of the Chesapeake ecosystem. The trails are all easy to follow, with improvements that include steps, benches, boardwalks, and a footbridge. Trail junctions are signed. Hiking on all trails is easy. Hikers should be aware that the trails are popular and often crowded. A handicapped-accessble nature trail with 14 stations and picnic tables is located at a separate trailhead just N of the main trailhead.

# Pohick Bay Regional Park

It's something of a stretch to include this highly-developed park in a guidebook to the Virginia backcountry. With facilities that include 2 boat storage areas, a jet-ski slalom course, championship golf course, mini- and frisbee-golf courses, a large picnic area, and a swimming pool, pristine natural areas are not really a major consideration. It's included for two reasons: a car campground and boat access to the Potomac River. The park sits on Mason Neck, adjacent to Mason Neck State Park and Mason Neck National Wildlife Refuge; with the campground, it makes an excellent base to explore either area or both, whether on foot or in a canoe or kayak. The park is open year round.

Lorton (NW) and Woodbridge (W) are the closest towns.

**contact:** Pohick Bay Regional Park, 6501 Pohick Bay Dr, Lorton, VA 22079; 540/339-6104.

**getting there:** From the S, take I-95 to exit 160. Turn N on US-1 and go 1.5 mi to VA-242 (Gunniston Rd). Turn R and go 3.2 mi to the park entrance, L. • From the N, take I-95 to exit 163. Turn L on Lorton Rd and go to Armistead Rd. Turn R and go to US-1. Turn R and go to VA-242. Turn L and go 3.2 mi to the park.

**topography:** The rolling piedmont plateau extends all the way to the waterline here. Forest cover is mixed pine and hardwoods, with large areas of the park cleared and landscaped. **maps:** USGS Fort Belvoir.

**starting out:** Except for the residents of the 3 surrounding counties, there's a $4/vehicle entrance fee. Restrooms, water, a pay phone and vending machines are located at the visitors center. There's also a concession stand there that sells snack food. The park is very popular and is often crowded on peak weekends in spring, summer, and fall.

Alcohol is prohibited. Swimming in the bay is not allowed.

**activities:** Camping, Canoeing/Kayaking, Fishing

**camping:** The large car campground has 150 sites in 2 different areas. In the larger loop, the sites are large but close together, offering little privacy. The smaller loop is better, with heavier forest cover providing a measure of isolation. This loop isn't always open, however. All sites have a picnic table and grill. Restroom/shower facilities (hot water) are located in both areas. A small campstore carries a limited supply of food and camping supplies. Sites cost $12/night; $14/night with hook-up. As you might expect, the campround is more popular among the RV set than with backpackers. It's open year-round.

**canoeing/kayaking:** Although the busy, noisy area around the boat launch seems less than promising for backcountry paddling, as you follow the shoreline southeast you soon round Hallowing Point and leave the noise (most of it, at least) behind. Around the point begins a 5-mi shoreline within Mason Neck SP and Mason Neck NWR (see separate entries below). Another option is to cross Pohick Bay and enter Accotink Bay, a part of the Accotink Bay Wildlife Refuge (see separate entry above). Both of these environments offer plenty to the unobtrusive paddler: pristine estuary habitats and the abundant wildlife they nurture and support. Great blue herons, wood ducks, Canada geese, muskrats, and even bald eagles can be seen. From the put-in to Accotink Bay is 1 mile; to the boat launch at Mason Neck SP is about 10. If you decide to spend more than a day paddling in the area, you can make base camp in Pohick Bay Park, the only camping facility on Mason Neck (backcountry camping is not allowed). A $4 launch fee for canoes and kayaks is charged in Pohick Bay Park.

**fishing:** Pohick Bay is part of the Potomac River. The park provides access to the water at the boat launch. Bank fishing isn't really a possibility, due to the limited shoreline in the park and the business of the boat launch/marina area. Sport fish in the Potomac River include striped bass, bluefish, sea trout, croaker, flounder, spotted sea trout, red drum, chain pickerel, bullhead catfish, white catfish, channel catfish, black bass, yellow perch, white perch, American shad. A marine fishing license is required to fish this part of the river.

# Mason Neck National Wildlife Refuge

Located on a broad peninsula that juts out into the Potomac River, the refuge is one component in a group of federal, state, and local holdings on Mason Neck working together to preserve as much of the 8,000-acre peninsula as possible as habitat for bald eagles and other wildlife. The 2,276 acres of the refuge abut Mason Neck State Park and Gunston Hall Plantation. Together with nearby Pohick Bay Regional Park, more than 5,000 acres are being managed for natural resource protection and outdoor recreation. On the refuge these resources include Great Marsh, the largest freshwater marsh in northern Virginia, and a deciduous forest that is working through the stages of succession to climax stage. With facilities limited to a pair of hiking trails, the most popular activity on the refuge is wildlife observation. There's plenty to observe, with more than 200 species of birds observed, including Canada geese, great blue herons, wood ducks, least bitterns, osprey, and of course bald eagles, for whom the refuge was created. Among mammals are white-tailed deer, beaver, and muskrat. The refuge is open daily during daylight hours.

Woodbridge (W) is the closest city.

**contact:** Refuge Manager, Mason Neck NWR, 14416 Jefferson Davis Highway, Suite 20, Woodbridge, VA 22191; 703/690-1297.

**getting there:** From the jct of US-1 and VA-242, take VA-242 E 3.7 mi to SR-600. Bear R and go 0.6 mi to SR-5733. Turn R and go 0.7 mi to the refuge access and parking lot. Access to the *Great Marsh Trail* is on SR-600, 1.1 mi S of its jct with SR-5733.

**topography:** The majority of the refuge is covered by a deciduous forest. The remainder is freshwater marsh and sandy shoreline. Elevations on the refuge do not exceed 50 ft. **maps:** USGS Fort Belvoir, Indian Head.

**starting out:** The only facilities on the refuge are an information kiosk and port-o-san at the small parking area. A refuge brochure, trail map and bird list are available there.

Pets must be kept on a leash.

**activities:** Hiking, Kayaking/Canoeing.

**hiking:** The 2 trails on the refuge are the 3-mi *Woodmarsh Trail* and the 0.75-mi *Great Marsh Trail*. The shape of the former vaguely resembles a guitar, with a long, straight section that branches off into an oval loop. The trail passes through the hardwood forest and skirts one edge of Great Marsh. An extensive system of boardwalks provides access to the marsh and permits excellent opportunities for wildlife viewing out across its expanse. A few benches for this purpose are placed along the trail. Hiking on the single-track path is easy. The trailhead is at the parking area. Access to the shorter *Great Marsh Trail* is on SR-600. Also designed to maximize wildlife observation, it passes into the Great Marsh on an elevated boardwalk. Both trails are popular with birders and other lovers of wildlife.

**kayaking/canoeing:** Although there's no river access on the refuge, the stealth and mobility afforded by a canoe or kayak make them ideal vessels for exploring its borders. The boat ramps at Mason Neck SP and Pohick Bay SP (see separate listings) are close enough to make day-trips possible. If you put in at the state park, you have about 2 miles of paddling to reach the NWR. From Pohick Bay, it's about 5 miles. Paddlers should anticipate open water conditions on the Potomac River.

# Mason Neck State Park

Mason Neck State Park is one element of the cooperative plan to protect as much of the Mason Neck peninsula as possible in order to provide undisturbed habitat for bald eagles. The park occupies

1,804 acres of the neck's western edge, fronting Belmont Bay, a protected anchorage of the Potomac River. The eagles that visit the area are most commonly seen between late fall and early spring. Other wildlife that has benefited from the protected habitat includes white-tailed deer, red fox, wild turkeys, beavers, Canada geese, and great blue herons. Except for the secretive fox, there's a good chance of seeing one or more of these species on a visit. The park's natural environments include both upland forest and low-lying wetlands. Outdoor recreation in the park is consistent with habitat preservation, and low-impact travel is the rule. Hiking trails meander through the different regions of the park and a picnic area with several dozen tables and grills is located in a bayside meadow. The park is open daily during daylight hours. With no camping facilities, only single-day visits are possible.

Woodbridge (W) is the closest city.

**contact:** Mason Neck State Park, 7301 High Point Rd, Lorton, VA 22079; 703/550-0960

**getting there:** From I-95, take exit 161 to US-1S. From the jct of US-1 and VA-242, take VA-242 E 3.7 mi to SR-600. Bear R and go 0.6 mi to SR-5733. Turn R and go 0.9 mi to the park entrance.

**topography:** The primary natural habitat in the park is hardwood forest. There is also a fairly extensive freshwater marsh, with some meadows. Terrain combines flat coastal plain with gently rolling upland. **maps:** USGS Ft Belvoir, Indian Head.

**starting out:** An entrance fee of $1/vehicle weekdays and $2 on weekends is charged. Facilities in the park are at the picnic area (restrooms, water) and visitor center (water, pay phone). The visitor center can also provide you with a map of the park that shows hiking trails, natural habitats, and scenic spots. Several exhibits there reveal aspects of the natural and cultural history of the area, with a focus on the Mason Neck peninsula. The visitor center is open daily during summer and on weekends in Apr, May, Sep, and Oct.

Public use or display of alcohol is prohibited. Pets must be kept on a leash. Swimming from the park is not allowed.

**activities:** Hiking, Canoeing/Kayaking, Fishing

**hiking:** Although the trail network covers only 3 miles, it packs a lot of highlights into that small distance. The 1-mi *Bayview Trail* is a self-guiding interpretive trail with plaques that describe the environment of a marsh. The trail passes through uplands and wetland areas, with good views out over the bay. Another trail, the *Kane's Creek Trail*, wanders through hardwood forest before ending at a viewing blind from which bald eagles can often be seen. Both trails begin near the visitor center. The trailheads are signed, as are trail jcts. Trail improvements include extensive boardwalks, benches, and stairs. Hiking the trails is easy.

**canoeing/kayaking:** The park put-in for canoes and kayaks is located beside the visitor center. From the park, paddlers enter Belmont Bay, where they have the option of exporing a part or all of Mason Neck. In either case, open water conditions can be expected, with wind and tides both a factor. Mason Neck has a shoreline of more than 10 miles, most of which is publicly owned and managed for wildlife habitat protection. Traveling south and then east, you come to the shoreline of Mason Neck NWR and then to Pohick Bay regional park, where there's another boat ramp, making possible one-way trips with a short vehicle shuttle. For a shorter trip across open water, head southwest across Occoquan Bay to Leesylvania SP, where you can take out or turn around and go back to Mason Neck. One way, the trip is 5 miles. Although you're likely to encounter motor boats out on the bay, traffic is not usually opressive.

**fishing:** Fishing on Belmont Bay has suffered in recent years due to a loss in aquatic plants that provide important habitat for the food that fish eat. If you want to give it a try anyway, you can fish from either a boat or on shore, where there's plenty of open shoreline from which to cast. Species most commonly caught here are largemouth bass, black crappie, and bluegill. You can fish these waters with a VA, MD, or Potomac River Fisheries Commission freshwater fishing license.

# Leesylvania State Park

Leesylvania—the name means Lee's woods—State Park is located on the shore of the Potomac twenty-five miles south of Washington, D.C. The 508-acre park is rich in history. Though it was in the

Lee family for five previous generations, the property is most often associated with Henry Lee III, better known as "Light Horse Harry," a governor of Virginia, member of the Continetal Congress, and U.S. senator. He was also the father of Robert E. Lee. The park's historical significance is combined with opportunities for outdoor recreation. It is a popular launching site for power boats running up and down the Potomac. Quieter pursuits are also facilitated, by the park's network of backcountry trails and by a secondary boat launch for canoes and kayaks on the relatively serene Powell's Creek. Other facilities include a large picnic area with tables, grills, and shelters. A unique—and occasionaly irksome—feature of the park is that an active railroad line runs right through its middle. While there are other parks in the vicinity that offer more extensive backcountry and are geared more toward preserving natural habitats, none surpasses Leesylvania in its combination of outdoor recreation and historical significance. The park is open daily between dawn and dusk.

Woodbridge (N) and Dumfries (SW) are the closest cities.

**contact:** Leesylvania State Park, 16236 Neabsco Rd, Woodbridge, VA 22191; 703/670-0372

**getting there:** From I-95, take exit 156. Turn E onto SR-784 and go 1.3 mi to US-1. Turn R and go 0.2 mi to Neabsco Rd. Turn L and go 1.5 mi to the park entrance, R.

**topography:** Park terrain is primarily gently rolling hillside blanketed with hardwoods. Some areas of the park along the river have been cleared to provide a park setting and to accommodate the marina. **maps:** USGS Quantico, Indian Head.

**starting out:** The entrance fee is $2/vehicle on weekdays, $3 on weekends. Facilities (restrooms, water, pay phone) are located at the marina store. For sale there is fishing tackle and snacks. While a steady stream of trucks pulling boat trailers seems to enter the park on peak season weekends, and the area around the marina is often very busy, the park's backcountry is inevitably relatively empty.

Public use or display of alcohol is prohibited. Pets must be kept on a leash. Swimming in the Potomac from the park is not allowed.

**activities:** Hiking, Kayaking/Canoeing, Fishing

**hiking:** 2 main trails provide access to the forested backcountry that gives Leesylvania its name. 2 other trails follow the Potomac shoreline. Combined the trails cover 6 miles. The 2 upland trails are both interpretive trails with accompanying guides available at the respective trailheads. The 2-mi *Powell's Creek Nature Trail* wanders through rolling upland forested with hardwoods before descending to Powell's Creek and surrounding wetland habitat. The trail guide describes the natural processes that are essential to a healthy ecosystem. The trailhead is near the entrance station, and is marked by a petrified tree stump. The focus of the *Lee's Woods Trail*, also 2 miles, is historical. The pamphlet describes 10 sites along the trail in terms of dates ranging from 1608 to 1978. The colonial and Civil War period are emphasized. The trailhead is at the end of the park road. Hiking on all park trails is easy to moderate. The trails are easy to follow and use is moderate to heavy.

**kayaking/canoeing:** Paddlers can put in from a cartop boat launch area located on Powell's Creek, away from the bustle of the marina and main boat launch. From there, it's possible to explore the quiet, intimate waters of Powell's Creek, or to venture out into the Potomac, where the concentration of powerboats can be pretty heavy on busy weekends. If you're interested in a longer trip, paddle northeast up the Potomac and across Occoquan Bay to Mason Neck. Once there, you can expore the shorelines of Mason Neck SP and Mason Neck NWR. You might even see a bald eagle in the area. A boat ramp is located in Mason Neck SP, where you can take out, or you can turn around and head back to Leesylvania. In either case, expect open water conditions on Occoquan Bay and the Potomac. Both bodies of water are tidal, and choppy conditions and strong winds are common. Conditions on Powell's Creek are much tamer, though it too is tidal and feeds into the Potomac.

**fishing:** Fishing is possible in both Powell's Creek and in the Potomac River. Whichever one you decide to fish, a canoe will allow you to cover the most water. Although there are places from which to fish along the shore, these are not real popular due to heavy boat traffic. Species most commonly taken in the area are largemouth bass, black crappie, and bluegill. A VA, MD, or Potomac River Fisheries Commission freshwater fishing license are all valid to fish these waters.

# Caledon Natural Area

A National Natural Landmark, this 2,579-acre preserve exists primarily to protect the habitat of bald eagles. In summer as many as eighty have been counted on its land along the Potomac River. One or two nesting pairs are also making their permanent home in the area. Lands that now form the preserve were once the property of Scottish settler and tobacco farmer John Alexander, who named the area aftern Caledonia, the great forest of Scotland. Much of the preserve is still covered in forest, with stands of old growth at the upper elevations. In addition to the bald eagles, the preserve provides a haven for more than 100 other species of birds, including the great blue heron, turkey vulture, red-tailed hawk, osprey, pileated woodpecker, ruby-throated hummingbird, red-bellied woodpecker, and tufted titmouse. Among mammals, white-tailed deer are most prevalent on the preserve. In fact, their numbers have surpassed the level that is condsidered the natural limit. As a result, managed deer hunts were instituted in 1995. Recreation in the preserve is very limited, due to the wildlife conservation objective. Only hiking is permitted, and only on the part of the preserve away from the eagle habitat. To allow visitors to see the eagles, field trips are conducted twice daily during summer. The Preserve is open daily all year from 8 AM to sunset.

Fredericksburg (W) is the closest city.

**contact:** Caledon Natural Area, 11617 Caledon Rd, King George, VA 22485; 703/663-3861

**getting there:** From the jct of US-301 and VA-3, take VA-3 N 4.1 mi to VA-206. Turn R and go 6.3 mi to VA-218. Turn L and go 0.9 mi to the entrance, R.

**topography:** Natural habitats in the park include river frontage, marshland, open fields, and upland hardwood forest. Terrain is hilly, with gentle ridges that slope down to small drainages. Elevations are between sea level and 160 ft. **maps:** USGS King George.

**starting out:** Facilities (water, restrooms, pay phone) are located at the visitor center. A smal gift shop has a good selection of field guides for sale. Trail maps of the preserve are available for free. The center is open 9 AM to 5 PM Wed–Sun. Eagle tours are offered at 10

AM and 2 PM between mid-June and Labor Day. Reservations are recommended.

Between Apr 15 and Oct 15 boating within 1000 ft of the shoreline is not allowed in order to protect the eagle habitat. Public use or display of alcohol is not allowed.

**activities:** Hiking

**hiking:** A network of 5 interconnected trail loops covers a total distance of 5 miles. The loops are stacked one on top of the other, allowing loop hikes of varying distance. The trails occupy only a small part of the preserve, winding through mature hardwood forest at the upper end of the preserve. Spotting bald eagles from them is unlikely, due to the dense forest cover. All trails are accessed from a single trailhead, located near the preserve office. A small picnic area with tables and grills is located there. The trails are improved with footbridges and benches. Hiking along the mild terrain is easy.

# Westmoreland State Park

1,300-acre Westmoreland State Park is perched atop the Horsehead Cliffs overlooking a particularly scenic stretch of the Potomac River. The cliffs form part of a 1.5 mile river frontage on Virginia's northern neck. They're studded with fossils of prehistoric sharks, dolphins, and whales left over from the Miocene epoch when the river was part of a vast sea. Fossils, shark's teeth, and fragments of whale bones can still be found in the area, though removing them is prohibited. The park's historical significance extends into the modern era, as its lands were once home to the Powhatan Indians, one of the Algonquian tribes. And the birthplaces of George Washington and Robert E. Lee are both just outside park boundaries. Outdoor recreation in the park centers around the river and the backcountry forest. On the river there's a boat ramp, boat rentals, a sandy beach and picnic area with tables, grills, and shelters, and a swimming pool with bathhouse that's open from Memorial Day to Labor Day, the park's peak season. A network of trails winds through the backcountry, where there's a car campground, cabins for rent, an unobtrusive restaurant, and a visitor center with exhibits on local ecology, geology, and history. The park is open all year from

sunrise to sunset.
Colonia Beach (N) is the closest town.

**contact:** Westmoreland State Park, Route 1, Box 600, Montross, VA 22520; 804/493-8821

**getting there:** The park entrance is located at the jct of VA-3 and VA-347, about 10 miles S of Colonia Beach.

**topography:** Park habitats include low-lying wetlands and upland hardwood forests. Most of the park sits on a flat plateau that drops 100 ft on cliffs to the river. Some areas have been cleared to create an open park setting. **maps:** USGS Stratford Hall, Colonial Beach South.

**starting out:** Entrance fees are $1/vehicle on weekdays, $2 on weekends. A visitor center has exhibits on area wildlife, prehistory, and history. You can pick up a trail map and park brochure inside. Park facilities include restrooms, water, and a pay phone.

The public use or display of alcohol is not allowed. Pets must be kept on a leash.

**activities:** Hiking, Camping, Canoeing/Kayaking, Fishing

**hiking:** A network of 7 short trails covers a total distance of 6 miles. Trails reach into all regions of the park, with scenic highlights that include exceptional views of the river, the Horsehead Cliffs, an observation tower overlooking Yellow Swamp, and an interpretive trail that describes the lives of the Powhatan Indians at the time when the first European settlers were making their way up the Potomac. Hiking along most of the trails is easy, with a few moderate stretches. Trails follow both single-track paths and old logging roads. The clearly signed trailheads are located along the main park road. Trail use is moderate to heavy.

**camping:** The car campground has 3 loops located in different areas of the park. In all, there are 118 sites. The loops are all similar, with the sites set in heavily wooded areas. Unfortunatley, the sites are pretty small and close together. If the campground is crowded, as it often is during summer, privacy is about nil. Each site has a picnic table and grill. Shower/restroom facilities are located near the center of each loop. Sites cost $12/night, $17 with hookups. The campground is open Mar 1 to Nov 30.

Group campsites are also available.

**canoeing/kayaking:** The stretch of the Potomac that runs along the park provides paddlers with a scenic setting and moderately challenging conditions. It's a good place to upgrade sea-kayaking skills from novice to moderate. You can explore the line of cliffs and sandy beach that front the river, or duck into one of several creeks and bays in the vicinity. More ambitious paddlers can cross the river to the MD shore—a 6-mi trip one-way, or explore lengthy stretches of the VA shore. In either case, shoreline development is minimal, as is boat traffic. The Potomac River is tidal, and subject to stiff winds. Be sure to check local conditions before heading out. A boat ramp is located at the end of the park road.

**fishing:** Fishing in the Potomac River is possible from a boat or from the shoreline. One popular spot for bank casting is near the boat ramp. Hiking about a mile on the *Turkey Neck Trail* will take you to a more isolated stretch of beach. Species taken from the river's brackish water include bluefish, striped bass, and spot. A freshwater license from VA or MD is required.

Another option for anglers is Rock Spring Pond, a small farm pond that supports populations of largemouth bass, catfish, and balck crappie. Only shoreline fishing is available. You reach the pond by hiking a short distance on *Laurel Point Trail.*

# Beaverdam Park

This Gloucester County park is situated on the middle neck between the Rappahannock and York Rivers not far from the historic town of Gloucester. The park's centerpiece is 635-acre Beaverdam Swamp Reservoir, a scenic impoundment open to fishing and boating. The park rents canoes, and there's a lakeside picnic area with tables, grills, and a shelter. The park was only opened in 1992; it's already become quite popular, and warm weekends find it fairly busy. The park's appeal for backcountry enthusiasts is the attractiveness of the lake and the hiking trails that wander through the lush hardwood forest that surrounds it. If you're in the area, it's worth a visit. Park hours are 6 AM to sunset. Gloucester (S) is the closest town

**contact:** Gloucester County Parks and Recreation, P.O. Box 157, Gloucester, VA 23061; 804/693-2355; Park Office 804/693-2107.

**getting there:** From I-64, take exit 220 (VA-33). Turn E onto VA-33 and go 18.3 mi to US-17. Turn R and go 12.4 mi to US-17 BUS and the town of Gloucester. Turn L and go 0.3 to SR-616. Turn L and go 2.5 mi to the park entrance.

**topography:** The man-made lake is surrounded by very gently rolling terrain forested with upland and bottomland hardwoods. Elevations do not exceed 50 ft. **maps:** USGS Gloucester.

**starting out:** Park activity centers around the main parking area on boat ramp. Modern restrooms, water, and a pay phone can all be found there. The park office handles all fees and boat rentals, and can provide you with a free trail map and nature guide.

Alcohol is not allowed in the park. Pets must be kept on a leash. Swimming in the lake is not permitted.

**activities:** Canoeing/Kayaking, Fishing, Hiking

**canoeing/kayaking:** The small lake offers an attractive locale for a short paddle or a day-long fishing trip. Away from the boat ramp, the lakeshore is quite scenic, with a lush hardwood forest that crowds the banks. Several arms provide quiet places to explore or moor. A daily $3 boating permit is required. The park rents canoes for $10/day. Boat traffic is moderate to heavy. Boats with gasoline motors are not allowed on the lake.

**fishing:** Fishing from a boat is most popular on the lake, although the fishing pier always seems to attract a small crowd. If you want to fish from the shore, you'll find plenty of room near the picnic area, though this is also the busiest part of the park. Fishing from canoe is recommended, since you'll be able to cover the most water that way. Largemouth bass, crappie, catfish, and bluegill are all commonly caught in the lake.

**hiking:** A single nature trail is laid out in 4 interconnecting loops that cover a total distance of 3.5 miles. A guide to more than 50 stations along the route is available from the park office. The trail is worth hiking, as the diversity of flora is impressive, and the lake views are excellent. Hiking the trail is easy. The signed trailhead is located behind the restrooms at the main parking lot. Use is heavy.

# York River State Park

2,505-acre York River State Park is situated on the southern shore of the river not far from historic Williamsburg. The park's natural habitats include uplands hardwood forests and brackish marshes. A part of the park is included in the National Estuarine Research Reserve. Located on the lower neck, the park provides an important natural habitat in a region that has been transformed by agriculture in the past three centuries. In fact, the park was once the site of a tobacco warehouse. Today, the woods and estuary provide a haven for wildlife: beavers, deer, raccoon, wood ducks, osprey, great blue herons, mink, northern harrier, and bald eagles can be seen at different times. At the time when the area was first being settled by Europeans, it was the home to Powhatan, father of Pocahontas and leader of the Algonquian tribes. Low-impact backcountry travel is the focus of outdoor recreation in the park. A large trail network—open to hikers, bikers, and equestrians—extends into most regions of the park. A boat ramp on the York River is located on one end of the park, and canoe rentals and guided trips are available during the peak summer season. Other park facilities include a small picnic area and visitor center with exhibits. The park is open all year daily 8 AM to dusk.

Williamsburg (S) is the closest city.

**contact:** York River State Park, 5526 Riverview Rd, Williamsburg, VA 23188; 804/566-3036

**getting there:** From I-64, take exit 231B (SR-607). Go E on SR-607 0.8 mi to Riverview Rd (SR-606). Turn R and go 1.6 mi to the park entrance, L.

**topography:** The central part of the park is situated on a bluff overlooking the York River. Park uplands are generally level and forested; some areas have been cleared and landscaped. Low-lying areas include Taskinas Creek and several brackish marshes. **maps:** USGS Gressitt, Toano.

**starting out:** The entrance fee is $1/vehicle on weekdays, $2 on weekends. Facilities (water, pay phone, toilets) are at the visitor center, where you can also pick up a park map. It's open weekdays 9 AM to 5 PM, weekends 10 AM to 4 PM. Also on site are exhibits on local history, geology, and ecology. Restrooms and water are also available at the boat ramp.

Public use and display of alcohol is not allowed. Pets must be kept on a leash.

**activities:** Hiking, Mountain Biking, Canoeing/Kayaking, Fishing

**hiking:** Most of the parks uplands are covered by an extensive trail network. In all, 16 miles of multi-use trails amble through the woodlands and marsh areas. Loop hikes of many different lengths are possible. Scenic highlights include views of the river and a good chance to spy wildlife in the different park environments. Bird watching in particular is rewarded with frequent sightings of dozens of species. The trails follow a combination of old roadbeds and single-tracks. Hiking throughout the park is easy. Most trails can be accessed from the visitor center. Moderate to heavy use keeps the trails well defined and easy to follow. Boardwalks cross wet areas. *Taskinas Creek Trail* is a self-guided interpretive trail. A guide is available at the park office. Some of the trails are open to horses and mountain bikes.

**mountain biking:** 6 miles of trails are open to bikes. These trails generally follow old roadbeds through hardwood forest. One trail leads to the York River with good views. Riding on the mostly level, well-maintained trails is easy. Access is at the visitor center. A couple of the trails are open to horses too.

**canoeing/kayaking:** Paddlers have a choice of travelling across two very different bodies of water. On the one hand, there's the York River, one of the major waterways on the coast. At the park, it's more than a mile across. Canoeists and kayakers should expect trips to be influenced by tides and winds, which can be quite strong. Although the York River is popular with motor boats, its size prevents traffic from being much of a concern. Development on both shores is minimal, leaving plenty of undisturbed marsh and beach habitat to expore. The option is Taskinas Creek, a small, flatwater creek that resembes a snake as it winds through brackish marsh. Although there's no boat access to the river from the park, it's only a short paddle down the York from the boat ramp. During peak season the park rents canoes on the creek. Either body of water or a combination of both has much to offer paddlers. To reach the boat ramp leave the park and turn R on SR-606 (Riverview Rd). Go 1.6 mi to SR-607 (Croaker Rd). Turn R and go 1.9 mi to Croaker Landing Rd (SR-605). Turn R and go 1 mi to the boat ramp.

**fishing:** 3 bodies of water provide angler with very different fishing conditions. Within the park Woodstock Pond is a 7-acre freshwater farm pond that supports populations of largemouth bass and bluegill. Fishing is from the banks only, where there's a large cleared area.

The York River can only be fished from a boat, as there is no shore access from the park. The major game species present are sea trout, spot, croaker, and catfish. A saltwater fishing license is required. To launch a boat, follow the above directions to the boat ramp.

Taskinas Creek also must be fished from a boat. It contains catfish and white perch. A saltwater or freshwater license is valid.

# Waller Mill Park

A scenic, 343-acre lake sits in the middle of this popular 2,400-acre park. The lake was built in 1942 and is used today to supply water to the city of Williamsburg. The park is located in York County just outside of the historic city that was once the state's capital. The lake and surrounding woodlands provide a natural oasis amidst urban and suburban development. Outdoor recreation and wildlife habitat are the main benefits of the park. Wildlife is abundant and regularly seen. Canada geese, swans, and ducks all gather around the lakeshore, and turtles can be seen sunning themselves on the lake. Flora in the mature hardwood forest is diverse, and includes species such as white ash, black cherry, American holly, flowering dogwood, oaks, and hickory. Mammals occasionally seen include river otters, beavers, white-tailed deer, opossums. Recreation on the lake is provided by fishing and boating, with canoes and jon boats the favored crafts. On land, a small network of hiking and biking trails wind through the forest and along the lakeshore. Other facilities include extensive picnic areas with tables, grills, and shelters; a fitness trail; seniors' walking course; and rowboat, canoe, and pedal-boat rental. Without camping facilities, the park is best suited to a day visit. Families in particular seem to enjoy the park's natural, but comfortable surroundings. The park is open daily from March to mid-December betweeen sunrise and sunset.

Williamsburg (S) is the closest city. Thanks to Rich Anderson.

**contact:** Waller Mill Park, Route 645, Williamsburg, VA 23185; 757/220-6178

**getting there:** From I-64, take exit 238. Just past the exit turn R onto E. Rochambeau Dr and go 1.3 mi to Airport Rd (SR-645). Turn L and go 0.4 mi to the park entrance, L.

**topography:** The terrain of the park has features more comonly associated with the piedmont than with the coastal plain: gently rolling hills blanketed with a mixed hardwood/pine forest surround the man-made lake. **maps:** USGS Williamsburg.

**starting out:** Facilities in the park are centered around the boat dock area. There you'll find the park office where you can pick up a trail map. Facilities are there too: restrooms, water, and a pay phone. Fees are charged for several park activities. Launching a canoe or kayak is $3; fishing from a boat costs $4/person.

Alcohol is prohibited in the park.

**activities:** Hiking, Canoeing/Kayaking, Fishing, Mountain Biking

**hiking:** 2 trails cover 4 miles of forested shoreline near the lake's midsection. These trails afford good views of the lake and offer a chance to get away from the often busy dockside part of the park. Both trails are loops that begin on the lake's eastern shore. The 1.5-mi *Bayberry Nature Trail* is a self-guiding loop with 75 stations. A trail guide is available at the park office. The trailhead is at the footbridge near the boat dock. The other trail is 2.6-mi *Lookout Tower Trail*. It begins beside Aiport Rd near the park entrance. Trailheads to both trails are signed. Trails are not blazed, but are easy to follow due to heavy use. Hiking is easy on both.

**canoeing/kayaking:** The lake affords a very pleasant setting for an afternoon's or day's paddle, particularly in combination with fishing. Although the 343-acre lake doesn't really offer the room for a long trip, the scenic shoreline and quiet setting help compensate its small size. The boat ramp is located near the park office. Before putting in, you have to check in at the park office and pay the launch fee. Boat traffic is light to moderate and is mostly canoes and jon boats, as boats with gas motors are not allowed on the lake.

**fishing:** Fishing in the lake is one of the main attractions in the park. Most anglers choose to fish from a canoe or jon boat, as it allows for greater water coverage. A boat launch fee must be paid before heading out onto the water. Landbound fishing is possbile, but not recommended, as the number of open places on the shoreline a few, and are mostly near the busy boat dock area. There's a small fishing pier there as well.

**mountain biking:** Across Airport Rd from the park entrance is the Dogwood Trail, a 4.5-mi trail open to mountain bikes. The wide dirt single-track follows the countours of the hilly terrain through scenic forests and long the lakeshore. The trail is well maintained, and riding it is not difficult. Trail use is moderate.

# Newport News Park

Newport News Park is a vast park located at the edge of the Newport News–Hamton metropolitan area found at the bottom of lower neck. On its 8,000 acres are extensive woodlands, a large car campground, a 650-acre lake, hiking and biking trails, picnic areas, and a golf course. Fortunately, the golf course is isolated from the rest of the park. The busy park offers a full range of service to outdoor enthusiasts, including canoe, jon- and paddle-boat rentals, bike rentals, an interpretive center with exhibits on local flora and fauna and area history (a Civil War battle was fought here), large picnic grounds with shelters, tables, and grills, and fishing in a stocked lake. Probably the major benefit of the park to backcountry travelers is the large campground, the only one in the area. Although the park isn't the destination for a rugged wilderness experience, on its sprawling grounds are many arcas where wildlife flourishes. More than 200 species of bird visit or nest in the park; mammals such as white-tailed deer, river otters, beavers, and woodchucks can be seen; and the pine–hardwood forest includes a surprising diversity of species. The park is an ideal stopping-off place for a short visit, or as an overnight base for explorations of the area. It's open year round.

**contact:** Newport News Park, 13564 Jefferson Ave, Newport News, VA 23603; 757/888-3333

**getting there:** From I-64, take exit 250B. Turn N onto VA-143 and go 0.4 mi to the park entrance, R.

**topography:** Park terrain is almost flat, with only gentle swells in the uplands around the lake. Large parts of the park are forested, although there are also large areas that have been clear and landscaped to facilitate the park atmoshpere. **maps:** USGS Yorktown.

**starting out:** Maps, brochures, and other info are available at the park headquarters/tourist info center just inside the main entrance (open 9 AM to 5 PM daily). Other places to get info are the campground office (opoen 24 hrs) and the interpretive center. Restrooms, water, and pay phones are located at all 3 locations. A small selection of supplies can be bought at the campground store.

Swimming in the reservoir is not allowed. Pets must be kept on a leash.

**activities:** Hiking, Camping, Canoeing/Kayaking, Fishing, Mountain Biking

**hiking:** The park features 6 miles of hiking trails and a 5.3-mi trail open to hikers, bikers, and equestrians. The longest hiking trail is the 2.6-mi *White Oak Nature Trail*. Passing through hardwood forest and a swamp and over several footbridges, it includes 23 stations that highlight park ecology. An accompanying guide is available free at the interpretive center. The signed trailhead is located across the road from the center at the footbridge across the lake. Heavy trail use keeps the trail well defined and easy to follow. Hiking is easy.

**camping:** The large, popular car campground is one of the park's main attractions. It has 188 sites arranged in 4 main loops. Despite its size, it offers more privacy than many smaller campground. The sites are generally large and well spaced, and they are located according to type of use: tent, RV with full hookup, RV with partial hookup. Each site has a picnic table and grill. Hardwoods provide shade and add at least a measure of isolation. Tent sites cost $14.50/night. Bathhouses with showers and modern restrooms are located in the center of each loop. The campground's large size means that sites are almost always available. The registration office is open 24 hours a day. The campground is open all year. Campsites can be reserved for the year beginning on Jan 1. Call 888-3333.

**canoeing/kayaking:** Lee Hall Resrevoir offers a pleasant location for a short paddle or fishing trip. Scenery around the lake is only average; a powerline and pipeline across its middle don't help. If you don't bring a boat with you, you can rent one from the park. If you use your own, a permit is required. You can put in at the boat ramp near the campground or at the boat dock and rental station. Traffic on the lake is moderate to heavy.

**fishing:** Largemouth bass, black crappie, bluegill, white and yellow perch, chain pickerel, channel catfish, flathead catfish, and northern pike are all stocked in the lake. Anglers can fish from the shoreline, where there's plenty of open space, or from a boat. Shoreline fishing costs $1.50/day.

**mountain biking:** The mountain bike is a 5.3-mi loop that winds through a forest on a wide path of dirt and crushed gravel. The trail begins and ends at the campground store. Riding is easy. The park rents bikes.

# Grandview Beach Preserve

The only way to get to this 578-acre preserve is to walk or paddle. The walk isn't long, about a quarter-mile, but it insures that the preserve's mission of providing flora and fauna with a relatively undisturbed habitat will not be jeopardized. The preserve is located at the wide mouth of Back River where it empties into the Chesapeake Bay, not more than a couple miles from busy, hyper-developed Hampton. Habitats on the preserve include a 2.5-mile beach that ends in a long narrow spit of sand, an extensive dune system, shrub thickes, and marshes. Across Back River is Plum Tree Island NWR. Visitors to the undeveloped preserve come to walk the long sandy beach, birdwatch, fish, or simply to enjoy an undisturbed natural setting. Paddlers can experience the preserve by putting in at a boat ramp located on the preserve's back side. Shore birds are abundant on the preserve, and some species of mammals such as woodchucks and white-tailed deer can sometimes be seen. With no camping allowed, the preserve is designed for day trips only. The preserve is open all year during daylight hours.

Hampton (SW) is the closest city.

**contact:** Grandview Nature Preserve, Hampton Parks & Recreation, 22 Lincoln St, Hampton 23669; 757/727-6347

**getting there:** From I-64 take exit 263. Go E on US-258 3 mi to VA-169. Turn L and go 2.9 mi to Beach Rd. Turn L and go 2.7 mi (at 1.9 mi you can turn L onto Dandy Point Rd and go 0.9 mi to the boat ramp) to State Park Dr, L. Parking for the preserve is along the road. Parking there is not allowed between sunset and 7 AM.

**topography:** The terrain includes several habitats typical of low-lying coastal areas: sandy beach, dunes, shrub thicket, wetlands, and stands of pine. Elevations do not exceed 20 ft in the preserve. **maps:** USGS Hampton.

**starting out:** The preserve is entirely undeveloped, with no facilities at all. Be sure to bring enough water for the day, since none is available.

Pets must be kept on a leash.

**activities:** Hiking, Fishing, Kayaking/Canoeing

**hiking:** Although there are no developed hiking trails in the preserve, the 2.5-mi stretch of beach offers ample space for a short stroll. Visitors also hike along informal trails between the dunes and shrub thicket, where songbirds and and small reptiles can often be seen. All hiking is easy, but deep sand can make going a little slow. Access to all hiking areas is at the main gate. Along the beach and in the dunes

**fishing:** Anglers can fish from the long, sandy beach. The beach fronts the Chesapeake Bay, with is home to dozens of saltwater game fish. Among those commonly taken are bluefish, striped bass, black drum, spot, croaker, flounder, and tautog.

**kayaking/canoeing:** Paddlers can explore the long sandy beach or narrow Long Creek, which flows through the backcountry marshland. Outside the creek, be prepared for open water conditions and strong, unpredictable currents. The extensive saltwater marshes of Plum Tree Island NWR are only 2 miles from the put-in, less than 1 mile from Northend Point at the end of the peninsula. The boat ramp is just outside the preserve, on its back side. Directions are given above.

# Chippokes Plantation State Park

This 1,683-acre park is one of several state parks that combine historical significance with natural preservation. In the case of Chippokes Plantation, preservation includes the historical, as the plantation is still a working farm and the house and outbuidings are open to the public as living museums. The park is located along a two-mile stretch of the lower James River in Surry County directly across from Jamestown Island. Ownership of the land dates to 1619, and Chippokes is thought to be one of the oldest working farms in America. Park grounds include a nineteenth century mansion, a farm complex of seven buildings that house thousands of antique implements and tools, and formal gardens. Other park facilities include a visitor center; swimming pool; picnic grounds with shelter, tables, and grills; and small trail network. Although most of the park remains in the "settled" state of a plantation, there are areas of undeveloped woodlands and wetlands to explore. Particularly attractive is the shoreline of the James River and Lower Chippokes Creek. The park is open year-round from 8 AM to dusk.

Surry (W) is the closest town.

**contact:** Chippokes Plantation State Park, Route 1, Box 213, Surry, VA 23883; 804/294-3625

**getting there:** From downtown Surry, take VA-10 E 1.8 mi to SR-634 (Alliance Rd). Turn L and go 3.6 mi to the park entrance, L.

**topography:** Rolling hillside is alternately covered in forest and cleared for agricultural plantings. A narrow sand beach forms the shoreline on the James River. Elevations are between sea level and 60 ft. **maps:** USGS Hog Island.

**starting out:** The entrance fee is $1/vehicle on weekdays, $2 on weekends. You can pick up a park map and other info at the visitors center, where there's an exhibit on area history. Also there are restrooms, water, and a pay phone.

Public use or display of alcohol is not allowed. Pets are allowed, but must be leashed. Swimming in the James River is not permitted.

**activities:** Hiking, Mountain Biking, Fishing, Canoeing/Kayaking

**hiking:** The small network of park trails allows you to wander around the grounds of the historic buildings that dot the park, or explore the forest and shoreline of the James River. The most remote and scenic hiking is not on a trail, but along the 2-mi sandy beach on the James. Depending on the tide, you might get your feet wet if you hike it. Park trails total a little over three miles. There really isn't much backcountry to speak of; the attractions here are the historic plantation and the scenery along the James. Trails follow a combination of old plantation roads and single-tracks.

**mountain biking:** Although not worth a special trip, 2 miles of trails are open to bikes. Most interesting of these is the 1.3-mi *College Run Trail*, a very attractive trail lined by rows of bald cypresses. The trail passes the river house and outbuildings and ends at the mansion, where it connects to the 0.5-mi *James River Trail*, a double-track plantation road that ends at the river. Trails are level and well maintained. Biking is easy.

**canoeing/kayaking:** The combination of historical significance, natural beauty, and wildlife habitat make the lower James one of the most interesting and rewarding paddling environments on the coastal plain. Although there's no boat ramp in the park, paddlers have a couple of options for getting on the water. One is to make about a 50 yd portage through an overgrown field to the river. The park doesn't advertise that this can be done, but if you ask a ranger, he'll show you where the shortest crossing is. This is a good option for two people. The other possiblity is to drive a short distance to Hog Island WMA (see next listing below) and put in there. From the WMA, it's a little over 2 miles back up river to the park. Paddlers should be aware that the lower James River is a large body of water with open water conditions. Tides, choppy water, and stiff winds are all factors to consider when planning a trip. The park is located on a wide bend in the river. Straight across it's 5 miles, though it's only about 3 miles to Jamestown Island. River traffic is relatively light in the area.

**fishing:** Fishing in the James River can either be done from the park shoreline, or from a boat. The shoreline is mostly a narrow strip of sand that is relatively off the beaten path. If you're lucky, you'll have it to yourself. If you're going to fish from a canoe, see above for info on river access. The game fish commonly caught in the area are striped and largemouth bass, walleye, white perch, and blue catfish. A freshwater license is required to fish downstream as far as Hog Pt. Beyond that, a saltwater license is required. Fishing pressure is light.

# Hog Island Wildlife Management Area

The 3,908-acre Hog Island WMA sits on a narrow peninsula known as Gravel Neck in Surry County overlooking a curve in the James River almost directly across from Jamestown, the earliest English settlement in Virginia. The river surrounds the WMA on three sides and comprises a large portion of its interior as well. With elevations that are mostly no more than a couple feet above sea level, habitats on the refuge are primarily aquatic: impoundments, slow-water creeks, and marshes cover the majority of acreage. Small pockets of uplands with adequate drainage support small pine forests. The WMA's primary mission is wildlife habitat management, with outdoor recreation—hunting and fishing primarily—related objectives. There are few facilities on the refuge, and visitors will find gated roads the only alteration to the backcountry. Aside from action that appeals to sportsmen, the WMA provides excellent opportunities for birders and nature photographers. Winter in particular provides a great opportunity to observe dozens of species of waterfowl and shorebirds such as the great egret, snowy egret, great blue heron, wood duck, and Canada geese. The refuge is open all year during daylight hours only.

Surry (W) and Smithfield (S) are the closest towns.

**contact:** Hog Island WMA, 5806 Mooretown Rd, Williamsburg, VA 23188; 804/253-7072.

**getting there:** From the crossroads community of Bacon's Castle, take VA-10 E 0.8 mi to SR-650 (Hog Island Rd). Turn L and go 6.2 mi to the WMA entrance. The road (now gravel) continues 2 mi to the WMA office.

**topography:** The majority of the WMA consists of impoundments and surrounding marsh areas. Small pockets of pine forest have established themselves in areas with sufficient drainage. The terrain is level, and does not exceed 20 ft. **maps:** USGS Hog Island

**starting out:** Facilities on the WMA are very limited. There's a WMA office, though it's not run to provide the public with information. If it's open, you can probably stop in and get a map of the WMA. If not, track down a ranger and ask. There are no public restrooms or water supply on the WMA.

**activities:** Hiking, Kayaking/Canoeing, Fishing, Mountain Biking

**hiking:** 10 miles of gated roads on the Hog Island Tract provide hikers an excellent oppotunity to explore the wetland habitat of tidal marshes and impoundments. Viewing wildlife is all but assured, particularly in winter, when thousands of birds descend on the WMA. With the exception of the main WMA access, all roads are gated and closed to motor vehicles. Trailheads are located along the main road. The roads connect with one another to form loop hikes of various distance. Hiking is easy.

**kayaking/canoeing:** The Hog Island Tract is surrounded on 3 sides by a bend in the James River. Lawnes Creek runs between the Carlisle and Stewart Tracts before emptying into the James. Hog Island WMA is defined by water. A canoe or kayak are therefore ideal vessels from which to explore its environment. You can put in at the boat ramp on Lawnes Creek or from one of the designated fishing areas in the Hog Island Tract. To reach the boat ramp on Lawnes Creek, leave the WMA and go 2.2 mi on SR-650 to Landing Dr. Turn L and go 1.3 mi to the boat ramp. In either case, you'll be paddling the waters of the James. Expect open water conditions, with wind, tides, and choppy water are all factors to consider. The Hog Island Tract has 6 miles of river frontage; Hog Island Creek

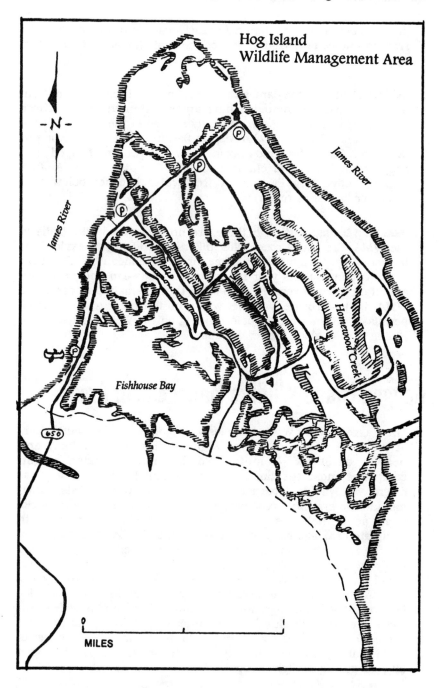

provides access to its interior. Another possible trip is to cross the river to Jamestown Island, site of the first English settlement in America.

**fishing:** Fishing in the James River can be done from a boat or from one of several designated fishing areas within the WMA. These areas are located along a wide sandy stretch of the shoreline near the entrance. Canoeists who wish to fish from a boat can also put in there. Game fish most commonly caught are striped and largemouth bass, and channel and blue catfish. Note: Anglers fishing above Hog Pt need a freshwater license; below it a saltwater license is required.

**mountain biking:** Although there are no designated bike trails in the WMA, the gravel roads offer bikers a good way to explore the backcountry, though it's no place for an extended ride. The main road is open to bikes year round; gated roads can only be ridden at certain times of year. Keep in mind that the main purpose of the WMA is to provide wildlife with undisturbed habitat. Seek permission from a ranger before riding on the WMA's gated roads. Riding is easy along the level roads.

# Ragged Island Wildlife Management Area

The Ragged Island WMA occupies 1,537 acres on the south shore of the James River in Isle of Wight County near the busy and heavily developed Hampton Roads area. Brackish marsh comprises most the land area, providing habitat for a great diversity of wildlife. Most readily seen are the wading birds, which include the graceful great blue heron and great egret, and ducks such as buffleheads and mallards. Pockets of upland with adequate drainage support stands of pine. Dense thickets of wax myrtle and other shrubs are also encountered. In the wooded areas are small populations of white-tailed deer, red fox, and other small mammals. With limited facilities and opportunity for backcountry travel, the preserve is best-suited to short visits for birdwatching or photography. Since most of the land is wide open, views are generally superb. A well-designed hiking trail provides access to some of the marshland and a boat ramp allows canoeists and kayakers to explore the area from the water. The WMA is open all year during daylight hours.

Newport News (NE) is the closest city.

**contact:** Ragged Island Wildlife Management Area, 5806 Mooretown Rd, Williamsburg, VA 23188; 804/253-7072.

**getting there:** From the jct of VA-10 and US-258 in Benns Church, take US-58/VA-32 N 2.8 mi to a traffic light and the jct with US-17. Turn L on US-17/US-258/VA-32 and go 5 mi to a WMA parking area, R, just before the bridge.

**topography:** The large majority of the preserve is marshland. Scattered pocket of upland support stands of pine. Elevations do not exceed 25 ft. **maps:** USGS Newport News S, Beens Church.

**starting out:** There are no facilities at all at the WMA. Be sure to bring enough water for your visit.
   The public use or display of alcohol is not allowed.

**activities:** Hiking, Kayaking/Canoeing, Fishing

**hiking:** A short, one-way trail leads from the main parking area to the banks of the James River. Along the way, the trail passes over a lightly wooded hummock and then crosses a brackish marsh on a long boardwalk that ends at an observation platform. The chances of observing wildlife—wading birds and fiddler crabs are most prominent—is very high. The only drawback to this otherwise remarkable trail is that the sounds of traffic crossing the bridge to Newport News is a constant presence. The trail is 0.3 miles one way. The trailhead is at the main parking area. hiking is easy.

**kayaking/canoeing:** The canoe/kayak put-in is located at the end of the main access road, not more than a stone's throw from the bridge across the James. Although the roar of traffic is constant and annoying, once you're on the water you can easily escape it by heading downriver along the banks on the WMA. Scenery in the area is mixed. On the one hand, the Hampton Roads area is one of the most heavily developed in all of Virginia. Commercial vessels and a horizon of towering buildings is just acrossthe river. On the other hand, inlets such as Ragged Island Creek, Chuckatuck Creek, and Nansamond River provide sheltered havens where herons and egrets will probably be your only company. To sum up: there are certainly more remote and pristine paddling environments on the Virginia coast, but if you're looking for a challenge and a change of scenery, Ragged Island WMA is a good spot for a day's paddle. On the open water of the James, tides, wind, and choppy water should all be taken into account when planning your trip.

**fishing:** Despite the incessant noise from traffic crossing the bridge across the James River, the shoreline at the main parking area is a popular spot with local anglers. A somewhat quieter location is the small pier at the end of the hiking trail described above. Your best bet, however, is to put a canoe on the water and paddle around to the south side of the preserve, away from the maddening sounds of traffic. Croakers are most commonly caught here. Other species include spot, bluefish, flounder, and gray trout. A saltwater fishing license is required. Fishing pressure is moderate to heavy from the shoreline, lighter in the surrounding waters.

# Lone Star Lakes Park

Lone Star Lakes Park offers a serene, backcountry setting in an area that is becoming increasingly developed. Located in county-sized Suffolk, the centerpiece of the 1,172-acre park is a series of exceptionally scenic lakes. Formerly marl pits, today the lakes are surrounded by dense hardwood forests that provide habitat to a wide range of fauna. The park is particularly amenable to birds, and birdwatchers will find wading birds (great blue herons and great egrets are common) and songbirds in significant numbers. Outdoor recreation in the park is geared toward paddling and fishing. Each of the lakes has boat access, and several game species of fish provide a challenge to anglers. Other facilities include a handful of small, very scenic picnic areas, an archery range, and dirt roads for hiking or biking. The park is well-suited to families and to beginning paddlers, though it is recommended to anyone who enjoys the outdoors and pristine natural environments. The park is open from sunrise to sunset between Apr 1 and Oct 31; Nov 1 to March 31 it's open 8 AM to 5 PM.

Smithfield (NW), Suffolk (S), and Portsmouth (E) are the closest cities.

**contact:** City of Suffolk, Dept of Parks & Recreation, Birdsong Recreation Center, Suffolk, VA 23439; Lone Star Lakes Park:

757/925-6325. Phone at the entrance gate is 757/255-4308.

**getting there:** From Smithfield go 7.4 mi S on VA-10 to VA-125. Turn L and go 0.4 mi to the Bob House Pkwy (SR-761), L. The park entrance is half a mile down the road. • From downtown Suffolk, go 10 mi N on VA-10 to the jct with VA-125. Turn R and follow directions above.

**topography:** As is typical of the coastal region, park terrain is flat. What is not so typical is the impressive diversity of hardwoods—cedars, sycamores, and sweetgums, among many others—that surrounds the lakes. Some parts of the park have been cleared. **maps:** USGS Chuckatuck, Benns Church.

**starting out:** An entrance fee of $1/vehicle is charged. Launching a boat or fishing costs $2/person. A park map and brochure are available at the entrance station. If no one is there, you can track a ranger down in the park. Facilities in the mostly undeveloped park are limited. A pit toilet is located in the small playground across from the entrance, and a hand water pump is in one of the picnic areas. If you're going to spend the day on the lakes, be sure to bring enough water with you.

Alcohol is not allowed in the park. Swimming in the lakes is prohibited. Pets must be kept on a leash.

**activities:** Canoeing/Kayaking, Fishing, Hiking, Mountain Biking

**canoeing/kayaking:** 9 lakes offer paddlers some of the prettiest inshore paddling in the coastal region. Several of the small lakes (none are larger than 50 acres) are interconnected; all are surrounded by lush hardwood forests with some openings that attract wildlife. Boat ramps or put-in spots can be found on each of the lakes. Because boats with gasoline motors are not allowed, traffic levels are typically quite low. With 9 different bodies of water and so many nooks and coves to explore, the Lone Star Lakes Park provides a great place to spend a lazy day on the water.

**fishing:** The 9 park lakes offer anglers various fish habitats. Some of the lakes are very deep with clear water, others are shallow blackwater habitats. Species include striped and largemouth bass, bluegill, catfish, white perch, crappie, and sunfish. The best fishing is from a canoe, where it's easiest to enjoy the park's scenery and to cover the most water. Bank fishing is also possible, with designated locations on many of the lakes. Bank fishing outside these locations is not allowed.

**mountain biking:** The park's 5 miles of dirt roads offer bikers a short, scenic ride. From the entrance station, the road runs right and left. Right is a loop with several very pleasant picnic areas; L the road is a dead end, requiring a backtrack. Roads are flat and riding is easy.

**hiking:** Hiking trails are limited in the park, where the main attraction is the lakes themselves. In addition to 5 miles of double-track dirt roads, there are 4 hiking trails that cover 1.5 miles. These are short nature trails that are little more than leg-stretchers. The trailheads are signed along the main park road. The trails are level and hiking them is easy.

# Kiptopeke State Park

One of the newer state parks, Kiptopeke occupies 375 acres and nearly a mile of waterfront on the lower Chesapeake Bay at the southern end of the Eastern Shore. From 1949 until the Cheasapeake Bay Bridge-Tunnel was opened in 1964, Kiptopeke was the northern terminus of the ferry that provided access between mainland Virginia and the remote eastern shore. Remnants of those days are still visible in the park. Although the bridge-tunnel has connected the Eastern Shore to the rest of the state, the region remains a land apart, with a slow pace of living and minimal development. Most of the land is agricultural, with large areas of pristine waterfront still intact. The state park is located directly in the migratory path of the thousands of raptors—hawks, falcons, osprey, and kestrels—that fly down the Delmarva Peninsula each year and get funnelled into its narrow southern tip. The park has become an important area for observation, study, and banding of the birds. Spring and fall are the best times to observe the birds.

Outdoor recreation in the park is centered around the water, with only limited opportunities for backcountry travel on land. The most popular draw is probably the long swimming beach, which is open and supervised by a lifeguard between Memorial Day and

Labor Day. The large car campground makes an excellent base for exploring the park or the rest of the Eastern Shore, as camping facilities elsewhere are very limited. Other park attractions include a large picnic area with tables, grills, and shelters; and a series of long boardwalks and steps that connect park uplands with the dunes and beach. The park is open all year.

Cape Charles (N) is the closest town.

**contact:** Kiptopeke State Park, 3450 Kiptopeke Dr, Cape Charles, VA 23310; 757/331-2267

**getting there:** From US-13 (approximately 3 mi N of the Chesapeake Bridge Tunnel toll plaza), turn W onto SR-704 and go 0.5 mi to the park entrance.

**topography:** The bayside topography of the park is a combinations of wide sand beach, sea grass-covered dunes, and uplands forested with pines and hardwoods. Elevations in the park are between sea level and 40 ft. **maps:** USGS Townsend.

**starting out:** The parking fee is $1/vehicle on weekdays, $2 on weekends. Restrooms, water, and a pay phone are all located within the park. The park office can supply you with a trail map and brochures that describe the park's history and ecology. It's hours are 8 AM to 4:30 PM M–F. The swimming beach is open from 10 AM to 7 PM daily.

The public use or display of alcohol is not allowed. Pets must be kept on a leash.

**activities:** Hiking, Camping, Canoeing/Kayaking, Fishing.

**hiking:** In addition to almost a mile of beachfront, the park has a single designated hiking trail that covers 1.4 miles of forested upland and open field. The main highlight of the *Bay Woods Trail* is the opportunity to observe the bird banding station in action and to perhaps spot one of a dozen species of raptors that migrate through the park each year. The trail follows old roadbeds in a loop that begins near the hawk observatory. Hiking is easy. Trail use is heavy, particularly during periods of bird migration.

**camping:** The car campground has 121 sites in the park's upper section. Most of the sites are laid out in rows in a large cleared and landscaped area. Trees provide shade for some, but many are completely in the open. Most sites are close together and not very large; privacy is minimal. Each site includes a picnic table, grill and water spigot. Sites cost $16/night, $20 with hookup. One small cluster of sites in a wooded grove offers larger sites with considerably more privacy. There's a centrally-located bathhouse with hot water. The campground is open from Mar 15 to Nov 30.

**canoeing/kayaking:** Although a boat doesn't offer the best way to see the park, the lower Chesapeake Bay offers an outstanding paddling environment. From the put-in/take-out next to the ferry terminal, it's possible to travel up or down the unspoiled coast for miles. Heading south, it's a 5-mi trip to Fisherman's Island, a National Wildlife Refuge that's home to an amazing diversity of shorebirds. A round-trip would be a full day's paddle. Heading north, it's also miles to Old Plantation Creek. Once there, you can leave the bay and expore the quieter waters of the creek, or continue N another 2 miles to the small port town of Cape Charles. Conditions on the Chesapeake are variable, depending on time of year, weather, tides, and winds. In any case, be prepared for open water conditions, with stiff winds, choppy water, and tidal currents all common.

**fishing:** Anglers have the option of surf-casting from the beach or putting a boat in the water and trying their luck in open waters. The area surrounding the breakwater is reputed to have some of the finest fishing in the bay. Species commonly taken are bluefish, flounder, tautog, striped bass, spot, and cobia. A saltwater fishing license is required to fish.

# Eastern Shore National Wildlife Refuge

The 725 acres of the Eastern Shore of Virginia NWR are located at the southern tip of the Delmarva Peninsula. The refuge was established in 1984 for the protection of habitat crucial to migratory birds and endangered wildlife species. The location of the refuge is key, because as birds migrate south each year the narrowing of the Delmarva Peninsula forces them onto a relatively small stretch of land before they make the crossing over the mouth of the Chesapeake Bay. Refuge habitats, which include saltwater marsh, agricultural fields, maritime forest, and freshwater impoundments, are managed primarily for the benefit of wildlife. Low impact outdoor recreation is a secondary benefit. Although the refuge doesn't offer the extensive backcountry that some of the other coastal national wildlife refuges do, it does provide an excellent opportunity to observe and photograph almost 300 species of birds in a small area. The best viewing times are from late August to early November. Before it provided a safe haven for birds, refuge lands played a strategic military role. During World War II, a pair of 16-inch guns—capable of hurtling 2,000-lb projectiles 25 miles—were positioned to defend the military installations at Virginia Beach and Norfolk. Vestiges of this earlier role can still be seen on the refuge.

In keeping with the wildlife conservation mission of the refuge, facilities for outdoor recreation are limited. Aside from a visitor center with exhibits on local ecology, a short hiking trail leads to observation decks that afford superb views of refuge habitats. The refuge is an excellent starting point for any trip to the Eastern Shore. It's open year round during daylight hours only.

Cape Charles (N) and Virginia Beach (S) are the closest towns.

**contact:** Refuge Manager, Eastern Shore of Virginia NWR, 5003 Hallet Circle, Cape Charles, VA 23310; 757/331-2760.

**getting there:** From US-13 (0.4 mi N of the Chesapeake Bridge-Tunnel toll plaza), turn E onto SR-600. The refuge is 0.2 mi ahead.

**topography:** Refuge habitats include marshland, impoundments, shrub thickets, open fields, and stands of maritime forest. Most of the refuge is at sea level or less than 10 ft above. **maps:** USGS Townsend, Fisherman's Island.

**starting out:** Facilities (restrooms, water) on the refuge are at the visitor center. It's open weekdays from 8 AM to 4 PM. You can pick up a refuge map, brochure, and bird list. Exhibits describe the local flora and fauna. The refuge itself is open daily from thirty minutes before sunrise to thirty minutes after sunset.

Pets must be on a leash.

**activities:** Hiking.

**hiking:** There are only abot 0.5 miles of trails on the refuge. Their main purpose is to permit observation of the hundreds of species of bird that visit or nest on the refuge. There are 2 observation decks along the trails. One overlooks an interior impoundment, while the other affords expansive views out over the salt marshes and Atlantic Ocean. The trails follow refuge roads and cinder paths. Signed trailheads are located at a parking area. Hiking on the trails is easy.

# Mockhorn Island Wildlife Management Area

Located on the Atlantic coast of the Eastern Shore near the southern tip of the Delmarva Peninsula, Mockhorn Island WMA comprises two separate tracts. The larger of the two is Mockhorn Island, which is actually a jigsaw puzzle-like mass of many islands separated by narrow channels and creeks. It lies a little more than a mile off the coast and covers more than 7,000 acres. A low-lying environment of saltwater tidal marshes dotted with hummocks that sprout thickets of wax myrtle and stands of loblolly pine and red cedar, much of it disappears under water at high tide. The other tract of land is the 365-acre GATR Tract, which is located on the mainland at water's edge. Mockhorn Island is part of a complex of tidal marshes and barrier islands that stretch the length of the Eastern Shore. It is the wildest, most natural environment in all of Virginia. Earlier attempts at developing some of the islands were thwarted, and now most of the land is owned by The Nature Conservancy. The primary aim of the WMA is wildlife habitat management. Among visitors, bird-watching, fishing, and photography are the major activities. Among the species of birds and waterfowl regularly seen on and around the island are great blue herons, great egrets, gulls, ospreys, bufflehead ducks, and black ducks. The refuge is open during daylight hours only and can only be reached by boat. Whether you come to paddle these waters for a day or a week, it's an experience you're not likely to forget soon.

Cape Charles (W) is the closest town.

**contact:** Mockhorn Island WMA, 5806 Mooretown Rd, Williamsburg, VA 23118; 757/253-4180

**getting there:** The only way to reach Mockhorn Island is by boat. The paddle from boat ramp to island is a little more than a mile. From the eastern shore end of the Chesapeake Bay Bridge-Tunnel, take

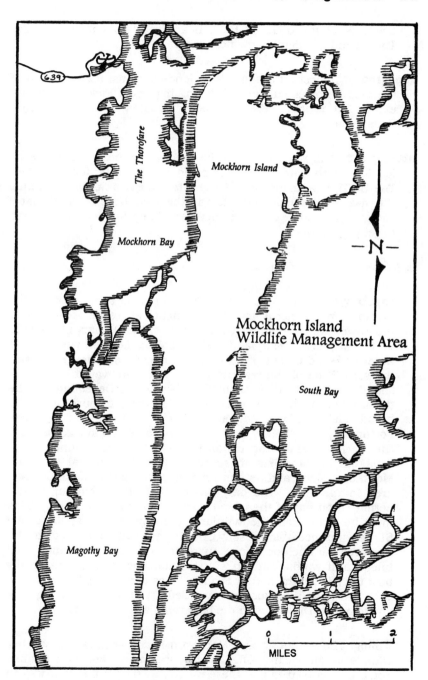

US-13 N 11 mi to US-13 BUS. Bear R and go 1 mi to SR-639. Turn R and go 2.6 mi to the boat ramp.

**topography:** Almost all of the WMA's lands are tidal marsh. Much of the area becomes submerged during high tide. Elevations do not exceed 5 ft. **maps:** USGS Townsend, Cheriton, Cobb Island, Ship Shoal Inlet.

**starting out:** The WMA can only be reached by boat. There are no facilities at the site. Be sure to bring enough water for your visit. The USGS topo maps or NOAA charts are essential for navigating the maze of channels and inlets in the area. Keep in mind that if you get into trouble out here, there isn't likely to be anyone around to get you out of it.

**activities:** Kayaking/Canoeing, Fishing

**kayaking/canoeing:** Mockhorn Island is part of a complex of tidal marshes and barrier islands that stretches along the ocean side of the Eastern Shore from the southern tip of the Delmarva Peninsula all the way to the Maryland state line. This isolated world where water and land mingle precariously is one of the wildest regions in the state. One of the reasons is that the only way to reach the islands is on a boat. Even then, it isn't easy. Depending on the tides, much of the land is either under water or surrounded by broad tidal flats with not more than a couple inches of water. Fortunately, the shallow draft and low profile of a kayak makes it the perfect vessel for exploring such an environment. For kayakers or canoeists in search of pristine coastal habitats, Mockhorn Island and its surrounding environment offers the best area in the state. The only drawback is that camping is not permitted on any of the islands. That means that multi-day trips must be based from the mainland (the campground at Kiptopeke SP is one possible base). Conditions paddlers need to be prepared for include tricky currents, a maze of channels and inlets, stiff winds, sudden storms, and choppy seas, especially past the edge of the barrier islands. Trips of any length from a day to a week will be amply rewarded in this amazing aquatic environment. Directions to the boat ramp are given above.

**fishing:** The waters around Mockhorn Island and the many other islands in the vicinity offer some outstanding saltwater fishing. You'll need a boat to fish these waters, as there's no other way to get to them, although you can fish the surf from some of the barrier islands once you reach them. The area is reputed as having one of the best (locals say *the* best) flounder fisheries in the state. Other species commonly taken are bluefish, gray trout, black drum, channel bass, croaker, and tarpon.

# Saxis Wildlife Management Area

5,574-acre Saxis WMA is located on the Chesapeake Bay at the northern end of the Virginia Eastern Shore. Primarily saltwater marsh, the two main tracts that comprise the refuge are separated by Messongo Creek. Smaller creeks separate the mainlands from adjacent islands and snake through the refuge's interior. Unlike other wildlife management areas, which are natural oases located in areas altered by the hands of humans, the Saxis WMA differs little in appearance from its surroundings. Most of the surrounding shoreline is equally undeveloped and equally scenic. This affords the backcountry traveler a great chance to explore a very large area of almost pristine wilderness. The only signs of civilization you're likely to encounter on a visit are crabbers and fishermen. More likely, you'll have shorebirds and waterfowl for companions—black ducks, canvasbacks, redheads, mallards, pintails, and Canada geese are all found in the area. The best way to view the preserve is from a boat. Opportunites for travel on land are slight, due to the marshy nature of the area. For serious sea-kayakers, the WMA and surrounding area offers some of the best paddling on the Chesapeake. The WMA is open during daylight hours only.

Chincoteague (E) and Pocomoke City, MD (NE) are the closest large towns.

**contact:** Saxis Wildlife Management Area, 5806 Mooretown Rd, Williamsburg, VA 23118; 757/253-4180.

**getting there:** From US-13 S of Temperanceville, Turn W onto SR-692 and go 8.6 mi to SR-695. Turn L and go 0.9 mi to SR-788. Turn L and go 0.9 mi to the Hammock Landing boat ramp. Another boat ramp is located at the end of SR-695.

**topography:** Both tracts of the preserve are predominantly saltwater marsh. Small pockets of upland are found near the interior edge of

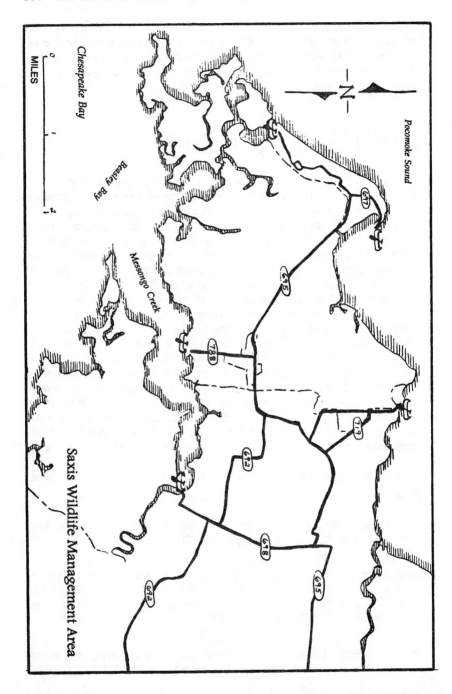

the preserve. elevations do not exceed 5 ft. **maps:** USGS Saxis.

**starting out:** Apart from the roads and boat ramps, there are no facilities of any kind on the WMA. If you're going out on the water, be sure to bring an adequate supply of water with you. Hunting takes place on the WMA's upper tract in fall and winter.

**activities:** Kayaking/Canoeing, Fishing

**kayaking/canoeing:** Paddlers have no fewer than six put-ins on and around the WMA to choose from. That should serve as a hint that this is prime paddling territory. Of course the boat ramps are also used by other vessels, but not so many that they're likely to spoil the scenery. As far as the actual paddling goes, really you could travel for days and not grow tired of the scenery. The entire bay side of the Eastern Shore is almost uniformly undeveloped, and the Maryland shore north of the WMA isn't any different. The only real drawback is the lack of places to camp. Multi-day trips will have to be based on the mainland. Commercial campgrounds on Chincoteague Island are a possibility. Hazards to beware of on the bay are sudden storms, strong winds, and seas that can get pretty choppy once you get out from the mainland a little.

**fishing:** Anglers in the area pursue gray trout, flounder, striped bass. bluefish, channel bass, and croaker. If you want to fish, you'll need a boat. There's really no other way to get to the water. A VA or MD saltwater fishing license is valid on the bay.

# Chincoteague National Wildlife Refuge

Chincoteague NWR occupies the southern half of Assateague Island, one of the long series of barrier islands that front the Atlantic Ocean along much of the east coast. The entire island—stretching from Ocean City, MD to Tom's Cove Hook in VA—is publicly owned. Chincoteague NWR occupies the VA end of the island; Assateague Island National Seashore and Assateague State Park comprise the MD section. All three sites are managed with a similar objective: conservation of a threatened coastal habitat and the wildlife it sustains, combined with low-impact outdoor recreation. At Chincoteague, which was established in 1943 for the protection of waterfowl, conservation takes the upper

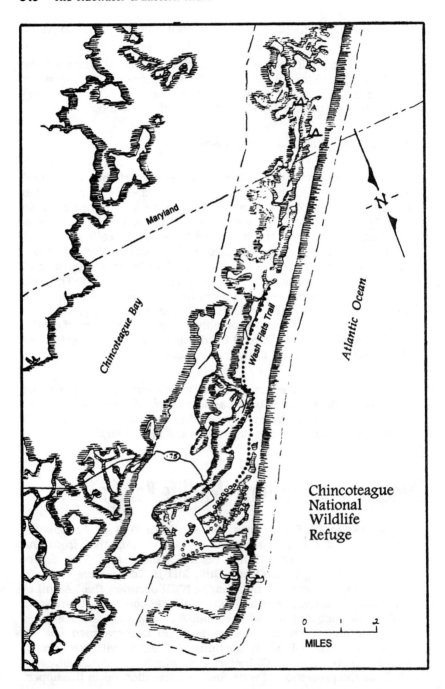

Maryland

Chincoteague Bay

West Flats Trail

Atlantic Ocean

Chincoteague
National
Wildlife
Refuge

N

0   1   2
MILES

hand. Bird-watching and nature photography are primary activities, with a network of hiking trails designed to bring visitors closer to wildlife without jeopardizing their habitat. While the refuge is host to more than 300 bird species, including the greater snow goose, Canada goose, snowy egret, common loon, brown pelican, and blue-winged teal, two non-native mammal species seem to receive the most attention. The Sika deer, an oreiental elk, and the famed herd of wild ponies are both frequently seen and often photographed. Unlike the adjacent national seashore, there are no camping facilities on the NWR, which is only open during daylight hours. Visitors wanting to come for a weekend or longer can camp at one of the developed campgrounds or at any of six backcountry camping areas on the Maryland side of the island. Visitor facilities in the refuge include a visitor center with exhibits on local history and ecology, wide beaches with lifeguards on duty during summer, and designated sites on the bay side for canoeists and kayakers to put in and take out. The refuge's most popular event each year is the pony auction. On the last Wednesday and Thursday of July the horses are driven across the channel to the Chincoteague carnival grounds where some of the herd is auctioned off. The rest are returned to the refuge. Refuge hours vary seasonally. Open times are: from May to Sep 5 AM to 10 PM, Apr & Oct 6 AM to 8 PM, Nov to Mar 6 AM to 6 PM.

Chincoteague (W) is the closest town.

**contact:** Refuge Manager, Chincoteague National Wildlife Refuge, P.O. Box 62, Chincoteague, VA 23336; 757/336-6122.

**getting there:** From the jct of US-13 and VA-175 4 mi S of the VA/MD state line, take VA-175 E 10.6 mi to Main St in downtown Chincoteague. Turn L and go 0.4 mi to Maddox Blvd. Turn R and go 1.8 mi to the refuge entrance. The visitors center is another 0.3 mi ahead, L. To reach the Assateague Island National Seashore visitors center, continue ahead another 2 mi.

**topography:** Chincoteague NWR is located at the S end of Assateague Island, one of a string of barrier islands that line the south Atlantic coast. Habitats include wide sandy beaches, dunes, shrub thickets and forests, and tidal marshes. Elevations are between sea level and 25 ft. **maps:** USGS Chincoteague E, Chincoteage W, Boxiron, Wallops Island.

**starting out:** An entrance pass (good for 7 days) is $4. Facilities (restrooms, pay phone) are at the visitors center. You can pick up maps and brochures at the NS visitor center, where there's also a pay phone. Inside, a small selection of guide books is for sale. The center is open 9 AM to 4 PM. 2 bath houses (open seasonally) with restrooms and water are located near the visitors center. The swimming area is open between Nov 1 and Mar 31 from 6 AM to 6 PM; Apr 1–30 and Oct 1–31 from 6 AM to 8 PM; May 1 to Sep 30 from 5 AM to 10 PM.

Alcohol is not allowed on the NS. Nude sunbathing is prohibited. Pets are not allowed. Toms Cove Hook is closes from Mar 15 to Aug 31 for nesting piping plovers.

**activities:** Hiking, Kayaking/Canoeing, Fishing, Mountain Biking.

**hiking:** In addition to almost 20 miles of sandy beach to hike, there are 15 miles of designated trails on the refuge. Between the beach and the trails, all areas and habitats of the refuge are covered. The most popular trail is probably 3.2-mi *Wildlife Loop*. It follows a paved road around Snow Goose Pool, a favorite gathering place of duck, geese, and other waterfowl. The trail is open to motor vehicles between 3 PM and dusk. At all other times it's only open to hikers and bicyclists. The trailhead is located behind the visitor center. Also popular is the 1.5-mi *Woodland Trail*, a paved loop open to hiking and biking. Trail users bring binoculars and cameras in the hope of spotting the refuge ponies from the observation deck. The trailhead is on the main refuge road. For a more strenuous, backcountry hike try the gated 7.5-mi road that leads north to Wash Flats. From there you can hike along the beach into Maryland or turn back south and complete a 15-mi loop. Whichever trail you decide to hike, all are clearly signed, level, and well-maintained. Hiking is easy. 2 of the trails are nature interpretive trails with guide booklets available at the trailhead or visitor center. Trail improvements include boardwalks, benches, and observation platforms.

**kayaking/canoeing:** Tom's Cove, Assateague Channel, and Chincoteague Bay are all first-rate paddling locations. The major drawback is that fishing boats are fairly prevalent in the area. The best way to avoid them is to stick close to land and travel through the channels that are too shallow to accommodate their drafts. With the bay side of the barrier island and mainland and the ocean around the other side, paddling trips of almost any length are imaginable. Although there's no camping on the VA side of the island, there are 4 backcountry primitive camping areas on the adjacent NS in Maryland. A permit is required, and can be picked up at the Tom's Cove visitor center. The put-in for the bay side of the island is at parking lot #4 near the visitor center. A short portage is necessary. Paddlers should check with the ranger at the visitors center for up-to-date status on put-in and take-out points. Paddling hazards include shallow, open waters prone to windy conditions and sudden storms, particularly in summer.

**fishing:** Anglers have the option of surf-casting from the beach or putting a boat on the water and fishing the ocean or bay. Surf-casters go after flounder, bluefish, striped bass, red drum, black drum, gray trout, croaker, and spot. The shallow waters of Chincoteague Bay hold the same species, but they can only be fished from a boat. See above for put-in spots for canoes and kayaks.

**mountain biking:** Although a mountain bike is an excellent way to get around the refuge, there really isn't any opportunity for off-road riding. 2 trails, covering a total of 4 miles, are open to bikes, but both are paved. Trail access is at the visitor center and along the main refuge road. Riding on the beach is not allowed.

# Seashore State Park & Natural Area

With more than 1,000,000 visitors each year, Seashore is the busiest state park in Virginia. Part of the reason is its location at the edge of Virginia Beach, a heavily developed resort area with miles of pristine beaches. Another reason is its combination of park facilities and extensive unspoiled backcountry. The park's 2,770 acres of beach, swamp, dunes, and forest are a natural oasis amid a sea of concrete and pavement. Perched at land's edge where the Chesapeake Bay meets the Atlantic Ocean and backed by Broad Bay, the park is almost entirely surrounded by water. Outdoor activities in the park are centered around the 1.25-mile beach and the large network of multi-use backcountry trails. The trails offer a chance to get an up-close glimpse of the myriad habitats that make up an Atlantic coast ecosystem. Cypress swamps, where the trees are draped dramatically with Spanish moss, maritime forests, and dunes harbor wildlife such as

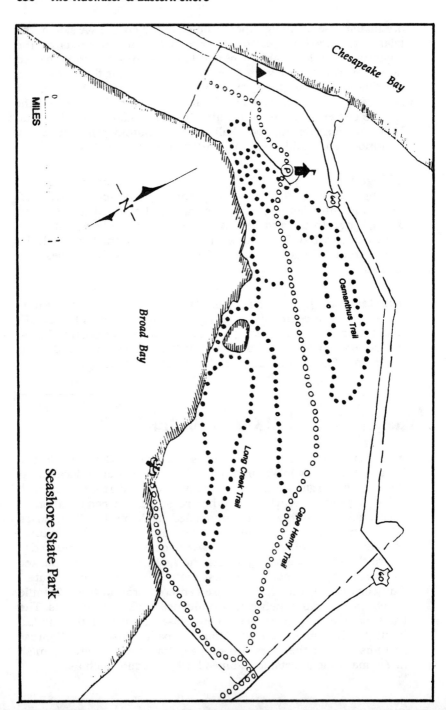

Chesapeake Bay

MILES

Broad Bay

Osmanthus Trail

Long Creek Trail

Cape Henry Trail

Seashore State Park

ospreys, great blue herons, great egrets, pileated woodpeckers, and gray foxes. The endangered chicken turtle is found nowhere in Virginia outside the park. And the poisonous cottonmouth snake reaches its northern limit here. Park amenities include a massive car campground, visitor center, a large picnic area with shelters, tables and grills shaded by live oaks, and a boat ramp on the bay. The park is open year-round from 8 AM to dusk.

The park is located within the city of Virginia Beach.

**contact:** Seashore State Park and Natural Area, 2500 Shore Dr, Virginia Beach, VA 23451; 757/481-2131.

**getting there:** From the W: from the jct of US-13 and US-60 just S of the Chesapeake Bridge-Tunnel, take US-60 E 4.5 mi to the park entrance at a traffic signal. From the E along the Virginia Beach waterfront: Park entrance is located on VA-343. From Atlantic Avenue, take Shore Dr (US-60) 3.6 mi to a traffic light and the park entrance, L and R.

**topography:** From beach to backcountry dunes and forest, the terrain of Seashore SP undulates in gentle rises and drops. Elevations are between sea level and 30 ft. **maps:** USGS Cape Henry, N Virginia Beach.

**starting out:** A parking fee of $1/vehicle on weekdays, $2 on weekends is charged. Restrooms, water, and pay phones are located at the park office and visitor center. Also available there are park maps and brochures. The visitor center is closed from Dec 1 to Apr 1.

The public us or display of alcohol is prohibited. Pets must be kept on a leash.

**activities:** Hiking, Camping, Mountain Biking, Kayaking/Canoeing, Fishing.

**hiking:** The park's trail network extends into all corners of the backcountry, covering almost 20 miles. The longest of these is the 6-mi *Cape Henry Trail*, open to bikes but particularly popular with trailrunners. The trails are laid out in a manner so that loops of differnet lengths can be formed by hiking more than one trail. Hiking on all trails is easy, and trail use throughout the park is heavy. Although this is not the place to come to disappear into remote backcountry, the trails are uniformly excellent and provide the chance to observe wildlife and learn about coastal habitats. Especially worthwhile is the *Bald Cypress Trail*. A 1.5-mi loop, it's an interpretive trail with observation stations that winds through a stunning cypress swamp. Hike it and you'll forget you're next door to a major metropolis. All trails are blazed and easy to located and follow. Improvements include boardwalks, benches, and observation platforms. Trailheads are signed, as are trail jcts. Access to the trails is at the visitor center.

**camping:** The large 230-site car campground sprawls across several acres on the landward side of the dunes that front Chesapeake Bay. Despite its size, the division of the campground into 8 smaller loops and the thick groves of live oaks make it one of the most attractive car campgrounds in the state. One minor drawback is that traffic from US-60 can be heard from some of the sites. The sites are generally large, well-spaced, and shaded by live oaks. Privacy is for the most part excellent. Each site has a picnic table and grill. Long boardwalks provide access across the dunes to the beach. Shower/restroom facilities with hot water are located near the center of each loop. The fee is $20/night. Despite its size and high price, the campground often fills up during the summer—come early Friday to get a site or reserve one in advance. The campground is open Mar 1 to Dec 1.

**mountain biking:** The park's longest trail, the 6-mi *Cape Henry Trail*, is also its only one open to bikes. The one-way trail begins near the main park entrance and ends at the boat ramp at The Narrows. It can be ridden round-trip or a loop can be formed by riding US-60 around the park's edge, a relatively scenic ride for a primary highway. For most of its length, the trail is a wide path of packed sand and dirt. It is also popular with trailrunners. Riding on the trail is easy.

**kayaking/canoeing:** The park boat ramp is located on its back side, on Broad Bay. Across the bay, the shoreline is developed with homes. The bay's waters are quiet, but scenery is not great. Still, there are plenty of channels and inlets to explore in the vicinity—at least a day's worth. You can reach the Chesapeake by paddling about four miles, but it's not really worth the effort, as the area is pretty intensely developed. If you do decide to paddle the open waters of the Chesapeake, make sure you're prepared for conditions that can include strong winds, choppy water, and nasty currents. The park is located where bay and ocean meet. The put-in is at the 64th St boat ramp. To get there, leave the park and head E on US-60. At 3.5 mi reach the jct with Atlantic Ave. At 4.8 mi reach 64th St and the access to the boat ramp, R.

**fishing:** Despite being surrounded by water, the park isn't really such a great location for backcountry angling. There are two reasons for this: the park waterfront areas are often crowded, and outside the park backcountry, the area is heavily developed. Which isn't to say that there no fish here. Far from it, the mouth of the bay is considered to offer some of its finest fishing, with almost all species of Virginia saltwater game fish available at one time of year or another. The best fishing is from the beach, where you at least have the freedom to find an isolated spot. Chesapeake Bay game fish include bluefish, striped bass, flounder, gray trout, croaker, spot, and tautog. A saltwater fishing license is required to fish these waters.

# Great Dismal Swamp National Wildlife Refuge

Once upon a time, the Great Dismal Swamp was a vast wetland of more than a quarter million acres. Two centuries of drainage, road-building, and timber extraction, however, have altered its makeup radically. The entire swamp has been logged at least once. Where previously stands of Atlantic white cedar and cypress stood, the forest is now dominated by red maple, a more common species. Some of these alterations date back to colonial days. The swamp features prominantly in early American history. William Byrd II surveyed it in order to draw the state line between Virginia and North Carolina. George Washington founded the company that dug many of the the canals that drained large portions of it. By modern standards, the swamp is still quite large, covering 107,000 acres in Virginia and North Carolina. The land that today surrounds the refuge is primarily agricultural, evidence of past draining. The refuge is managed mainly for the protection of wildlife and other natural resources. Refuge counts of various species of flora and fauna underscores the crucial importance of wetlands. 209 species of bird have been observed here, 34 species of mammal (including balck bear, bobcat, and white-tailed deer), 21 species of snakes (3 poisonous), 19 species of toads and frogs, and 27 species of fish. A secondary, related objective is low impact outdoor recreation. The refuge has two designated trails and a

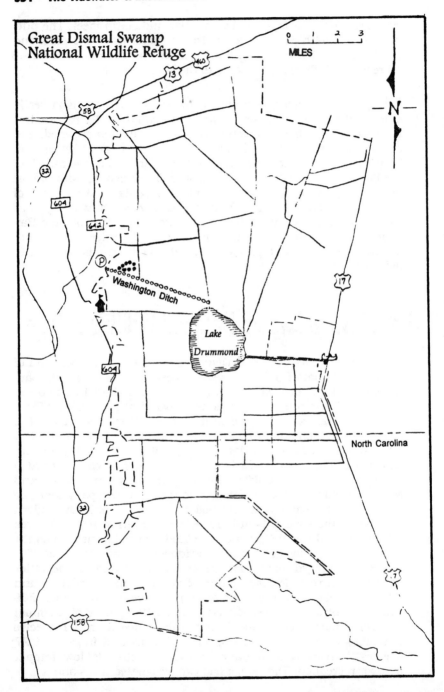

Great Dismal Swamp
National Wildlife Refuge

MILES

N

Washington Ditch

Lake
Drummond

North Carolina

feeder ditch that leads from a boat ramp to Lake Drummond offers canoeists and kayakers a remote, other-worldly paddling environment. In addition to the trails, a large network of abandoned, gated logging roads provides a means of exploring the refuge's nether regions. Wildlife observation and photography are two amply rewarded activities on the refuge. With no camping allowed, visits are limited to daytime only. The refuge is open all year from thirty minutes before sunrise to thirty minutes after sunset.

Suffolk (NW) is the closest city.

**contact:** Refuge Manager, Great Dismal Swamp NWR, P.O. Box 349, Suffolk, VA 23439; 757/986-3705.

**getting there:** From the jct of US-58 BUS (Washington St) and VA-32/US-13 in downtown Suffolk, take VA-32/US-13 S 3.6 mi to the fork of VA-32 and US-13. Bear L on VA-32 and go 4.5 mi to Cypress Chapel Rd (SR-675). Turn L and go 0.5 mi to White Marsh Rd (SR-642). Turn L and go 1.8 mi to a crossroads at Desert Rd (SR-604). To reach the refuge office turn R and go 1.7 mi. Or, continue straight 1 mi to the Washington Ditch entrance, R. The parking lot is ahead 1 mi at the end of the gravel road.

**topography:** The entire region is defined by water, from Lake Drummond in the middle to the network of drainage ditches to the surrounding bottomlands that lack drainage sufficient to ever completely dry them out. Elevations on the refuge vary little, with few areas more than 10 ft above sea level . Most of the land is forested, with bottomland and swamp hardwoods most prevalent. **maps:** USGS Lake Drummond, Lake Drummond NW, Suffolk, Corapeake.

**starting out:** Facilities on the refuge are limited. A visitor center is open weekdays 8 AM to 3:30 PM. Restrooms and water are inside and you can pick up a refuge map and brochure along with a bird list. The Washington Ditch entrance is open daily Apr 1 to Sep 30 6:30 AM to 8 PM; Oct 1 to Mar 31 6:30 AM to 5 PM. Portions of the refuge close in fall during the deer hunt.

**activities:** Hiking, Mountain Biking, Canoeing/Kayaking, Fishing.

**hiking:** The refuges 2 designated trails, the Dismal Town Boardwalk Trail and the Washington Ditch Trail are only the beginning of the story for hikers on the refuge. More than 100 miles of abandoned former logging roads crisscross the refuge. All trails and roads on the refuge are level and easy to hike. The challenge is in not getting lost. If you do decide to venture away from the 2 main trails, be sure to bring a topographic map and compass. After a while all the old gated logging roads begin to look the same, and the flat terrain doesn't provide many clues about your location. Not to be missed is the Dismal Town Boardwalk Trail. As its name suggests, it follows a boardwalk through a large area of swamp. The mile-long trail offers a great chance to observe swamp habitats up close. There are benches along the route for resting or observation. The Washinton Ditch Trail (open to bikes too) runs 4.5 miles in a straight line to Lake Drummond. Access to these 2 trails and the network of refuge roads is at a signed trailhead at the Washington Ditch parking area.

**mountain biking:** All former logging roads on the refuge are technically open to moutain bikes. In practice though, many of them will only appeal to the most ardent adventurist, as they are no longer maintained and offer some pretty rough riding. The Washington Ditch, on the other hand, is a smooth ride from the entrance gate all the way to Lake Drummond, a one-way trip of 4.5 miles. Apart from the difficulties of choppy roadbeds, riding in the refuge is easy, since the terrain is tabletop flat. The network of old logging roads covers every cordern of the refuge, a distance of more than 100 miles. Trail access is at the Washington ditch entrance. If you're going to venture into the backcountry, be sure to bring a good topo map and compass. Getting lost is a real possibility here.

**canoeing/kayaking:** The only boat access to the refuge is at the E end of the feeder ditch that runs E of Lake Drummond to US-17. The boat ramp is on the highway 3 mi N of the VA/NC state line. There's a single easy portage over a water control structure between the put-in and Lake Drummond. Paddling the 3,100-acre lake is like going back in time. In all likelihood you'll be the only one on the water. The nearly round bowl of water, surrounded by nothing but forest and an immense sky, seems to be totally removed from the rest of the world. Paddling is easy, except when the wind is up, when it can be downright dangerous. Opportunities for bird-watching and other wildlife observation are excellent. Plenty of room for paddling on the large lake.

**fishing:** Bank fishermen on 3,100-acre Lake Drummond have to be content with a small pier at the end of the *Washington Ditch Trail*. Other than that, fishing from the shoreline isn't really a possibility, due to the dense forest that crowds the water. A better bet is to put a boat on the water at the boat ramp and paddle up Feeder Ditch to the lake. The fishing pressure is so light some days it's nonexistent. Species of game fish in the lake are largemouth bass, chain pickerel, channel and white catfish, black crappie, bluegill, and yellow perch.

# Northwest River Park

This 763-acre park and nature preserve is located in Chesapeake City. Situated on the banks of Indian Creek and the Northwest River near the North Carolina state line, it's about as far from an urban setting as you can imagine. Except for a network of trails, its extensive backcountry of upland hardwood forest, bottomland swamp, and a 29-acre lake and canal system exists in an unspoiled natural state. Park facilities are clustered near the entrance and include boat rentals for the lake, an extensive picnic area with shelters, tables, and grills, a car campground, and a camp store. The lake is part of the new Urban Fishing Program and is stocked with trout in winter. It provides fishing more typical of the coastal plain at other times of year. The park is an excellent destination for families wanting to spend a day or weekend in the outdoors, but still have some of the amenities of civilization nearby. More rugged journeys are possible by putting a canoe or kayak on the Northwest River and paddling through the remote swamp forest that crowds its banks. The park is open all year fronm sunrise to sunset.

Blackwater (E) is the closest town.

**contact:** Northwest River Park, 1733 Indian Creek Rd, Chesapeake, VA 23322; 757/421-7151.

**getting there:** From the jct of Blackwater Rd (VA-165) and Pungo Ferry Rd (1.5 mi W of the bridge across North Landing River, go S on VA-165 1.9 mi to Indian Creek Rd. Turn R and go 4.3 mi (at 2.8 mi bear R) to the park entrance, L. • Or from the W: from the jct of VA-168 and Indian Creek Rd, go E on Indian Creek Rd 3.2 mi to the park entrance, R.

**topography:** Located at the confluence of a coastal river and creek, park terrain combines floodplain bottomland with substantial pockets of upland. Most of the land is heavily forested, except where landscaping has been used to create the park setting. **maps:** USGS Moyock.

**starting out:** Facilities in the park are centered around the lake, where there's a camp store, campground registration and facilities (restrooms, water, pay phone). Additional facilities are located at the picnic area. The park office can supply you with a map of the park showing trails and boat ramps. The area around the boat rental dock is typically crowded. The backcountry, by comparison is often relatively empty.

Pets must be kept on a leash. Alcohol is not allowed in public areas. Swimming in the lake is not allowed.

**activities:** Hiking, Camping, Canoeing/Kayaking, Fishing.

**hiking:** Almost 10 miles of trails wind through the hardwood forest and bottomland swamp in the park's backcountry. The trails are laid out in interconnecting loops, allowing hikes of various lengths. The trails are well constructed and well maintained. They follow a combination of roadbeds and single-tracks. Improvements include boardwalks, footbridges, benches, and observation decks over the lake. Trailheds, located near the park office and picnic areas, are clearly signed, as are trail jcts. One unique trail is the Frangrance Garden, a 600-ft loop designed for the visually impaired. The trail is planted with various species of trees, shrubs, and flowers. Several of the trails are open to horses too.

**camping:** The park's car campground has 72 sites in 2 large loops. The campground is located in a quiet corner of the park in a sparsely wooded area. The trees provide an element of shade, but do little to increase privacy, which is minimal when the campground is crowded. The sites are large and fairly well-spaced. Each site has a picnic table and grill. Some have electrical hookups. 2 restroom/shower facilities are centrally located. The sites cost $12/night. The campground is open from Apr to Nov.

A backcountry group camping area is reserved for groups of 10 or more. Each of the 4 large sites has picnic tables and a grill. The sites have no water source. The hike to reach the camping area is about a half mile from the main campground.

**canoeing/kayaking:** The park offers canoeists and kayakers 2 distinctly different paddling environments. Within the park, there's a 29-acre lake with a long, narrow profile that extends from the park entrance to the Northwest River at the park's S boundary. Private boats are not allowed on the lake, so you have to rent a canoe, paddle boat or jon boat from the park. This is a good options for families or other paddlers who would like to spend a couple of hours on the water without the hassles of transporting a boat. The backcountry environment here is surprisingly scenic and serene—well worth a short visit.

For more ambitious paddlers, or those merely wanting more of a wilderness experience, or a longer trip, a boat ramp on Indian Creek is located just outside the park. Indian Creek is a narrow, isolated creek that meanders through bottomland hardwood and swamp forest. From the put-in, it flows S about a mile before emptying into Northwest River, another remote slow-moving coastal river. A boat ramp is located near the confluence. If you continue downstream, you'll cross into NC after about 2 miles; another 7 miles brings you to the river's mouth at Tull Bay. From there, you can either turn around and paddle upstream (depending on the current) or paddle 5 miles E across the North Landing River to Mackay Island NWR, where there are take-outs (open seasonally; see *North Carolina: A Guide to Backcountry Travel & Adventure* for details). Paddling along this entire route is easy. To reach the boat ramp outside the park, leave the park and turn L. Go 0.9 to the boat ramp, L. Creek is about 20 yds across.

**fishing:** Like canoeists and kayakers, anglers have the option of fishing the park's 29-acre lake or in one of the rivers that forms most of the park's boundaries. The park lake is stocked with trout in winter as part of the Urban Fishing Program; it also supports populations of largemouth bass, channel catfish, crappie, bluegill, and white perch. Bank fishing is a very popular method. To cover the most water, however, it's best to rent a boat. A trout license is required to fish between Nov 1 and Apr 30.

Northwest River and its tributaries can be fished from canoes or other small craft. Species most commonly caught are largemouth bass, crappie, and sunfish. See above for directions to the boat ramp and a description of the rivers.

# Back Bay National Wildlife Refuge

7,732-acre Back Bay NWR was created in 1938 to provide a habitat for migratory waterfowl. Located in the southeast corner of the state south of Virginia Beach, the area was once popular with waterfowl hunters. Refuge holdings, which include part of a barrier spit and a wide expanse of bay that includes islands, marshes, and flats, were once the site of several local hunt clubs. The refuge is managed primarily for the protection of wildlife. Snow geese and a variety of species of ducks are the most numerous inhabitants, with brown pelicans, osprey, bald eagles, peregrine falcons, and piping plovers among 300 species of birds observed. Maximum numbers of migratory waterfowl occur in December. Mammals that inhabit the refuge include the white-footed mouse, raccoon, muskrat, feral hog, river otter, nutria, red fox, and whited-tailed deer. Although habitat management is the refuge's primary goal, outdoor recreation consistent with that goal is encouraged. The refuge offers exceptional opportunities for birding, kayaking and canoeing, and fishing.

**contact:** Refuge Manager, Back Bay National Wildlife Refuge, P.O. Box 6286, Virginia Beach, VA; 757/721-2412.

**getting there:** From the jct of General Booth Blvd (US-60) and Princess Anne Rd S of Virginia Beach, go E on Princess Anne Rd 0.8 mi to Sandbridge Rd. Turn L and go 3.7 mi (at 1.6 mi bear R at a fork) to Sandpiper Rd. Turn R and go 4.2 mi to the refuge entrance.

**topography:** Habitats and terrain are typical of a barrier island environment. Beach, dunes, shrub thicket, maritime forest, and freswhater marsh are all present. Except for the system of dunes backing the beach, the refuge is flat. **maps:** USGS North Bay, Knotts Island.

**starting out:** The refuge is open daily year-round during daylight hours only, except Saturday Dec to Mar, when it's closed. An entrance fee of $4/vehicle or $2 if entering on foot or bike is charged. The visitors center is open weekdays 8 AM to 4 PM, weekends 9 AM to 4 PM. Facilities there include restrooms, a pay phone, water, and a small collection of wildlife exhibits. A refuge map and brochures are available as well.

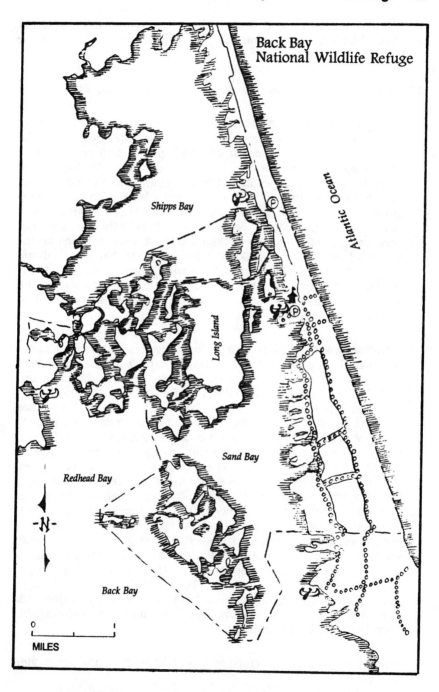

Back Bay
National Wildlife Refuge

Atlantic Ocean

Shipps Bay

Long Island

Sand Bay

Redhead Bay

-N-

Back Bay

0
MILES

Swimming, surfing, and sunbathing are prohibited. Pets are not allowed between Apr 1 and Sep 30. At other times they must be kept on a leash.

**activities:** Hiking, Mountain Biking, Kayaking/Canoeing, Fishing.

hiking/**mountain biking:** About 6 miles of trails follow the refuge dikes and cross over the dunes to the beach. Almost all of the trails follow refuge roads of crushed graved and packed dirt. They're open to both hikers and mountain bikers. The trails allow ample opportunity for wildlife observation and improvements such as long boardwalks and observation decks have been constructed to make viewing easier. Although the trails are not blazed, they're easy to locate and follow. Access to all trails is at the visitor center. Another option for hikers and bikers is the 4 miles of beach on the ocean side of the refuge. Hikers wanting a longer trip can continue on to False Cape State Park, adjacent to the south. In winter, refuge trails close to all uses to prevent disturbance of the migratory birds that use the refuge. The beach is still open to hikers and bikers during this time.

**kayaking/canoeing:** Since a majority of the refuge is bay, islands, and tidal flats, probably the best way to experience the refuge as a whole is from a kayak or canoe. The area between the mainland and the barrier spit is actually a series of bays: North, Shipps, Redhead, Sand, and Back. These waters offer paddlers the chance to travel on open water and also to wind through narrow channels and coves defined by a number of large and small islands. The refuge waters are ideal for a day trip, with longer trips possible by paddling S to False Cape SP (where there are waterside campsites) and beyond. Another option is to put in on the ocean side just N of the refuge at Little Island Park. Keep in mind that there's no inlet from bay to ocean in VA. Although the bay is relatively sheltered, and beyond the range of tidal action, wind and waves consistent with open water conditions are often present. In winter large sections of the bay freeze over. Within the refuge, you can put in on the bay behind the visitor center. On the mainland, you can put in at the Back Bay boat ramp. To get there from the refuge, backtrack to the jct of Princess Anne Rd and Indian River Rd. Turn S on Princess Anne Rd and go S 5.2 mi to Mill Landing Rd. Turn L and go 2.9 mi to the boat ramp.

**fishing:** Fishing in the refuge is permitted on both the ocean side and the bay side. Surfcasters will find 4 miles of nearly deserted beach. Sport fish commonly taken from the surf include bluefish, black drum, channel bass, flounder, gray trout, speckled trout, and spot. On the bay side, there are a few places from which it's possible to fish from land, including a small pier. A better bet is to take a boat out onto the bay. You can fish from the boat or get out and wade in the shallows. Because the nearest ocean inlet is so distant, there's no natural salt content in the water. Sport fish present are largemouth bass, crappie, white perch, bluegill, and catfish.

# False Cape State Park

Not far south of the busiest park in the state park system (Seashore SP), is the one that receives the fewest visitors each year, only about 25,000. Not that False Cape State Park is lacking in attractions. Far from it. In terms of remote, pristine backcountry, it is undisputably the jewel of the entire system. The reason for the low numbers is access. Located at the very bottom of the barrier spit that Back Bay separates from the mainland, the only way to reach False Cape State Park is to hike, bike, or come by boat. The 4,321-acre park lies along a 6-mile stretch of beach- and bayfront between North Carolina (S) and Back Bay National Wildlife Refuge (N). The park is a haven for waterfowl and other wildlife. Among mammals, white-tailed deer, nutria, feral hogs, and wild horses are all regularly seen. On the bay and impoundments inside the park, you're likely to see dozens of species of waterfowl and shore birds. Viewing blinds have been constructed to assist in this. The place didn't always belong to the birds and animals, however. During the last century and into the first half of this one, a community of 300 named Wash Woods flourished. They even built a methodist church with planks of cypress salvaged from a shipwreck off the coast. Ocean washovers and other difficulties of living in such a harsh environment eventually led to the disbanding of the community. Signs of it past, including a cemetery and the church steeple, still remain, however, and can be seen along the hiking trails. Throughout the park, interpretive panels describe the natural forces that have shaped the seaside environment, local history, and some of the species of flora and fauna encountered in the park. Park facilities include primitive campsites, boat docks on the bay side, a network of trails that extends into all regions of the park, and a

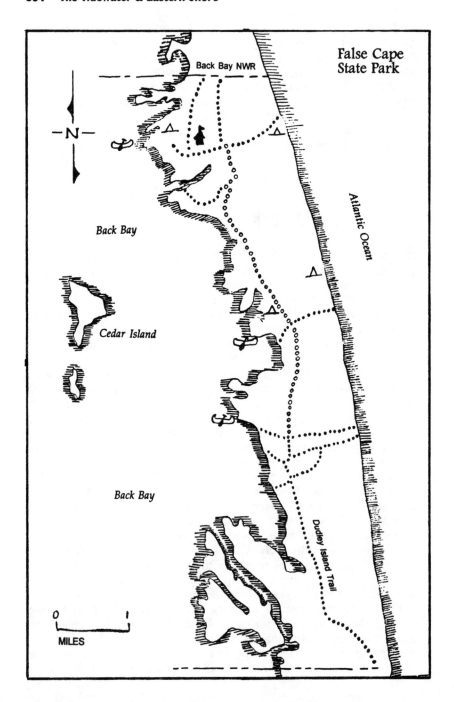

small clapboard visitor center. Best of all, though, is the miles of empty beach and the undisurbed maritime habitats. The park is a perfect locale for a weekend visit. It's open all year.

Virginia Beach (N) is the closest city.

**contact:** False Cape State Park, 4001 Sandpiper Rd, Virginia Beach, VA 23456; 757/426-7128.

**getting there:** There is no vehicle access to the park; visitors arrive by foot, bike or boat. If you're visiting for the day, you can leave your car at Back Bay NWR, adjacent to the N. If you're planning on camping in the park, you'll have to park overnight at Little Island Park, 0.5 mi N of Back Bay NWR. Depending on where you park, the hike or bike into the park is 4.5 or 6 miles. See above for directions to Back Bay NWR. If you arrive by canoe or kayak, you can take out at any one of three landings in the park.

**topography:** The terrain and habitats in the park are characteristic of barrier islands and land masses: beach, dunes, shrub thickets, maritime forest, shallow impoundments, and marsh are all encountered. **maps:** USGS Knotts Island, North Bay.

**starting out:** There are few facilities in the park. The visitor contact station can provide you with park maps and brochures. It's open Apr–Oct M–W, F from 8 AM to 3 PM; weekends & holidays 9 AM to 3 PM. A pay phone is there too. Pit toilets are located in the primitive camping areas. Although a few hand pumps in the camping areas provide water, they are not always reliable. There are no other sources of water in the park. Because the park is isolated and not accessible by car, it is never crowded.

The following are prohibited in the park: open fires, off-trail hiking, and alcohol. Pets must be leashed. All trash must be packed out.

**activities:** Hiking, Kayaking/Canoeing, Camping, Mountain Biking, Fishing.

**hiking:** Any hiking trip in the park begins with a 5-mile trek through Back Bay NWR. You can hike along refuge roads (closed in winter) or on the beach. Hiking along the beach is not difficult, though it's easiest at low tide, when you can walk on hardpacked sand. Count on about a 2-hr hike if going along the beach, a little less on refuge roads. Inside the park, there are about 9 miles of trails (not counting the beach). Most of the trails are seldom-used roadbeds of crushed gravel and packed dirt. These paths get most of their traffic when a hurricane is imminent; the park is part of the evacuation route from NC. Other trails follow sandy single-tracks. Trails are all clearly marked and easy to follow, with signs at trail intersections. As in most coastal environments, the terrain is generally level and the hiking easy, slowed at times by deep sand. Improvements along the trails include viewing blinds, benches and interpretive stations. The trails offer an excellent chance to explore the various flora and fauna of a barrier land mass.

**kayaking/canoeing:** With ocean and bay frontage, the park offers an ideal habitat for trips of varying length, including what is probably the best opportunity for kayak/canoe camping in VA. In the bay, paddlers can explore the shallow waters of 25,000-acre Back Bay, freshwater marshes, and abundant waterfowl up close. The ocean side offers the chance to follow a pristine beach and paddle in challenging conditions. Within the park there are 3 boat landings on the bay side, 2 of which are near primitive camping areas. The other 2 camping areas are on the ocean side, allowing for multi-day ocean kayaking trips. Getting to the park by boat is relatively easy. N of the park, you can put in at Little Island Park on either the ocean or bay side. From there, It's about a 6-mile paddle past Back Bay NWR to the park. On the mainland across the bay are 3 more launch sites, all on roads accessible from Princess Anne Rd. From any of these launches, the paddle across the bay to the park is 5-7 miles. Although Back Bay is sheltered and the shallow water often calm, winds and wind-tides are not uncommon. Be prepared for open water conditions. Because the nearest ocean inlet is 70 miles south, lunar tides are not a factor in the bay. In winter, large portions of the bay freeze over, but usually only for short periods. On the ocean side, tides and strong currents are of course a factor.

**camping:** There are 12 primitive backcountry campsites in 4 different areas of the park. Each of the large sites has a picnic table; groups of sites share a pit toilet. The sites are located in various surroundings, some among the dunes near the beach, others near the bay and sheltered by live oaks. Once you reach the park, the hikes to the various sites are pretty short, between 0.5 mi and 2 mi. Sites cost $7/night. Securing a campsite is a fairly involved process, but worth the effort. First, a permit must be picked up in person at Seashore SP in Virginia Beach. During warm weather, reservations should be made 2 or 3 weeks in advance. This can be done over the phone. First-time campers are required to watch a 10-minute slide/audio presentation on the ecology of False Cape. Go to the visitor contact station, except for Dec–Mar, when permits are picked up at the park office near the park campground. The park office is open 8–4:30 Mon–Fri. At other times, you'll have to track down a park ranger. For camping info, call 704/481-4836.

**mountain biking:** Riding along the beach or on the gravel roads of Back Bay NWR, a mountain bike is the fastest way to get to the park. Once there, there's another stretch of wide, deserted beach and a handful of trails and park roads open to bikes. On Virginia's Atlantic coast, the combination of the refuge and the state park offer the best biking in the region. On the beach, low-tide leaves a wide swath of hard-packed sand exposed, making it the best time to travel to the park. Within the park, the dirt road that runs down the park's spine and a couple of spurs are open to bikes. In all, there are probably twenty miles of riding between the refuge and park. The riding is easy, and offers the best way to cover a lot of ground in the area.

**fishing:** Anglers have the choice of fishing the shallow waters of Back Bay or of surf-casting from the oceanside beach. You'll want to have a boat to fish Back Bay. Although you can fish from some of the boat landings, this method doesn't allow you to cover much water. Back Bay is located 70 miles from the nearest inlet to the Atlantic. For this reason, it's primarily a freshwater fishery, although a few saltwater species can be found in its waters. Species commonly taken are channel catfish, white perch, largemouth bass, black crappie, bluegills, and flounder.

Oceanside angling is from the beach. Because you have to hike or bike to reach the park, this stretch of beach is almost always deserted. Game fish taken from the surf are bluefish, flounder, black drum, gray trout, croaker, spot, and striped bass, among others.

# Outfitters & Supply Stores

The following businesses sell gear or offer services for the outdoor activities covered in this book. These stores are arranged here geographically, by city, following the general west-to-east pattern of the book. Within a given city, listings are alphabetical. Fishing supply stores and bike stores have not been included; you'll find them in just about any town near a popular fishing or mountain biking area.

Key to some terms used below: camping=tents, backpacks, sleeping bags & clothes; paddling=canoes, kayaks & accessories; topos=USGS 7.5 minute topographic maps.

## Bristol

Mountain Sports Ltd—1021 Commonwealth Ave; 540/466-8988
M–F 9 am–7 pm, Sa 9–5:30, Su 1–5 pm
Sells: camping, paddling, mtn biking, topos

## Damascus

Mt Rogers Outfitters—110 Laurel Ave;540/475-5416
M–Sa 9 am–6 pm, Su 12–5 pm
Sells: camping; Rents: camping, mtn bikes; Shuttles

## Dublin

Tangent Outfitters—Route 4; 540/674-5202
M–F 9 am–6 pm, Sa 9 am–8 pm, Su 10:30 am–8 pm
Rents: paddling, fly fishing, mtn bikes
Trips: hiking, paddling, fly fishing, mtn biking; Shuttles

## Blacksburg

Backcountry Ski & Sports—3710 S Main St; 540/552-6400
M–F 10 am–8 pm, Sa 10 am–5 pm, Su 1–5 pm
Sells: camping, paddling, topos; Trips: paddling

Blue Ridge Outdoors—211 Draper Rd; 540/552-9012
M–F 10 am–9 pm, Sa 10 am–6 pm, Su 12–5 pm
Sells: camping, topos

## Roanoke

Blue Ridge Outdoors—4362 Tanglewood Mall; 540/774-4311
MF 10 am–9 pm, Sa 10 am–9 pm, Su 1–6 pm
Sells: camping, topos; Shuttles

## Lynchburg

Timberlake Sporting Goods—10119 Timberlake Rd; 804/239-3474.        M–F 9 am–6 pm, Sa 9 am–5 pm
Sells: camping, paddling, fly-fishing; Rents: Canoes

## Lexington

Rockbridge Outfitters Ltd—112 W Washington St; 540/463-1947
M–F 10–5:30, Sa 10–5 pm
Sells: camping, mtn biking, topos; Rents: mtn bikes

## Waynesboro

Rockfish Gap Outfitters—1461 E Main St; 540/943-1461
M–F 10 am–6pm, Sa 10 am–5 pm
Sells: camping, paddling, mountain bikes, topos

## Harrisonburg

Wilderness Voyagers—1544 E Market St; 540/434-7234
M–F 10 am–6 pm, Sa 9 am–5 pm
Sells: camping, paddling, topos; Rents: camping; Shuttles

## Charlottesville

Blue Ridge Mtn Sports—Barracks Road Shpg Ctr; 804/977-4400
M–F 10 am–8 pm, Sa 10 am–6pm, Su 12:30–5 pm
Sells: camping, paddling, topos; Rents: camping, paddling;
Trips: hiking

## Front Royal

Front Royal Canoe Co—P.O. Box 473; 800/270-8808
M–F 9 am–6 pm, Sa, Su 7 am–7pm
Rents: paddling; Shuttles

## Winchester

Mountain Trails—212 E Cork St; 540/667-0030
M–F 10 am–7 pm, Sa 9:30 am–5 pm
Sells: camping; Rents: camping

# Richmond

Alpine Outfitters—11010 Midlothian Tpk; 804/794-4172
M–F 10 am–9 pm, Sa–Su 10 am–5 pm
Sells: camping, paddling, topos; Rents: camping, canoes

Alpine Outfitters—7107 W Broad St; 804/794-4172
M–F 10 am–9 pm, Sa 10 am–5 pm
Sells: camping, paddling; Rents: camping, paddling

Blue Ridge Mtn Sports—Chesterfield Town Ctr; 804/794-2004
M–Sa 10 am–9 pm, Su 12:30–5:30
Sells: camping

Rowlett's Bicycles—1904 Staples Mill Rd; 804/353-4489
M–F 10 am–7 pm, Sa 10 am–5 pm
Sells: canoeing, mountain biking

# Glen Allen

Blue Ridge Mtn Sports—10164 W Broad St; 804/965-0494
M–F 10 am–9 pm, Sa 10 am–6 pm, Su 1–5 pm
Sells: camping; Rents: camping; Trips: hiking

# Fredericksburg

Outdoor Adventures—4721 Plank Rd; 540/786-3334
M–F 10 am–8 pm, Sa 10 am–6 pm, Su 12–5 pm
Sells: camping, paddling, fly fishing, topos
Rents: camping; Trips: hiking, paddling, fly fishing

# Springfield

Hudson Trail Outfitters, Ltd—Springfield Mall; 703/922-0050
M–Sa 10 am–9 pm, Su 11 am–5 pm
Sells: camping, paddling, fly fishing, mountain biking, topos
Rents: camping, paddling; Trips: paddling, mountain biking

# Oakton

Appalachian Outfitters—2938 Chain Bridge Rd; 703/281-4324
M–F 10 am–9 pm, Sa 9 am–6 pm, Su 12–6 pm
Sells: camping, paddling, topos; Rents: camping

## Fairfax

Eastern Mountain Sports—12997 Fair Lakes Ctr; 703/968-7595
M–Sa 10 am–9 pm, Su 12–5 pm
Sells: camping, kayaking, topos; Rents: camping

Hudson Trail Outfitters—11750 Fair Oaks Mall; 703/385-3907
M–Sa 10 am–9 pm, Su 11 am–5 pm
Sells: camping, paddling, fly fishing, mountain biking, topos
Rents: camping, paddling; Trips: paddling, mountain biking

Hudson Trail Outfitters—9683 Lee Highway; 703/591-2950
M–Sa 10 am–9 pm, Su 11 am–5 pm
Sells: camping, paddling, fly fishing, mountain biking, topos
Rents: camping, paddling; Trips: paddling, mountain biking

## Falls Church

REI—3509 Carlin Springs Rd; 703/379-9400
M–F 10 am–9 pm, Sa 10 am–7 pm, Su 11 am–6 pm
Sells: camping, paddling, mountain biking;
Rents: camping, paddling

## Washington, D.C.

Hudson Trail Outfitters—4530 Wisconsin Ave; 202/363-9810
M–Sa 10 am–9 pm, Su 11 am–5 pm
Sells: camping, paddling, fly fishing, mountain biking, topos
Rents: camping, paddling; Trips: paddling, mountain biking

## Williamsburg

Blue Ridge Mtn Sports—1248 Richmond Rd; 804/229-4584
M–F 10 am–9 pm, Sa 10 am–5 pm, Su 1–5 pm
Sells: camping, kayaking; Rents: camping, kayaks.

## Newport News

Open Road Bike Shop—12715-H Warwick Blvd; 757/930-0510
M–F 10 am–8 pm, Sa 10am–5pm
Sells: camping, mtn biking, topos

## Chesapeake

Expedition Outfitters—801 Volvo Pkwy, #142; 757/436-4925
M–F 10 am–7 pm, Sa 10am–6pm, Su 12–5pm
Sells: camping, mtn biking, topos; Rents: camping

## Virginia Beach

Blue Ridge Mtn Sports—762 Hilltop N Shpg Ctr; 757/422-2204.
M–F 10 am–9pm, Sa 10 am–6 pm, Su 12–5 pm
Sells: camping, canoes, topos; Rents: camping

Wild River Outfitters—3636 Virginia Beach Blvd; 757/431-8566
M–F 10 am–8 pm, Sa 10 am–6 pm, Su 12–5 pm
Sells: camping, paddling; Rents: camping; Trips: Paddling